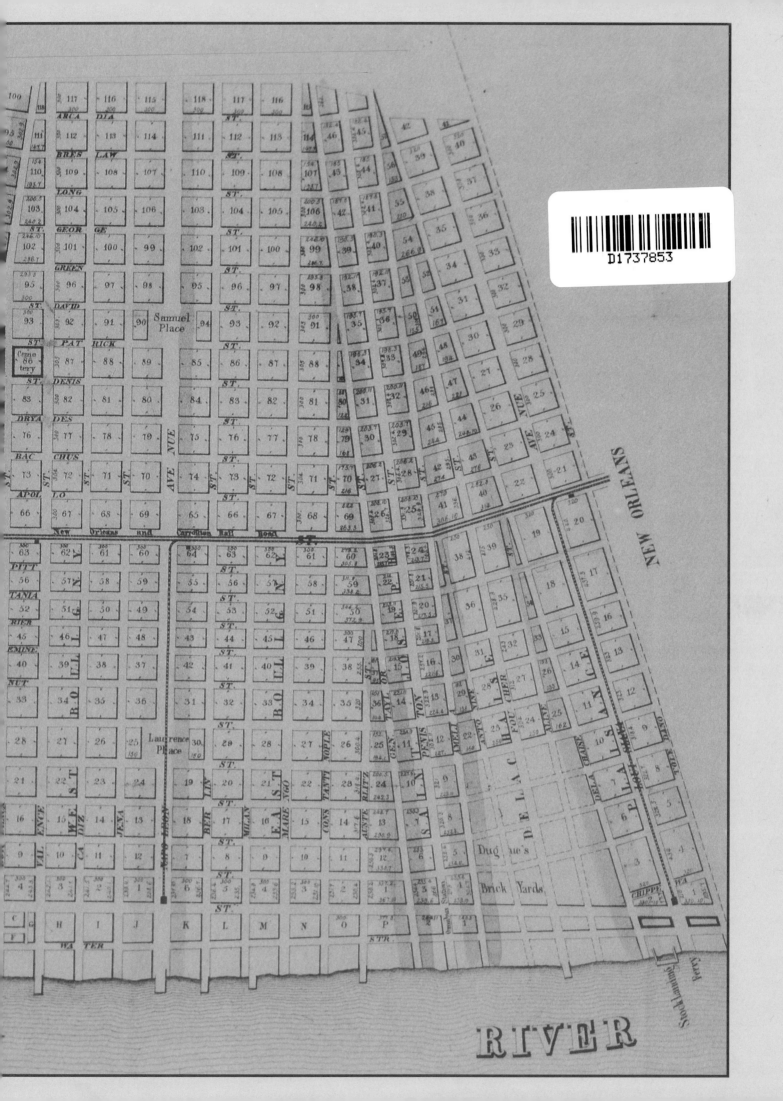

NEW ORLEANS ARCHITECTURE

VOLUME VII:
Jefferson City

4424 Constance Street. Front porch detail.

NEW ORLEANS ARCHITECTURE

VOLUME VII:

Jefferson City

Toledano Street to Joseph Street
Claiborne Avenue to the Mississippi River

By The Friends of the Cabildo
    Associates of the Louisiana State Museum

Compiled and edited by:
DOROTHY G. SCHLESINGER
ROBERT J. CANGELOSI, JR.
SALLY KITTREDGE REEVES

Contributing authors:
BERNARD LEMANN
SAMUEL WILSON, JR.
SALLY KITTREDGE REEVES
JOHN E. WALKER

Photographs by:
Walter B. Moses, Jr.

PELICAN PUBLISHING COMPANY
GRETNA 1989

International Standard Book Number: 0-88289-668-7

City of Jefferson Bond, June 1, 1856.
(Courtesy Louisiana State Musuem.)

Library of Congress Cataloging-in-Publication Data
(Revised for volume 7)

Friends of the Cabildo.
    New Orleans architecture.

    Vol. 4 compiled by R. Toledano, S. K. Evans, and
M. L. Christovich.
    Includes bibliographies and index.
    Contents: v. 1. The Lower Garden District.—
v. 2. The American sector (Faubourg St. Mary)—[etc.]—
v. 7. Jefferson City.
    1. Architecture—Louisiana—New Orleans.
2. New Orleans (La.)—Buildings, structures, etc.
I. Wilson, Samuel, 1911–   . II. Christovich, Mary
Louise, ed.   III. Toledano, Roulhac, ed.   IV.   Title.
NA735.N4F74   1971   720′.9763′35   72-172272

Library of Congress Cataloging-in-Publication Data

ISBN 0-911116-51-6 (v. 1)

Manufactured in the United States of America
Published by Pelican Publishing Company, Inc.
1101 Monroe Street, Gretna, Louisiana 70053

CONTENTS

3512 St. Charles Avenue (demolished). Da Ponte residence. Ornate parlors and hallway. (Courtesy: Southeastern Architectural Archive, Tulane University Library. Thomas Sully Office Records—Gifts of Jeanne Sully West.)

PREFACE AND ACKNOWLEDGMENTS

At the inception of the *New Orleans Architecture* series in 1965, plans included a volume on Uptown New Orleans. But because so many other areas of the city were in danger of demolition—by premeditation or neglect—there was a consensus that the alarm for those areas should take precedence. Uptown was relatively safe, or so it was thought. Unfortunately, the past twenty-four years have witnessed many changes and intrusions in the name of progress or gentrification or renovation—both good and bad. Now that Uptown New Orleans, from Louisiana Avenue to Lowerline Street, has received an Historic District designation in the National Register of Historic Places (accomplished while this book was in progress), there is an added impetus to research thoroughly the important, and many times obscure, facts and features of the area that once was Jefferson City.

Assembling a book of this nature is similar to working on a gigantic multi-dimensional jigsaw puzzle, knowing beforehand that some of the pieces are missing. It is an exhilarating experience to correlate seemingly disparate facts, and a demanding exercise to fit together the pieces of this super puzzle. Most of the records are in order, but some are missing, others burned or water-soaked. Our purpose has been to assemble, research, digest, evaluate, and ascertain all the facts available about the land that once was the City of Jefferson. This volume will define the area geographically, recount the history and development, point up the socio-economic factors, describe building types and styles, and inventory some typical and atypical structures that comprise the neighborhoods of this heterogeneous, yet relatively stable, segment of New Orleans. Some structures are not included because severe alterations have destroyed their architectural integrity. Robert Cangelosi, Jr., Bernard Lemann, Sally Reeves, and Dorothy Schlesinger accomplished the inventory selection.

Since the first announcement of this publication, many individuals volunteered valuable information and old photographs that would not have been available otherwise. Without this enthusiastic response, this book would have been simply a factual account; with it, our endeavor has become a living entity with unusual information. Those who have been most helpful are: Doris F. Albers, Sandra Barnett, B. Raymond Bordelon, Helen Brown, Chris Canan, Priscilla and Edgar Casey, John Clemmer, Claire Creppel, James H. Crosby, Becky Currence, Edmond A. d'Hemecourt, Jean M. Farnsworth, William H. Forman, Terry Paul Gautier, Dr. Arnold and Gail Gelfand, Randal C. Griest, Maunsel W. Hickey, Hilary S. Irvin, Pickslay and Davis Lee Jahncke, Jr., Leon Mann, Frank Masson, Katherine McFetridge, James Mills, Marguerite Montgomery, Rita Odenheimer, Gloria and Bruns Redmond, Marcia Saitta, J. Raymond Samuel, Coralie Schaefer, Patricia Motte Segleau, Garrett G. Stearns, Suzanne Stewart, Sara Stone, Charlene and Curt Weaver, Caroline Weiss, Dr. Harold Wirth, and Albert J. Wolf, Jr.

Intensive research was done in all local primary source repositories. Without exception, the professionals working in the libraries and archives went out of their way to be helpful. They are:

Confederate Memorial Hall:
   Pat Eymard.

The Historic New Orleans Collection, Museum/Research Center:
   Stanton Frazar, Dode Platou, Judith H. Bonner, Robert Brantley, Charles Buchanan, Susan Cole, Howard Estes, Kitty Farley, Eloise Gamble, Barbara Guillaud, Florence Jumonville, Cathy Kahn, John Lawrence, Alfred Lemmon, Kellye Magee, John Magill, John Mahé, Richard Marvin, Victor McGee, Judith McMillan, Pat McWhorter, Jessica Travis, Jan White, and Michele Wyckoff.

Jackson Barracks:
   Mary B. Oalmann.

Louisiana State Museum Historical Center:
   Edward F. Haas, Deena Bedigian, Burt Harter, Rose Lambert, and Steven Rhinehart.

Louisiana State University Library, Baton Rouge:
   M. Stone Miller, Jr., Thomas Robin.

New Orleans Conveyance Office:
   Ronald Vignes.

New Orleans Historic District Landmarks Commission:
   Saundra K. Levy, Bayard T. Whitmore.

New Orleans Notarial Archives:
   John Hainkel III, Ernest Crayton, Irving Crayton, Steven Crayton, Harold Hand, and Hugh Mahoney.

New Orleans Office of Property Management, Division of Real Estate and Records:
   George Kaltenbach, Rita Medus, Joyce Phipps, and Elwood Verrett.

New Orleans Public Library, Louisiana Division:
   Collin B. Hamer, Jr., Wayne Everard, Ernest Brin, Liz Gilbert, Jean Jones, and Suhad Khalaf.

Tulane University, Howard-Tilton Memorial Library:
   Louisiana Collection:
      Jane Stevens, Gay Craft, Madeleine Blanchard, Victoria Howell, Jane Johnson, Catherine Marchese, Susan McClellan, Mac Myers, Leslie Palmer, Nichole Theriot, and Bethany Urschel.
   Microforms Division:
      Mary Yordy.
   Rare Books and Manuscripts Division:
      Wilbur Meneray, Doris Antin, Jeannine Eckholdt, Guillermo Nanez Falcon, Mary LeBlanc, Clemencia Molina, and Terry Sinclair.
   Southeastern Architectural Archive:
      William Cullison, Geoffrey Kimball.

University of New Orleans, Earl K. Long Library, Archives and Manscripts:
   Clive Hardy, Marie Windell.

Title Researchers:

Diana Earhart, Farleigh Earhart, Sarah Labouisse, Vicki Lazarus, Mary Morrill, Paul Mutty, Bettie Pendley, and Joy Plauche'.

Others who have been supportive:

John J. Avery, Jr., Barbara Kraus, A.L. Schlesinger, Jr., Charles Stich, and Martha H. Walker.

Behind the scenes heroines were Ann Conroy, who copyread the text, and Linda Dawson, who entered the manuscript and inventory on computer. Computer technology facilitated the production of this volume, through the courtesy and cooperation of Koch and Wilson Architects.

A generous family wishing to remain anonymous, F. Evans Farwell, and the Alex Berger Foundation underwrote pre-publication costs. Walter B. Moses, Jr. did all the photography, unless otherwise noted, and donated his expertise, time and photographic supplies for this publication.

The experience of being involved in this book is difficult to describe in all its aspects. It has meant new friends and associates, a learning phenomenon impossible to anticipate, a familiarity with the halls of academia, and archives plumbed in depth. All this and more have contributed to a remarkable personal engagement that has enhanced my awareness of our precious architectural heritage and the need for its protection and preservation.

DOROTHY G. SCHLESINGER

Corner Louisiana Avenue and Laurel Street, backed by Constance and Delachaise.

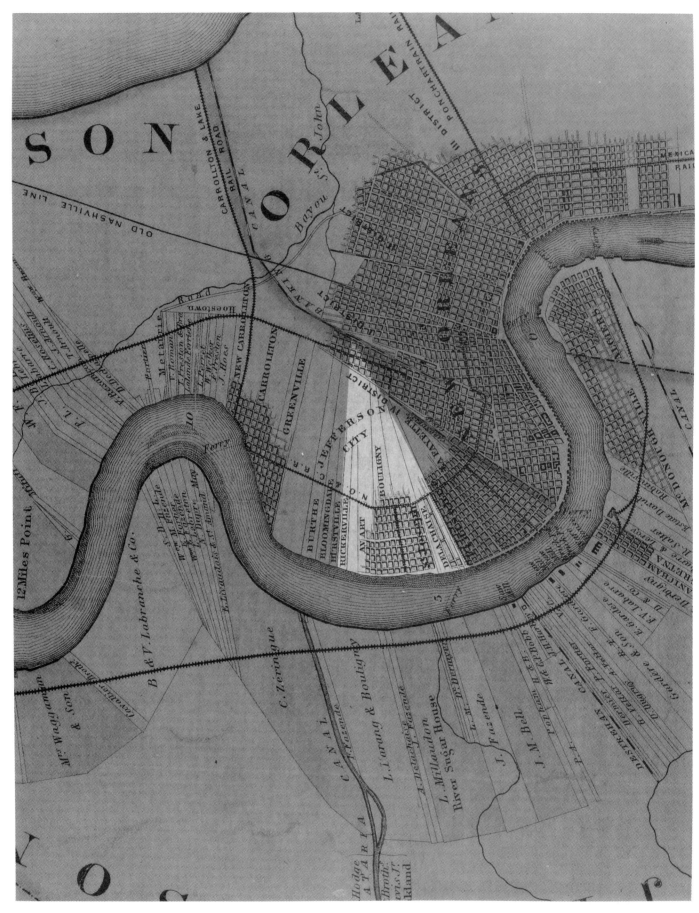

Detail of "Norman's Chart of Lower Mississippi River." A. Persac, 1858. (Courtesy The Historic New Orleans Collection, Museum/Research Center, Acc. No. 1947.1.)

FROM THE PRESIDENT

In 1971 Friends of the Cabildo president J. Raymond Samuel wrote of the dedication of the editors of the first volume of *New Orleans Architecture*. That commitment has become a hallmark of the entire series, and this seventh volume is no exception. Having been involved with the book since 1983, I have been fortunate to experience that dedication first-hand. Working as a team, the authors have combined their expertise and personal approach to architectural and urban history, yielding a well-rounded product. The captain of our team, Dorothy Schlesinger, kept us moving forward—often when we resisted. She has allowed us to commandeer the Schlesinger home as an office, and for the past seven years has planned her life around the production of this book.

Over the years, the Friends have taken pride in their leadership role in the preservation movement. No other city in the nation has attempted such a comprehensive analysis of its architectural heritage. While that leadership role is, of course, ancillary to the Friends' primary role as a support group of the Louisiana State Museum, our dedication to this series has not diminished. This seventh volume is the mid-point of a revised schedule adopted by the Friends' board in 1987 to carry the series into the next century. It will cover in subsequent volumes, the University section, Carrollton, the old City of Lafayette, Algiers, the Vieux Carré, Faubourg St. John, Mid-City, and the Gentilly-Lakefront area.

Since *New Orleans Architecture, Volume VI,* was released in 1980, we have mourned the loss of three individuals who have left a significant mark on the City of New Orleans, the Louisiana State Museum, and the Friends of the Cabildo. We dedicate this book to the memory of those men—F. Monroe Labouisse, Jr., Leonard V. Huber, Sr., and Stanton M. Frazar.

Monroe Labouisse, a noted preservation architect, author and community activist, was a long-time member and supporter of the Friends. He served as the architect for the restoration of Madame John's Legacy, a Louisiana State Museum property, as well as for numerous other historic structures. Everyone who knew Monroe will remember his intelligence, ability, and quick wit.

Leonard Huber, historian, author, collector and businessman, was a past president and long-time board member of the Friends. His interest in local history was widely recognized. As a strong voice in the local preservation movement, Leonard authored and co-authored many books for the Friends, among them, *The Pontalba Buildings and the Remarkable Woman Who Built Them*, *The Cabildo on Jackson Square*, *The Presbytere on Jackson Square*, *Jackson Square Through the Years*, and *New Orleans Architecture, Volume III: The Cemeteries*. The second volume of this series, which focused on the Central Business District, was published during his presidency.

Stanton "Buddy" Frazar, an executive and public relations expert, was also a former Friends' president and a long-time board member. His leadership and enthusiasm reinforced the Friends' prestige in the community. During his presidency, Buddy matured into a dynamic civic leader and became the director of The Historic New Orleans Collection. Volumes III and IV of this series were released while he was president.

We remember these three men for the significant roles they played in helping to preserve New Orleans' architectural heritage and for their contributions to the Louisiana State Museum.

Robert J. Cangelosi, Jr., President
Friends of the Cabildo

3528 Magazine Street. Jigsaw poetry.

INTRODUCTION

With the publication in 1971 of *New Orleans Architecture, Volume I: The Lower Garden District*, the first book of this series, a realization was expressed that other areas of New Orleans besides the Vieux Carré and the Garden District needed protection. Our precious architectural heritage was going down the drain. Aside from the efforts of the Louisiana Landmarks Society, the Orleans Parish Landmarks Commission, and a few vocal citizens, very little was being done to save irreplaceable treasures. The Friends of the Cabildo stepped beyond its role as associates-supporters of the Louisiana State Museum and undertook the project of alerting New Orleanians that the city had unique buildings and neighborhoods worth saving.

The Vieux Carré Commission dates from 1936, and the United States Department of the Interior designated the Vieux Carré a National Historic Landmark in 1965. Eleven years later, the New Orleans City Council awarded Historic District status to the Lower Garden District and St. Charles Avenue. In 1978 the Council established the Picayune Place Historic District, the Lafayette Square Historic District, the Warehouse Historic District, and the Faubourg Marigny Historic District. A year later the Esplanade Ridge Historic District joined the list. With the exception of the St. Charles Avenue Historic District, the impact of the Friends of the Cabildo Architecture Series was a positive factor in these Historic District designations. Building Watchers tours and the Preservation Resource Center were outgrowths of the first two volumes.

An energetic, creative, intelligent cadre produced the preceding volumes. The standards set by Mary Louise Christovich, Roulhac Toledano, Betsy Swanson, Samuel Wilson, Jr., Sally Evans Reeves, and all who participated are beacon lights for others to emulate and follow. Just as the first and subsequent volumes were the successful results of dedicated volunteers and professionals working together, so this, too, is the product of trained experts and non-professionals collaborating in a meaningful way.

For purposes of this book, we chose boundaries that contained the City of Jefferson as a workable historic designation. The Borough of Freeport, incorporated by an act of the Legislature on May 27, 1846, preceded by a little more than three years the incorporation of Jefferson City in the 1850 session of the State Legislature. The Borough of Freeport extended from Toledano Street to the Bloomingdale Line (a line in the middle of the squares between State and Webster streets), but Jefferson City's upper limit was Joseph Street. Jefferson City survived as an entity for twenty years until New Orleans absorbed it in 1870. Considered a great distance from the city, the early nineteenth-century French influence justified the term "faubourg" (suburb). Faubourg Plaisance was adjacent to the City of Lafayette, and upriver from it were the Faubourgs de la Chaise (later

3811 St. Charles Avenue, now Columns Hotel. Entrance Hall. (From family collection of Miss Tawney Harding, great-granddaughter of Simon Hernsheim, original owner. Courtesy Claire Creppel.)

3811 St. Charles Avenue, now Columns Hotel. Parlor. (From family collection of Miss Tawney Harding, great-granddaughter of Simon Hernsheim, original owner. Courtesy Claire Creppel.)

Delachaise), St. Joseph, East Bouligny, West Bouligny, Avart, and Rickerville. The boundaries were from Toledano to Joseph and from the river "back to the woods."

Many factors, both natural and man-made, contributed to the development of this area. The Mississippi River was a focal point for the location of plantations and the subsequent rural character of the land. The river was the transportation route and along it developed landings, brickyards, lumberyards, sawmills, cotton mills, and other industries. The State Legislature approved the charter for the New Orleans & Carrollton Rail Road Company in 1833, and its growth and expansion impacted the development of the area by providing a network of public transportation. When the Carrollton Line (later the St. Charles Line) started operation September 26, 1835, the *New Orleans Bee* reported: "The railroad from the city to Carrollton on the Mississippi, distant about four and a half miles, was opened to travel on Saturday last. The route passes through a level and beautiful country; very high, dry and arable land." In the days before the development of a mechanical drainage system, "high" and "dry" were of the utmost importance. Held in what is now Audubon Park, the financially disastrous World's Industrial and Cotton Centennial Exposition of 1884 contributed positively to Uptown growth.

City of Jefferson Improvements Bond, January 29, 1870. (Courtesy Louisiana State Museum.)

The transfer of real estate by subdivision, sheriffs' sales for non-payment of taxes, donation, succession, auction, and confiscation during the Civil War reflect socio-economic trends. Notarial acts also mirror the ensuing cataclysm of Reconstruction, followed by an upsurge of activity in land transfers and the building of large residences. From the mid-1880s until well after the turn of the century, huge single-family residences were constructed on St. Charles Avenue and other thoroughfares such as Napoleon and Marengo. Many of these fine residences have been destroyed or allowed to deteriorate. In some cases, only vacant lots are grim reminders of the past. On other sites, unattractive, large, multi-family structures have replaced the old mansions, with irreverent disregard for the surrounding neighborhood.

Rows of identical houses punctuate many Uptown streets. This repetitive rhythm that is so familiar is a forerunner of tract housing. It was economically advantageous to use the same plan for multiple dwellings, to get the materials in bulk, and to have the workmen repeat the same tasks and skills in the immediate area.

Relocating large houses was not an unusual occurrence. Soards' 1899 *Directory* lists four house-moving companies. Most of the records relating to this activity no longer exist, but notarial acts and maps substantiate movement of structures to less conspicuous locations and subdivision of valuable land. The simple economics of subdividing sizeable lots has resulted in a density that really began about one hundred years ago. More recently a profusion of town houses is literally wall to wall! In some cases, a house facing St. Charles or another prestigious street, remained in its original location and less pretentious dwellings filled surrounding lots. With a keen eye and a little imagination, it is not difficult to visualize how many of the fine homes must have looked without twentieth-century surroundings.

Gone are significant institutions and organizations whose roles either changed or became obsolete. De La Salle High School on St. Charles between Valmont and Leontine replaced New Orleans University (later Gilbert Academy), the first local institution of higher learning for emancipated blacks. Two orphanages flanked New Orleans University—the Asylum for Destitute Orphan Boys on the downtown side, and the Jewish Widows' and Children's Home (now the site of the Jewish Community Center) on the uptown side. There is no sign now of the American Athletic Club, with its natatorium and shooting range, that was prominently located facing Napoleon in the square bounded by Constance, Laurel and Gen. Pershing; or of the New Orleans Bicycle Club, built at the same time in 1892 in the square bounded by Baronne, Dryades, Constantinople and Gen. Taylor. The New Orleans & Carrollton Rail Road Company had extensive offices and stables in the two squares facing St. Charles between Napoleon, Gen. Pershing, Carondelet, and Pitt. The Stock Landing, the sawmills, brickyards, cotton mills and other businesses located on or near the river have disappeared.

The streets are all paved. There is no more "Rosetta Gravel," granite stone, planking, shell dressing, or "Shillinger"—a patented pavement of the Fritz Jahncke Company. As late as 1909, St. Charles was graveled on the lake-side and asphalt-paved on the river-side. Cisterns for collecting rainwater for household use are relics of the past, with only one extant, but not usable, within the boundaries of Jefferson City.

Although a number of significant structures have been built in this area since World War II, we have limited our inventory to the ninety years preceding that war—from 1850 to 1940. Archival research reveals that although there were numerous buildings in the area in the first half of the nineteenth century, none are extant. Demolitions and fires have taken their toll.

It is important to make explanations about two sets of city maps that have been vital to our research. The *Atlas of the City of New Orleans* by Elisha Robinson, published in New York in 1883, while important for its delineation of structures on site and identification of many property owners, contains inaccuracies which careful title research has corrected. C.A. Braun compiled the basic atlas information about 1873, and Robinson assembled more facts over a five or six year period (1875-1881). The atlas is not current to its date of publication. The *Insurance Maps of New Orleans, Louisiana* of 1887, 1893, 1896 and 1909 by the Sanborn-Perris Map Company of New York are extremely accurate, not only in outlining the shapes of the structures, but also in delineating the number of levels, types of materials used, the use of the building, street paving, and house numbering. It should be noted that Soards' 1896 *Directory* states that "the new, or decimal, system of house numbering was not entirely completed till about December 1, 1895."

City directories, too, are important in this type of research. New Orleans directories published before 1870 were not always precise on Jefferson City—still sparsely settled and distant from the city. With the publication of Soards' *New Orleans City Directory* of 1874 and for sixty years thereafter, accuracy and reliability resulted.

From the vantage point of a seven-year involvement in production of this publication, the story of Jefferson City emerges as a vital segment of the history of New Orleans. With Samuel Wilson's deft grasp of early history, Bernard Lemann's impressionistic essay, Sally Reeves' intriguing insight about the people and politics, John Walker's knowledge of surveyors and their profession, and Robert Cangelosi's architectural expertise, the whole effort comes together in sharp focus. This publication is truly a case of the whole being greater than the sum of its parts.

NEW ORLEANS ARCHITECTURE

VOLUME VII:
Jefferson City

Valence between Pitt and Prytania. (Photo credit: Alan Karchmer.)

St. Charles Avenue between Bordeaux and Cadiz (Lakeside). (Photo credit: Alan Karchmer.)

The Uptown Experience

BERNARD LEMANN

What is Uptown? Where is it?

There has been a sense, there is still a more or less general agreement, that the significant edge is Canal Street, the historic, traditional, perpetual division between the lower and the upper city. But today the Central Business District above Canal Street is the very center of Downtown, and only occasionally is it seen as "Up." This leaves Uptown, its extent and its position, always viewed ambivalently, according to the station point of the observer at any particular moment, and always certainly according to the attitude of any homebody.

Under these changeful conditions, Uptown must unavoidably be defined as a state of mind. In this sense it can be said that there never was, and never will be a shift in Uptown.

It can also be said that the City of Jefferson is geographically the very core of the amorphous Uptown spread. Uptown Square, the interesting commercial enterprise, for example, is located, unlike such district centers as Jackson and Lafayette squares, at the distant edge of Uptown and so necessarily out of the book. The City of Jefferson is hardly recognized or recalled today, except passingly when advertised at Mardi Gras by the old marching parade, the Jefferson City Buzzards.

Unfortunately, our crowded pages leave no space for Upper Uptown, especially the divisions of Burtheville, Bloomingdale, and Greenville (near the universities, the large park, and affluent families)—a truly reluctant omission, since in many respects this is the locale of the very heart of the Uptown attitude. Rich in landmarks and fine houses, the University Area, along with Carrollton and its Riverbend and Uptown Square, will have to await a future publication. Such a volume would be the counterpart to our *New Orleans Architecture Volume I: The Lower Garden District*

Virtually two distinct cities were separated at Canal Street. The lower one clung to the unchanging ways of old world character and the upper went in for a popular American sport called "Leadership." Even with this marked separation, an interesting play of give-and-take, within the surrounding circumstances of land, water, and history, combined to make New Orleans an unrepeatable phenomenon. Much of the city's initiatives in intellectual, civic, and commercial affairs tend to develop more conspicuously from the upper region, though never without some subtle influences from the old lower city's cultivation of music and leisure, creative cookery, and good times. Thus the distinctive New Orleans atmosphere continues to hover over the inner Crescent City as a whole, which will survive the current flight to the new residential outer regions.

Approaching the middle years of the last century, as the forces of American acumen were gathering momentum, the New Orleans & Carrollton Rail Road line became the spine of expansion linking the Uptown faubourgs. Expansion was fairly rapid throughout the remainder and past the turn of the century, in a chronological-linear thrust, combined with a hastening spatter pattern of new sites (like the spotting and gathering of first raindrops on a pavement). The acceleration was noteworthy. Kerr's 1856 city directory listed hardly more than two hundred fifty households, while Gardner's directory of 1868 had almost ten times that number. The town's 1860 census reported a population of 5,107, of whom 131 were "free persons of color." In 1870 Jefferson City's 25,000 expanded the 191,000 of New Orleans.

These few figures can lead us to visualize the cinematic picture of progressive changes: first the suburbanite villas, amply spaced, and nearby the fields and prairie land of former plantations, the layout of muddy streets and ditches, the gathering of sparse villages in a lengthening stretch accessible to the rail line and the old river road. A glance at the map may help to explain the relatively inland plotting of the railroad, a kind of compromise between the lengthy crescent curve and a direct New Orleans-to-Carrollton straight line, which would have reached too deeply toward the marshy middle of the crescent. With the extraordinary mechanical drainage system of the early 1900s, following the linkage of all suburbs into one single Uptown New Orleans, the direction of urban growth crept ever inward toward the "back o' town" streets, where already some modest rental row housing had evolved. The back land, especially of Bouligny, had been somewhat filled by alluvial deposit that spilled across the rear from Sauvé's upriver crevasse in 1849.

In sum, the scenario of this actively shifting urban pattern has been a complex function of three major factors: transportation service, available land, and cultural divergencies.

A broader perspective over the city might validly contrast the open spacing and greenery of Uptown (above the Central Business District) with the more closely urbanized environment of the lower city. A wide bird's-eye view over the Vieux Carré and beyond in all directions gives a strong impression of clustered rooftops

Around the St. Charles Belt. Complimentary publication of New Orleans & Carrollton Rail Road Light and Power Co., ca. 1906. (Courtesy Ben Bavly.)

Detail from "Topographical and Drainage Map of New Orleans prepared for Joseph Jones, M.D. by T.S. Hardee, Civil Engineer," 1880. (Courtesy J. Raymond Samuel.)

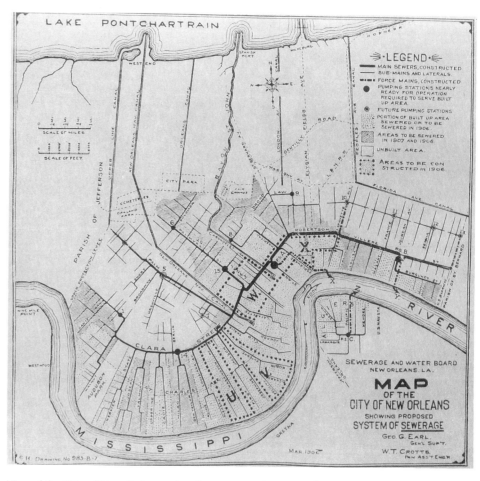

Map of the City of New Orleans showing proposed system of sewerage. *Architectural Art & Its Allies*, Vol.II, Nov. 1906. (Courtesy Louisiana Collection, Tulane University Library.)

and few trees. (Notable exceptions are Esplanade, Ursuline Avenue, and North Dorgenois.) Correspondingly, the upriver perspective hides the buildings in wreaths of subtropical forestry. Trees and flowering shrubs are unmistakable manifestations of Uptown (except for industrial areas near the river). The characteristic streetscapes, green tunnels lined with filtered glimpses of houses, cannot adequately be taken in by the camera eye. Only the roving glance of the pedestrian can absorb the experience from both sides, as well as in depth. For this reason, the most notable instances must be signaled here:

> Camp Street from Delachaise to Peniston
> Delachaise from St. Charles to Carondelet
> Delachaise from Magazine to Camp
> Foucher from Chestnut to Magazine
> Chestnut from Aline to Delachaise
> Carondelet from Amelia to Delachaise
> Carondelet from Gen. Taylor to Peniston
> Baronne from Soniat to Dufossat
> Soniat from Magazine to Constance
> Dufossat from Magazine to Constance
> Magazine from Bellecastle to Valence
> Magazine from Jefferson to Valmont
> Valmont from St. Charles to Blanc Place
> Blanc Place from Valmont to Dufossat
> Leontine from Coliseum to Prytania
> Chestnut from Octavia to Joseph
> and the major boulevards, St. Charles and Napoleon, full-length within
> our boundaries.

Other streets are handsomely shaded by large oaks leaning overhead from one side.

The overall character of Uptown was modified in certain details after significant developments in water supply, drainage, and sewerage—almost concurrently with the closing years of the district's dominant period. It is not possible to make a firm estimate of how many dwellings of about a century ago had rather conspicuous cypress cisterns, or what Victorian-Edwardian dwellings originally lacked bathrooms, a circumstance plainly disclosed today in those unseemly upstairs bulges.

The problems of supply and control of water in our swampy land have had a troubled history, reaching back throughout the nineteenth century and liberally dramatized in financial liquidations and numerous court battles. On January 19, 1869, the city acquired the waterworks from the Commercial Bank—as published in 1902 in the twenty-fourth annual report of the New Orleans Waterworks Company, Inc., which purchased the system on April 9, 1878. Separately, there had also been a New Orleans Sewerage Company. After complaints about excessive rates, the state legislature created the Sewerage and Water Board in an extra session in 1899. Following Legislative Act 111 (July 1902) and further litigation in the highest court, the New Orleans Drainage Commission (organized in 1896) was formally merged with the Sewerage and Water Board in January 1903.

Roger Baudier, in the sixteenth and final article of his interesting series on "Sanitation in New Orleans" (in *The Southern Plumber*, November 1930–April 1932), tells of the early years of the modern system. During the city's last yellow fever epidemic, in 1905, all cisterns were screened and oil spread over their water surface to seal off breeding places of stegomyia mosquitoes, the carriers of the disease. The result vindicated the mosquito theory, in spite of some scattered skepticism among the medical profession. Baudier tells that "eventually after full operation of the water system, cisterns were banished in New Orleans." Construction for sewerage began in June 1903, and the system went into operation in October 1907. Upon completion of the East Bank purification plant, filtered water was pumped into the system on February 6, 1909. During the first two decades of the Board, licensed plumbers were actively employed connecting households to the ever expanding water and sewer network. Meanwhile, drainage channels were extended, cleared of debris or vegetation, and gradually enclosed, ever increasing the livability of Uptown. Storm water, originally drained by gravity back into the woods, is now evacuated, even from the pocket below mean sea level, by the world-famed twelve-foot screw pumps designed by Baldwin Wood, who has been called "one of the fathers of Modern New Orleans."

It is interesting to note how the various components of Jefferson City have spontaneously zoned themselves, prior to official regulation, into separate but related neighborhoods. The river frontage still has some recall of early residential sites. As today, there was the necessity of commercial or industrial land use: the brickyards, saddlers, stables, the livestock landing, and slaughterhouse (the buzzards!). St. Charles Avenue (Nayades), a gracefully bending grand boulevard, still retains its splendid stride of large, spaced masses set back from the landscaped street, although more than half of its mansions of the 1890s have been destroyed. (Throughout the length of Jefferson City the avenue was the lineup of Thomas Sully's best work, and a few good examples remain.) Handsome large family dwellings on slightly smaller lots tend to gather in the side streets on either side and collectively constitute a kind of upper St. Charles artery. Magazine Street was once predominately residential, but has tended to become a commercial corridor. Beyond Magazine toward the river were the less pretentious dwellings,

7

tightly spaced and near the front property line. The same street character prevailed beyond St. Charles towards the "woods" (as old-timers used to say). It seems noticeable that the cross streets have more front yards and better houses than the up-down streets, which may have been considered less choice because of the numerous clattering lines of public transportation. Yet small businesses did not seem unwelcome in residential areas. The corner grocery is a familiar type; also the pharmacy or small family business—even to some extent on St. Charles Avenue. They were convenient for home deliveries or as meeting places for neighborhood conversation. Their gradual disappearance is to be regretted.

This prevailing scheme can be recognized in the nineteenth century directories as beginning to shape up, and its layout of buildings and streets can be seen as virtually completed in the Robinson *Atlas* of 1883. The grand parade of civic and commercial leaders stretched along the avenue, their co-workers in the vicinity. Farther away gathered the clerks, crafts people, domestics, laborers, and the rows of shops, services, and comestibles were midway and accessible to all.

Compared with previous volumes in this architectural series, our inventory is somewhat less a collection of romantically choice historic specimens. More significant than any single building or type is the coherence and workability of the whole seamless spread. The appreciation of urban form—the city as "autonomous structure" or as collective artifact extended in time—is a concept or attitude that has been growing among architects and theorists, even among bureaucrats who try to collect statistics on "environmental impact." It now has its verbal formulation in *Architecture of the City* by the Italian architect Aldo Rossi. The view of Uptown as a consciously willed joint creation of a community complex justifies this as a panoramic scene, a non-tourist, lived-in neighborhood. It scans an area that is generally overlooked, even taken for granted by Uptowners themselves. As

Roman Candy Wagon on St. Charles Avenue. (Photo credit: A.L. Schlesinger, Jr.)

BURGLAR ALARMS,
ELECTRIC BELLS,
Electric Supplies of all Kinds.
AMERICAN DISTRICT TELEGRAPH CO.
No. 47 Camp St.
Public Telephone Call 300.

Burglar alarm advertisement that appeared in Soards' 1885 *Directory*. (Courtesy Louisiana Collection, Tulane University Library.)

we move into the next century, the historic consistency of this widespread district will be increasingly recognized and valued for its unusual size and the quality of its visual message.

In this newer manner of overview, our compilation should take into account not only buildings and trees, the brick sidewalks and grassy trenches of earlier drainage, but also the mobile peopling of the streets, the passing vehicles, and the intangibles of the environment; the heavy, saturated atmosphere, tentative whiffs of sweet olive or night-blooming jasmine, the fierce sunlight, the drenching cloudbursts, the welcome movement of air and foliage or dramatic wind gusts, the city sounds and lingering ghostly remembrances that have been all but totally dissolved by time, economics and air conditioning. Rocking chair porch watching was permissable in the St. Charles artery, and stoop sitting was an enormously influential factor of social intercourse in the streets of banquette-aligned shotgun houses. Middle-aged and older residents should be able to recall the street cries of the *ramoneur* (chimney sweep), the vendor of clothes poles, the blackberry woman with bandanna and balanced basket, the clap-clop sound of the milk wagon and vegetable cart. Too long ago, but memorialized by hearsay, are the bottle collectors who traded goodies or trinkets with their young suppliers, the knife and scissors sharpeners, and the organ grinders, with or without a pet monkey. With windows closed, no longer do we notice the plaintive river sounds, but modern times have brought us the excitement of frequent fire engine and police sirens, the jazz of political loudspeakers, and the ding-dong ice cream truck. Only the Roman Candy man's grandson carries on in his picturesque mule cart, his distinctive bell a comforting reassurance that the Uptown experience is a continuing reality. His white wagon, a family heirloom, should join the St. Charles Avenue streetcar among the items in the National Register of Historic Places.

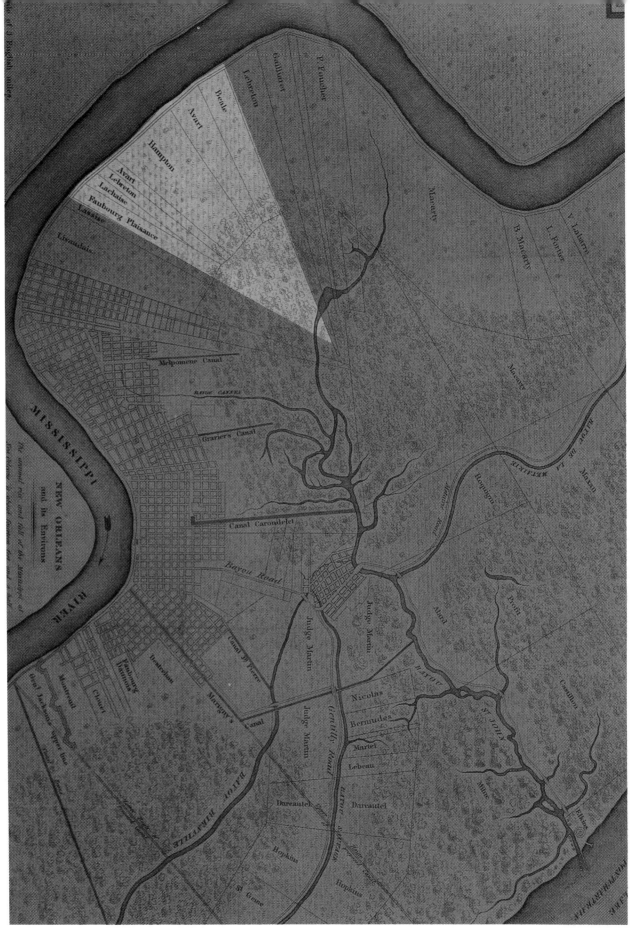

Detail from "New Orleans and its Environs," F.B. Ogden, 1829. Shows pre-Jefferson City land divisions. Note that Wade Hampton owned all the land that eventually became Faubourg Bouligny. (Richard Koch Collection. Courtesy The Historic New Orleans Collection, Museum/Research Center, Acc. No. 1971.21.)

Early History

SAMUEL WILSON, JR., F.A.I.A.

The area of Uptown New Orleans that was incorporated as Jefferson City in 1850 and consisted of the Faubourgs Plaisance, Delachaise, St. Joseph, East and West Bouligny, Avart, and Rickerville, was annexed to New Orleans in 1870. It was once part of the vast east bank plantation that was granted to the city's founder, Jean Baptiste LeMoyne, Sieur de Bienville, by the Superior Council of Louisiana on March 27, 1719.

After the French crown refused authorization to hold such extensive lands, Bienville, in January 1723, began to subdivide the part of his plantation upriver from an area that he later sold to the Jesuits. He granted these parcels, ranging from six to eighteen *arpents* to various settlers, mostly German immigrants, on a perpetual ground rent basis.

In 1737, on Bienville's orders, François Saucier surveyed each grant, including one of six *arpents* owned by the Sieur Raymond Amyault d'Ausseville, Attorney of Vacant Estates. In the *procès-verbal* of survey, Saucier stated that the six *arpents* had originally belonged to one André Crestmane, who was "possessor of said land by virtue of the cession made to him directly by my said Sieur de Bienville, Lord and proprietor of this land by contract passed before Rossard, Notary Royal in Louisiana on the first of January, one thousand seven hundred and twenty three, at a rental of eight *livres*, three *sols*, four *deniers* of rent for each *arpent* beginning on the first of January, one thousand seven hundred and twenty five, as also of six *capons* and ten days of labor for each year."

Saucier described D'Ausseville's plantation as "a tract consisting of six *arpents* fronting on the River Saint Louis by forty in depth, situated at a distance of one league above New Orleans, the said land protected by a levee along the river, having the quantity of seventy-two *arpents* in area cleared on which land we have found a barn built on ground sills and fifteen negro cabins, the said land culti-vated in food stuffs." D'Ausseville had bought the plantation on August 5, 1735, from Pierre Voisin, who had acquired it from Sieur Buchet on November 27, 1731. Buchet had purchased it from the original grantee, André Crestmane, on June 22, 1730.

According to the 1737 Saucier surveys, the plantation upriver, adjacent to that of the Sieur D'Ausseville, belonged to the Sieur François Joseph Couturier, an employee of the King in the Bureau of the Marine. It was described as a "tract of eight *arpents* and fifteen *toises* front by forty *arpents* in depth . . . protected by a levee along the river . . . on which land we found a house on ground-sills, another of posts in the ground, an old barn, a dovecote of brick and timber framing and two negro cabins."

When Saucier made his survey of the Couturier plantation in October 1737, he noted that it had been purchased only recently on August 17, 1737 from Dame

Elizabeth Guiolle, wife of Sieur Cesar de Blanc, Captain of a detached company of the Marine. De Blanc was granted this eight *arpent* tract on May 1, 1728 by the Sieur de Noyan, acting on behalf of his uncle, Bienville.

Next above Couturier's land was the eight and one-half *arpent* plantation that the Sieur de Noyan, acting for Bienville, on the same day, May 1, 1728, granted to the Sieur Pacquier, Counsellor in the Superior Council. The land was cultivated in vegetables and indigo. The only buildings on the land were twelve negro cabins and a storehouse. A census made of the area in 1724 indicates that the Couturier and Pacquier tracts had previously been granted to others who had probably abandoned them or failed to pay the agreed upon rental fees, and the land reverted to Bienville.

The six *arpent* tract on the downriver side of D'Ausseville's plantation, according to Saucier's 1737 survey, belonged to Charles Petit, Esquire, Sieur de Levillier, Captain of a detached company of the Marine. The land was cultivated in rice and corn, and on it was a one-room house on ground-sills and a kitchen with a framework of *poteaux en terre*. Petit had bought the land from Louis Roys and his wife, Marie Jeanne, on June 24, 1737. Louis Roys was probably the same Louis Roisset, who purchased the land on April 10, 1727 "from one Jacques Ouvre, a German and Barbe Chauvinne, his wife." Jacques Ouvre (or Oubre) was a French spelling of the German name Jacob Huber, to whom Bienville had granted the land on January 1, 1723.

Downriver and adjacent to the Petit tract was another six *arpent* plantation owned, according to Saucier's 1737 survey, by the Sieur Livaudais, Captain of the Port of New Orleans. It had originally been granted by de Noyan, acting for Bienville, on November 20, 1726, to Gaspart Keel, a German. Keel sold the land to Louis Vigier who, on October 20, 1729, sold it to Livaudais and a Monsieur de Mondreloir. Livaudais then acquired de Mondreloir's half-interest on January 16, 1732. Forty-eight square *arpents* of the Livaudais plantation were "cleared and sown with foodstuffs, on which land we found a barn and five negro huts." Livaudais descendants owned several other plantations in what is now Uptown New Orleans, one of which in 1832 was sold and subdivided to become most of today's Garden District.

From Bienville's original grants to German families, many of these tracts passed into the ownership of the most prominent of Louisiana's French colonial families.

From the mention of buildings existing on these plantations in the 1737 surveys, it would appear that the owners did not live on the plantations, for few of them had even a small house for brief visits or for an overseer. In the entire area from the upper limit of the Jesuits' plantation as far up as the present Jefferson Parish line, only seven of the more than twenty plantations had any sort of house.

The most elaborate was that of the Sieur Hubert Bellair in the name of his wife, the widow of Etienne Roy, to whom Bienville had granted the land on September 1, 1723. According to the 1724 census, Etienne Roy was then thirty-three years of age, a native of Montreal, Canada and a nephew of Monsieur Chauvin. On his ten *arpent* plantation he lived with his wife and a female Indian slave and one cow. The census record notes that "he is served only by his female savage and with the help of 14 days-work-negroes for de-stumping on his land where he has cut the first canes. He counts on harvesting 200 barrels, having more than 200 sheaves in his barn, and he will be able to extract around thirty barrels from the second cutting, which he hopes to make, provided that a freeze does not supervene. The rice is almost ripe."

The buildings on the former Roy plantation belonging to Hubert Bellair, according to the 1737 survey, were "a house on ground sills consisting in a salon, a chamber, and a cabinet; a shed, a store house, a dovecote, a poultry house, a kitchen and five negro cabins."

These buildings were probably of the simple frame or *colombage* construction that had been used by the French in Louisiana since the earliest days. Heavy timber sills were placed on the ground, into which vertical timbers were mortised and tenoned, as also into a plate at the top. On this plate, trusses were erected to form a hipped roof, which was then covered with split shingles or bark roofing. Doors and windows were framed between vertical wall timbers with sills and heads, sometimes cut in a segmental form, mortised and tenoned between them. The walls were then covered with horizontal boards on the exterior and sometimes on the interior. Generally the door and window openings were closed with batten shutters without glazed sash. The spaces between the wall timbers were sometimes filled with bricks between posts, or with a mixture of mud and moss known as *bousillage*.

An interesting contract for such a house was passed between Michel Vien and Raymond Amyault, Esquire, Sieur D'Ausseville, for a house to be built on his plantation in 1730. The location of the plantation is not given, but it was probably not the one that eventually became part of the Faubourg Bouligny, which D'Ausseville did not acquire until 1735 and on which in 1737 there was only "a barn built on ground sills and fifteen negro cabins." This contract, dated June 27, 1730, is as follows:

> We undersigned—Raymond Amyault, Esquire, Sieur D'Ausseville and Michel Vien have agreed to what follows, To wit:—that I the said Vien obligate myself to build on the plantation of the said Sr. D'Ausseville a house of forty-five to fifty feet long by twenty-two or more wide as the length of the wood will permit, the said building with two frame cross walls which will form three chambers; twelve windows and a gallery five feet wide all around the said house, on sills well timbered and with St. Andrew Crosses in all the voids and elevated above some blocks of four to five feet high, the rafters strong and set close enough one to the other in order to be roofed with double planks in the Canadian manner. At which building I the said Vien obligate myself to work regularly, beginning Monday next, because he will furnish me with Negroes to set up and erect the timbers, and there will be paid to me after the said house is done, the sum of two hundred fifty *livres*, money of this country. To all of which we have obligated ourselves, each of us in whatever concerns us, under penalty of all expenses, damages and interests, the one towards the other. Done and signed in duplicate at New Orleans the twenty-seven of June, one thousand seven hundred thirty.

On October 18, 1730, D'Ausseville filed suit against his builder Vien, claiming various omissions and modifications from the terms of the contract. D'Ausseville complained that "Among other faults the house is only about a foot and a half above ground level, instead of 4 to 5 feet. Neither was the work done in time stipulated. Vien and his partner were fed over and above the bargain and also received a bonus of wine. Let Vien be cited to make due alterations, and let him be sentenced to 500 *francs* by way of damage for delay."

The matter was submitted to arbitration. Jean Coupart, representing D'Ausseville, found various positive departures from the contract in respect to dimensions and spacing and reduced number of windows. He admitted, however, that the quality of construction was good, the house was very solid and well built and capably joined. Michel Vien's representative generally agreed that the plan was

13

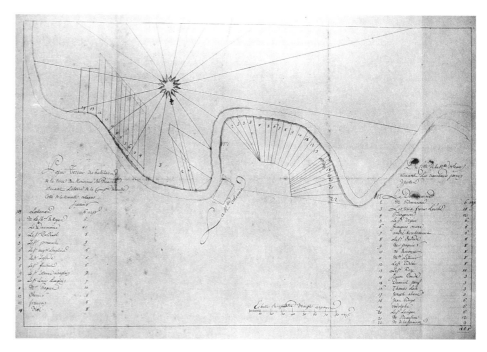

Bienville's Land Grants from King Louis XV (ca. 1725). Lower line of #2 is Felicity Street and upper line of #22 is the Protection Levee at Carrollton. Book of Concessions, Louisiana State Museum. (Courtesy Samuel Wilson, Jr.)

not carried out to the letter, but that the construction was sound. It was finally decided on December 5, 1730 that Vien would make the specified changes as called for in the original contract or else D'Ausseville could employ carpenters to make them at Vien's expense.

D'Ausseville died in 1746, and his plantation, which then contained seventeen *arpents*, was sold by his succession to Robert Avart. After Avart's death, his widow, Jeanne Joseph Piquery, married Louis Piot de Launay. After her death, a controversy arose between de Launay and Louis Le Blanc and Valentin Robert Avart, stepson and son of Robert Avart. It was then agreed that certain slaves belonged to de Launay and the seventeen *arpent* former D'Ausseville plantation should be equally divided between Le Blanc and Avart, each receiving eight and one-half *arpents*. This agreement is recorded in an act passed before the notary J.B. Garic on January 21, 1772.

After the death of Avart's neighbor, Joseph Dubord, the younger Avart bought Dubord's twelve *arpent* plantation on February 7, 1778 before Garic. He further enlarged his holdings when on November 29, 1787, before the notary Fernando Rodriguez, he purchased the nine *arpent* plantation of his neighbor Réné Huchet de Kernion. This de Kernion plantation had been sold by Genevieve Babin, widow of Jacques Livaudais, on November 5, 1777, by an act passed before the notary Andres Almonester y Roxas. This may have included the six *arpents* originally granted to Livaudais by Bienville in 1726.

By the time of his death on August 2, 1807, Valentin Robert Avart's plantation contained thirty-eight *arpents*, fronting the river by the usual depth of forty *arpents*. He had apparently acquired the other eight and one-half *arpents* that had originally been given to his half-brother, Louis Le Blanc.

After Avart's death, an inventory of his estate was made by the Deputy Register of Wills, Pierre Ambroise Cuvillier, on October 13, 1807. He recorded that he left the city at eight o'clock in the morning to go up to the Avart plantation "at around four miles from the city." There he met the five sons of Valentin Robert Avart: Louis, François Robert, Celestin, Valeri, and Erasme, all more than twenty-one years of age. Also present was Jean de Lassize, representing his wife Eulalie, Avart's daughter. De Lassize was the owner of a downriver plantation whose upper boundary, now Toledano Street, eventually became the lower line of the City of Jefferson.

The inventory was begun in the principal house of the plantation, a house with a plan similar to that of a typical French colonial house. Three rooms across the front consisted of the salon in the center with a bedroom on each side. Across the back, in the center, was the dining room with a smaller room on each side. The kitchen was a one-room structure in the yard. The furnishings of each room were then listed in the inventory, including two door curtains and two window curtains in the salon. Next came a listing of the farm animals, followed by lists of the numerous male and female slaves.

The plantation was inventoried as "thirty-eight *arpents* of land facing the river, by forty *arpents* of depth, bounded on the upper side by the plantation of Madame Widow Ducros and on the lower side by the plantation of Mr. Joseph Wiltz." The buildings were listed as being located on three different sections of the plantation. On the upper part were "a house of around sixty feet in length by around thirty of width, composed of eight apartments [rooms]; dependent from the said house, a storehouse in bad condition, having around thirty-five feet of length by twelve of width; four wretched negro cabins of sixteen feet by twelve feet in width."

The principal house was located in the center section of the plantation and was described as "having around seventy feet of length including the galleries, by around forty-six of depth including the gallery, the said house in very bad condition; a storehouse of around fifty feet of length with a surrounding gallery, posts in the ground, the said store house having around twenty feet of width, divided into three compartments; a wretched kitchen of around thirty feet of length by around fifteen of width, falling into dilapidation; a shed surrounded with stakes, of around forty feet of length by thirty of width, having a gallery in front, also of around ten feet in width; an old building serving for drying indigo, having around thirty feet of length by around fourteen of width and a gallery of around eight feet. Three wretched empty poultry houses; twenty-four negro cabins, good as well as bad; a brick sugar house of around ninety feet of length by forty four of width or thereabout, with all its dependences, to wit: a complete equipage, two cisterns containing around ninety *bon caux four* wood coolers of cypress, two large boilers also for cooling."

In the lower part of the plantation was "a brickworks established in a new shed of around ninety feet in length including the galleries, by around fifty feet of width also including the galleries; a brick kiln of around thirty feet of length by twenty feet of width, to provide baking after a bit, eighty thousand bricks, four kneading troughs, a chaplet pump with its wheel for furnishing water to the said troughs."

Three of the Avart brothers—Louis, François and Celestin—objected to including these brickyard buildings in the inventory, saying that about two years previously their father had verbally given them permission to build these buildings on this part of the plantation, and that the buildings belonged to them, not to their father's succession. Their other two brothers, Valeri and Erasme, and their brother-in-law, Jean de Lassize, acting for his wife, their sister Eulalie, agreed,

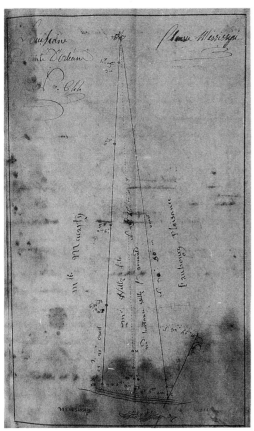

Survey of Division of Wiltz Property. Surveyor and date illegible. Attached to Notary Public Michel de Armas, Acts 6/350, July 8, 1811. New Orleans Notarial Archives. (Photo credit: Bert Myers.)

saying that "they had a perfect and entire knowledge that the late Valentin Robert Avart, their father, at around two years ago, permitted the said Sieurs Louis, François and Celestin Avart to establish for their own account, a brick works on a piece of land where the said brick works is presently situated, agreeing to let them enjoy it as long as they wished, or that in case that it was ever necessary to prevent them from it that their expenses would be reimbursed and they would be left free to take away and take down all their buildings of whatever nature they might be. . . . They also declared that they would never oppose, in their capacities, what the said Sieurs Louis, François and Celestin Avart continue to work and to leave their buildings on the said piece of land as long as the said plantation shall remain to the community." This was probably the brickyard that was later owned by P.A. Delachaise, and produced bricks for many New Orleans buildings in the 1830s.

In addition to the brickyard, this lower section of the Avart plantation also contained "a house of around thirty-two feet of length by twelve feet of width, on ground sills with galleries in front and rear, posts in the ground, divided into three rooms; six negro cabins of around sixteen feet of length by twelve of width, a wretched dovecote of twelve feet of length by eleven of width; and finding also around one hundred fifty *arpents* of sugar cane . . . the most part quite puny and promising little." The total value of the plantation, according to the 1807 inventory, was estimated at $130,815.25.

The *Louisiana Courier* for July 31, 1811 carried the following advertisement for the sale of a plantation adjacent to the Avart brickyard, but did not give the name of the owner of the property, who was also probably the builder of the "newly built" mansion house and other buildings mentioned.

FOR SALE—A Plantation situated about a league above the city, containing six *arpents* fronting the river, by forty *arpents* in depth, joining on one side the plantation of the widow Louis Avart, and extending above as far as the brickyard of Mr. Robert Avart. There are on said plantation a mansion house, stores, sheds, coach houses, and negro cabins, the whole newly built, an orchard planted with vines and fruit trees from Philadelphia, with a crop which brings in a daily revenue.

There will be sold with the plantation, the cattle and implements of husbandry, as also several slaves of both sexes, as well creoles as natives of Guinea.

In cases persons would wish to purchase a part of said plantation, the land will be divided into lots of one or two *arpents*, as the purchaser may think proper.

FAUBOURG PLAISANCE

The Faubourg Plaisance, in 1807, was the first subdivision of a plantation in the area that eventually became Jefferson City, being preceded in the nineteenth century only by the Faubourg Marigny in 1805 and the Faubourg Annunciation in 1806. It was also one of the smallest, measuring only about four *arpents* of front to the river.

It was purchased by Joseph Wiltz in 1800, and in 1807 he had a handsome plan for a subdivision drawn up by the architect Jean Hyacinthe Laclotte, and gave it the name of Plaisance (Pleasure), from which the name of Pleasant Street was derived. To the principal avenue he gave his own name, calling it the Grand Cours Wiltz, which eventually became Louisiana Avenue. A parallel street, unnamed on the plan, became Delachaise Street and formed the boundary between the Wiltz and Avart properties. Part of this Avart holding subsequently became the plantation of Philippe Auguste Delachaise.

Laclotte's drawing was entitled: "Quartier de Plaisance/Plan/of the Plantation of Mr. Jh. Wiltz/at 2½ miles above the city/Divided into lots spacious enough in order to there establish Country Houses, Road-side Inns, Gardens, etc./Note: The Lots numbered and colored in Red are the only ones to be sold for the present./New Orleans the 22 June, 1807/Drawn by H'the Laclotte, Arch't."

The drawing was presented in two parts, at different scales. The half to the right showed the layout of the streets and lots, extending from the river to the cypress swamp, or *cyprière*, in the rear. The other half of the drawing was a large-scale suggested development of one of the typical lots facing the Grand Cours Wiltz, showing the plan of a house with an elaborate layout of formal gardens, *parterres*, and avenues of trees. The well-studied plan of this elaborate country estate was one of Laclotte's earliest projects after he came to New Orleans from his native city of Bordeaux, France. It was entitled "Plan of Arrangement of a Lot of 180 feet of front by 340 of depth."

It is doubtful if such a splendid house and garden were ever built on the Grand Cours Wiltz, or if indeed the avenue itself ever came into being for many years. Apparently the purchasers of the lots were responsible for the building of the roads and the planting of the fine avenues of trees as envisioned by Laclotte. Wiltz, in a lengthy note written on Laclotte's plan, explained the privileges and responsibilities of the purchasers:

> The portion of frontage, of Batture, of Savannah and of cypress swamp, corresponding to the forty-two sites put up for sale for the present, and conforming to the titles of ownership of the vendor, is abandoned in perpetuity in favor of the purchasers to be enjoyed by them in common, with this sole condition that the said purchasers can send into the common pasture only at the rate of three heads of animals for each lot and may cut wood in the *cyprière* for their own use and not for commerce.
>
> The two large roads are each one hundred feet in width and the two others ninety feet.
>
> The trees along the roads and the canals or drainage ditches will be planted and done by the purchasers as well as the roads.
>
> New Orleans, the 22 June 1807
> Joseph Wiltz

One of the first sales of property in the Faubourg Plaisance was made by Joseph Wiltz to his son Louis J. Wiltz, who acquired lots 22 and 23 on the Grand Cours Wiltz at some distance back from the river, each lot being 180 feet front by 340 feet. Several lots were sold on July 10, 1807, one to Charles Victor Mansury de Pelletier, an engineer and surveyor who bought Lot No. 2, 170 feet facing the river, and 360 feet along the lower side of the Grand Cours Wiltz, for which he paid $2,100. According to the terms of the act of sale, "the vendor promises and obligates himself to immediately build the road marked on the square insert of the said plan, having ten feet of banquette starting from the lots facing the river and forty feet of road as far as the ditch." Four lots on the upper side of the Grand Cours were sold three days later to Pierre François Dubourg de St. Colombe, and two others to Jean Gourjon (Goujon).

Joseph Wiltz had been acquiring plantations in this area since at least 1797, but did not live to see his Faubourg Plaisance become a successful development. It was not until after the building of the New Orleans and Carrollton Rail Road in 1834 that the Grand Cours Wiltz, renamed Louisiana Avenue, really began to develop.

On July 8, 1811, Wiltz's son and daughter, his sole heirs, divided the remainder of his property, a plantation of four *arpents*, sixty-six feet, adjacent upriver to the

Detail of Laclotte Plan. Notarial Archives, Plan Book 28, Folio 1.

Faubourg Plaisance and bounded on the upper side by the tract of Mlle. Jeanne Macarty. Wiltz's daughter Hortanse (Hortaire), wife of Jean Arnauld (Arnault, Arnaud), received the half of the plantation adjacent to Plaisance, with the buildings, while her brother, Louis Joseph Laurent Wiltz, received the other half. He apparently operated the old Avart brickworks on his sister's half of the plantation, for which he paid a rent of $1,500 per year and was also allowed to use two negro cabins.

FAUBOURG DELACHAISE

The two halves of the Wiltz plantation inherited by Joseph Wiltz's son and daughter in 1811 were eventually acquired by Philippe Auguste Delachaise. On July 22, 1820, before the notary Michel de Armas, Delachaise purchased a half interest in the tract that had belonged to Hortanse Wiltz Arnauld, and on May 18, 1822, before the notary G.H. Stringer, he acquired the other undivided half from noted Louisiana historian François Xavier Martin. Then on October 6, 1823, before Marc Lafitte, notary, he acquired the half of the plantation that Louis Joseph Laurent Wiltz had inherited from his father.

Delachaise later enlarged the former Wiltz plantation by purchasing from Jean Baptiste François Le Breton an additional two and one-half *arpents*, the small tract that had formerly been owned by Mlle. Macarty. The act of sale was passed before the notary Carlisle Pollock on February 14, 1831. The whole of the eight *arpent* plantation was part of the land of thirty-eight *arpents* that had comprised the plantation of Valentin Robert Avart at the time of his death in 1807.

By the late 1830s most of the Avart plantation had been subdivided as the Faubourg Bouligny, leaving only the Delachaise plantation and a small plantation of the Widow Louis Avart, as well as a larger one of F.R. Avart, above Bouligny still in agricultural use. When P.A. Delachaise died in 1838, his estate was inherited by his widow Marie Antonine Foucher, and his three minor children, Pierre Auguste, Elizabeth Lucienne, and Louis Philippe Delachaise. An inventory of his Jefferson Parish plantation was then made on June 12, 1838, beginning in the principal house, "the late domicile of the said Philippe Auguste Delachaise, deceased, at their plantation adjoining Plaisance, situated on the left bank of the River Mississippi."

The house was not a large one and included a parlor, used also as a library, in which there were 522 books. There was also a dining room with a small *cabinet* next to it, and two pantries. There were three bedrooms—the master bedroom, one for the daughter, and one for the two sons. The contents of each room was listed, as well as the contents of the cellar, the agricultural tools, the horses, mules, cattle, and other stock, and eighty-seven slaves attached to the plantation were listed by name, age, sex, and occupation. Then there was listed the following:

Landed Property
Buildings, Improvements, &c.

A tract of land or plantation together with the right of batture . . . situated in this Parish of Jefferson on the left Bank of the River Mississippi measuring eight *arpents* more or less front on said River by a depth growing narrower, according to the titles, bounded on one side by *Quartier de Plaisance*, on the other side by the property of Widow Avart and composed of

1st. Two *arpents* and thirty feet . . . next to *Quartier de Plaisance* . . .

2nd. The balance of the eight *arpents*, composed of three tracts purchased of Fonvergnes, Mon—— and Le Breton valued . . . at an average of fifteen thousand dollars an *arpent* $120,000.00

The Dwelling House on the two *arpents* and thirty feet of ground next to *Quartier de Plaisance* . . . valued by the experts at . . . $1,500.00
All the buildings and improvements on the plantation consisting of one brick kitchen, one brick pigeon house, four brick furnaces, four sheds for bricks, six *petrines pour briques* (troughs for bricks), one corn store, two stables, two small houses, one for the overseer and one for the gardener, the fences in bad order, valued together . . . $20,000.00

Then were listed a number of lots in the Faubourg Plaisance inherited by Madame Delachaise from her late father, Pierre Foucher.

The total value of the land and buildings was estimated at $173,960. Charles F. Zimpel's "Topographical Map of New Orleans and Its Vicinity" of 1834 shows the Delachaise plantation, its front section along Levee Street divided into three sections. On the lower section adjacent to the Faubourg Plaisance, the plantation house and its outbuildings are shown with elaborate gardens in front. In the center section are the various yards and buildings of the brickworks, probably somewhat enlarged from the earlier brickyard of the Avart brothers. Delachaise brick was a popular building material in New Orleans in the nineteenth century. In the third or upper section are shown two buildings with a rectangular area behind them of undesignated use.

It was not until 1855 that the Delachaise heirs finally had the family plantation subdivided into squares and lots to which they gave the name Faubourg Delachaise. This was the last of the plantations to be subdivided in what has become Uptown New Orleans, as far up as the Bloomingdale Line between State Street and Webster/Palmer Avenue. The streets in the new faubourg perpendicular to the river were given names of the Delachaise family—Delachaise Street forming the boundary between it and the adjacent Faubourg Plaisance. The next street, Aline, was named for Aline Delachaise, wife of François Enoul Dugué de Livaudais. Foucher and Antonine streets were named for Antonine Foucher, wife of Philippe Auguste Delachaise.

According the 1883 Robinson *Atlas*, the Delachaise Brick Works was then still in operation and occupied a four-block area bounded by Foucher, Amelia, Tchoupitoulas, and Laurel streets—the same area occupied by the brickyard as shown on the Zimpel map. The adjacent four squares between the brickworks and the Faubourg Plaisance in 1883 was an open area designated as Delachaise Park, bounded by Delachaise, Foucher, Tchoupitoulas, and Laurel streets. This was the area occupied by the Delachaise Plantation house, according to Zimpel's 1834 map. Both these areas were subsequently subdivided into building lots with Aline, Antonine, and Annunciation streets being extended through them to divide each of the areas into four squares. All are now built up with houses or other buildings.

FAUBOURG ST. JOSEPH

Extending along the river between what are now Amelia and Gen. Taylor streets was a small plantation of three *arpents*, immediately upriver above the Delachaise plantation. This plantation was part of the estate of Louis Robert Avart inherited by his widow, Claude Augustine Eugénie Delachaise. The widow Avart subdivided the property into squares and lots according to a plan dated March 1, 1849, drawn by the surveyor Benjamin Buisson, and she named her new subdivision Faubourg St. Joseph. Two of the three streets of the faubourg, Amelia and Peniston, were named for Madame Avart's adopted daughter Amelia Duplantier, the wife of Dr. Thomas Peniston. The third street, Gen. Taylor, was named in honor of Zachary Taylor, then the popular hero of the Mexican War, and Louisiana's only president of the United States.

FAUBOURG BOULIGNY

Just above the small Faubourg St. Joseph was the largest of the faubourgs that eventually were incorporated as Jefferson City. It was part of the thirty-eight *arpent* plantation of Valentin Robert Avart. After Avart's death in 1807, the plantation was divided between his widow and their children. His widow, Julie Allain, eventually acquired a total of twenty-three and one-half *arpents*, including her own inheritance as well as acquisitions from other heirs. In 1816, Gen. Wade Hampton of South Carolina purchased these twenty-three and one-half *arpents*, seventeen *arpents* from Abner L. Duncan, and six and one-half *arpents* from Pierre Laurans. Duncan sold his seventeen *arpents* to General Hampton on March 26, 1816, only ten days after he had purchased them from the Widow Avart before the notary Michel de Armas on March 16.

General Hampton called his plantation "The Cottage" and owned it until 1829 when on April 7, before the notary Louis T. Caire, he sold it to Louis Bouligny. Two years later, on April 19, 1831, before the same notary, Bouligny sold the lower half of the plantation to Samuel Kohn and Laurent Millaudon. On the same day, again before the same notary, Kohn and Millaudon leased back to Louis Bouligny for a period of eight years, the eleven and three-quarter *arpents* they had just purchased, excepting from the lease "the batture that is located on the river in front of the said eleven and three-quarters *arpents* . . . of which the Sieurs Kohn and Millaudon are already in possession." Also excluded from the lease was "all the front of the half of the plantation . . . that is to say a portion of the land facing the public road and extending from the limit of Lady Widow Louis Avart as far as that of the said Sieur Louis Bouligny by two *arpents* of depth, this portion of land being at this time planted with canes. The said Sieur Bouligny shall have possession and enjoyment of it until the first of January eighteen thirty-two, at which time the said Sieurs Kohn and Millaudon will be put in possession and enjoyment of the said portion of land to do and dispose of as might seem good to them."

A few days before his act of sale for the Cottage Plantation was passed in 1829, Louis Bouligny entered into a building contract before the notary Louis T. Caire with Michael Jones, a master builder who, according to the terms of the contract of April 4, 1829, "does bind himself to build and finish well, duly and in a workmanlike manner, a house to be erected on Mr. Bouligny's plantation at about one league from the City and on the same side of the river Mississippi at such a distance from the public road as the proprietor will designate."

At the time of passing this contract, Bouligny was a resident of Plaquemines Parish and evidently intended to establish himself on his new property in Jefferson Parish. The contract is unusual, as it is written in both French and English, each page being divided by a line from top to bottom, with the text in English on the left and in French on the right. Plans of the house were signed by the owner and the builder, but unfortunately, a copy was not attached to the contract, nor is it stated by whom the plans were drawn.

The house was to be fifty-one feet across the front and forty-four in depth. It was to be raised eight feet above the ground on brick pillars, the walls above to be "filled with bricks between posts and the frame at each corner and inside shall have French braces." A twelve-foot-wide gallery "with a bannister breast high"

Detail from Plan Book 110, Folio 9. Drawing by Jacob Rothaas, December 22, 1833. New Orleans Notarial Archives. (Courtesy Samuel Wilson, Jr.)

extended across the front of the house, and three rooms of equal size, each with its fireplace and wood mantel, opened onto it. Behind these three rooms were a dining room fourteen feet by twenty-two feet, with a twelve by sixteen foot small room or *cabinet* at each end. The contract also mentions that "as Mr. Bouligny intends, after a while, to divide the ground floor in several rooms, said master builder does hereby bind himself to build chimneys that will correspond with that of the upper part of the house." The house was to be completed within three months of the date of the contract for the total price of $2,730. There is no indication of the exact location of this typical French-style house of the early nineteenth century, which was built before the streets of Faubourg Bouligny were laid out.

Another early house in the Faubourg Bouligny faced the river and, after the streets were laid out, is believed to have occupied the square facing Laurel between Valence and Bordeaux streets. This house is shown in an interesting watercolor drawing by Jacob Rothaas dated December 22, 1833, filed in Plan Book 110, folio 9 in the New Orleans Notarial Archives. The house is shown as an impressive hipped roof structure with a deep cornice supported on eight Doric columns with a wood railing between them and a stair in the center bay leading from the ground to the gallery. Five french doors open onto the gallery across the front of the house, a single window is shown in the left end wall, and two dormers are shown in the front slope of the roof. At the left rear corner of the house is a tall wood cistern, and across the front of the property is a handsome wood picket fence with heavy square wood fence posts topped by round balls. The house appears to be raised about five or six feet above the ground. To the right, facing the side of the house, is a one-story, gable-end building with tall, slender, wood columns across the front, probably a kitchen. Further to the right are two tall, square *pigeonniers* with pyramidal roofs and a simple barn-like structure. These outbuildings appear behind a *pieux* fence, and as a final pastoral touch, the artist depicts in the foreground a shepherd with his dog and several cows and sheep. The accompanying plan shows only the outline of the various buildings, but indicates that the main house had a five-bay recessed rear porch, beyond which was a small, formal garden flanked by symmetrically placed cisterns. Possibly this was the house that Louis Bouligny built in 1829, with some changes in the design as originally specified in the contract.

A map of West Bouligny made by Zimpel for the April 10, 1834 sale at the Exchange shows houses existing on two squares in the area, one in Square No. 10 bounded by Jersey (now Annunciation), Cadiz, Laurel, and Valence streets, and the other in Square No. 13 bounded by Laurel, Napoleon, Live Oak (now Constance), and Jena streets. One of these houses may be intended to be the handsome house shown in the Rothaas drawing of 1833. This map, and Zimpel's great "Topographical Map" of 1834, show public squares on Napoleon Avenue at nearly equal distance from St. Charles Avenue (then called Nayades). The square closer to the river, between Camp and Magazine, was called "Laurence Place" in honor of Laurent Millaudon, and the other was "Samuel Place" for Samuel Kohn, indicating that Kohn and Millaudon, who bought the lower half of the Cottage Plantation from Bouligny, also had an influence on Zimpel's plan of the Faubourg Bouligny. These two little parks survive today as Lawrence and Samuel Squares.

On July 4, 1832 Louis Bouligny's title to the plantation was confirmed by the United States. In 1834 the New Orleans and Carrollton Rail Road began operations along Nayades Street, running through Bouligny's Cottage Plantation. Bouligny then had his half of the plantation laid out in streets, squares, and lots by the surveyor Charles F. Zimpel, whose plan was dated March 18, 1834. The next day, the following advertisement appeared on the front page of the *New Orleans Bee*:

By Tricou & Canonge & R.J. Domingon

Will be sold on Thursday, the 10th April next and following days, at 12 o'clock, at Hewlett's Exchange, Mr. Louis Bouligny's property, on the left side of the Mississippi, situated about a league above the city. Said property will be divided into lots agreeably to a plan made by Mr. Zimple [*sic*], deputy surveyor and that will be deposited at the Exchange before the day of sale. The proximity to the city, and the advantages this situation offers to the brick yard, saw mills and Carrollton railroad, which runs through the said property, deserves the attention of speculators.

The front lots of ground will be sold, with the rights of batture without any reserve.

The purchasers will have the right to the immediate enjoying of the streets, shown on the plan, in all the depth up to and including the Carrollton railroad.

As to that portion of the *habitation* which lies on the other side of said railroad, the streets will be open and delivered only when, at least, a lot in each square will have been sold.

Also offered for sale in the same advertisement were "50 talented and choice negroes, such as masons, blacksmiths, mechanics, carpenters, sellers, coachmen and house servants. . . . The acts of sale to be passed before Louis T. Caire, n.p., at the expense of the purchaser. The purchasers will use Mr. Zimple [*sic*], deputy surveyor, to put them in possession at their expense."

Although the plan of Faubourg Bouligny was drawn by Zimpel, the design and naming of the streets has generally been credited to Pierre-Benjamin Buisson, Jefferson Parish surveyor and a former captain of artillery under Napoleon. An article, "A Soldier of Napoleon," by James Beard in the *Daily Picayune* of December 24, 1911 notes of Buisson:

After arriving in the Crescent City he engaged in his profession of civil engineer, and in this capacity Captain Buisson surveyed and mapped most of the uptown section of New Orleans, and it became his duty during the work to choose names for many of the streets. As might be expected, the names reflect the history of the man whom all his life he most admired, his general and emperor, Napoleon. Many of the streets are named for battles, such as Milan, Berlin, Cortez, Jena, etc. The wide avenue with the neutral ground in the middle received the name of Napoleon. His friends and family watched with much amusement the remembrances of his old life and ideals creep into his new work, and were fond of suggesting, when a street was laid out and was waiting for a new name, that it be called Moscow or Waterloo. The old soldier, however, did not care to joke on the subject, and his boys usually made sure that they were at a safe distance before offering any advice in map-making.

Unfortunately this interesting succession of street names relating to Napoleon was interrupted when the name of Berlin Street was changed to Gen. Pershing in a misdirected wave of World War I patriotic fervor. Cadiz, not Cortez, is one of the streets of Bouligny, others being Lyons, Bordeaux, and Valence above Cadiz, with Marengo, Constantinople, and Austerlitz below Milan. Zimpel's "Topographical Map" of 1834 shows all these streets parallel to Napoleon Avenue. With the sale of lots in 1834, the development of this large area of Uptown began.

FAUBOURG AVART

At the same time that Congress confirmed Louis Bouligny's claim to the twenty-three and one-half *arpent* plantation that became the Faubourg Bouligny, the adjacent upriver tract of eight and one-half *arpents* was confirmed to François Robert Avart. It was described in House Document No. 73, January 31, 1834, as:

> A tract of land, situate in the parish of Jefferson, on the east bank of the river Mississippi, and about three and a half miles above the city of New Orleans, containing eight and a half *arpents* front, by the ordinary depth of forty *arpents*, and bounded above by land now or formerly belonging to widow Joseph Marie Ducros, and below by land of Louis Bouligny.
>
> The said tract of land is claimed in virtue of purchase, founded on ancient and uninterrupted possession; having been constantly inhabited and cultivated, by claimant and those under whom he holds, for more than forty years past. We are therefore, of opinion that this claim ought to be confirmed.

François Robert Avart died in 1838, and when the inventory of his estate was made by the Jefferson Parish notary J.F.E.D. Livaudais (fo. 6, p. 768) on March 19, 1838, the plantation was described as being bounded by Daniel Walden above and the Faubourg Bouligny below. It was noted that he had acquired it from his mother, Julie Allain, widow of Valentin Robert Avart, by an act passed before the notary Michel de Armas on April 22, 1811. The Avart family had owned plantations in this area at least since the time that Valentin Robert Avart had bought a nine *arpent* tract from Réné Huchet de Kernion in 1787.

Charles F. Zimpel's 1834 "Topographical Map of New Orleans and Its Vicinity" shows the Avart tract under cultivation, with a master house approximately in what is now the square bounded by Upperline, Constance, Robert, and Laurel. In the rear were several outbuildings and to the left of this service area was a large formal garden, probably a vegetable garden or orchard. In front of the house, a long *parterre* garden was bisected by a walk or driveway leading to Tchoupitoulas Street, a distance of about two and one-half blocks. Adjacent to this garden, on the upper side and facing Tchoupitoulas Street, were large brickworks and on the batture at the upper end of the property, additional brickyard structures are indicated near the river bank. The Avart inventory of 1838 mentions "the brick establishments thereon as also 200,000 bricks not yet burnt and the piles of River sand already trawled in the brick yard."

The inventory also lists "the dwelling house, out houses, hospital, pigeon houses, negro huts," besides the brickworks. The eight and one-half *arpent* plantation with its outbuildings was valued at $75,000. There were also sixty-five slaves attached to the plantation, valued at $34,500; cattle, horses, mules, etc., $729; and "instruments of husbandry." The estate also included properties with buildings in the City of Lafayette, on Jackson Avenue between Tchoupitoulas and Rousseau, valued at $6,500, besides $2,400 in bank stock, and $7,945 in cash and other assets.

No description of the master house has been found, but the inventory indicates that it consisted of a parlor, dining room, and three bedrooms, all of which were simply furnished. In the parlor was an old mahogany sofa, twelve straw chairs, two mahogany card tables, a set of andirons, shovel and tongs, a bellows, two "spit boxes," and a brass fender. A looking glass, a clock, two flowerpots, and two cylinders, probably on the mantel, completed the contents of the parlor, all valued at a total of seventy-five dollars.

Also inventoried were the contents "in the cellar" and in the kitchen, which was undoubtedly an outbuilding. In a room in the pigeon house were two old cypress *armoires*, a small glazed-door *armoire* (old), an old bedstead, one large old table and a small one, besides two bathing tubs.

In 1841 the Avart plantation was subdivided into squares and lots, the streets of the Faubourg Bouligny being extended through it. The streets parallel to Upperline, the upper limit of the Faubourg Bouligny, were named Soniat and Dufossat for both Valerien Gustave and Martin Valmont Soniat Dufossat, who had married Marie Louise Artimise and Louise Almaïs, François Robert Avart's daughters. Robert Street was named for Avart himself, and Bellecastle is said to have been named after a branch of the Soniat family in France. These Avart heirs had the subdivision plan drawn by the architect-surveyor Henry Mollhausen, dated October 26, 1841.

RICKERVILLE

The eight *arpent* tract forming the upper boundary of Jefferson City extended from Valmont Street, the upper limit of the Faubourg Avart, as far up as Joseph Street. A plan for its subdivision into squares and lots was made by the surveyors Benjamin Buisson and W.T. Thompson, dated March 23, 1849. However, Maurice Harrison's "Maps of the City and Environs of New Orleans," authorized in 1845, shows this area already divided by streets in almost the same configuration as exists today. This map does not give the names of any of the streets above Upperline, the upper boundary of the Faubourg Bouligny.

Charles F. Zimpel's "Topographical Map" of 1834 shows this tract, like the adjacent Avart tract, as still being under cultivation, with a master house being located near the lower river corner. The tract that eventually became Rickerville was, at the time of the 1834 map, in the possession of D.T. Walden. His house was located between what were to become Magazine Street, Jefferson Avenue, and Leontine Street, probably the site today of the Poydras Home. The house faced the river and an avenue of trees led to it from the Public Road, now Tchoupitoulas Street.

When Walden's plantation was subdivided as Rickerville, it was owned by several different owners—a one-half interest belonging to the City Bank of New Orleans; one-tenth to the noted lawyer, Christian Roselius, and two of his associates, William C. Micou and John M. Bach; two-tenths to Samuel Ricker, Jr.; one-tenth to Léontine and Octavine Ricker; and one-tenth to the minor Samuel

Ricker. This partition of ownership was effected by an act passed before the notary L.R. Kenny on March 7, 1849.

The principal avenue of the new subdivision was given the name "Peters," possibly for Samuel J. Peters. The name was changed in the 1920s to Jefferson Avenue, as it was felt that there were too many streets in the city with the name Peters or one similar to it. The two flanking parallel streets were named for the Ricker ladies, Léontine and Octavia.

The Rickerville property had been acquired by Daniel Treadwell Walden from the heirs of Thomas Beale on March 19, 1831, the act of sale being passed before the notary Theodore Seghers. The year before, the property had been put up for sale by United States Marshal John Nicholson in the case of John Wister vs. the heirs of Thomas Beale, Sr. in the District Court for the Eastern District of Louisiana. The sale, advertised in the *Louisiana Courier* of March 8, 1830, was to take place at the Exchange Coffee House that stood on the corner of Chartres and St. Louis streets, where the Royal Orleans Hotel now stands. The sale was for:

> The undevided [*sic*] moiety of a PLANTATION or Tract of Land situate [*sic*] on the left bank of the river Mississippi, and about one league and a half above the city of New Orleans, containing about eight *arpents* front on the river, and extending in depth about one hundred *arpents* by lines which terminate on a point forming a triangle—bounded above by the lands formerly belonging to the late E. Boree, and below by lands of Robert Avart, being the same described in the act of sale made on the 29th April, 1818, by the late John Poultney to the late Thomas Beale, Senr., before the late Philip Pedesclaux, notary public, in New Orleans—seized and sold as the property of the defendants to satisfy the judgment in the above case.   Terms:— cash.

The Beale heirs became the purchasers, as it was they who sold the plantation to Daniel T. Walden the following year for $23,900. Walden owned the plantation when it reverted to the heirs of Thomas Beale as the result of a lawsuit, No. 20677 in the 1st Judicial District Court (Jefferson Parish Records, Book 12, folio 834). The Beale heirs were James Beale, Céleste Beale, Octavine Beale, and the minor children Samuel Ricker, Jr., Eliza Céleste Léontine Ricker and Eliza Octavine Clemence Ricker, heirs of their mother, Eliza Beale, deceased wife of Samuel Ricker, Sr.

When the eight *arpent* plantation was purchased by Daniel Walden in 1831, it was sold "together with dwelling house, out houses and other improvements." After Thomas Beale bought the property from John Poultney in 1818, he sold it to his son Thomas Beale, Jr. on April 27, 1819 before Michel de Armas, n.p. Thomas Beale, Jr. died a few years later and Mrs. Beale, his widowed mother, bought the plantation back at a public sale held on March 20, 1824. The act of sale was later passed before the notary G.R. Stringer on March 10, 1825.

The plantation had had many changes in ownership, but for many years retained its original dimensions. John Poultney had owned the plantation for only a few months when he sold it in April 1818, having bought it from the heirs of the widow of Joseph Ducros on November 17, 1817 before the notary Philippe Pedesclaux. The Ducros family had owned the plantation for more than thirty years after Joseph Ducros acquired it from Duforest Walker, widow Revoil, on August 30,1785. It had belonged for a few months to Joseph Foucher when he sold it to the widow Revoil on November 22, 1782, buying it on May 8, 1781 from J.B. Macarty, agent for Alexandre de Clouet before the same notary, Leonardo Mazange. The names of most of these former owners of the plantation that became Rickerville in 1849 have been prominent in Louisiana history.

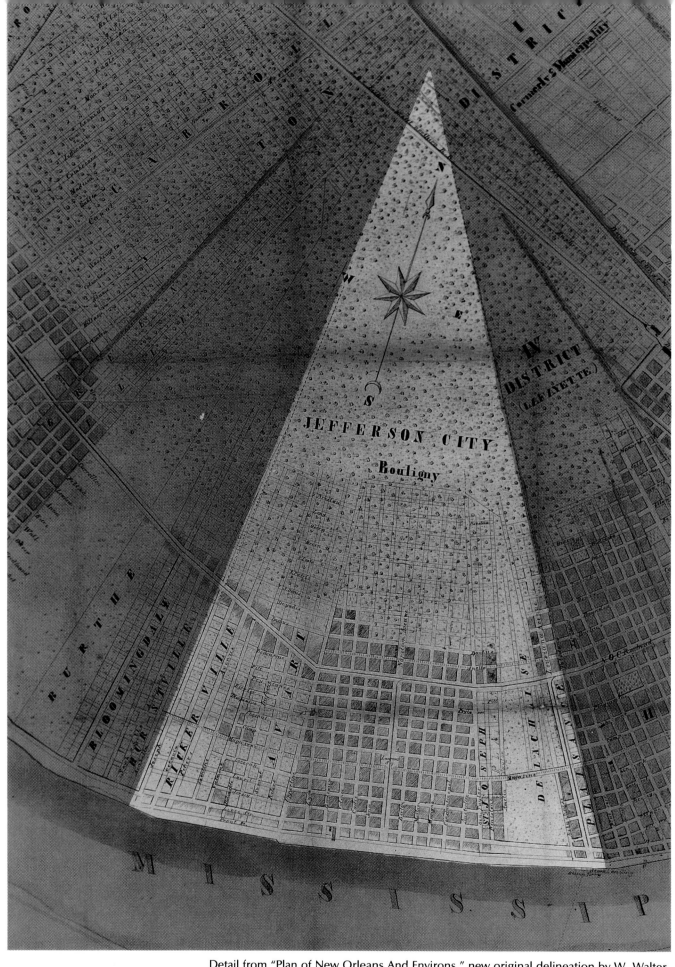

Detail from "Plan of New Orleans And Environs," new original delineation by W. Walter, published by A. Bronsema, 1855. Collection of Samuel Wilson, Jr. (Courtesy The Historic New Orleans Collection, Museum/Research Center, Acc. No. 1945.4.)

The Founding Families and Political Economy, 1850–1870

SALLY KITTREDGE REEVES

Jefferson City, Louisiana, that piece of Uptown New Orleans lying between Toledano and Joseph streets and today a major part of New Orleans' Sixth Municipal District, was, during the nineteenth century, a municipality in its own right. The sparsely-settled New Orleans suburb, an amalgam of seven privately-developed, individual faubourgs, received a city charter from the state legislature in 1850. For twenty years after that, Jefferson City had an independent existence complete with its own mayor, aldermen, courts, public schools, cemeteries, public market, port, and other facilities. In 1870, however, the legislature decreed that Jefferson City, along with the little West Bank town of Algiers, should be annexed to New Orleans. This expansion came not as a step in New Orleans' natural economic evolution but, as we will see, as evidence of the brute political power of state government during Reconstruction. It would, moreover, prove to be a penultimate step in New Orleans' corporate growth. The Crescent City annexed the Town of Carrollton in 1874, and has not annexed a suburb since.

If Jefferson City's corporate life was brief, the town's twenty-year political, social, and economic experience nevertheless gives abundant testimony to the kinds of forces that shaped nineteenth-century urban America. Jefferson City grew out of antebellum prosperity, and from demographic and technological change. German, Irish, and a few French and Italian immigrants gave it a population boost that built on the base of its founding families, and on the migration of free persons of color to its waiting homesites. The founding families, one by one, had subdivided and developed their plantations into faubourgs as the older generations died off, and the newly-founded New Orleans and Carrollton Rail Road increased the prospect of land profits for their heirs. Growth, however, was slow at first.

The slow growth pattern evidently doomed the fortunes of Jefferson City's brief political forerunner, the Borough of Freeport. Freeport's boundaries were slightly larger than those of Jefferson City, extending from Toledano to just past State, and including Hurstville and Bloomingdale. Incorporated in 1846, with limited police and taxing powers formerly reserved to the Jefferson Parish Police Jury,[1] Freeport lasted only four years. Its "Board of Council" found it difficult to enforce those powers, since its political and economic clout was yet unformed when it was incorporated. A strong challenge to its very existence arose at the end of its first year.

In 1845 the Jefferson Police Jury had authorized businessmen Paul Lacroix and Lewis Ackerman to build and operate a tallow factory at the foot of Louisiana Avenue. The factory received cartloads of animal fat from the many local butchers of the Plaisance, or Louisiana Avenue, neighborhood, and melted it down into tallow for soap. The adjacent City of Lafayette had evicted this facility for being a nuisance, but when it relocated upriver, the owners promised better environmental controls. Indeed, they persuaded Victor Burthe, judge and committee chairman for the police jury, that their fifty-foot smokestacks would carry all of their factory odors far away from residential areas. They promised, moreover, to use only fresh, not putrid fat, and to keep their place "perfectly clean."[2]

The tallow factory had been operating less than a year when neighborhood objections to it coalesced. Mr. S.S. Burdet, a Freeport public school teacher, complained that the disagreeable smell disrupted his evening Bible classes. John G. Wilson of Bouligny complained that the stench threatened to "knock him down" when he tried to take his evening walk. Baker Woodruff, a landlord in Freeport, said the odor was causing him to "lose fifteen per cent" of his rents. Woodruff said he had to breathe into his handkerchief when he passed the factory. Lafayette resident Benjamin Florence also complained that "emanations from the tallow plant drove his family from the dinner table." John Morris Bach, a Bouligny resident, summed up the commentary. The tallow factory's exhaust, said Bach, was the "*Ne Plus Ultra* of all nuisances, or the Royal Stench of all Stench."[3]

Freeport's town council tried to close the factory, but it defied them by operating at night. Taken to court by Mayor Charles Barnes, the owners relied on their police jury permit. They had received no complaints until "the little rustic Borough of Freeport sprang into existence," they chided. Freeport was too *rural* to claim police powers, they argued. "It will be some time yet before the little rustic plaintiff will be able to boast other than its present 'far and far between' population," with "whole plantations dividing the contiguity of its streets," they noted.[4]

Borough of Freeport record book. Freeport was Jefferson City's brief political forerunner, lasting only four years. (Courtesy Louisiana Division, New Orleans Public Library; photo credit: Bert Myers)

Mayor Barnes won his case, but the lawyers' patronizing tone surely touched a concern. Freeport was indeed rustic and unpopulated. Two entirely undeveloped plantations (Delachaise and Madame Louis Avart) separated its one populous area along Louisiana Avenue from the next, near Napoleon. Upriver, Rickerville had a name but was as yet undivided pasture, and the two faubourgs above it had just seceded from the town after only a year's participation. Freeport's incorporation was, in fact, premature, and in just a few years the town would be dissolved. In its place, however, the City of Jefferson would be born.

Jefferson City was incorporated sixteen years after its first faubourg, West Bouligny (Napoleon to Upperline), was subdivided. It was now 1850, and the town's economy grew steadily while meeting New Orleans' increasing demands for meat, dairy products, building materials, and waste disposal. Butchers, operating cottage-industry slaughterhouses near the town stock landing at the foot of Louisiana Avenue, and dairymen, pasturing cattle on the abundant "woods" side land north of St. Charles above Napoleon, were mainstays of local employment. The stock landing itself provided employment to common laborers, while numerous "bull drivers" found work herding animals through the streets to the local slaughter shops.[5]

The butchers worked quickly, in late morning during winter and at dusk in summer. With a beef, they strung a rope through the nose, felled the animal, and hung it on a hook via pulley and chain. They then carved the meat and salted the hide. Pork men scalded their hogs in kettles, hung them up, and made blood pudding and sausage. It took about an hour to kill and prepare an animal, and some little time more to put the bloody refuse outside for the cart drivers.[6]

Flourishing at the top of the meat industry were stock auctioneers and dealers such as the company of Hortaire Inbau and Jordan T. Aycock, who leased space on the stock landing where they received shipments of beef, calves, sheep, and

Except for the Boulignys and Plaisance, the faubourgs of Freeport were hardly more developed during the late 1840s than they had been when Charles F. Zimpel's "Topographical Map Of New Orleans and Its Vicinity" was published in 1834. (Map detail courtesy The Historic New Orleans Collection, Museum/Research Center, Acc. No. 1945.13.)

Stock landing on the Mississippi River between Louisiana Avenue and Delachaise Street. Detail from "Plan of 2 Lots and Ground with Right to Batture at the Stock Landing, Jefferson City." Drawing by Charles A. de Armas, October 4, 1865. Plan Book 77, Folio 24, New Orleans Notarial Archives. (Photo credit: Robert J. Cangelosi, Jr.)

hogs from Texas, Kentucky, Tennessee, and Missouri. Inbau, Aycock & Co. then stabled the animals nearby, selling them at auction to their regular customers, all local butchers. There were, by the late 1860s, eight livestock dealers in Jefferson City.[7]

In addition to the stock trade, the local Delachaise-Dugué and Avart-Dimier brickworks and the Ocean and Braun sawmills, all located along the town's riverfront, could ship their building products to the city via the Mississippi's convenient downriver drift. Just as conveniently, if less salubriously, those same waters were called upon to carry away the town's garbage, privy refuse, and noxious slaughterhouse leavings of bone, heads, feet, blood, fat, hide, and entrails; for Jefferson City, like Freeport before it, was a land of nuisances. These nuisances indeed gave it life.[8]

Animal slaughtering had been under governmental regulation in Louisiana from colonial times when the *abattoir* was relegated to the West Bank, and that regulation continued to push the slaughtering industry farther into the suburbs during the nineteenth century. After receiving its own municipal charter in 1805, New Orleans allowed slaughtering on the East Bank, but under strict provisions for cleanliness. City ordinances on the books as early as 1812 and 1816 limited slaughtering licenses to previously existing ones, while later ordinances required butchers to "bury all blood and entrails, or cause them to be thrown into the river." By the 1850s the area's expanding population had greatly increased the need for meat in the local markets, but slaughtering restrictions were so tight in New Orleans and Lafayette that incoming German and French butchers, and their by-product processors, were locating farther upriver. The center of the slaughtering industry had moved first from New Orleans to Lafayette, and then just upriver from Lafayette to the Plaisance or Louisiana Avenue region when Jefferson City built an ambitious stock landing at the foot of Louisiana Avenue. Noxious businesses like Lacroix and Ackerman's Tallow Factory followed the butchers.[9]

The City of Jefferson, unlike its downriver neighbors, not only welcomed the meat processing and by-product industry, but took on the waste disposal industry as well. From the foot of Delachaise, the town built a projecting structure uneuphemistically called a "nuisance wharf," from which "nuisance contractors," working jointly for New Orleans and Jefferson City, heaved slaughterhouse refuse, animals found on the streets, residential garbage, and privy refuse into the Mississippi River. Necessary but undesirable industry, in short, provided the fledgling Jefferson City with population and employment. No matter that the "nuisance wharf" was just a mile upriver from New Orleans' water intake.[10]

Population and employment was, of course, a boost to the town's real estate industry. A whole class of land speculators, notably Laurent Millaudon, John Morris Bach, Raymond Pochelu, Alvin Rocherau, Samuel, Carl and Joachim Kohn and many others, made money from the town's development. Some purchased land at the original plantation auctions, staying by to watch while both prices and neighborhoods rose. Others held lots in speculation as second, third, and fourth-generation buyers. In Rickerville, squares lakeward of the present Newman School, facing attractive blocks of Jefferson, Octavia, and Joseph streets, were still being held in speculation after the turn of the twentieth century. The building boom in this and many other more modest neighborhoods on the river side of Prytania Street eventually required the rise of the savings and loan industry to come about. It is no accident that predominant architectural styles in these areas reflect the trend of stock, if attractive, production.[11]

Following close to the real estate people were the politicians and lawyers who made a living feeding on the town's governance, and the contractors who attended them. John T. Michel, who served successively (and sometimes concurrently) as city comptroller, third ward alderman, justice of the peace, Jefferson Parish Recorder, fire company president, and Mayor of Jefferson City, was probably the town's most well-known and successful politician. He got his start, not surprisingly, representing numerous clients in Second and Third Judicial District Courts, the "people's courts" of nineteenth-century Jefferson Parish.[12]

Patronage and paternalism kept contractors, lessees, and other employees busy providing services to the town. Ocean Saw Mill owner Joseph Carbo or contractor E.R. Chevally received much of the town's business building planked roads, raising and maintaining levees and the flatboat and stock landing wharves, clearing ditches, and building bridges over the ruts that passed for gutters. Both patronage and paternalism ordained that the town should have a single market with a single lessee, lest easily spoiled foods—vegetables, melons, potatoes, onions, fish, shrimp, crabs, crawfish, turtle, and game—be sold in unsanitary surroundings. Ordinary nineteenth-century paternalism also had it that the council should strictly control the price of bread, staple of all diets. Ten cents was the maximum price for a loaf, but the bakers found a way to follow the letter of the law and still vary its size. When flour was $4.00 a barrel, their loaves were over two and one-half pounds; at $16.00 per barrel for flour, however, the still ten-cent loaves shrank to sixteen ounces. Finally, patronage also fed, if quite modestly, the politically-appointed teachers who staffed the town's four public schools.[13]

Patronage aside, Jefferson City's charter called for a modest amount of government. There were only about thirty city employees, including higher elected officials, middling figures such as harbor master, streets commissioner, or city surveyor, and lower level employees such as schoolteachers, policemen, and ditch diggers. Council members personally supervised the public schools, and the mayor superintended the tiny police force. All firemen were volunteers, organized into the Home Hook and Ladder, Pioneer, and Star Hook and Ladder companies.[14]

The city's income derived from fees on commercial vehicles, river vessels, trades and professions; from franchises on the market, port, ferries, and street railway; and from a one percent ad valorem tax on real estate and slaves. Each year the council appointed three private citizens to act as assessors for the latter tax. Police powers were limited, and a full third of the charter dealt with procedures safeguarding property rights involved in expropriations for the opening or widening of streets, a major item on the municipal agenda.[15]

If the charter was simple, it merely reflected then-current values of minimal government in America. The charter largely tracked that of the nearby Town of Carrollton, established in 1845, and was in miniature a forerunner of New Orleans' amended charter of 1852, if omitting New Orleans' perhaps too-powerful recorder posts. Jefferson City officials, however, would ask the state legislature to amend their charter four times in less than a decade during the 1850s.[16] In retrospect one can understand this, for they were working out the complexities of a growing nineteenth-century American municipality.

Both the original Jefferson City charter and 1850 federal census data can be taken as guides to the city's population density. The charter gave the First Ward faubourgs, Plaisance and Delachaise, three aldermen; but St. Joseph and East Bouligny in the Second Ward received only two. West Bouligny (Napoleon to Upperline) had three aldermen by itself, and all of Avart and Rickerville (Upper-

Home Hook & Ladder fire company, 824 Marengo, ca. 1890. From Thomas O'Connor, *History of the Fire Department of New Orleans*. (Courtesy A.L. Schlesinger, Jr.)

line to Joseph) had only one.[17] Ruth Koons Hollis, in a recent thesis on Jefferson City, has analyzed the town's population characteristics further from 1850 federal census data. These show that truck and dairy farms filled the upriver section above Napoleon, while "by-product users" such as tanners, curriers, and soap and sausage makers could be found in abundance downriver. Among the small population of 1,500 there were nearly twice as many Germans as French, and three times as many Germans as Irish, American, Italian, Swiss, or Spanish.[18]

By 1860, reports Hollis, the population had mushroomed to over 4,500, of which Germans accounted for about forty-five percent. There were over 900 French, 600 Irish, and a mixture of Americans, English, Spanish, Italian, and Swiss. There were still as many as forty farms and dairies above Upperline, and the town supported no less than eighty-four slaughterhouses.[19]

Both the town's economy and its political structure survived intact up to and even through the Civil War, but failed to survive Reconstruction. By the stroke of a pen, the 1870 annexation to New Orleans completely eradicated Jefferson City's municipal independence, along with its attachment to Jefferson Parish. At the same time, a state-orchestrated removal of its meat processing industry to a location downstream from New Orleans efficiently quashed the town's economy.[20] The area would, however, live to be rekindled during the Gilded Age as one of the premiere residential districts of a major American city.

THE FOUNDING FAMILIES

We move now to a discussion of the plantation families who fashioned the seven faubourgs that made up Jefferson City. One wonders if they were lucky or wise, making gains that kept their descendants prosperous and socially prominent for a century or more. Perhaps some, less fortunate or more foolish than others, failed to conserve the wealth that might have been theirs for having owned the site of Uptown New Orleans when it was developed. Did any of these families become the old money of Uptown New Orleans? Did they pass their strengths from generation to generation, imparting stability and cohesion to New Orleans society? To do this, it seems, they must need, not only to have had money in the early generations, but also to produce in subsequent generations children capable both of maintaining a sense of family identity, and of repairing or restoring the family fortune. These children must obviously live long enough to marry and have children of their own, and it seems that they must also have enough energy and morality to impart stability to their immediate families. Finally, it seems obvious that they must stay in town. The children cannot grow up and move back to France, and still be counted as having imparted stability and cohesion to the society in which their grandparents gained prominence. The application of these criteria seems to be an appropriate framework for examining the lives of Jefferson City's founding families. Few, it seems, met the mark.

FAUBOURG AVART

Perhaps the earliest and most important of Jefferson City's founding families was that of Avart. Associated with this family was the co-patronymic Robert, which most of the Avart men and some of the women carried as a middle name. As Samuel Wilson, Jr. has reported earlier in this volume, the first Avart to appear in the future Jefferson City arena was Robert Avart, who purchased seventeen upriver *arpents* as early as 1746. In 1770, Alexandro O'Reilly's official Louisiana census identified his plantation on the east bank river coast as one of some seven or eight *habitations* on the "Chapitoulas."[21]

Avart's son, Valentin Robert Avart [1740–1807], inherited a share of his father's land in 1773. In time, this successful second-generation Creole expanded his holdings to thirty-eight *arpents*, stretching from Valmont to Foucher streets, by today's measuring. At the age of thirty he married Julie Allain of Pointe Coupee Parish, and at thirty-seven joined the Louisiana militia. Avart served over twenty-five years as a volunteer militia officer while cultivating a plantation, prominent marks of social attainment.[22]

Of six Avart children in the third generation, two—François-Robert and Louis Valentin—retained ownership in land that would one day form two of Jefferson City's faubourgs. François-Robert [1777–1838], by inheritance and purchase from his mother, acquired a modest eight and one-half *arpents* in the Upperline-Soniat-Dufossat region that only after his death became known as Faubourg Avart.[23] His older brother Louis [ca. 1772–1809] acquired an even more modest two *arpents* in the Peniston-Gen. Taylor area, died young, and left the land to his widow, who many years later fashioned Faubourg St. Joseph from it.[24]

François-Robert Avart was a conservative Creole of the type who considered their Louisiana militia membership the highest form of social activity, and preferred to maintain their plantations in agricultural and industrial use rather than developing subdivisions from them. One suspects that he was probably crushed when, after practically growing up in the Louisiana militia, he was too ill to fight in the Battle of New Orleans when the most important moment came to defend his country. Avart was so ill in the fall of 1814, just when the British were advancing, that he made his "last will," expecting to die at the age of thirty-seven. In this will, Avart left his then-modest estate to his only daughter, Azéma. Avart did not die then, but ended up having three daughters and accumulating a sizable estate.[25]

Avart's wealth in later life accumulated largely from his brickyard, which he operated from youth until death. As Samuel Wilson, Jr. has pointed out, for a time after his father's death in 1809, Avart shared a brickyard with his brothers Louis and Celestin on family-owned land. By 1820, however, François-Robert had founded a brickyard of his own between today's Robert and Dufossat streets, extending from Tchoupitoulas to the river. He invested heavily in the slave and animal labor and equipment needed to run it, and by 1826 the facility could make 28,000 to 30,000 bricks a month and was claiming to be the largest brickworks in the region. The building complex consisted of three galleried octagonal structures connected by two sheds, along with a large kiln, storage buildings, and slave cabins. Avart's son-in-law, Guy Duplantier, had designed the octagonal buildings and superintended their construction by builders Robert and Benjamin Fox.[26]

Avart was evidently content to grow corn, keep orchards, and raise animals on the plantation behind the brickyard while enjoying life in a fine country home and occasionally visiting the family town house in the Vieux Carré.[27] He seems to have had little use for development, and felt injured when the New Orleans and Carrollton Rail Road extended its tracks across what was then the rear of his land.[28] In spite of this anti-growth attitude, Avart lived to accumulate a net worth of about $125,000 by the time of his death in 1838, of which the plantation, brickworks, forty-seven slaves, and equipment amounted to ninety-five percent.[29] In twenty-seven years, he had increased the value to that amount from $20,000, the sum he had paid his mother for the land in 1811. This was, of course, a notable increase, but the amount pales when compared to the profits Avart's

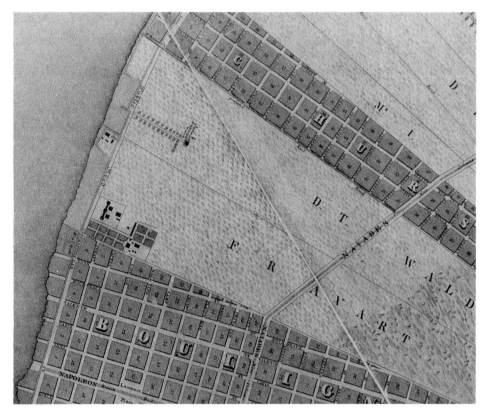

François Avart Plantation, showing brickyard near river (with three connected octagonal buildings) and family plantation complex (at Upperline between Laurel and Magazine). From Charles F. Zimpel, "Topographical Map of New Orleans and Its Vicinity," 1834. (Courtesy The Historic New Orleans Collection, Museum/Research Center, Acc. No. 1945.13)

widow and children realized just a few years after his death from selling off the brickworks and subdividing the old man's cattle pastures and fruit orchards.

François-Robert and Louis Avart each married a third cousin, Amélie and Eugénie Delassize, respectively. The Delassize sisters had been orphaned as children, and actually grew up in the Avart household.[30] Roman Catholic, strong-willed and long-lived women, they proved to manage both money and people well. François-Robert's wife, Amélie Delassize Avart [1776–1856], bore her husband three daughters and outlived not only him, but also one of the daughters and two sons-in-law. When her husband died in 1838, she bought out the childrens' interest in their father's estate, had it surveyed and subdivided, and managed the brick factory for a time. About a half-mile downriver, her sister Eugénie outlived husband Louis Avart by over forty years. Childless, Eugénie became so attached to her sister's grandson, Joseph Allard Peniston, that she adopted him, left him her fortune, and named her faubourg (St. Joseph, from Amelia Street to Gen. Taylor) for him.[31] New Orleans society referred to these two widowed sisters by distinguishing names. Eugénie was "the Widow Avart," while Amélie was simply "Madame Avart."[32]

During the decade of the 1840s, Amélie sold a few lots in Faubourg Avart, but spent most of her energies building a new house and reserving choice squares along Tchoupitoulas Street and the future St. Charles Avenue for her daughters and grandchildren. On a large site slightly removed from the river at what is today Laurel and Upperline streets, she had a impressive new residence built within a sprawling orchard of orange, pecan, plum, and persimmon trees. The one-and-one-half story manor house, surrounded by columned galleries, passed on Madame's death to her daughter Louise Almaïs, wife of Valmont Soniat Dufossat, and survived until 1923.[33]

By the early 1850s, Mme Avart was ready to promote her faubourg more aggressively. She had three hundred handbills posted, distributed two hundred plans, ran advertisements in the newspaper, and staged a major auction. From this sale she realized over $100,000 profit after paying less than $2,600 in state and city taxes, real estate commissions, and advertising costs.[34]

Amélie Delassize Avart died in 1856, three years after this auction, but not before selling off the old brickyard at another respectable profit. The purchaser was Louis A. Dimier, who changed the name to Dimier's Brickyard, a label so designated on old maps of Jefferson City. In 1866 Dimier sold out to Jacob Von Hoven for $24,000. This price included a raised home, two brick kilns, machinery, and several drying sheds, much of which must have dated from the era of François-Robert Avart.[35]

The three daughters of François-Robert and Amélie Delassize Avart were the only representatives of the fourth Avart generation in New Orleans. The oldest daughter was Azéma [b. 1805], who married Guy Duplantier [d. 1835], had one daughter, and was widowed quite young. Her younger sister, Almaïs [d. 1878], married Martin Valmont Soniat Dufossat [1811–1877], and the youngest sister, Arthémise, married his brother, Valerien Gustave Soniat Dufossat [1814–1855]. This generation lived through a transition from the old agrarian-industrial pattern of Louisiana life to one characterized by suburbanization and a *rentier* mentality.

The Soniat men had been born to wealth and were experienced in politics and real estate, qualities that served them well in dealing with Faubourg Avart land sales. Their parents were Joseph Soniat Dufossat, a third-generation Creole, and his wife Louise Duralde, owners of the thousand-acre Tchoupitoulas Plantation in East Jefferson at Twelve-Mile Point.[36] Martin Valmont served on the Jefferson Parish Police Jury, and Gustave was secretary-treasurer of the Borough of Free-port. Gustave was evidently the family real estate manager, and Mme Avart made him her testamentary executor in a will, not knowing that she was going to outlive him. Gustave had been left to manage the real estate that his three sons inherited from their mother when Arthémise met an early death about 1847. Unfortunately, in 1855 Gustave also died, leaving the boys orphans.[37]

The fifth generation, children of the Soniats and the Duplantiers, were the last of the family to own land in Faubourg Avart. In this group were the three children of Arthémise Avart and Gustave Soniat—Gustave, Alfred, and Théodore Soniat, who were orphaned by 1855; the three children of Almaïs Avart and Martin Valmont Soniat—Valmont, Edgar, and Arthémise Soniat; and the daughter of Azéma Avart and Guy Duplantier, Amélie. This generation's share of the Avart and Soniat estates left them quite well endowed. As children, for example, the orphans Gustave, Alfred, and Théodore Soniat received from their Avart grandmother some valuable property on Tchoupitoulas Street, then the business part of Jefferson City, along with property fronting St. Charles Avenue, eight blocks deep, in the Upperline-Soniat neighborhood. From their Soniat grandmother, Théodore and his brothers inherited over $9,000 in 1855. The mother and father, then, both died young, leaving the boys orphaned but in possession of the parents' sizable estates.[38]

Of all seven cousins, only the youngest orphan, L. Théodore Soniat [1844–1924] would prolong the Avart family line in New Orleans. Théodore was left the only

This posthumous portrait is believed to be of Amélie Delassize Avart. Simply titled "Mme Avart" (the name by which she was known) it was painted in 1860, four years after her death, by Peter Schmidt. Oil on canvas. (Courtesy Louisiana State Museum.)

one after all his brothers and cousins either died or moved away. Gustave, Théodore's oldest brother, sold his New Orleans property in 1859, and after that moved first to Havana in 1864, and then, by 1867, back to the family's native Paris, where he remained. The middle brother, Alfred, died before attaining the age of twenty-one.[39] Théodore's cousin, Amélie Duplantier, married Dr. Thomas Peniston and died quite young, leaving a son who believed that he was cheated out of his inheritance by lawyers and did not remain in New Orleans.[40] The other cousins—Valmont, Edgar, and Arthémise Soniat—returned to France with their parents, who died during the late 1870s. There, Arthémise gave up her fortune and entered the Visitation monastery at Moulins, taking the name Sister Marguerite Marie. Her brothers not only settled in Paris, but went so far as to change their family name back to its original Saunhac du Fossat. They actually had their baptismal records in St. Louis Cathedral altered to the old form, as if to eradicate the traces of their American sojourn.[41]

Théodore, after attending Georgetown University, went to Paris himself at the beginning of the Civil War, but only to study the classics at the Sorbonne. Returning to New Orleans, he married his first cousin, Emma Soniat, in 1864, fathered eight children, and followed the life of the *rentier*, living from his propertied income, reading the classics, basking in the services of three unmarried daughters, and disdaining work as the fare of the bourgeois. He named his sons for himself and his two brothers, and sent them to the Jesuits and to the Brothers of the Sacred Heart to be educated. He named his daughters for his wife, mother, and grandmother, and sent them to the Sacred Heart to be educated. The daughters produced no heirs, although one married. All four sons entered business in New Orleans—in coffee, dry goods, insurance, and real estate. They continued Théodore's line with at least sixteen grandchildren and fourteen great-grandchildren, many of whom have been prominent in local business, law, and medicine. At this writing, there are twenty ninth-generation New Orleans descendants of the first Robert Avart, who first purchased Uptown land during the 1740s.[42]

FAUBOURG ST. JOSEPH

The second Avart whose land became one of the Jefferson City faubourgs was François-Robert Avart's brother, Louis Valentin Robert Avart. Louis acquired his small *habitation*, located in the present Peniston-Gen. Taylor area, after his father's death in 1807.[43] A good Creole like his brother and father, Louis served over ten years in the Louisiana militia, mostly during the 1790s.[44] As previously mentioned, he married a Delassize, as did his brother and a sister, Eulalie Robert Avart. Louis died young, in 1812, leaving no children. His widow, Claudia Augustine Eugénie Delachaise, retained their property for quite a few decades before finally having it subdivided in 1849. During those years she maintained a town house on St. Peter Street in the Vieux Carré, along with a suburban home on Annunciation near Peniston. Without direct heirs, Eugénie bequeathed her estate to a favorite great-grand-nephew, Joseph Allard Peniston, in 1855. Joseph's father was Thomas Peniston, a physician and native of Virginia. His mother was Amélie Duplantier, the daughter of Azéma Avart and Guy Duplantier, whom the Widow Avart had adopted.[45]

Amélie Duplantier married Dr. Peniston about 1840, but died at quite a young age in 1845. Left to manage their son's inheritance from his mother, Peniston functioned as Joseph's tutor for nearly twenty years after his wife's death, occasionally buying land in Faubourg St. Joseph for his account. He remained close to the Widow Avart, who approved his handling of Joseph's finances, and there was never any major disagreement between them. In 1855 the Widow Avart died, making Joseph Allard Peniston her universal heir to more real estate and valuables. After that, Dr. Peniston's tutorial responsibilities increased.[46]

A year after the Widow's death, Dr. Peniston married Néomi Lallande, a native of New Orleans and daughter of Joseph and Marie Rush Lallande.[47] However successful the marriage was, Dr. Peniston's personal happiness declined after that. He had already lost a daughter, and in 1858 another daughter died at the age of two. During the second marriage Dr. Peniston intended to transfer all of Joseph's real estate and rents to his name, but he did not get around to doing so before 1863 when, sick and depressed, he died at the age of 48.[48]

"It is my ardent wish and desire," Dr. Peniston had written in an 1860 will, "that my beloved family shall keep together. In the present gloomy state of the future, it is impossible for me to say more. Adieu. To be continued life permitting."[49]

Peniston's last wishes had little fulfillment. In 1862 they lost four-year-old William; then Peniston himself died. Joseph Allard Peniston soon opposed the settlement of his father's succession on the grounds that Dr. Peniston's administration had deprived him of his great-aunt's bequests. He also opposed his stepmother's role as his tutrix, claiming that a conflict of interest made her ineligible to manage his affairs. For her part, Mrs. Peniston felt that she should be accepted as acting in good faith as Joseph's tutrix, since Dr. Peniston had appointed her executrix in his will.[50]

Joseph now challenged not only his stepmother's administration, but the earlier settlement of his own mother's succession. He charged that the sum offered him by the lawyers and an earlier executor amounted to less than a third of the legacy due him. His claim was nearly $200,000; the executor proposed to remit $64,000. To make matters worse, while Joseph's lawsuits were pending, a notarial office where all of Dr. Peniston's tutorial account books were being audited burned with all the books and papers inside it.[51]

Joseph Allard Peniston eventually won his lawsuits before the Louisiana Supreme Court, receiving a judgment for the amount he claimed as his inheritance. Still, the legal victory was not guaranteed to produce money, nor in the end did it ensure Joseph's financial position in New Orleans. He died at St. Paul, Minnesota, in 1881, relatively unknown in the place of his birth. His stepmother Néomi Lallande Peniston lived on in New Orleans until her death in 1899, and the Peniston name died out in the city soon thereafter.[52]

FAUBOURG DELACHAISE AND FAUBOURG PLAISANCE

Another family with a one-time strong presence in the New Orleans Uptown area was that of Philippe Auguste Delachaise [1791–1831]. The Delachaise roots in Louisiana were over a century old when Philippe August first bought Uptown land in 1820. Delachaise's earliest Louisiana ancestor was Jacques Delachaise [1666–1730], who arrived in Louisiana in 1723 as an agent of the Company of the Indies sent to investigate criticisms of Governor Bienville's third administration. After his arrival, the Delachaise progenitor functioned as general director of the colony.[53]

Philippe Auguste Delachaise was born in the fourth generation of Jacques Delachaise's line in Louisiana. His grandfather, Jacques Delachaise *fils* [d. 1768], was King's Storehouse Keeper, *Procureur* [Attorney] *General* of the Superior Council, and a pioneer in Louisiana sugar-making. Philippe's mother was a Chrétien, a family prominent in Opelousas where he was born. His father, Honoré [1749–1820], and uncle, Charles Delachaise, were both long-time Louisiana militia captains and participants in the 1779–1780 anti-British campaigns of Spanish Governor Galvez. Thus, while the family name is remembered today chiefly from its street name in old Faubourg Delachaise, the family has had a longer and more important role in Louisiana affairs than the simple development of a street.[54]

About 1818, Philippe Auguste received an appointment as justice of the peace in Orleans Parish, which meant that he held court in the Cabildo.[55] He also owned a Royal Street town house, but his primary business and home were not in the Vieux Carré but on the outskirts of the city where he operated a brickworks. His partner in this venture was Louisiana Supreme Court Judge François Xavier Martin. Martin and Delachaise had operated a brickyard in Gentilly for a few years before 1820 when they purchased a home in Faubourg Plaisance on the former Wiltz-Arnault tract (Delachaise to Aline Street).[56] At that time they may have begun to lease the nearby Avart brickworks, then owned by Jean Baptiste LeBreton. This facility was at the river between Amelia and Delachaise streets.[57]

The brickmaking business was an attractive investment for Delachaise, Judge Martin, the Avarts, and many other nineteenth-century New Orleanians, because the expanding city provided an excellent market for their product. The Mississippi River batture provided a ready quarry for sand and clay; river transportation was available for the heavy materials; and slaves provided the labor. Brickmaking, however, was not without its share of business problems. Delachaise and Martin frequently sued or were sued for payments involving deliveries or other disputes, and a lawsuit, even won, could hamper business for months at a time.[58] Delachaise was also sued occasionally in his capacity as magistrate,[59] spending what was probably not an inordinate amount of time in courts for a magistrate-industrialist of his day.

In the midst of a spate of business problems in the spring of 1822, Philippe Delachaise married Marie Antonine Foucher [d. 1854], daughter of Pierre Foucher, sugar planter and part-developer of the Annunciation suburb.[60] The following month, Delachaise bought out Judge Martin's interest in the plantation home on the former Hortense Wiltz Arnault tract[61] (Aline to Delachaise), evidently to make way for his bride to move in. In the summer of the same year, Delachaise purchased the riverfront portion of the Louis Joseph Wiltz tract (Aline to Foucher), and the following year acquired the rear of this tract.[62] Finally, in 1831, Delachaise acquired the old Avart brickyard tract (Amelia to below Antonine), which he had probably been leasing.[63] Thus in several parcels did Philippe acquire the land that would one day become Faubourg Delachaise.

For the next few years, Delachaise and his father-in-law, Pierre Foucher, systematically acquired lots on and near Louisiana Avenue in nearby Faubourg Plaisance,[64] which had been abortively subdivided many years earlier. Without much evidence as to their ultimate plans for this land, one supposes that they saw it as a good investment based on the impetus of the New Orleans and Carrollton Rail Road, or that they perhaps intended to form their own subdivision in time. In any case, the death of Philippe August Delachaise in 1838 at the age of forty-seven probably cut short their plans.

Delachaise had lived a relatively short, but respectable and productive life. It had the marks not only of material success, but also of culture, and of a healthy family life. He was born to old money, which he built upon and increased through skillfully executed business ventures. He married quite well and was able to increase the wealth his wife brought to the community. At the time of his death in 1838 he had sold a million and one-half bricks, had built six Vieux Carré stores on land his wife inherited, owned numerous other commercial properties in the Vieux Carré, had hundreds of shares of bank stocks, and had a luxuriously furnished town house in the 400 block of Royal Street. He conducted his brickmaking business with the labor of eighty-seven slaves, who also staffed his country seat overlooking the river at the foot of the street that now bears his name.[65] His children would profit from selling the land he had purchased next door in Faubourg Plaisance, and his own plantation would one day become Faubourg Delachaise.

Delachaise can also be fairly safely judged a cultured family man. At a time when books were scarce, he kept a library of over five hundred volumes at the plantation home and of another seventy-five volumes at the town house. Among his papers was an 1834 [Charles F.] Zimpel map of New Orleans, already worth fifteen dollars, in which Delachaise had wisely invested when it was new. The Delachaise family commissioned their silver from talented New Orleans silversmith, Jean Lamothe, and the family used French crystal, white French porcelain table service, and fine faïence. As we have seen, Delachaise also had the civic credits of having served in the militia and in the judiciary.[66]

Delachaise and his wife had two sons, Pierre Auguste, called Auguste, and Louis Philippe, called Philippe, and a daughter, Elizabeth Lucienne, called Aline. After the father's death, these children and their mother might have lived to see the transition of their family plantation into an important segment of a thriving Jefferson City, but it was not to be. Auguste, the oldest [b. 1822], married Sophie Dugué Livaudais and lived most of his life while the Delachaise Plantation remained unsubdivided. After his mother's death in 1855, he and his wife received the Delachaise plantation home and grounds (near Magazine and Delachaise streets) in a family partition,[67] but Auguste did not survive many years after that. He fell dead from "apoplexy" (probably a heart attack or stroke) while walking down a city street in 1861.[68] Just a few years previously (1858), he and his brother and sister had first promised the Jefferson City Board of Aldermen to open the streets of Faubourg Delachaise, but the proposition was expensive, and there were quite a few homes and fences that did not conform to the surveyor's street lines.[69] It was ultimately left to others than Pierre Auguste to develop Faubourg Delachaise.

Pierre Auguste's sister, Aline [b. 1824], had married her brother-in-law, François Dugué Livaudais, in 1840.[70] Fifteen years after that, the mother died and Aline and her brothers partitioned their interests in Faubourg Delachaise and had it subdivided. At that time, each received sole title to some fifteen to twenty squares, Aline and her husband taking over the family brickyard "with the intention of continuing to manufacture bricks." The facility soon came to be known as Dugué's Brickyard, and continued as such until 1866 when Aline and François leased it to Benjamin Franklin Smith. Smith's lease was to run three years, but he soon subleased the property to the New Orleans Manufacturing and Brick Company. While the value at this time was set at an impressive $300,000, the Delachaise brickyard did not stay in business, and the land was soon turned into a baseball park. Widowed, Aline eventually moved to Paris. In 1891 she had her land sold at auction, leaving to others the task of developing the property.[71]

Louis Philippe, the youngest child, was born in 1830 and lived until after Jefferson City was incorporated into New Orleans. Like Auguste, Philippe was not a witness to this political event, nor did he effectively participate in the development of Jefferson City. In the family partition of 1855, he received quite a bit of land in the industrial riverfront section of Faubourg Delachaise,[72] but he did not develop it. After a divorce from his wife Victoria Gasquet, and just before the fall of New Orleans in 1862, Philippe sold most of his land to Raymond Pochelu,[73] who with William Hepp and Alvin Rochereau, was hoping to get a franchise on a consolidated slaughterhouse there.[74] Like so many other Creoles of that era, Philippe then left New Orleans and removed to Paris to live on the Place de la Concorde. He died there in January 1887, with no ascendants, descendants, or other forced heirs, leaving his entire estate to a New Orleans cousin, food broker Philip Thompson.

Philippe was evidently somewhat estranged from his immediate family in New Orleans. In a will made the summer before he died, he left nothing to his sister Aline, merely "recommending" her to Thompson. As to his nephews, sons of his late brother Auguste, Philippe specifically wrote them out. "Above all the youngest," he noted.[75]

In 1888, cousin Philip Thompson sold all of the land he inherited from Louis Philippe to the socially prominent businessman John T. Hardie. Thompson then used the money to buy out his partner, Nicholas Burke, in their food brokerage business. Before long, what remained of the Delachaise family land in Faubourgs Delachaise and Plaisance was sold. By the early twentieth century, the Delachaise name, like that of Avart and Peniston, was no longer extant in New Orleans.[76]

RICKERVILLE

The least attractive history of the Jefferson City founding families is that of the Rickerville founders. Rickerville was a four-block, eight-*arpent* property that stretched from Valmont to Joseph streets and, like the other faubourgs, from the river back one hundred *arpents* to approximately Claiborne Avenue. It covered the Octavia Street-Jefferson Avenue region, which today would include such institutions as the New Orleans Lawn Tennis Club, Poydras Home, Jewish Community Center, and Isidore Newman School.

Around the turn of the nineteenth century, the Joseph Ducros family of St. Bernard Parish owned this small plantation. In 1817 the Ducros heirs sold out, and less than a year later the place had become the property of Thomas Beale.[77] Beale acquired the place toward the end of a checkered career, one that seemed somehow destined to doom the fortunes of Rickerville.

Known to history primarily as the plucky captain who recruited and led a rifle company to share the glory of Andrew Jackson's right flank during the Battle of New Orleans, Thomas Beale in 1815 had already known the vagaries of fortune and had experienced the consequences of his own occasionally intemperate lifestyle. He had spent a great deal of time at Vieux Carré gambling houses, playing craps, drinking "drog," and frequently losing large sums of money. During the winter of 1810, Beale lost more than he could afford to lose at the gaming house of Jean Baptiste Soubié. He signed promissory notes for these debts, but never made good on them. Two years later, in the spring of 1812, he declared bankruptcy.[78]

Beale had a silent partner in the merchant Samuel Kohn, with whom he had earlier owned and operated a combined inn, tavern, and gambling house on Chartres and St. Louis streets. Beale drew from the business such pay as Kohn allowed him, but by the time of his bankruptcy he had driven his losses up to $26,000 against about $13,000 in credits. Beale did little to satisfy his creditors, and eventually went to jail for debt.[79]

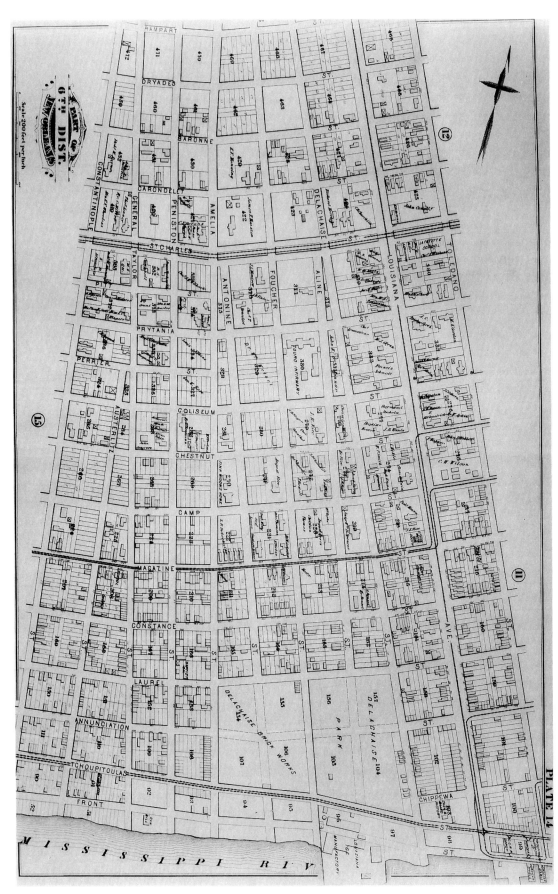

Atlas of the City of New Orleans—1883, plate 14 (Toledano to Constantinople). Elisha Robinson. (Courtesy The Historic New Orleans Collection, Museum/Research Center, Acc. No. 1952.8.16.)

Beale survived these escapades and, never the worse for wear, was by 1814 capable of recruiting the rifle company to help defend New Orleans from the British. One might imagine that he found his followers within the group of rakes who frequented the tavern with him. In any case, by 1815 he was a hometown hero and ended up in 1817 with a political appointment as "Register of Wills." This position was a courthouse sinecure that allowed Beale time to get back in the hospitality business and even buy and operate an Uptown plantation (the future Rickerville) with Samuel Kohn's money. Beale's illegitimate son, Thomas Beale, Jr. did most of the work there.[80]

The younger Beale, whose mother, Chloë Delancey, lived in Virginia, was as upright and economical as his father was rash. He ran the family hotel on Chartres Street very industriously, saw that it was finely furnished, and offered excellent meals. The object, in fact, of buying the Uptown plantation, was to cultivate a vegetable garden and pasture stock for use in the hotel kitchen.[81]

In 1819 the senior Beale conveyed this plantation to his son. The sale included nineteen slaves, hundreds of sheep and hogs, over a dozen horses, and many farming implements. The following year, the father died, and Thomas, Jr. was left to carry on the business alone. He did this quite well, soon moving from Chartres Street to larger quarters at the Planters and Merchants Hotel on Canal Street. Young Beale had builder Jeremiah Fox erect a home on the Uptown land, and little by little over the course of four years, paid off its mortgage to Samuel Kohn. Unfortunately, just three years after his father, Thomas Beale, Jr. died, still quite a young man.[82]

Thomas Beale, Sr. had been married to the former Céleste Grandpré of New Orleans, and had four legitimate children. In 1824 his widow purchased the plantation from Thomas Beale, Jr.'s estate, and three years later filed the first of many suits that would claim fraud in the handling of this plantation. In this case, Céleste Beale sued Thomas Beale, Jr.'s mother and only heir, Chloë Delancey, to recover the money she had paid for the property. She claimed that her late husband had sold the place to his illegitimate son by a simulated sale that was actually a disguised donation. The donation, she argued, was illegal under Louisiana law, because it was given to an illegitimate son while legitimate heirs existed. Litigation between Mrs. Beale and Chloë Delancey continued until about 1830, when Mrs. Beale finally won.[83]

In spite of her legal victory, Mrs. Beale was now in serious financial straits. Nathaniel Chamberlain, a cattleman who had contracted with her to graze 250 head of cattle on her property, had to sue to retrieve his cattle because Mrs. Beale could produce only five head by the end of 1830. During the summer of that year, Mrs. Beale had tried to sell the plantation in two separate auctions, but no buyers materialized. Finally, in the spring of 1831, the property sold to speculator Daniel Treadwell Walden, much to his later regret.[84]

The Widow Beale now packed up with her children and moved to Baton Rouge to be near the Gerard Favrot family, their closest friends. Her daughter Eliza, however, stayed in New Orleans to contract a fateful and controversial marriage to a man of whom the Favrots strongly disapproved.[85] He was Samuel Ricker, Jr.

Ricker was probably a native of Cincinnati who had moved to New Orleans during the 1820s to make his fortune. He mixed with polite society and soon made himself welcome in the Beale household. By 1830 he had persuaded the Widow Beale to endorse one of his promissory notes for a personal debt. His predictable default on the note the following year might have been a warning about his character, but it came too late, after he and Eliza Beale were married.

Ricker soon had his mother-in-law in even deeper financial trouble for endorsing the note that he failed to pay.[86]

Ricker's next move was to advise Mme Beale that her late husband had left quite a few debts. He counseled her to conceal her ownership of her slaves from her late husband's creditors by a simulated sale putting the title to them in his wife Eliza's name. Mrs. Beale did that, but retained the use of the slaves and of the income from hiring them out. This was her principal support.

In 1835 Octavine Favrot, Eliza Ricker's closest friend, wrote from Baton Rouge of her chagrin over their estrangement, which had resulted from Eliza's marriage to Ricker. Although Octavine reassured Eliza of her love and support, the coolness between them persisted. The following year, Eliza died, leaving two daughters, Léontine and Octavine (Octavia). To everyone's later regret, Ricker became their legal tutor.[87]

While Léontine and Octavia Ricker boarded year-round at the Ursuline Convent, Ricker maintained control of their mother's estate. He managed it poorly, and between 1836 and 1847 lost three properties they had owned at Pass Christian, at Biloxi, and near the Homochitta Swamp.[88]

In 1845 Eliza Beale's surviving brother and sisters—James, Céleste, and Octavia Beale Cavelier, along with Ricker, representing his children, sued Daniel Treadwell Walden to recover their community half of the New Orleans plantation that the Widow Beale had sold him in 1831. They claimed that Mrs. Beale, not having letters of administration to dispose of Beale's estate, had sold their half illegally. When the Louisiana Supreme Court agreed, Walden had to return a half-interest in the plantation, and the four Beales each received a tenth interest after selling their remaining tenth to investors. After that blow, Walden went bankrupt, and the City Bank, represented by president Samuel J. Peters, foreclosed on his mortgage and took over his fifty percent.[89]

Ricker now determined to get his sisters-in-law and brother-in-law's interests in the Beale land. For $3,000 each, a sum they would later claim was less than half the actual value, he bought out James and Céleste Beale's one-tenth interests. Meanwhile, he remarried, and had his new wife, Sophie Probst, purchase sister-in-law Octavia Beale Cavelier's remaining one-tenth interest. When Ricker's second wife died a few days after giving birth to a son, the infant, Ernest Samuel Ricker III, inherited that interest, and Ricker assumed control of it, too.[90]

Through tutorship and bargain purchases, Ricker now controlled forty percent of the former Beale plantation. Being a wide-open space close to Jefferson City slaughterhouses, the place, now known as "Ricker's," had become valuable pasturage. Ricker made quite a bit of money pasturing government stock on it during the Mexican War in 1847 and 1848, and had up to 2,000 animals roaming all over the place from the river to the house and beyond, all the way to the other side of the railroad. He also rented the home to a Mrs. Mount for $650 a year.[91]

During the 1840s Ricker also formed a partnership in the freight forwarding business with John H. Pearson & Co. of Boston. True to form, however, he had within a few years failed to account for $32,000 worth of goods that Pearson had ordered and paid for but never received. When it was clear that Ricker was never going to ship the goods, Pearson sued to attach Ricker's assets. In 1847 he won a judgment against Ricker's land interests for the amount of the debt.[92] Two years later, when Rickerville's multiple owners and mortgagors agreed to subdivide the place, Pearson had thirty-seven shares seized to recover the amount of his judgment.[93]

Subdivision did little to settle the many differences among Rickerville's various owners, mortgagors, claimants, and debtees. These included Peter Conrey for the City Bank, with fifty percent interest tied up; J.M. Bach, Christian Roselius and William C. Micau, holding a tenth interest jointing and filing petitions to dissolve encumbering mortgages; Ricker, holding tenuously to his forty percent; the Beale heirs, feeling discontent and cheated, preparing to sue Ricker; Pearson, holding his mortgage from the freight judgment; Ricker's daughters, concerned about their inheritance; Jefferson City, suing for back taxes; and even a carpenter, J.M. Butchert, suing Ricker to be paid for wooden banquettes he had built in Rickerville.[94]

The complaints held among these parties, unfortunately, all emanated in some way from Samuel Ricker's poor business ethics. He had, it seemed, habitually neglected to pay his debts. He was, in fact, prone to cheating. It mattered not whether his dealings were with powerful business acquaintances, family, the tax collector, or small tradesmen. His practices inevitably drew lawsuits.

In 1851, sister-in-law Céleste Beale sued him after realizing that she had sold out too cheaply. Ricker had not only tricked her, she claimed, but in two years had not made a payment on the paltry selling price. Backing her claim was a lineup of New Orleans real estate experts—Louis Bouligny, Gustave Soniat, John Morris Bach, Benjamin Buisson, Edward Gottschalk, J.R. Beard, John Hoey, and others—who testified that Rickerville land was worth about double what Céleste had received for it.[95]

Just a year later, Ricker's daughters, Léontine and Octavia, sued their own father for fraudulent handling of their mother's estate. In the suit they claimed that Ricker had squandered their Mississippi properties, had failed to remit both the rent from the plantation house and the income from pasturage, and had appropriated to himself the hire of their slaves. They claimed a privileged mortgage on Rickerville land, now four years after its subdivision.[96]

To further complicate matters, Bostonian John H. Pearson now intervened in the ladies' suit. The suit itself was a ruse, he claimed, one filed in perfect bad faith to assist Ricker in sheltering assets from his creditors by encumbering them with false mortgages. The girls had no claim to the fruits of Rickerville because their living expenses boarding at the Ursuline Convent during the disputed period had more than offset their plantation income. And the slaves they claimed, he noted, were actually their grandmother's property, held fictitiously in their late mother's name to further defraud creditors.[97]

Pearson won this suit before the Louisiana Supreme Court, in a victory that was a chilling indictment of Ricker's character. The Court's June 1856 opinion vindicated Pearson's argument that Ricker had indeed used his daughters to encumber his own property by a false mortgage. The false mortgage was designed to defraud creditors, and the daughters' claim against their father was fictitious and void. Justice demanded that Rickerville be seized and sold to satisfy the creditors' claims.[98]

By 1854 Samuel Ricker could not be found by authorities in New Orleans, Washington, D.C., or Cincinnati. Léontine Ricker had married John Solomon Lakin in 1853 and moved to Cincinnati, and her sister, Octavia, had married Joseph H. Guttierez of New Orleans. The couple, as may be expected, could not be found in Rickerville. As for the Beale heirs, they had moved permanently to Baton Rouge in 1846. Ernest Samuel Ricker III, Ricker's son by the unfortunate Sophie Probst who died a few days after giving birth to him in 1847, was growing up in New Orleans without ever hearing from his father. Fourteen years later, at the age of twenty, he would file a court petition for emancipation so as to manage his affairs free from his father's legal tutorship. Samuel Ricker had "altogether neglected and failed to support him," he would write.[99]

Rickerville trailed the prosperity of other Jefferson City faubourgs, and during the years after the Civil War, city directory agents could find only fifty-three householders there. Most of these were poor folk—coffeehouse keepers, gardeners, grocers, and day laborers. Only three or four prominent persons lived on or near St. Charles and Jefferson avenues—wine importer O.H. Karstendiek, manufacturer James J. Waldo, and the Robert Broome family.[100]

THE BOULIGNYS

The heart of Jefferson City was Napoleon Avenue, which divided its two remaining faubourgs, East and West Bouligny. These faubourgs were not originally separate sections of the same development, nor is Bouligny an entirely appropriate appellation for them. The two faubourgs (Gen. Taylor to Napoleon and Napoleon to Upperline) were actually Avart lands during the eighteenth century, and remained only briefly—two years in one case and six in the other—in the hands of Louis Bouligny.

The Bouligny faubourgs largely lack a founding family in the sense of having a subdivision formed by the heirs of an old family-owned and occupied plantation. As Samuel Wilson, Jr. has noted in this volume, Louis Bouligny did undertake to have a home built in 1829 on the former Cottage Plantation, site of the Bouligny faubourgs, but his efforts to establish himself there failed.

In 1829 Bouligny purchased the wide expanse of land between today's Upperline and Gen. Taylor streets with the intention of establishing a sugar plantation.[101] For this purpose he bought a large number of slaves and erected several agricultural buildings and a home. Perhaps to raise capital, Bouligny in 1831 sold the lower (Napoleon to Gen. Taylor) half of this property to speculators Samuel Kohn and Laurent Millaudon, while agreeing to lease it back from them for sugar farming for eight years.[102] Unfortunately, a hurricane soon destroyed a large portion of Bouligny's establishment, along with the prospects for his crop. An outbreak of cholera (probably in 1832) followed this disaster, carrying off most of his slaves. Bouligny then planned to auction his remaining assets (in the upper half), but the sale was a failure. By February 1834 the farming lease was cancelled and he was in court seeking protection from his creditors.[103] The following month, he had the land subdivided into squares and lots to form Faubourg West Bouligny (the part above Napoleon). Kohn and Millaudon then purchased fourteen prominent West Bouligny squares, especially along Napoleon and St. Charles avenues, adding to their control of the Bouligny properties.[104]

Laurent Millaudon [1786–1868] had been born in France and had migrated to New Orleans in 1802. From penniless beginnings he slowly accumulated savings, became a merchant, and invested in real estate. In spite of huge losses in 1825 and 1837, Millaudon accumulated a massive fortune and ended up owning the largest sugar-producing plantation complex in the state, worth a half-million dollars in 1860.[105] A co-founder of the New Orleans and Carrollton Rail Road and owner of nearly $300,000 of its stock, Millaudon invested in and sold vast amounts of property along the railway's route from Jefferson City through Carrollton.[106]

Samuel Kohn [d. 1853] was a native of Bohemia who as a youth "was known all over the countryside as a good-hearted, hare-brained ne'er-do-well, fond of the tavern and the lassies, and fonder still of a game of cards." Some time before 1806

Laurent Millaudon. Cohen's *New Orleans & Lafayette Directory*, 1853. (Courtesy The Historic New Orleans Collection, Museum/Research Center.)

he lost everything he had, tramped to Hamburg, and worked his way to New Orleans on a sailing vessel. Arriving in New Orleans, he did what he knew best, getting into the tavern business. By 1806 he was a half-owner of a tavern on Bayou St. John, and by 1808 had begun to invest in property north of Baton Rouge.[107] As noted earlier, Kohn was Thomas Beale's silent partner in a Chartres Street gambling house about 1810, and had endorsed Beale's Uptown plantation note by 1818. Kohn eventually made a considerable fortune in New Orleans as a banker financier, and real estate magnate, sharing an office on Gravier Street with his brother, Joachim Kohn, before moving permanently to Paris in 1832. He died there in 1853, leaving his fortune to his brother and nephews Joachim, Carl, and Edward Kohn, who for many years had represented his interests in New Orleans.[108]

The Kohns and Laurent Millaudon were the real developers of the East and West Bouligny faubourgs. They were selling lots in East Bouligny as early as 1833, and by the middle 1840s their faubourgs were the only populated sections of Freeport outside of the slaughterhouse area of Louisiana Avenue.[109] By the end of this decade there were enough Roman Catholics living near Napoleon Avenue and Magazine Street to warrant the city's first Catholic parish, St. Stephen's, founded by the Congregation of the Mission or Vincentians in 1849. The first St. Stephen's church was built on Napoleon at Camp in 1851, and nearby the Vincentians staffed a seminary for the Catholic Diocese while operating the forerunner of St. Stephen's Parochial School at Jena and Camp.[110] In 1854 the Kohn heirs held a highly successful land auction of East Bouligny lots, which sold at excellent prices.[111] In 1864 the Lutheran Church Society, led by its president Adam Droll, built its First German Evangelical Lutheran Church at the corner of Camp and Milan. The following year, the Congregation of the Mission, led by the Reverend John Hayden, built at Camp and Jena on the other side of Napoleon Avenue.[112]

Because Carl Kohn was astute enough to offer the Jefferson City Council ten prime lots at Magazine and Berlin (Gen. Pershing) for $5,000 in 1858, with the then privately-owned Lawrence Place thrown in as a public square—just when the aldermen were thinking about moving the council hall and market house from Valence and Levee streets to a more central location, the Magazine-Berlin intersection in particular, the region around Magazine and Napoleon in general, and became the civic center of Jefferson City. Not only the "council hall," but also the town jail, the city corn mill, the post office, the police station, four firehouses, the public market, the gas light company, the Jefferson School, the *Jeffersonian* newspaper office, all the lawyers' offices, and even the city pound ended up in East Bouligny, near the intersection of Magazine and Napoleon.[113]

And so it was at Lawrence Place in East Bouligny that the ultimate political crisis came to Jefferson City, after the Civil War, with Louisiana under military rule and its townsfolk still ready to do battle for independent government. Jefferson City residents had readily supported the Confederacy, had formed their own company of soldiers and officers who fought for it, and had given their share of financial support for it. It was on the riverbank of Faubourg Bouligny that the Tift brothers strained to complete the ill-fated ironclad Confederate gunboat *Louisiana*. At least thirty Jefferson City property owners contributed significantly enough to the Confederate cause in a political or financial manner to have their properties confiscated by Federal agents after the fall of New Orleans in 1862. Prominent among these were Edwin T. Merrick, chief justice of the Louisiana Supreme Court, Lafayette Napoleon Lane, owner of a cotton mill at Valence and Tchoupitoulas, and attorneys George W. Race and E. Warren Moise.[114]

Samuel Kohn, portrait on wood by unknown artist. With Laurent Millaudon, Kohn and his family were the real developers of the Bouligny faubourgs. (Courtesy Maunsell Hickey.)

As Hollis has pointed out, Jefferson City council members had stoutly resisted Federal occupation officials during and after the Civil War, and because of their stubbornness, Gen. Philip H. Sheridan had removed them from office and replaced them with his own nominees. In 1868 when a new Jefferson City administration opposed Reconstruction Gov. Henry Clay Warmoth, the ruthless governor ordered his personal police force, the Metropolitans, to occupy the police station and jail. He then had the Jefferson City charter amended in order to vacate all city offices.[115]

Through the first half of 1869, Jefferson City's elected leaders contended with Warmoth's appointed officials over the town's rightful municipal officers and against an attempted Metropolitan Police takeover. The struggle turned violent in May 1869, when residents met Metropolitans in a shootout in which two persons died and twenty were wounded. A tense showdown followed.[116]

On May 20, 1869, in a nightmarish show of force, Warmoth and Union General Mowry rode their horses into Jefferson City at the head of a column of three to four hundred infantry armed with muskets and howitzers. The soldiers marched up the residential lanes of St. Charles Avenue, turned down Napoleon, arrived at Lawrence Square, and set up their guns. Following a gun battle at the police station, the Metropolitans entered and searched St.Stephen's Church for resistors, and later arrested the town's elected officials. The Federal army, four years after Appomattox, occupied Jefferson City.[117]

After the takeover, Warmoth's appointees appropriated Jefferson City's offices, but did little governing. After a few months they devised a scheme to pay themselves three percent of all taxes collected, but when they quarreled over the spoils and the town became bankrupt, the pretense of government stopped.[118] Not long after its standoff with Reconstruction, Jefferson City's short municipal life ended.

In a special session of March 1870, Governor Warmoth pushed nearly two hundred bills through the legislature. One of these amended the New Orleans city charter to redefine its boundaries, simply embracing Jefferson City. This effective annexation vacated the town's municipal offices and eliminated its entire corporate life. Naturally, the bill also gave Warmoth power to appoint all municipal officials in the expanded city. This was a scenario repeated in several other Louisiana cities given new charters at the time. By the end of the special session, Warmoth had collected appointive powers over some important municipal offices in Louisiana.[119]

Political annihilation was not the legislature's only tool in dealing with the upstart Jefferson City. Another was, in effect, to destroy the town's economy. In 1869 the legislature ordained that all future animal slaughtering in the New Orleans area be done at a site below the city limits of New Orleans, and only at the facilities at the Crescent City Livestock and Slaughterhouse Company. No longer could animals be unloaded at Jefferson City's stock landing, and no longer could its butchers work in their own shops.[120]

In vain the butchers organized a union; filed lawsuits; exposed bribery. Their argument that Crescent City Livestock not only had no prior experience in butchering, but had paid no bonus for its exclusive franchise on a "coveted and necessary trade" fell on deaf judicial ears. Evidence that the slaughterhouse monopoly bill went beyond police regulation to corrupt restraint of trade found no hearing; and in vain did the butchers found their own slaughterhouse downriver, for the courts enjoined its operation.[121]

The butchers' suits against the slaughterhouse monopoly eventually became a national *cause célèbre* as the first test of the newly-passed Fourteenth Amendment. The suits failed, nevertheless, as the Republican U.S. Supreme Court decided that the state could regulate its butchers as it saw fit. In the end, Jefferson City butchers and stock dealers were forced to use the monopoly slaughterhouse or go out of business. Eventually all New Orleans area slaughtering was removed to sanitary facilities downriver, where the industry remained until the middle of the twentieth century.[122]

The strong arm of politics thus shaped a purely residential destiny for Uptown New Orleans. By the turn of the twentieth century, Jefferson City had evolved from a town that nurtured and thrived on nuisance industries to a primarily upper-class residential neighborhood with a few industrial facilities tucked safely on the river side of Tchoupitoulas Street. Only on street corners could be found remnants of the old town life within family-operated grocery stores, bars and restaurants, while the old founding families had largely died out or moved away. In 1929 when New Orleans passed its first comprehensive zoning ordinance, the Sixth District received the city's most restrictive residential status. Since that time, Uptown residents have zealously safeguarded that status.[123]

As for New Orleans and its suburbs, Louisiana law no longer provides for easy annexations. Perhaps annexations were never easy, politically speaking. As Jefferson City's case shows, Louisiana municipalities occasionally found their boundaries expanded not at their own request, but by the terms of new charters imposed by politicians who found it expedient to do so, and who knew the suburbs lacked the political clout to prevent themselves from being swallowed up. Today, quite a few Louisiana cities have home rule charters, but the state legislature continues to exercise great power over them, particularly over their taxing powers. Having felt only modest pressure from its urban lobby, the legislature, for today's political reasons, has generally precluded municipal annexations in favor of suburban growth, which is one big reason why New Orleans has not increased in size in over a century.

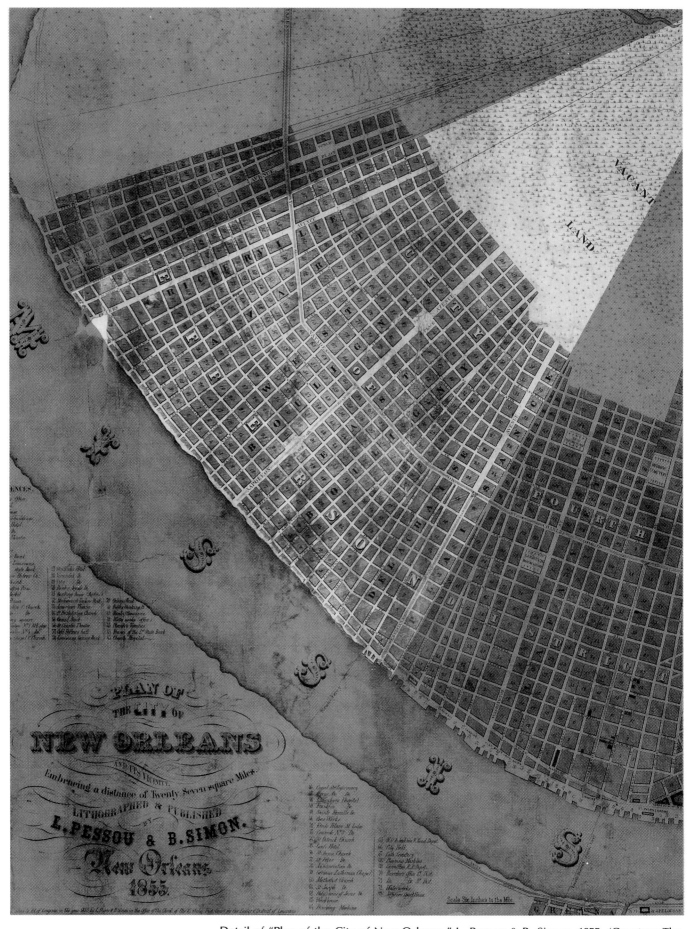

Detail of "Plan of the City of New Orleans." L. Pessou & B. Simon, 1855. (Courtesy The Historic New Orleans Collection, Musuem/Research Center, Acc. No. 1959.201.24.)

Surveyors and Surveying

JOHN E. WALKER, C.E.

Time has softened the lines of Uptown New Orleans considerably since the city began its expansion upriver in 1788 to accommodate an influx of new residents. Gradually the division lines between the plantations and great estates have disappeared from view and are recognized only by those who have been trained to seek them out.

To imagine the appearance of the Uptown section in the middle of the nineteenth century, one needs only to ascend the river levees in some of our upriver rural parishes and use a small amount of poetic license. Once you have removed the electric lines, automobiles, and ships, and put in their place steamboats, wagons, and livestock, you will visualize the terrain of the time. There were more and larger trees, perhaps, and some of the homes present today could be observed then.

New Orleans' population increased from 33,000 to 41,000 between 1815 and 1820. As late as 1807, during the territorial period, its population was only 15,000. By the year 1840, with 102,162 residents, New Orleans had become the fourth city in population size in the United States.[1] Elected officials of the time experienced the same problems brought on by rapid growth being faced by our leaders today: housing, drainage, sanitation, law enforcement, transportation, pure water, and levees. In addition there were several concerns that we do not have today, such as yellow fever, bubonic plague, cholera, malaria, and financial panics.

Land surveyors have played a necessary and important part in the development of New Orleans from its beginning as a colonial outpost to the present metropolis. Every mayor, every plantation owner, and every land speculator eventually found his way to the office of the land surveyor of his time in order to divide properties in the suburbs and towns that now comprise the city. In the next few pages, some light will be shed upon the profession of land surveying and the men who practiced it in New Orleans.

The story of the growth of the Jefferson City area begins in the 1830s and continues into the present century. At the beginning of this period, all of the royal surveyors who had held official positions under the French or Spanish were gone. Barthelemy Lafon died in 1820, Charles Laveau Trudeau in 1816, and Vincente Pintado in Havana in 1829. These men had been employed by the government to perform all of the surveying and mapping required under the colonial and territorial land grant system, and to mark off and lay out new streets, canals, and levees. Their successors, the public or city surveyors, continued to perform these tasks and many others.

These surveyors were known as *voyers de la ville* (road surveyors) because much of their work involved the design and location of the city streets. The correspondence and specification books of several of them have been preserved in the city archives in the Louisiana Division of the New Orleans Public Library, from which we derive a detailed account of their daily activity. They established proper slopes for the drainage ditches that carried the rainfall from the city back into the *marais* or swamps, and later into canals that drained the swamp by way of steam-driven draining machines or pumps. Owing to the imperceptible slope of the land from the Mississippi River to the swamp, the proper evaluations and gradients for the new streets were determined with great care by the city surveyors so that the natural slopes were not hindered in carrying off rainwater, and the drainage was improved wherever possible.

Another task which apparently required eternal vigilance was the supervision of the several contractors who were employed by the city to maintain the ditches and roads. The surveyors' books contain many letters, always couched in elegant but firm language, informing the recipient that in the event certain work was not done promptly, the surveyor would employ workmen at the contractor's expense to correct the problem at hand. The letters must have been effective in eliciting the required action, for seldom was the same matter dealt with in successive correspondence.[2]

A great deal of the surveyor's time was spent in laying out and supervising the construction of new streets. Shells were commonly used in the construction of streets in the years following the Civil War. Another surface that was tried was the "Nicholson Patented Pavement," a stratified plank and wood block surface, coated in tar and pitch,[3] with the crevices filled with hot gravel, tar, and pitch. Banquettes, or sidewalks, were planked and later bricked. Citizens who developed petitions requesting a certain type of improvement for their block had to be willing to bear part of the expense. The city council considered these petitions, then directed the surveyor toward appropriate action. At the end of the last century, the office of City Surveyor was renamed City Engineer, and now bears the title of Director, Department of Streets.

The land surveyor in private practice met many of the public's needs, and is still the surveyor people are most apt to recognize in the profession. These men bore the general title of *arpenteur*, which literally means one who measures *arpents*. The *arpent* was a French unit of measurement equivalent to 0.835 acres, and could be defined as a square having 180 French feet on each side. Each French foot was equal to 1.06575 English feet; thus the *arpent* as a lineal measure is 191 feet, 10 inches long in our present system.[4] Most of the *voyers de la ville* were also *arpenteurs*, sometimes engaged in private practice in addition to their public duties.

The *arpenteurs* marked off lots for people to buy, and drew individual maps of their work for purchasers to attach to their deeds. Plantation owners sometimes had their boundaries re-marked by the *arpenteur*, but more frequently they required their division into smaller tracts for their several children, or even into a subdivision of lots and blocks. These new subdivisions were styled either suburb or faubourg, followed most frequently by the name of the owner or developer.

U.S. Deputy Surveyors were contract surveyors whose work was required by the federal government in the final determination of land ownership under terms of the Louisiana Purchase. Napoleon sold Louisiana to the United States with the proviso that all colonists with legitimate titles to land in the territory would continue in their ownership undisturbed, and the remaining land became federal land, to be sold, given to schools, veterans, and to states, as the government deemed best.

Federal surveyors were very late coming to the metropolitan area for several reasons. The process of validating titles was not popular with the citizenry, and initially many refused to come forward with their proof of ownership. Many of them had no proof of ownership, owing to the destruction of records in the major fires of 1788 and 1794. Others who did bring their deeds found that the Americans did not understand the Spanish or French grant ordinances, or else they were advised that their proof was insufficient. Meanwhile, the city grew rapidly, and no contract surveyors could be found who could perform the extremely complex task of sorting the multitudinous boundaries in the city at the fees being permitted by the federal Surveyors General. Finally in 1872 the government contracted with men who were partially compensated by the municipality in order to get the work completed.[5] All governors of Louisiana, from the time of Villere to the War Between the States, were critical of the federal treatment of this state in the surveying and disposition of public lands.

All of these—the *voyers de la ville*, *arpenteurs*, and U.S. Deputy Surveyors— were mathematicians trained in geometry and trigonometry, and so it is today. Aspirants to the profession cannot master it unless they are proficient in these branches of mathematics.

In the field, surveyors most frequently used the magnetic compass and the Gunter's chain, a chain thirty-three or sixty-six feet in length made of steel wire links joined together with steel rings. There was an adjustable link at one end to compensate for the stretching of the chain caused by wear at the joints. The four-pole (rod) chain of sixty-six feet had one hundred links, and was devised as an aid in measuring land in the English system. Ten square chains equal one acre, and this fact facilitated computations of area for the surveyors. It did not provide any shortcuts in the measurement of *arpents* and other French units, however.

Transit instruments, the telescopes mounted on tripods so common today, were not found in every office. The first transit made in the United States was crafted in 1831,[6] but the device was not in general use until the end of the nineteenth century. Federal instructions for deputy surveyors permitted either compasses or theodolites (transits) in the township surveys until 1894. When the magnetic compass was replaced, it was not supplanted by the transit, but rather by another instrument, the Burt Solar Compass, which relied upon the unerring orbit of the earth about the sun to find true north, rather than the vagaries of the magnetic pole. The magnetic needle had the further deficiency of being affected by iron ore deposits in many areas, although that was not the case in New Orleans.

Transportation in the early years of the nineteenth century depended upon horse-drawn buggies or wagons, gradually augmented later by street railways in the city. Surveyors in New Orleans frequently traveled to plantations above and below the city by rail or river steamer on professional assignments. They were provided with food and lodging by the plantation owner, who also supplied laborers to carry equipment, cut a line through briars and cane, and assist in measuring and marking boundaries. These men acted as guides, pointing out ancient landmarks known to them on the premises.

When the importation of goods from Europe increased in proportion to the rapidly growing population, ships no longer carried large supplies of ballast stone to New Orleans. The oldest markers on the oldest boundaries in New Orleans were always cypress posts or ballast stones. With a diminished supply of stone on hand, the surveyors continued to use cypress stakes and posts, but also turned to a ready source of scrap iron. Robert Fulton's steam engines, through careless or unskilled operation, frequently blew up. The iron grating which supported the burning wood and allowed the ashes to drop into a bin, was made up of a series of rectangular bars of iron, which were ideal markers for plantation boundaries.

Most of the plantations that were subdivided into the suburbs that make up Jefferson City were wedge-shaped. The crescent of the river formed the front, along which ran a levee and the old King's Highway, now Tchoupitoulas Street; the side lines converged as they ran toward the rear line deep in the cypress swamp. Colonial grants were made in terms of frontage along the river and a depth running normal to the river, so that adjoining landowners shared more or less equally as their boundaries converged or diverged toward the rear, as dictated by the sinuosity of the Mississippi River. A small plantation of the period might measure four *arpents* or 768 feet along the river and a depth ten times as large, forty *arpents* or 7,680 feet.[7] A prosperous planter might have five times as much frontage along the river, but the depth remained the same, by law.

In addition to being a skilled mathematician, the surveyor was required to understand enough astronomy to enable him to establish the cardinal directions. If his skill also embraced the ability to determine the latitude and longitude of a place, he was considered an exceptional practitioner of his art. He was then in demand for more important tasks, such as the survey of the international boundary between the United States and Spanish Florida.[8]

After the measurements had been taken in the field and notations placed in any convenient, pocket-sized memorandum book, the surveyor returned to his office to draft a map of the tract that had been surveyed. The rules, scales, pens, inks, and paper have changed little in the past two hundred years. Transparent paper was introduced to take advantage of the process of blueprinting, and pens and inks then were designed to achieve clear copies. However, a surveyor today could easily pick up and use the drafting pens displayed in the basement of Monticello that were used by Thomas Jefferson, or those at Mount Vernon that were used by George Washington.

The training of young men into the profession required some apprenticeship in an established office or formal training into the mysteries of the mathematics and mechanics of measurement and mapmaking. Such formal training was provided in military schools of the time as a necessary part of military engineering. The apprenticeship system flourished within family groups, as in the Pilié and d'Hémécourt families.

BENJAMIN BUISSON

Benjamin Buisson's mark is the most indelible one made by any land surveyor in Jefferson City. He subdivided four of the nine plantations between Toledano Street and Audubon Park. In addition he was Jefferson Parish Surveyor from 1832 to 1846, and from all accounts was a man few people would forget.

Buisson came to New Orleans in 1817 to escape the unhappy memories of the defeat of his leader, Napoleon, at Waterloo. Buisson was French, and was trained as an artillery officer at L'École Polytechnique in Paris during the years when Napoleon could not lose a battle. Buisson fought in a number of campaigns, but was not present at the Battle of Waterloo. Unhappy under the restored monarchy, he traveled to New Orleans to visit relatives who had emigrated there. He never returned to France.

Buisson was twenty-four years old when he arrived in New Orleans on Christmas Eve 1817. He brought with him one treasured possession, the Cross of

Lieutenant Pierre Benjamin Buisson, ca. 1818. Watercolor, unidentified artist, Paris. (Courtesy Louisiana State Musuem.)

the Legion of Honor, pinned on his jacket by Napoleon himself. In later years when Louis Napoleon was in power, all of Bonaparte's old "eagles" were given another decoration for their service, which Buisson pinned to his tunic alongside the first. He was a leader and a man of many talents. In addition to engineering and land surveying, he practiced architecture, wrote books on the subjects of astronomy and artillery, and for a short while published a newspaper in Natchitoches, Louisiana. He was the subject of several charming newspaper articles—interviews with his children and grandchildren—which gave firsthand accounts of his ability and personality.[9]

As Jefferson Parish Surveyor, Buisson's duties included surveying roads, and designing and constructing public works of all descriptions such as levees and drainage canals. He laid out the streets and lots in the subdivisions he designed— Faubourgs St. Joseph, Rickerville, Hurstville, and Bloomingdale. In his spare time, he organized an artillery unit of the militia and served as its captain. At the time of the War Between the States in 1861 he was commissioned as a general in the Confederate forces, but was too old for active military duty. He designed or supervised the construction of two structures intended to protect New Orleans— one a breastworks and powder magazine in Jefferson Parish near the present-day Causeway Boulevard; the other an artillery emplacement at a place called the Little Temple, a few miles below the town of Lafitte. The small battery commanded the route by water from Barataria Bay through Bayou Rigolets up to the city by way of Bayou Barataria. Buisson also spent some time improving the fortifications around Mobile, Alabama.

Few of his maps and plans survive today. The words written by his successor, William H. Williams, Parish Surveyor, on the flyleaf of a ledger book tell the story:

> On the morning of April 19, 1857, at about 2 o'clock the office of the undersigned, situated on Dublin Street near the corner of Hampson Street, in Carrollton, was destroyed by fire. A large quantity of archives, records and papers of a public and private nature were totally destroyed, and among them was the volume of Records of Surveys in the Parish of Jefferson, Louisiana. The lost volume contained the records of numerous surveys made by Mr. B. Buisson as Parish Surveyor, and also the records of all surveys made by me, the undersigned in my official capacity. The records of my own surveys, I propose to restore in this present volume, as far as it may be possible, from notes still in my possession, and from the certificates and plats found in the possession of those for whom surveys have been made. The records of my predecessor, it will not be in my power to restore.
>
> The said Record Book constituted all in the nature of Records or archives that belonged to the office for Surveyor of the Parish.[10]

Benjamin Buisson lived on into the Reconstruction Era, and died quietly in his eighty-first year, ending a lifetime of active participation in the growth of New Orleans.[11] He left many descendants who reside in the New Orleans area, none of whom continued his practice of land surveying.

THE PILIÉS

The Piliés were an illustrious family of land surveyors, two of whom dominated the office of *Voyer de la Ville* for a large part of the nineteenth century. Gille Joseph Pilié emigrated to New Orleans from Santo Domingo at some time prior to February 17, 1805, for on that date he signed a contract to work in Barthelemy Lafon's geographic office for a period of two years, "drawing, tracing, copying, etc., also geographical or geodesic operations if necessary." Lafon paid him a sixteen dollar monthly salary and provided food and lodging as well.[12] By 1808 he was in his own professional practice, advertising that he was a painter of portraits,

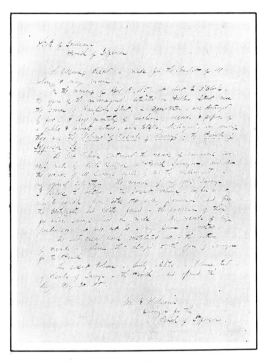

First page from William Williams's log book after fire, May 20, 1857. William H. Williams Papers, Folder #6, Mss 34. (Courtesy The Historic New Orleans Collection, Museum/Research Center. Acc. No. 76.42.L.)

landscapes, and flowers, would teach drawing, and could make architectural plans and charts. His professional stature grew rapidly, for he was appointed City Surveyor in 1818, and held that position until 1836. Owing to the division of New Orleans into three separate municipalities in 1836, he was appointed City Surveyor of the Second Municipality, our present central business district, and continued in that office until 1844. His professional career included surveying of both public and private works, as well as architectural plans. He designed the first iron fence around Jackson Square and the triumphal arch erected in the square for the visit of the Marquis de Lafayette to New Orleans in 1825.[13]

Joseph Pilié's son, Louis Henri, was born in New Orleans in 1820 and was educated at Janin's College on St. Louis Street. Louis entered into his father's employ, and in 1843 was appointed assistant surveyor to his father in the First Municipality. (By this time, Joseph Pilié was surveyor in both the First and Second Municipalities). Following the retirement of the elder Pilié from public life in 1844 due to poor health, Louis H. Pilié was elected Surveyor of the First Municipality in 1846, and in 1856 became surveyor of the consolidated municipality. He served in that capacity until 1867 when, because of his opposition to the use of Nicholson Patented Paving, he was dismissed by Gen. Philip Sheridan of the Reconstruction government. During the war years he had been removed from office and temporarily jailed by another Union general, Benjamin Butler.

Louis H. Pilié continued the public improvements begun by his father. In 1851 he designed and supervised the construction of the iron fence that stands today around Jackson Square. Many streets were improved during his terms as city surveyor, and he was responsible for the preparation of numerous maps for the sale of properties willed to New Orleans and Baltimore by John McDonogh in 1850.

In 1856 Louis Pilié prepared specifications for a general plan and index of the city to be made from an actual survey.[14] The rapid growth of the city in the first half of the century created numerous problems for the municipal assessors involving the proper identification of taxable lands. There were too many faubourgs, too many city blocks bearing identical numbers, too many streets in separate areas having the same name. Pilié required a renumbering of the old faubourg squares and an orderly projection of the city streets across surrounding vacant tracts to guide future subdividers. A contract was signed with Jules A. d'Hémécourt to perform this enormous task, but the War Between the States intervened, and the job was neither completed nor paid for.

Louis Pilié returned to private practice, but in his last years served as an assistant city surveyor. The account of his death in the *Times-Democrat* in 1886 bears the following tribute: "There were few men in the city better known or more generally esteemed than the deceased. Notwithstanding his long public career, he died leaving nothing, a proof of his honesty and integrity."[15]

A third generation surveyor in the Pilié family was Louis Henri's son, Edgar, who was born in 1844. At the age of seventeen he enlisted in the Confederate artillery and served in the Army of Tennessee for the duration of hostilities. He was employed during Reconstruction by Morgan's Steamship Company before taking up the profession of surveying. His practice was entirely in the private sector, although he was respected by both the bench and bar for his professional acumen.[16] Upon his death in 1912, the voluminous family surveying archives were purchased by the Louisiana Abstract Company, and are now in the Historic New Orleans Collection on Royal Street, only four squares away from Joseph Pilié's office and home.

C.J.A. D'HEMECOURT

Claude Jules Allou d'Hémécourt is thought by many to be the best surveyor who ever stretched a chain in the streets of New Orleans. This preeminence was achieved without the use of computers, electronic measuring devices, battery-powered metal detectors, or the host of other modern instruments that are in customary use in our time, more than one hundred years after his death. No modern survey of a Mississippi River bridge, an interstate highway, or a complex division of a large tract can approach the single masterpiece that entitles him to everlasting acclaim. Although he had a long and productive professional career, one survey—one that was never quite completed—provides sufficient evidence of his genius.

Born in France in 1819, d'Hémécourt came to New Orleans in 1831 with his parents and siblings. Family tradition indicates that his father, Jean Charles Allou d'Hémécourt, was a professor in the old College d'Orleans, and that connection may have precipitated the move to Louisiana.[17] Allou d'Hémécourt, as the father was known, was a competent civil engineer and land surveyor in New Orleans in the 1830s and 1840s, and examples of his work abound in the Notarial Archives. His home on Bayou St. John is now the property of St. Francis Cabrini School. Without a doubt, Allou had a strong influence on the education and professional thinking of his son.

In the notarial acts of Jean Agaisse for the year 1843, there is a marriage contract dated December 26, 1843, between Claude Jules Allou d'Hémécourt, son of Jean Charles Allou d'Hémécourt and his wife Marie Felicité Boisselin, and Mlle Victoire Émilie Rochefort, daughter of Pierre Rochefort and his wife Marie Julie Gabrielle Lemoine. As was the custom of that time, dowry and household goods of the bride are mentioned, as well as the contributions of the groom to the new family establishment. Jules's gift to the marriage included a house on Marigny Street between Craps and Great Men streets, a slave named Marie, and $1,000; his bride-to-be provided a dowry of jewelry and household goods valued at $500.

The marriage, so carefully planned, was shattered seven short years later by the death of the young wife at the age of twenty-four. Tragedy seemed to stalk the personal side of Jules's life, in spite of the success he achieved in his profession. Several years after Victoire Émilie's death, he married her younger sister Marie Rosa Rochefort. She died in 1871 at the age of thirty-three. He lived for nine years more before joining his family in St. Louis Cemetery No.2.

The New Orleans Notarial Archives contain hundreds of examples of d'Hémécourt's professional craftsmanship and skill. In 1859 he received an island in Bayou St. John as payment for surveying the Milne Asylum property in Gentilly.[18] The island was named Ile d'Hémécourt for a short while, and now is an exclusive residential area called Park Island. Bernard Marigny, who created the town of Mandeville, had also paid d'Hémécourt's father for professional services in lots in the new town across the lake.[19]

Jules's crowning work is the survey of the entire city of New Orleans undertaken in 1857. Common Council Ordinance No. 2795, dated May 28, 1856, authorized Mayor Charles Waterman to contract with J.A. d'Hémécourt to make a plan of the city, together with plan books showing each block in detail, and an index map for $30,000. The contract was executed before the notary Paul Emile Théard on December 1, 1856. Attached to the contract were detailed specifications defining the work, written by Louis H. Pilié, City Engineer.

The plan was an ambitious one, even though the city at that time began at Toledano Street and extended to Fisherman's Canal immediately below Jackson

Col. Valery Sulakowski. (Courtesy Confederate Memorial Hall)

Barracks. Ambitious, too, it would seem, because d'Hémécourt was required to complete the general plan and index map in one year, and the books of plans in two years from the signing of the contract. This schedule did not allow any time for field surveys or computations, and scarcely permitted the drafting of the plan. It appears that the contract was never completed nor paid for by the city. The work dragged on beyond the time specified, then finally the War Between the States disrupted the project for good.

The general plan on forty-eight large sheets of heavy buff paper was completed. Every block in the city was shown in outline form and given precise dimensions. Black india ink was used for the line work, lettering, and dimensions, but the angles at the corners were written in red ink. The drafting was done in one hand, and is of the highest quality, yet does not bear the signature of the delineator. Nothing is known of the index map, although one unsubstantiated story tells of its being lost at sea on its way to France to be engraved. This seems unlikely, considering the number of talented engraving firms at work in New Orleans at the time. Some of the plan books were partially done, but none was ever finished.

This was the only general survey of the city undertaken to this date. After J.A. d'Hémécourt's death, his son Paul sold the general plan to Col. Sidney F. Lewis for a few hundred dollars, and permitted the city, for a like sum, to make tracings of the sheets. While unofficial, the plan has been used by the city and other surveyors for every survey purpose since, and is an invaluable and monumental work. In 1937, John Hampton Lewis, son of Col. Sidney F. Lewis, donated the original sheets to the people of New Orleans, to be filed in the City Engineer's office for public use.[20] The donation was accepted by the Commission Council, and the plans may still be viewed in the Department of Streets in City Hall. The plan books and other d'Hémécourt maps are now in the Historic New Orleans Collection.

D'Hémécourt and his wife Marie were devout patrons of the Little Sisters of the Poor. A photograph of the couple was among the several papers and articles sealed in the cornerstone of the convent, constructed in 1872. One hundred years later, when the order moved its convent to Algiers, the older cornerstone was opened and the faded photographs came to light again, too faint to copy.[21] However, d'Hémécourt's maps remain as his memorial.

VALERY SULAKOWSKI

While Jefferson City was developing into a suburb of New Orleans, there were surveyors measuring large segments of land under contracts with the federal government. The United States township surveys were at the same time reprehensible and remarkable, and will forever affect private ownership of property in New Orleans. The system of surveying the countryside into six-mile squares, each designated by certain numbers to be a particular township, was ill-suited to deal with the whole of Louisiana. Some of the swamps are very difficult to survey by any system. In the Louisiana Purchase Treaty, the United States agreed to Napoleon's condition that all residents who had valid titles to property would maintain their ownership under the new government. The process of sorting through the titles and surveying all of the land in the state consumed the greater part of the nineteenth century. One federal surveyor who left his imprint upon New Orleans was Valery Sulakowski.

Sulakowski came to Louisiana in 1851 at the age of twenty-six, an exile from his native Poland, following his participation in an unsuccessful attempt to overthrow the Austrian and Prussian empire that ruled his homeland. Having received military training in his youth, he was able to find employment in New Orleans, primarily in the Federal Land Office, as an engineer and surveyor. He marked off a number of townships near Houma, and in all was the surveyor for almost four hundred square miles of public and private land in and around New Orleans.[22]

During his twenty-two year residence in Louisiana, he married Miss Simpson, daughter of a prominent lumber merchant in New Orleans. When the Civil War interrupted his surveying career, he quickly enlisted and was commissioned a colonel in the Fourteenth Louisiana Volunteers. On the way to northern Virginia, he quelled a riot among his troops by force, and following the construction of engineering works on the York Peninsula, resigned his command after one year. Later, he re-enlisted at the request of Gen. John B. Magruder, and was chief engineer under General Magruder during the design and construction of defense works along the Texas coast.[23] At war's end he was engaged in a plan to enlist Polish volunteers, many of whom had fled their homeland in 1863, after an abortive attempt to evict Russia from Poland. At the time of the collapse of the Confederate cause, Sulakowski was in Mexico awaiting passage to Cuba. From there he had planned to embark for southern Europe to enlist the Polish expatriates.

Before Sulakowski began his surveying work for the government after the war, the major tasks of running a central meridian—that is, a line running due north and south in the center of the state, and an east and west base line along the thirty-first parallel of north latitude—had already been done. Most of the township boundaries and their interior lines had been surveyed throughout the state. New Orleans was a special case because of the size of the task, and no surveyors could be found who were willing to engage in the work for the fees the federal government allowed. The matter of money was resolved by the city pledging to add $3,025 to $8,000 of federal funds, so that Sulakowski was engaged to survey an estimated 315 miles of claim lines for the princely sum of $35 per mile. The contract was executed in 1871, sixty-eight years after the Louisiana Purchase, and completed in less than four months. As a former Confederate soldier, Sulakowski was unable to take the prescribed loyalty oath, but did swear to "support and defend the Constitution of the United States against all enemies foreign and domestic."

The official maps of Township 12 and 13 South, Range 11 East, completed in 1872 by Sulakowski and on file in the State Land Office in Baton Rouge, give a clear picture of the plantations which developed into Jefferson City, as well as an indication of the extent that development had progressed beyond or back of St. Charles Avenue.

Faubourg Plaisance, between Toledano and Delachaise streets, appears to extend six squares lakeward of St. Charles Avenue. Faubourgs Delachaise, Joseph, and Bouligny all seem to have been developed for about three squares on the lake side of St. Charles Avenue. This evidence is confirmed in the official records of the Jefferson City Surveyor's office, now on file in the Louisiana Division of the New Orleans Public Library. These records indicate a great deal of street paving on Carondelet Street in 1869, the last year for which the records have been preserved. Faubourg Avart extended five squares back of St. Charles Avenue, a result, no doubt, of slightly higher land in that particular neighborhood.

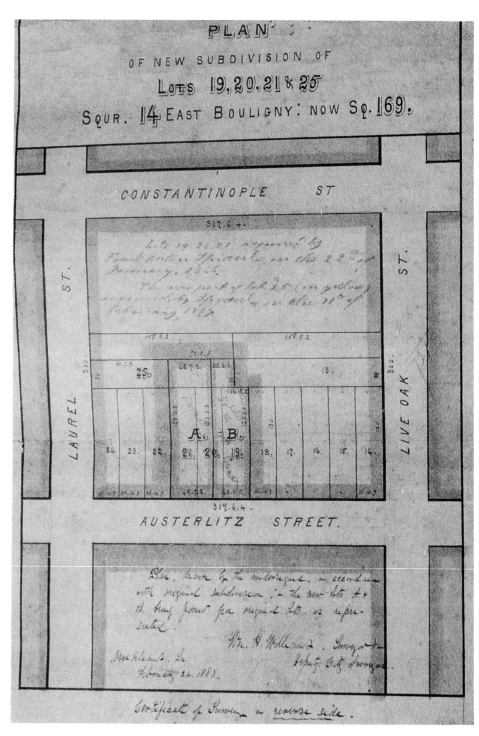

William H. Williams Survey of New Subdivision in East Bouligny. Feb. 24, 1881. Attached to Notary Public E. Commagere, Acts 9/90. New Orleans Notarial Archives. (Photo credit: Bert Myers.)

The clerks in the State Land Office today praise Sulakowski's neat field notes as exemplary. Some criticism was leveled at him by his peers, particularly that his plantation boundaries, as projected back into the swamps lying between the river and the ridge along Metairie and Gentilly bayous, were not correctly run. Hindsight permits those of us who are not enduring summer heat, yellow fever, malaria, and dengue, and other inconveniences such as mosquitoes, snakes, and swampy terrain, to require of him more rigid compliance with specifications than the ones which he was actually compelled to meet. Sulakowski was not a perfect surveyor, but a remarkable one under the circumstances. A man of talent and tenacity, undaunted by the physical hardships he endured. His untimely death at the age of forty-eight was the result of a stroke, and not of disease contracted walking countless miles through the inimical Louisiana terrain. Newspaper accounts of his day uniformly regretted the loss of a respected member of the community, whose talents, leadership, and literacy would be both missed and remembered.[24]

WILLIAM H. WILLIAMS

William H. Williams served as successor to Benjamin Buisson as surveyor for Jefferson Parish. Between his arrival in New Orleans in 1845 until his death in 1886, Williams lived a life that may qualify him as the "typical" surveyor of his time. This conclusion may be reached only after reading through his meticulous field notebooks, 123 in all, in the Rare Books and Manuscripts Section of the Howard-Tilton Memorial Library at Tulane University, and comparing them to the archives of his peers and to the state of the art today. These notebooks are pocket-size, each containing from thirty to sixty pages and with a beginning date recorded on each cover. Many of the notes are in narrative form, but sketches of lots, levees, and houses abound. They were usually recorded in pencil, but often enhanced later in ink. They describe his work of measuring property, setting grades for streets, repairing levees, recording the high water of the Mississippi River, and compensating for the annual variation of his compass from true north.

William H. Williams. (Courtesy Southeastern Architectural Archive, Tulane University Library.)

Williams came to New Orleans from Cincinnati, Ohio, at the age of twenty-eight, already trained as a civil engineer and surveyor. In the following year, 1846, he succeeded Buisson as Parish Surveyor. He held that position for a number of years, for it was in 1857 that he reported the fire in his office that destroyed the Parish Survey Record Book, which was mentioned earlier. In 1865 an announcement appeared in the newspaper, the *Daily True Delta*, that Williams had been re-elected to the office of Surveyor of Carrollton.[25] When he made the transition from one office to the other is not clear. One tends to associate Williams almost exclusively with the City of Carrollton. The home in which he lived and died was located at No. 65 Carrollton Avenue, across from the Carrollton Courthouse (now Benjamin Franklin High School). His office, before the fire, was nearby on Dublin Street. In 1876 he yielded to the entreaties of his fellow Carrolltonians and wrote a history of Carrollton as part of the celebration of the national Centennial.[26]

Williams's world extended farther than the city limits of Carrollton, however. One of his published works is a lithographic map, dated 1871, entitled "Carrollton and the Sixth District of New Orleans." Of all the surveyors in professional practice in New Orleans at that time, only Williams was qualified to produce such a map. His little notebooks contain entries and sketches of surveys in Jefferson City, New Orleans, and places as far away as Canton, Mississippi, and Chicot County, Arkansas. He traveled up the Mississippi River as far as Baton Rouge to

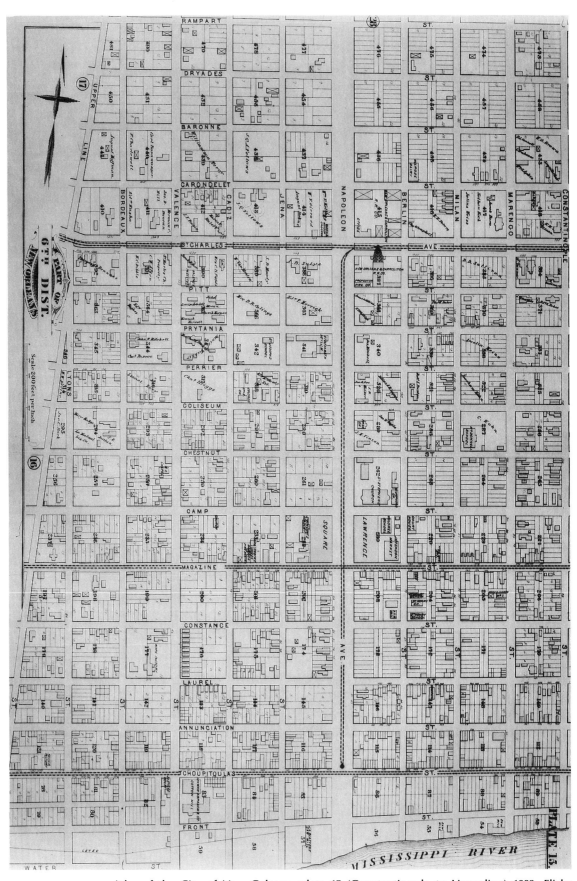

Atlas of the City of New Orleans, plate 15 (Constantinople to Upperline) 1883. Elisha Robinson. (Courtesy The Historic New Orleans Collection, Museum/Research Center, Acc. No. 1952.8.17.)

inspect and evaluate levee problems. A letter written in July 1865 to Gov. Madison Wells expressed concern over the condition of the state's levees, and suggested a plan of action.[27] This letter evidently bore some fruit, for Williams's notebook dated October 1865 lists the Levee Engineers of the First Division, with J.A. d'Hémécourt as Chief and himself as one of several assistants. Williams was responsible for the levees from Carrollton to Ascension on the left bank of the river.

Other entries in the field book tell about Williams's life and matters that concerned him. An entry dated Sunday, September 26, 1858, in Canton, Mississippi, reads: "Broke the Sabbath slightly, by computing my observations, and writing a letter to my wife." In an April 1861 entry there is a listing of the penetrating power, through "well-rammed earth," of shells of all sizes, from musket balls up to twenty-four pounders. Another entry, apparently a list of things to remember to take on one trip in 1863, is short and simple: "Pistol/Overcoat/Map of River." One book contains a memorandum regarding a mother's complaint of a teacher's excessive punishment of her son, and another lists materials required by the teachers in the school.

Accounts indicate Williams received a monthly salary of $150 when employed on levee work, and annual receipts ranging from $1,200 to $1,800. His assistants, hired by the day for the levee work and representative of unskilled workmen of the day, were paid $3 per day, as they were needed. Thus by prevailing standards, the surveyor received a respectable compensation for his efforts, albeit not a princely one.

The manner of charging fees for property surveys was established by governing bodies, and followed a format that continued into the early years of the present century. Country property was measured off for a fee of twelve and one-half cents per *arpent* along the front, where the land was generally clear, but the price rose to twenty-five cents per *arpent* for depth and rear measurements where the terrain was unusually rough. Stakes were set for one dollar each, and town or suburban lots were measured at the rate of one cent per foot of perimeter.[28] This last figure prevailed until the late nineteenth century, when it finally was increased to two cents per foot.

Williams worked until his death on March 6, 1886. His son, C. Milo Williams, continued his father's surveying practice into the twentieth century. The young man's first notes, in notebook 123 dated March 10, 1886, bear testimony to the esteem in which he held his father: "First day's work without Pa. Oh! God! How lonesome!"

CONCLUSION

Would Benjamin Buisson recognize his Jefferson City today? Perhaps the buildings that have been preserved would give him a vague sense of belonging, but it is unlikely that he would be able to find his way about with ease. Street signs in many cases call for new names, most of the street railways have disappeared without a trace, and the pastures and *marais* behind the city have vanished. However, surveyors have played an important role in the development of what once was Jefferson City, one that will never be diminished.

Fabacher's Row. Six two-story frame dwellings built for Lawrence Fabacher in 1892 for $25,000, facing Prytania, between Milan and Marengo, backed by Perrier. (Photo attributed to G.F. Mugnier. Courtesy Louisiana State Museum.)

5401 St. Charles Avenue (demolished). Built for John Byrne, 1878. C. Milo Williams, architect. (Courtesy Samuel Wilson, Jr.)

Architectural Styles

As the previous volumes in this series have amply demonstrated, each of New Orleans' historic neighborhoods has its own distinctive architectural flavor. From *The Lower Garden District* to *Faubourg Tremé*, New Orleans' buildings—and tombs—generally developed out of the city's own peculiar cultural traditions. With the present volume, however, our series has embraced a neighborhood in which international and national trends shaped the architecture in the district to a greater extent than did local traditions. It is thus appropriate to analyze the international and national origins of the architectural styles found today in Jefferson City. These styles generally developed between 1875 and 1925, when a majority of the houses in the Jefferson City area were built.

The Jefferson City that today forms the greater part of New Orleans' Sixth Municipal District, reflects the reality that post-Civil War America underwent a feverish metamorphosis from sparsely populated, agrarian, and rural, to well populated, urban, and industrial. Between 1870 and 1910 New Orleans grew from 191,000 to 339,000 inhabitants as the city swallowed up the bordering communities of Jefferson City, Carrollton, and Algiers, and pushed its own development toward Lake Pontchartrain. Jefferson City was born in an era when galleried, Creole-style farmhouses occupied whole squares of newly subdivided plantations, but matured in an era when newly rich families migrated to architect-designed homes along streets like St. Charles Avenue and Prytania to display their wealth in fashionable suburban residences.

Trollies during this interval had made urban growth possible and suburbs a reality. New Orleans' system of streetcars began as early as 1835 with the New Orleans and Carrollton Rail Road, and by 1881 seven lines had expanded into the Jefferson City area. By 1915, three more lines had been added, while the advent of the automobile was fueling urban sprawl.

America, meanwhile, was experiencing strong cultural crosscurrents that affected its architectural styles in a variety of ways. The 1876 Centennial Exposition in Philadelphia, attended by millions, spurred a sense of both national and regional heritage. This led directly to a taste for Queen Anne and Colonial Revival style architecture. While the country looked to its past, however, it also gave up isolationism, becoming a world power and even acquiring colonies after the Spanish-American War. That experience fostered a Spanish influence in American architecture—the "Spanish Eclectic," "Spanish Mission," and various forms of "Mediterranean." Other currents led to the adoption of Second Empire, Queen Anne, Tudor, Romanesque, and Renaissance Revival styles. Finally, a strong reaction to the Industrial Revolution brought forth architectural essays in "pure," "honest," and spontaneously "American" styles labeled "Craftsman," "Prairie," and "California Bungalow," all of which became enormously popular as modest-priced housing during the early twentieth century.

News of the latest in culture traveled quickly. A proliferation of magazines, books, art organizations, historical associations, and theaters were quick to publicize the most up-to-date inspirations of the muse in an increasingly "modern" era. University curricula, museums, and professional societies, meanwhile, increased not only professional standards, but levels of communication among practitioners of the arts. Among the museums founded during this time were the Chicago Art Institute (1878), the New York Metropolitan Museum of Art (1870), and locally, the Louisiana State Museum (1906) and Delgado Museum of Art (1911).

The works of Edison, Darwin, Freud, the Wright brothers, Ford, and Bell transformed American thought and urban life over a relatively short period of time. Science and technology also made possible new municipal services that affected home building. In New Orleans a drainage system went into operation in 1899, opening up vast mid-town areas for development. This revolutionary development followed closely on the introduction of telephones in 1879, electricity in 1882, and electric streetcars in 1893. A new city sewerage system went into operation in 1903, followed by a purified water system in 1909.

Owing both to the development of technology and to the widespread increase in printed communications, house designs in New Orleans inexorably came to resemble those found throughout the country. By 1908 a visiting architect would lament in a local magazine article that "out St. Charles Avenue, through probably the finest residential section of the city, one finds pretentious houses, as it were, transplanted from Chicago with all the meaningless collection of angles and turrets, [and] high pitched roofs to shed snow and ice which so rarely comes to New Orleans; all together giving the general suggestion of the Nouveau Riche taste, caring more for display than for common use." This observation the local editors shared. "The work of the past two decades might just as well have been done in Kalamazoo as in this city," they declared.[1]

What were these homogenous post-Civil War styles that had so overcome the distinctive spirit of local design? In general, they were of two types—the picturesque and free-spirited, as seen chiefly in the Queen Anne style that swept the nation after 1880, and a reversed trend, more academically correct, that often took its inspiration from classically inspired designs. This latter trend continued into the twentieth century, sharing the nation's attention with the first modern styles to have open planning and non-traditional ornament.

An increasing number of professional architects helped New Orleans keep pace with the nation. While city directories listed only ten architectural firms in 1883, by 1900 that number had risen to thirty-eight. Well-trained local architects such as Emile Weil, who subscribed to at least nine national magazines and had an extensive architectural library, kept abreast of national developments.

Weil and other professionals could also read of the latest fashions in the local press. New Orleans newspapers from the 1880s through the 1920s, for example, printed annual trade columns on builders and architects. The city actually supported two journals devoted to architecture—*Architectural Art and Its Allies* (1905–1912) and *Building Review* (1913–1923). These periodicals carried articles on national and local design trends and, importantly, featured photographs of local design.

While not all designs lend themselves to easy categorization, Jefferson City has seen at some time or another at least one or two examples of most nationally

Augustus Rice residence, built 1868-69 (demolished). Camp Street between Foucher and Antonine, backed by Chestnut. Now site of Frank T. Howard School No. 2 (New Orleans Free School). Note two-story cistern at left, rear. (Courtesy Charlene and Curt Weaver.)

prominent types and styles. Space limits a full discussion of them all, and some— the California-style bungalow, for example—will in any case be more appropriate for a full treatment in future volumes in this series. The present article will trace the origins and local expressions of Jefferson City's most prevalent architectural styles: Greek Revival, Italianate, Queen Anne, Eastlake, and Romanesque; Tudor, Spanish, Renaissance, and Colonial Revivals; and finally, Craftsman and Prairie.

GREEK REVIVAL, ITALIANATE, AND NEW ORLEANS BRACKETED

Greek Revival is one of the oldest surviving architectural styles in Jefferson City. While many Orleanians are so familiar with this form that they see it as a local expression, it is actually an international style that supplanted much of New Orleans' regional architecture. It relies on classical details, especially the Greek temple form. Architectural pattern books such as Minard Lafever's *The Beauties of Modern Architecture,* published in 1835, were responsible for much of its widespread dissemination during the nineteenth century. *New Orleans Architecture Volume I: The Lower Garden District* contains a more thorough treatment of this style.

In the Jefferson City area, Greek Revival structures comprise only three percent of the housing stock observed in a recent study.[2] These are generally located in close proximity to the river between Louisiana Avenue and Upperline or near St. Charles Avenue. Greek Revival had an early (ca. 1820) debut in New Orleans, but persisted in the vernacular form into the 1880s. 3303 Coliseum (see Inventory), a James Freret design of 1869, is a fine Greek Revival, while 712-14 Austerlitz, built in 1882, could be called a "poor man's Greek Revival."

As architects tired of the Greek Revival, they turned to the Italianate. New Orleans' version of the style, however, is almost alien to that promoted by its

1314 Napoleon Avenue. St. Elizabeth's Children's Home, ca. 1890. Enlarged and remodeled 1883-84, Albert Diettel, architect. *Art Work of New Orleans.* (Courtesy Louisiana Collection, Tulane University Library.)

Exterior detail, St. Elizabeth's. Diettel signature: curvilinear gable, ocular window, and wrought-iron cross.

national advocates—chiefly Andrew J. Downing, Calvert Vaux, and Samuel Sloan. The towers, flat roofs, broad overhangs, and masonry walls featured in Italianate houses elsewhere are not typical in New Orleans. Locally, brackets and segmental windows are the most common details, as are double galleries, not seen in national pattern books.

Italianate center hall cottages in Jefferson City date from the 1850s through the 1870s. The so-called "Italianate bracketed shotgun" comprises eighteen percent of the housing stock observed in the same study. This local vernacular house type grew in popularity in the 1880s, attained its greatest usage during the 1890s, and lasted as late as 1915, as seen, for example, at 3614-16 Saratoga. As this style has little to do with the national Italianate style, a more appropriate appellation might be "New Orleans Bracketed" style.

The appendix contains a list of extant New Orleans Bracketed houses found in city building permits for the Jefferson City area.

SECOND EMPIRE

The international Second Empire style takes its name from the French Second Empire of Napoleon III (1852–1870). The style, however, was not concurrent with Napoleon III's reign. In fact, more common names for the style were "French Roof" or "Mansard," a corruption of the name of the seventeenth-century French architect who developed this roof form, François Mansart. Its design was sculptural, heavily ornamental, and employed two identifying features—a pavilion motif, and a steep mansard roof with bold dormers. Local architects James Gallier, Sr., James Freret, and Albert Diettel traveled to France and experienced the style first-hand. Diettel designed the additions and alterations to St. Elizabeth's at 1314 Napoleon Avenue in 1883 (see Inventory).

Row of bracketed shotguns in the 500 block of Napoleon Avenue. (Photo credit: Robert J. Cangelosi, Jr.)

3453 Magazine Street (demolished). Built ca. 1860 for Peter H. Willard and remodeled for J.H. Keller by Thomas Carter, architect. Engelhardt, *New Orleans: The Crescent City*. (Courtesy Louisiana Collection, Tulane University Library.)

3905 St. Charles Avenue (demolished). Built for Thomas Janney, 1872. Known for many years as the Henry Beer residence. (Courtesy Coralie Schaefer.)

5018 St. Charles Avenue. Built 1902 for Charles E. Allgeyer (demolished). Favrot and Livaudais, architects. Engelhardt, *New Orleans: The Crescent City*. (Courtesy Louisiana Collection, Tulane University Library.)

Mansarded buildings first appeared in the United States during the late 1840s, and grew more fashionable in the 1850s, but did not achieve their greatest popularity until after the Civil War. The style became so prolific during President Ulysses Grant's administration that it was often called the "General Grant Style."

Early examples of the Second Empire were often Italianate structures with mansard roofs added. This combination continued throughout the history of the style, as Americans were reluctant to give up their favorite Italianate details. Consequently, the style is also referred to as Franco-Italianate.

A variety of mansard roof shapes, including straight, concave, convex, and S-curved, were hallmarks of the style. Architects often added mansards to existing structures to gain additional area or to modernize, as happened at 4801 St. Charles Avenue and 5520 Hurst (see Inventory), and at the Keller house at 3453 Magazine (demolished).

Large dormers were usual and more often than not, very elaborate. Well-detailed dormer frames took on a multitude of shapes and usually had scrolls at the base. A wooden curb around the top of the steep roof slope supported cast iron crestings, which have been lost on most examples. Roofs had patterned and polychromatic slates, and rested on distinctive bold cornices with either brackets, consoles, dentils, or a combination of these, similar to those found on Italianate structures. The windows were generally elaborate, hooded, bracketed, and scrolled at the base. Stilted segmental, flat-topped, or rectangular arches were commonly used for grouped windows on the major elevations.

Although alterations to the Cabildo and Presbytère in 1847 reflect an early local interest in the Second Empire, the style did not become popular until the post-Civil War era. In Jefferson City, the John L. Byrne house (demolished, formerly at 5401 St. Charles) was constructed in 1878, and the Thomas Janney house at 3905 St. Charles (demolished) was constructed in 1872. The *Daily Picayune* reported in 1884 that "Mr. Muir built for S.B. McConnico at Peniston and St. Charles a house two stories in height with a Mansard Roof."[3] The style remained popular in New Orleans throughout the remainder of the nineteenth century, for example, at the Edward Thompson house at 4209-11 Prytania (ca. 1891); at 5129 Camp, built in 1898 for Dr. B.A. Ledbetter; and 1817 Napoleon.

The Second Empire continued even into the twentieth century, as evidenced by the Charles E. Allgeyer residence (demolished), formerly at 5018 St. Charles Avenue. Allgeyer, a cotton broker, commissioned Favrot and Livaudais to design this large residence in 1902 at a cost of $20,000. It was of brick veneer with stone trimmings. Its designers considered it "the finest residence in the city."[4]

ROMANESQUE REVIVAL

The Romanesque Revival began in the United States during the mid-1840s, following a European lead in Munich beginning about 1830. Based on English (Norman) and Italian (Lombard) precedents of the ninth through twelfth centuries, this style came into use here during the 1850s and 1860s, primarily for religious, public, and commercial structures. Romanesque Revival was only rarely employed for residences, although many pattern books illustrated at least one example.

Since the style was a revival of the round-arched architecture of medieval Europe, most openings were semi-circular arches, and blind arches embellished wall surfaces. An arched corbel table was commonly used under string courses and eaves. Parapets or pyramidal roofs might top towers. Wall surfaces tended to be broad and smooth expanses of masonry with windows spaced far apart. Romanesque features were sometimes mixed with Gothic, especially in churches, or with Italianate or Renaissance details in secular buildings.

Local interpretations of the style in the Jefferson City area include St. Vincent's Academy, built on Napoleon Avenue in the mid-1860s, now demolished; the William Fitzner-designed Lane Cotton Mill No. 2, built in 1881; and Lane's Mill No. 3, designed by Diedrich Einseidel in 1893 (see Inventory). Later examples are St. Henry's Roman Catholic Church at 812 Gen. Pershing (Diboll and Owen, 1925, see Inventory) and Holy Ghost Catholic Church at 2015 Louisiana Avenue (Diboll and Owen, 1926).

The Romanesque Revival's greatest impact on domestic architecture began in the late nineteenth century, chiefly through the influence of one man, Henry Hobson Richardson. Richardson's interpretation of the style during the 1870s and 1880s was very different from previous American designs and from original Romanesque precedents. His very personal, uniquely American, late phase of the style is often referred to as the Richardsonian Romanesque. Known as an "architect's style" and confined to large, expensive structures, Richardson's style shows best in his own work. His imitators were often less successful, as is the case in many local examples. The style was picturesque, romantic, and typified by an overall massiveness, simplicity of form, and solidity. The random-coursed ashlar exterior, accompanied by deep window reveals and small roof overhangs, reinforced a sense of weight and made a significant departure from the delicate decorative detailing of the Queen Anne with which it co-existed. Richardson avoided monotony by using a different stone or contrasting textures for arches, lintels, and other structural features.

Stone arches were a key identifying feature of the Richardson Romanesque style. These occurred in association with windows, wall surfaces, porch supports, blind arches, arcades, or cavernous entrance alcoves. For the latter, the "cyclopean" Syrian arch, springing almost from the floor, was the most popular. Sometimes clusters of short, squat colonnettes with cushion capitals supported the arches. Arched windows were grouped and had colonnettes in lieu of jambs. With groups of three arched windows, the central one was often taller than the flanking two. Contrasting with the arch were rows of small, square-headed windows set in ribbon fashion often placed aloft in walls. Stone mullions supported the continuous lintel, and the transom bar was also often of stone. Most windows had single-pane sash.

Stone wall dormers were prominent elements and were usually Gothic in feeling. Alternately, eyebrow or hip-roof dormers could substitute. Romanesque details or a distinctive type of carved ornament known as "Byzantine leafwork" often enhanced column capitals, keystones, and wall surfaces. In theory, this ornament was not merely applied, but integral with the structural elements.

Roofs were usually tall and hipped, with decorative ridge flashing calling attention to their mass. Finally, blunt pinnacles silhouetted against the sky often surmounted dormers, corners, towers, and gables.

The interior plan was relatively open and tended to be asymmetrical, even rambling. Heavy dark wood paneling and beamed ceilings were decorative elements of major rooms.

Between 1890 and 1910, several large Romanesque residences were built on St. Charles Avenue. Perhaps the finest example was the Isidore Newman home at 3607 St. Charles (demolished), which was built in 1890 according to a design of

3607 St. Charles Avenue. Built 1890 for Isidore Newman (demolished). Sully and Toledano, architects. James P. Craig, *New Orleans: Illustrated in Photo Etching*.

Sully and Toledano. Surviving detail drawings indicate the architects' abilities, as do the fine stone carvings preserved from the house.

The Harris Hyman house at 4305 St. Charles, also demolished, was a square-massed, rock-faced residence with a steep roof punctuated by large dormers. Designed by Favrot & Livaudais in 1901, the house—particularly its entrance porch and fenestration—were atypical of the Romanesque style. The William Perry Brown residence (1904) at 4717 St. Charles (see Inventory), another Favrot & Livaudais design, is perhaps the best surviving example of the style. The structure at 3804 St. Charles (Emile Weil, 1905, see Inventory), is less sophisticated than 4717 St. Charles, but reflects many of the same characteristics once found in the demolished Newman residence. The large stair hall with its 'wood carpet' and inlay is particularly fine.

These rock-faced structures are alien to New Orleans' architectural traditions, as no building stone can be found in Louisiana. The style, however, has a place in the ambience of St. Charles Avenue.

QUEEN ANNE

Born in England as a middle-class reaction to contemporary values of the 1860s and 1870s, the Queen Anne style was a result of a nostalgic yearning for the simpler life of the pre-industrial period. It is not, as the name implies, a revival of styles from the reign of Queen Anne (1702–14), which were early Georgian, but an eclectic approach that freely combined seventeenth and eighteenth century architectural details, rendering an "English" appearance. Although the name was a misnomer, and recognized as such from the start, the public and professionals alike quickly adopted it. Some architects, however, preferred the expression "Free Classic," or even "Re-Renaissance," to Queen Anne.

4305 St. Charles Avenue. Built 1901 for Harris Hyman (demolished). Favrot and Livaudais, architects. (Courtesy Louisiana Collection, Tulane University Library.)

4717 St. Charles Avenue. Built 1904 for William Perry Brown. Favrot and Livaudais, architects. Engelhardt, *New Orleans: The Crescent City*. (Courtesy Louisiana Collection, Tulane University Library.)

3508 Magazine Street. Queen Anne detailing.

English architects Richard Norman Shaw, J.J. Stevenson, William Nesfield, Philip Webb, and George Scott developed the initial vocabulary of the Queen Anne style: asymmetrical massings of red brick, with steeply pitched, picturesque roof lines, elaborate, decorative chimneys, gables, leaded-glass windows, and terra-cotta ornament.

Picturesqueness was in fact the chief characteristic of the American Queen Anne style. Critic Talbot Hamlin in 1926 reflected on the Queen Anne era as "a drunken orgy of form and color."[5] Irregular planning and massing, accompanied by a variety of color, texture, and structural expression, was typical. Different shaped wood shingles arranged in a variety of designs were common. Every surface of the Queen Anne house was textured, making the skin of the house the dominant decorative feature. Building elements such as towers, oriels, entrance porches, wraparound verandahs, bay windows, cutaway corners, and projecting second floor gables were common. Roofs were steep and complex, often with cross gables and moderate overhangs. Polychromatic slates, elaborate terra-cotta ridge tiles, and decorative chimneys with large corbeled tops were usual.

Floor plans were informal and asymmetrical; rooms open, light and airy. The "living-entrance hall" made its debut, finished generally in dark oak or other stained wood, with large fireplaces and elaborate stairways illuminated by staggered stained glass windows. Grouped around the hall were the living room, study, and dining room, connected by large sliding doors. Projecting and inserted verandahs and porches were also integral parts of the floor plan.

Windows tended to be tall and thin, with a top sash divided into small colored panes surrounding a large central field, and with a single large lower pane or one divided by a single vertical muntin. Period catalogs labeled these "Queen Anne windows." Stained glass windows were common; Palladian and other forms of grouped windows were also used. Primary doors often had a large glass area, frequently leaded, and were commonly deeply recessed under a porch, vestibule, or second story overhang.

1716 Milan Street, ca. 1890. "Living Entrance Hall." (Photo courtesy Randal C. Griest.)

1716 Milan Street, ca. 1890. Double parlors. (Courtesy Randal C. Griest.)

During the 1880s, Eastlake spindlework (described in the next category) demonstrated a widespread influence on the Queen Anne style. The coming of this fashion brought delicate turned ornaments to porches and gables, and to bay windows under gabled roofs. By the late 1890s, however, a "free classic" adaptation had become more widespread as Colonial inspiration increased. Classical columns, often grouped and raised on a pedestal, now replaced turned columns, while Palladian windows, dentils, garlands, and other classical and colonial details became common. Although little separated later Queen Anne houses from early Colonial Revival ones, the Queen Anne tended to be more picturesque and asymmetrical.

In September 1884 the *Daily Picayune* reported that "for dwelling houses, the Queen Anne has recently secured considerable popularity." It noted two Queen Anne cottages designed by Thomas Sully at 4827 and 4831-4833 St. Charles (see Inventory). Two years later, the newspaper curiously described Sully's plans for Capt. J.L. Harris's St. Charles Avenue home (demolished) as being in the Queen Anne style and "a novelty in New Orleans."[6] Sully & Toledano also designed

4006 St. Charles Avenue. Built 1889 for Isidore Hernsheim (demolished). Sully and Toledano, architects. Hollander, *New Orleans of Today*.

4032 Prytania Street. Entrance door detail.

3706 St. Charles Avenue. Built 1896 for Mrs. John P. Richardson (demolished). Sully and Toledano, architects. Hollander, *New Orleans of Today*.

4132 St. Charles Avenue. Built 1890 for Henry Abraham (demolished). Sully and Toledano, architects; LeCorgne, builder. Hollander, *New Orleans of Today*.

Queen Anne style homes for Isidore Hernsheim at 4007 St. Charles; for Henry Abraham at 4132 St. Charles; and for Mrs. John P. Richardson at 3706 St. Charles, all unfortunately demolished.

An obituary for Canadian-born architect Louis Lambert credits him with introducing the Queen Anne cottage to New Orleans.[7] One of the most prolific architects working in the style, Lambert capitalized on speculative houses and houses offered on terms. He completed over twenty-seven designs in 1887 alone. Among Lambert's work in Jefferson City are the Ames residence at 4706 St. Charles (see Inventory), the Herman Meader residence at 4803 Carondelet, 1646 and 1648 Jefferson, and 3720 Prytania, all of which have been severely altered.

In September 1888 the *Daily Picayune* reported on the growing popularity of the style and its local variations:

3316 St. Charles Avenue. Built 1886 for Mrs. W. Fagan (demolished). Sully and Toledano, architects. (Courtesy: Southeastern Architectural Archive, Tulane University Library. Thomas Sully Office Records—Gift of Jeanne Sully West.)

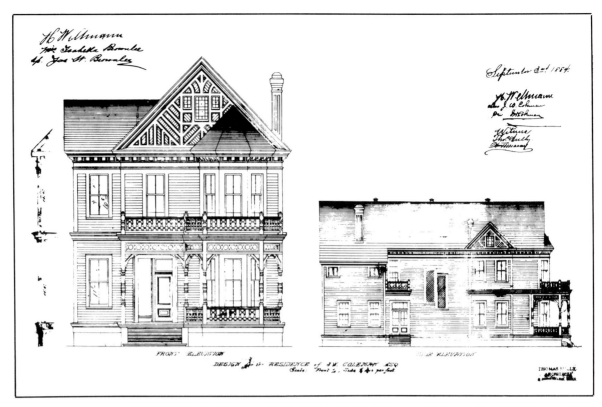

4827 St. Charles Avenue. Built 1884 for J.W. Coleman. This was the first Thomas Sully designed residence in New Orleans. (Courtesy: Southeastern Architectural Archive, Tulane University Library. Thomas Sully Office Records—Gift of Jeanne Sully West.)

4104 St. Charles Avenue. Built 1887 for Albert Mackie (demolished). Thomas Sully, architect. (Courtesy: Southeastern Architectural Archive, Tulane University Library. Thomas Sully Office Records—Gift of Jeanne Sully West.)

In dwelling houses the Queen Anne style of architecture appears to have become quite the rage and a large number of these ornamental and comfortable yet comparatively inexpensive buildings have been added to the dwellings in this city. These houses are not strictly speaking in the Queen Anne style, inasmuch as the original style has been so altered as to make them more suitable for this climate. The stories are higher, the balconies wider and the openings larger than in the original Queen Anne houses. These changes rather add to than detract from the beauty of the style.

Five percent of the structures in the area covered by this book are in the Queen Anne style, according to the study mentioned earlier. Refer to the Architectural Styles Listing for some of those not found in the Inventory.

EASTLAKE

The Eastlake style coexisted with the Queen Anne, and shared many of its planning and massing characteristics. A product of the chisel, gouge, and lathe, Eastlake ornament was three-dimensional, oversized, and robust. These features distinguished it from the Queen Anne. The style was named after Charles Locke Eastlake, an English architect and art critic who advocated nothing resembling the architectural style that bears his name. Eastlake actually promoted a style of furniture and interior detailing that was handcrafted and free of excessive ornament. Based on medieval precedents, his furniture, featured at the 1876 Philadelphia Centennial Exposition, was simple in form and attempted to reflect the style and principles of early manufacturers. American designers borrowed from these precedents and established their own interpretation of his style. The name thereafter gained widespread, but really meaningless popularity.

Buildings in the Eastlake style designed by Americans featured elaborately turned porch railings and spindles, decorative brackets, over-doors and windows, and elaborate ornament applied wherever and whenever possible, resulting in the appellation "gingerbread." The rapid growth of the lumber industry, especially in Louisiana, along with the technological advances in millwork machinery, was making ornamentation possible at affordable prices. Entire "stock" houses could in fact be mail-ordered from catalogs. The proliferation of millwork shops in New Orleans made Eastlake "gingerbread" both popular and affordable in the city, especially for small shotguns and two-story double residences. By 1884, "Eastlake style" was a recognized term in New Orleans, and four years later the *Daily Picayune* was writing that Eastlake was a prevailing style for "cottages and residences." The paper cited several residences under construction, noting in particular the works of Louis Lambert.[8]

Although the Eastlake style reached its greatest popularity in New Orleans during the 1890s, it continued into the twentieth century, and some local examples can be found from as late as the 1920s. In Jefferson City, the study indicated that seven percent of the residences are Eastlake. The appendix contains some of those in building permit listings.

NEO-GREC

Much Eastlake detailing can be traced to the Neo-Grec movement, which developed at the École des Beaux Arts during the 1840s as an attempt to reconcile modern technology with traditional forms. Simplified and stylized Greek ornament formed the basis for its incised linear ornament, used in combination with Second Empire and late Italianate detailing. The style's rectangular and machine-precise ornament was expressive of an industrialized technology. Planes and

1315 Louisiana Avenue. (Courtesy The Historic New Orleans Collection, Museum/Research Center. Acc. #1974.25.3.712 iv.)

1727 Napoleon Avenue. (Photo credit: Robert J. Cangelosi, Jr.)

1727 Napoleon, double doors, ca. 1898. Interior doors and transom of leaded glass.

3607 Magazine, entrance detail.

routers produced Neo-Grec ornament much cheaper than they did Italianate foliated consoles and acanthus leaves. The style was thus more economical than hand-wrought detail, considering the rising cost of postwar labor. Two preferred motifs of the Neo-Grec were a stylized flower known as the "Eastlake motif," and long, parallel, narrow channels known as "Neo-Grec fluting."

Despite New Orleans architect J.N.B. de Pouilly's early use of Neo-Grec during the 1840s, most local examples date from the 1880s and 1890s. Those in the Inventory are 3607 Magazine, 5414 St. Charles, 3418 Carondelet, 3939-41 Chestnut, and 4602 Perrier. Other examples are 724-26 Austerlitz, 5005-07 Perrier, 1109-11 Peniston, 740 Aline, 1420-26 Marengo, 4904 Magazine, and 1727 Napoleon. Shotgun elevations designed by A.C. Bell and illustrated in *Roberts Catalog* of 1880, also show Neo-Grec influence.

COLONIAL REVIVAL

The American Colonial Revival movement followed precedents derived from at least four European countries, including England, Holland, France, and Spain. Dutch, French, and Spanish Colonial revivals developed in their own right, and are distinctive subgroups, but only the Anglican and Spanish Colonial styles merit treatment here. Just a few Dutch and French Colonial styles exist in Jefferson City. The term, as used here, describes the revival of Colonial and early Republic architecture of the Eastern Seaboard.

Although Colonial Revival may be attributed primarily to the nation's Centennial celebration, interest in the country's architectural heritage began almost at its inception. From the beginning, the Colonial Revival was closely allied with the Queen Anne, having been developed simultaneously by many of the same architects. Contradictorily, its popularity was attributed to "a decided reaction from the extravagant crudeness of the so-called Queen Anne architecture,"[9] which so revolted young architects that they reverted to colonial buildings for models.

By the early 1870s, interest in colonial life and architecture had assumed the proportions of a genuine revival. Two factors seem to have been responsible for this—first, the rise of summer seaside resorts, which focused attention on picturesque Colonial towns such as Newport, Marblehead, and Portsmouth; and second, anticipation of the Centennial year, which inspired a flurry of nostalgic writings.

After the Centennial, American literature directly advocated an architectural revival. *American Architect* asked for measured drawings of old houses, which it subsequently published during the 1870s and 1880s. In 1877 noted architects Charles McKim, William Mead, Stanford White, and William Bigelow responded to this call by making a tour of the New England colonial buildings that were featured in professional journals. Sketching their way along the coast of Massachusetts and New Hampshire, the architects documented America's architectural heritage. From this they would build a "national style."

The Colonial Revival style continued to emulate these picturesque precedents through the remainder of the nineteenth century. Its massing, however, was more complex than that of actual colonial buildings, with steeply pitched roofs having well-detailed cornices employing dentils, modillions, or garlands. Elaborate dormers and roof-line balustrades were also common. Clapboard siding was the preferred external surface treatment, often combined with wood shingles and applied pilaster corners. Fanciful porches were integral with the design composition. While most windows were rectangular with single-paned, double-hung

2006 Milan Street. Built 1895 for Edmond P. White. Frank P. Gravely & Co., architects. (Courtesy Louisiana Collection, Tulane University Library.)

1421 Napoleon Avenue. Built 1896 for Emile Perrin. (Courtesy Louisiana Collection, Tulane University Library.)

Front and vestibule doors, reflecting Neo-Grec influence. Orleans Manufacturing & Lumber Co., *Cypress Sash, Doors, and Blinds*.

3628 St. Charles Avenue (demolished). Built 1893 for Gustave Lehmann, Sr. Sully and Toledano, architects; Kelly Brothers, builder. Hollander, *New Orleans of Today*.

sash, important windows had pediments for added interest. Side lights and transoms framed both single and double doorways. The style also featured exaggerated but delicate Georgian and Adamesque details, including broken pediments, goose-neck handrails, urns atop newels, garlands, and wreaths.

By 1896 architects and critics, fueled by photographs and measured drawings in architectural literature, were exhibiting a growing interest in simplifying the Colonial Revival. As New Orleans architect Suthron R. Duval noted, "The most marked feature of our new buildings is the departure from the conglomerated, hackneyed Queen Anne so-called style and the adaptation of the classic 'colonial,' the only approach to the 'style' devised since printing killed the noblest art—architecture."[10]

The residence at 5346 Prytania (1896) by Dannerman and Charlton is an early example of the trend toward simplification. In 1905, Soulé & McDonnell took this a step further at 4941 St. Charles (see Inventory), which the *Daily Picayune* described as being "two stories and an attic in height, of pressed brick and Colonial style, with the tile roof." Picturesqueness, however, continued through the first decade of the twentieth century, as the Frederick R. Hottinger residence at 2009-11 Milan, built in 1906, exhibits.

Later twentieth-century examples tended to be simple rectangular blocks with hipped roofs. Large wraparound porches had virtually disappeared, but entrance porches covering less than the full façade, along with flanking side porches, became common. Details remained Georgian in inspiration, taking some precedents from the Adam style. After 1910, details tended to become more correct, the hipped roof gave way to the side gable, and Federal style precedents became fashionable. A pediment supported on pilasters or slender columns often accentuated the front door. Windows usually had double-hung sash with small panes, and blinds normally had upper panels with small decorative cutouts. With the advent of brick-veneer construction, brick houses became more prevalent.

A 1915 article in the local *Building Review* noted that "many have appreciated the obvious dignity of the type we call 'Southern Colonial,' the tall colonnaded portico and the severe classicism."[11] The reference to Greek Revival as Southern Colonial was common in national publications as well as in local ones.

Because the Colonial could be produced inexpensively, and because the style was associated with quality craftsmanship, the early twentieth century saw numerous developer-built Colonial Revival bungalows and shotguns. Colonial Revival residences influenced by the Craftsman style were also common between 1909 and 1916, and appeared in the Jefferson City area as early as 1902.

The Depression of the 1930s led to further simplification and a reduction in scale of Colonial Revival houses. The Federal Housing Authority contributed to this trend by making modest housing available through low-interest loans. The local chapter of the American Institute of Architects also had a committee on small houses, and designed them for a modest three percent of construction costs. Examples included side gables with simple stylized door surrounds, cornices, and other details that suggested, rather than mimicked the original inspiration. Cape Cod and restored Williamsburg provided ideal precedents for this. Local examples of this last phase can be seen at 2827 Jefferson; 2115, 2721, 2735, 2815, and 2829 Joseph; and 2830 Soniat.

The study found that eleven percent of the structures in our historical boundaries are in the Colonial Revival style. The Architectural Styles Listing contains a list of some of those houses not contained in the Inventory.

5430-32 and 5434-36 Annunciation Street. "Southern Colonial." (Photo credit: Robert J. Cangelosi, Jr.)

2101 Jefferson Avenue. Twentieth-century Colonial Revival. (Photo credit: Robert J. Cangelosi, Jr.)

SPANISH COLONIAL (MISSION) REVIVAL

While residents of the eastern states "discovered" their architectural heritage, Californians realized that their legacy was different. This realization resulted in a revival of Spanish Colonial architecture, the architecture of the missions. As early as the 1860s, literature of the American West romanticized its missions. By the 1880s, both regional and national publications were eulogizing their demise, recognizing their state of neglect since their secularization in 1834.

During the late 1880s and early 1890s, several California architects began to advocate the Mission style. The 1893 Chicago World's Columbian Exposition also played a major role in the Mission Revival. Between 1895 and 1900 the style quickly matured and became the predominate residential fashion of Southern California. After the turn of the century, the Mission style appeared throughout the country, as mail order catalogs made Mission style bungalows affordable and popular, and the Arts and Crafts movement closely allied itself with the mission's regionalism, honesty, and simplicity.

Mission Revival buildings were rarely literal copies of their earlier models, but based loosely on them. Architects relied on details—arcades, parapeted scalloped gable ends with quatrefoil windows, low-pitched red tile roofs, bell towers, lanterns, and broad unbroken massive exterior surfaces of stucco, often with buttresses—to achieve their effect. Windows varied in placement and size, but characteristically had circular heads, some with decorative iron and wooden grills. Two-story examples often had wall dormers in a mission parapet. Since the original missions had usually been devoid of detail, the revivalists borrowed Islamic, Moorish, Romanesque, Spanish, Mexican, or Sullivanesque details for variation. This ornamentation was often concentrated around the openings. Because these elements were relatively few and had little to do with the floor plan, the style was adaptable to all sorts of building types.

Early Mission Revival houses employed an informal interior plan with a large living hall connected to the other rooms through wide, frequently arched or Moorish doorways. A simple dark trim was standard, and the floors were usually of oak or tile.

California-trained H. Jordan MacKenzie probably popularized the Mission style in New Orleans. The *Daily States* in 1906 described two residences he designed as a mixture of California mission and "MacKenziesque," a term the architect himself had coined to describe his distinctive designs. The Avenue Floral Company, built in 1904 at 3442 St. Charles Avenue, an Art Nouveau structure with an obviously Mission style parapet, was probably MacKenzie's work.[12]

The style was also very popular in New Orleans for churches. Two in the Jefferson City area are Our Lady of Lourdes (Diboll & Owen, 1923) on Napoleon Avenue between Freret and LaSalle, and 3500 St. Charles Avenue, built as a church but now converted into doctors' offices.

The best example of the style is the "Alamo" at 1215-17 Constantinople. Mission parapets are evident on Camp Street houses at 3936, 3944-46, 3948-50, and 3952-54; at 1420 Valence; and at 5317 and 5325 St. Charles. Though sparsely represented in the Jefferson City area, the Mission style is important as a basis for the Spanish Eclectic and Mediterranean styles that followed it.

SPANISH ECLECTIC

As architects exhausted new possibilities for the Mission style and clients demanded increased opulence and flexibility, the style evolved into a revival of

3952-54 Camp Street, Mission parapet. (Photo credit: Robert J. Cangelosi, Jr.)

2730 Jefferson Avenue. Spanish eclectic, Andalusian Mode.
(Photo credit: Robert J. Cangelosi, Jr.)

2809 Napoleon Avenue. Spanish Eclectic, Andalusian Mode.
(Photo credit: Robert J. Cangelosi, Jr.)

Spanish architecture in general. This phase looked for inspiration not only to sources in the American Southwest, but also to Spain, Mexico, and the colonies acquired by the United States after the Spanish-American War. It also emulated the architecture of the entire Mediterranean.

As early as the 1890s, buildings appeared in California with exuberant Spanish details. Not until the 1915 Panama-California Exposition in San Diego, however, did the style become popular and fashionable. After the Exposition, and especially during the 1920s, a profuse phase of the style reached its heyday. Examples of this mode were more opulent than Mission style residences, with elaborate cast or carved ornament surrounding major fenestration. Tile roofs with deep overhangs often dominated the massing. Wall surfaces were smooth with deeply recessed, often arch-headed openings. Period accounts described the Casa Grande at 4900 St. Charles (see Inventory) as "Spanish Renaissance." It manifests many of the above characteristics.[13]

Another source of Hispanic inspiration was the more restrained provincial architecture of Spain, especially Andulusia, and of Mexico and the United States. Buildings in this mode were conceived as sculptural volumes, well-anchored to the site, often with courtyards or patios. Smooth stucco surfaces, red barrel-tile roofs, arched windows, simple detailing, and lack of ornamentation characterized this style.

Some architects traveled directly to the source, rather than simply relying on the many publications that popularized the Spanish style. Local architect Richard Koch went to Spain several times and returned with volumes of photographs. After these trips, Koch popularized the typical "Spanish" courtyard motif with its hexagon-based fountain.

Examples of the Andalusian mode in this area are 2730 Jefferson; 2110-12 and 2809 Napoleon; 2628, 2701-03, and 2908 Octavia; and 5250 St. Charles. Another influence on the Spanish Eclectic style was the Craftsman movement, as may be seen at 4915 Chestnut; 5329 Dryades; and 2629-31, 2814, and 2830 Jefferson Avenue.

MEDITERRANEAN

Between 1910 and 1920, the Spanish Eclectic style broadened into the Mediterranean. This movement employed a wide variety of styles found along the sea, often mixing them indiscriminately. One variation, for example, employed the

1607 Napoleon Avenue, "The Teresita." Spanish Eclectic. (Photo credit: Robert J. Cangelosi, Jr.)

exotic styles of Islamic, Moorish, and Byzantine regions. Local examples of this mode include the Teresita Apartments at 1607 Napoleon; 2522-29 Jefferson; 2702 Robert; 1525-27 and 2406-08 Soniat; 2036-38 Marengo; 1417 Valence ("Blue Flower," designed by architect Morgan Hite as his home); and Palm Terrace Court (William Spink, architect, 1925).

More formal examples employed Italian villa precedents from northern Italy in a neo-Italianate mode. Stucco walls, big windows, and large tile roofs supported on deep brackets were typical. Some examples relied heavily on Italian Renaissance and are difficult to separate from the Renaissance Revival. Quite often designers actually described these buildings as Renaissance.

Local examples of the Italian villa mode include 1930 Jefferson (ca. 1912, B. Mass, owner-builder, Charlton & Dannermann, architects), 1535 Octavia, 5111 Pitt, 1524 Toledano, 5120 St. Charles (see Inventory), and 1523 Soniat.

Other variations of the Mediterranean were more American than Spanish in feeling. These hybrids were in a synthesized Mediterranean style, with low-pitched hipped roofs covered by barrel tiles, and wide overhangs supported on brackets. Upper windows were small, often casemented, nondescript, and deeply recessed into the wall plane. Lower openings were commonly arched with doors. Classical columns or pilasters or Spanish Renaissance details frequently articulated entrances. Wall surfaces were usually stucco, but occasionally brick. Recessed porches were common.

Most extant examples in Jefferson City are from the second and third decades of the twentieth century. These include Nos. 4 and 6 Blanc Place, 1424 Cadiz, 1550 Dufossat (see Inventory), 1668 Jefferson, 2636-38 Octavia, and 1636 Valence.

1699 Robert Street. (Photo credit: Robert J. Cangelosi, Jr.)

1620 Napoleon Avenue (demolished). Built ca. 1907 for Sam Bonart. Keenan and Weiss, architects. Catalogue of Keenan and Weiss.

1636 Valence Street. (Photo credit: Robert J. Cangelosi, Jr.)

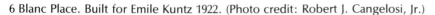

6 Blanc Place. Built for Emile Kuntz 1922. (Photo credit: Robert J. Cangelosi, Jr.)

1417 Valence Street, "The Blue Flower." Morgan Hite, architect-owner. (Photo credit: Robert J. Cangelosi, Jr.)

91

RENAISSANCE REVIVAL

During the 1820s, Renaissance style architecture was revived in Germany and then in England. In America, Renaissance details were first introduced in the East with the Georgian early in the eighteenth century, in the West with the missions, and in Louisiana with the French government's Louis XV style colonial buildings. By the late nineteenth century, American architects were seeking to restore order and discipline to their profession by returning to classicism. The design philosophy of the French École des Beaux Arts, which stressed the plan of the building, strongly influenced them. The massing developed as the result of a successful plan, while emphasizing Renaissance details.

While the Renaissance Revival work of architects McKim, Mead and White had the greatest impact on the profession, the 1893 Chicago World's Columbian Exposition made the style acceptable to the public. The Exposition advocated Renaissance building designs and promoted Renaissance urban planning—"The City Beautiful"—an attempt to restore order to the chaos of late nineteenth-century cities blighted with ghettos.

The largest Renaissance structure built in the Jefferson City area was the Jewish Widows' and Orphans' Asylum (demolished), designed by Thomas Sully and built

5342 St. Charles Avenue. Built 1887 as Jewish Widows' and Orphans' Home (demolished). Thomas Sully, architect. *Art Work of New Orleans.* (Courtesy Louisiana Collection, Tulane University Library.)

in the French genre in 1887 at 5342 St. Charles Avenue (see Inventory). Sully's firm (Sully, Burton and Stone) also considered the Alfred Hiller residence at 4417 St. Charles (see Inventory) "French Renaissance."[14] In 1905 the *Daily States* also referred to the Marks Isaacs house at 5120 St. Charles (see Inventory) as French Renaissance, though Mediterranean seems to be a more appropriate description today. Emile Weil used a French Renaissance motif for the 1907 remodeling of 5005 St. Charles (see Inventory), now the Orleans Club, and also for the 1916 Benjamin house at 5531 St. Charles (see Inventory). The Henry Alcus residence at 1645 Soniat was also a Weil design in a general Renaissance style.

Favrot & Livaudais used Italian Renaissance design elements for the Napoleon Avenue Branch Library in 1905, and Emile Weil chose the style for the Ewing Market Branch of the Canal Commercial Trust and Saving Bank on Magazine Street. The demolished Ghisalberti Apartments, formerly at 4301 St. Charles, designed by Robert Palestine, were also in the Renaissance style.

Spanish Renaissance motifs were also popular. As early as 1905, for example, a local newspaper described Toledano & Wogan's design for Mrs. E.T. Shepard's residence on Napoleon near S. Robertson as "designed after the Spanish Renaissance, with a flat roof so constructed to make it a roof garden."[15]

Some other houses in Jefferson City that reflect a Renaissance inspiration are 2709 Robert, 2005 Milan (Hubert Hundstein, owner; R.W. Markel, builder, ca. 1912); 4632 St. Charles, and 2212-14 Napoleon (Dr. H. Bayon, owner; John Lugenhuble, builder, ca. 1913).

CRAFTSMAN

The Craftsman philosophy encompassed a broad range of architectural styles, including Prairie, California, Mission, Tudor, and Art Nouveau. There is, however, a great deal of architecture operating within the Craftsman philosophy that does not fit neatly into these categories. Such designs demonstrate a lack of pretension, use of natural materials, integration with the site, and a dedication to simplification and utilitarianism. It is to these designs with a basic "arts and crafts" orientation that we apply the term Craftsman here.

The American Craftsman movement followed English movements that were reactions to the perceived corruption of artistic values associated with the Industrial Revolution. Early proponents of the Craftsman movement sought inspiration from pre-industrial Gothic architecture and philosophy. By the 1890s the movement was exerting influence throughout Europe and America.

Furniture manufacturer Gustav Stickley became America's greatest advocate of the movement, and his *Craftsman* magazine made the style commonplace throughout the United States. Stickley believed that houses should be utilitarian and economical. To him, the underlying principles of house designs should be "simplicity, durability, fitness for the life that is to be lived in the house and harmony with its surroundings."[16] Stickley's designs were consciously simple and devoid of historical precedent or applied ornament.

Craftsman houses were marvels of compactness and economy of arrangement, designed to lighten the "burden of housekeeping." Stickley found that a feeling of space and freedom was more attractive than shutting off rooms into separate compartments. He intended that the irregularity of room arrangement and the creation of nooks and alcoves should alleviate boredom. The "whole cannot be taken in at one glance," he wrote.[17]

To Stickley, the living room was not only utilitarian, but the symbolic center of family life, "unquestionably the most important room in the house." The dining

1645 Soniat Street. Built for Henry Alcus. Emile Weil, architect. *Architectural Art and its Allies*, October 1909. (Courtesy Louisiana Collection, Tulane University Library.)

room was the "center of Hospitality and good cheer," and considered the second most important room. Beamed ceilings and wainscots were common in them.[18]

The exterior of Craftsman houses had broad, shallow roofs with exposed rafter ends, purlins (horizontal members in a roof supporting the common rafters), and knee braces. The massing was picturesque, with broad porches, pergolas, terraces, and multiple windows. Exterior materials were preferably indigenous to the locale in which the house was built—thus brick, wood, stucco, and concrete were common.

Francis J. MacDonnell was the most prolific New Orleans designer who used concrete. *Architectural Art* featured his Jefferson City area designs of 5204 Prytania, 5210 Prytania, 4936 Pitt (demolished), and 2021 Gen. Taylor. Residential works by other architects published in *Architectural Art* include one by Frank P. Gravely & Co., 2028 Napoleon, and two by MacKenzie and Johnson at 4638 St. Charles, and 4938 St. Charles. The Paul Meyer residence at 5321 Prytania, designed by Nathan Kohlman, appeared in the national magazine *Architecture* in 1922.

Architect C. Milo Williams advertised in a New Orleans paper that he did residential work in block and reinforced concrete—materials that *Craftsman* and *Architectural Art* often featured in house designs. Williams was the first contractor in New Orleans to use reinforced concrete for residential work.[19] There are four surviving concrete block houses in the Jefferson City area: 2601 Gen. Pershing (Robert J. McQuiston, owner-builder, 1906), 4831-33 Chestnut, 2525 Milan, and 4832-34 Carondelet, all built prior to 1909. *Sanborn Insurance Maps* sometimes referred to these houses as "patent stone."

The Craftsman style began to falter in 1910 when Stickley confessed that he had never built even one of his designs, and therefore had never realized the deficiencies of the style. He also acknowledged that the houses were not as inexpensive to build as he had claimed. After that, the Craftsman movement, still on the decline, nevertheless continued until the financial crash of 1929. The demise of the style was inherent in its basic philosophy. Mass production of affordable handcrafted houses proved impossible as labor costs rose and technology became more efficient.

Many examples in the Jefferson City area date from the second decade of the twentieth century. These include three large structures at 3521-37 Camp; 5528-30 Coliseum; 1505-07, 2426, and 2822 Jefferson; 1506 Jena; five identical doubles 1721-23, 1725-27, 1729-31, 1733-35, and 1737-39 Gen. Taylor; 1334 Louisiana; 2017-19 Marengo; 1501 Napoleon (see Inventory); 1736 Napoleon; 2523 Octavia; 1905 and 2202 Peniston; and 3933 Prytania.

The Architectural Styles Listing includes Craftsman style residences cited in local building permits.

PRAIRIE

With the Arts and Crafts movement came a simplification of architecture and a reliance on nature for inspiration. Out of this philosophy grew the Prairie style in America's Midwest at the turn of the century. The style was referred to during its evolution as "Chicago School," "New School of the Middle West," and "Sullivan School of Design." New Orleans architect Morgan Hite used the term Prairie style as early as 1918. Frank Lloyd Wright wrote in 1936 that "the more ambitious began to call the new buildings that appeared upon the prairies from 1893 to 1920 'the prairie school.'"[20]

2525 Milan Street. Concrete block house built for Henry J. Rolling in 1907. (Courtesy Louisiana Collection, Tulane University Library.)

2202 Peniston Street. (Photo credit: Robert J. Cangelosi, Jr.)

2426 Jefferson Ave. (Photo credit: Robert J. Cangelosi, Jr.)

2523 Octavia Street. (Photo credit: Robert J. Cangelosi, Jr.)

The style was born early in the twentieth century in Chicago's Steinway Hall where a number of young architects had their offices. Soon the Steinway Hall group expanded into the "Group of Eighteen" and included others practicing elsewhere. While Louis Sullivan, a great advocate of simplification, was the spiritual leader of the movement, he did not offer any means of achieving his goals. It remained for Frank Lloyd Wright to offer a strong positive program of design. He quickly became the acknowledged leader of the group and taught many of the style's noted architects.

The Prairie style rejected historical ornamentation and strove for simple, "pure" organic designs. Many of its characteristics were derived from Wright's concept of "organic" architecture. As the architect wrote in 1908, "A building should appear to grow easily from its site and shape to harmonize with its surroundings if Nature is manifest there, and if not, try to make it as quiet, substantial and organic as she would have been were the opportunity hers."[21]

1707 Jefferson Avenue. Built 1911 for E.S. Maunsell. H. Jordan MacKenzie, architect. *Architectural Art and Its Allies.*

In plan, Wright eliminated compartmentalization and opened the interior to nature, just as Stickley had advocated. Low terraces, outreaching walls, and sequestering private gardens integrated the house to the site. Highly sophisticated spatial arrangements flowing freely from one function to the next defined space, but did not enclose it. Traditional rooms were combined into one compact living space and in lieu of walls, the various functions were sequestered or screened from one another. Changes in floor levels, combined with low walls, often achieved this objective. The use of multiple glass doors maintained a feeling of openness, even though the reduced scale of interior spaces resulted in lower ceiling heights.

"Taking a human being for my scale," explained Wright, "I brought the whole house down in height to fit a normal man."[22]

A broad wood-burning chimney, often free-standing, served as the pivotal design element in Prairie style houses. Furniture was often built in, fixtures assimilated into the structure, and artwork incorporated into the general design. Windows, often with geometric patterns, were set in horizontal bands with the sills forming a continuous line around the house and the heads lost in the roof overhang.

The Prairie style proved flexible in that it could be simple or complex in plan and mass. The simple cube was inexpensive to erect and maintain, and was the most popular in New Orleans. Its unpretentious appearance and simplicity of detail made it affordable.

Locally, Morgan Hite in 1911 illustrated an article he wrote on the bungalow with several Prairie houses. Several years later, however, Hite observed that the Prairie house, although popular in Chicago, had "found no favor in locations where traditional styles were already entrenched."[23] His observation was correct with respect to New Orleans, as to date only five local architects are known to have used Prairie designs—Edward F. Sporl, H. Jordan MacKenzie, Francis J. MacDonnell, Peter F. Donnes, and Robert Spenser Soulé. Prairie designs are nevertheless more common here than one might think, though far simpler than those of the Midwest.

Of three Sporl-designed residences for the D'Antoni family in New Orleans, only one is in the Jefferson City area, at 1516 Robert Street, and it is substantially altered. A MacKenzie-designed house at 2011 Peniston, built in 1911 as a square stucco box with pyramidal roof (also severely altered and recently damaged by fire), has a full-width front porch with emphatic horizontal bands, and bands of double-hung windows with geometric pattern glass. A good example of a stucco Prairie residence is 2000 Louisiana Avenue, built in 1925 as the home of Henry E. Braden. 2035 Jefferson Avenue (Charles Sinnott, developer, 1913) and 1330 Louisiana Avenue (David S. Haspel residence, 1913) are two similar stucco residences with symmetrical entrance porches. Wooden examples of the style include 4215 Freret, 1901-03 Gen. Taylor, and 2502-04 Milan, all of which have flat roofs with deep overhangs and modest entrance porches.

Several houses that are not necessarily classified as Prairie nevertheless exhibit the influence of the style. These include 2423 Gen. Pershing, 2120 Napoleon, and 1634 Robert. The Architectural Styles Listing lists others.

TUDOR REVIVAL

The Tudor Revival style (1890–1935) capitalized on the popular taste for English precedent established by the Queen Anne. It was, however, more faithful to English domestic architecture than was the free-spirited American Queen Anne. Like Queen Anne, the phrase Tudor Revival is a misnomer somewhat, as the style was eclectic, borrowing not only from Tudor (1485–1558), but also from Elizabethan (1558–1603) and Jacobean (1603–1624).

Tudor Revival houses tended to be picturesque, deriving their charm from simple materials and contrasting shapes rather than from ornament. Features included steeply pitched roofs with intersecting front-facing gables, often with dormers, elaborate chimneys with multiple flues, and elaborate chimney pots placed in a prominent location on the front or side of the house. The massing was typically irregular and complex. Projecting bays, wall dormers, bay windows, and

2011 Peniston Street. Built 1911. H. Jordan MacKenzie, architect. (Photo credit: Robert J. Cangelosi, Jr.)

2035 Jefferson Avenue. Built 1913. Charles Sinnott, developer. (Photo credit: Robert J. Cangelosi, Jr.)

1330 Louisiana Avenue. Built for David S. Haspel, 1913. (Photo credit: Robert J. Cangelosi, Jr.)

2000 Louisiana Avenue, window detail. (Photo credit: Robert J. Cangelosi, Jr.)

2000 Louisiana Avenue. Built 1925 for Henry E. Braden. (Photo credit: Robert J. Cangelosi, Jr.)

upper floors projecting over lower ones added to the complexity of the massing. Parapeted gables and elaborate verge boards were common on more expensive examples.

Half-timbering in a variety of patterns was common, and in fact a hallmark of the Tudor Revival style. A 1907 article in *Craftsman* noted that it was "an article of faith with us that it [half-timbering] should be made entirely 'probable,' that is, the timbers should be so placed that they might easily belong to the real construction of the house."[24] Half-timbering at this time was often merely applied ornament and not structural.

Patterned brick and stone, either solid or veneer, was also important to the Tudor style. Stucco was often used as infill for half-timbering, or for entire wall surfaces on less expensive houses. This was prior to 1920 when veneering was common. Windows were either casement or double-hung, and were often grouped together in bands of three or more. Small panes, often diamond-shaped and leaded, were common. Transoms were present, sometimes above major windows, and stone mullions divided windows in expensive examples. Cast or cut stone was frequently used as trim work above windows and doors and as

2725 Joseph Street. (Photo credit: Robert J. Cangelosi, Jr.)

2312 Louisiana Avenue, built 1910. E.A. Christy, architect.

quoins adjacent to fenestrations and at corners. Doorways, windows, and porches often employed a "Tudor arch," a distinctive, very wide, almost flat, pointed arch. Sometimes castellated parapets and railings were present, as were entrance porches. A particular type of ornament called strapwork, which consists of flat scrollwork that resembles leather straps, was often used for metal ornaments such as leaderhead straps and door hinges.

Interior details combined late Gothic and early Renaissance features, including large fireplaces, elaborate stairs, beamed ceilings, paneling and wainscoting—all closely allied to the Craftsman movement. Local examples of the Craftsman influence are 2701 and 2725 Joseph, and 4522 and 4526 Prytania.

The largest and best example of Tudor Revival in Jefferson City is 5010 St. Charles (see Inventory), designed by Robert Sporl in 1909 for Joseph Vaccaro. Early twentieth-century examples include the E.B. Hyman residence at 1800 Marengo (Favrot & Livaudais, 1901) and the Otto Walther residence at 1934 Marengo (see Inventory). In 1908 the *Daily States* reported that "a style of architecture known as English half-timbering has become very popular in New Orleans of late,"[25] citing numerous houses and their architects. The following year the same newspaper described the Jacob K. Newman residence at 4433 St. Charles, designed by Emile Weil (see Inventory), as "of English half-timber design with brick veneer"; the Sol Fechbeiner residence at 1509-11 Robert Street by Keenan & Weiss as "of Tudor English style"; and the Leopold Levy residence at 4729 St. Charles, also by Keenan & Weiss, as of the "Elizabeth style."

In 1909 *Architectural Art* published several designs of C. Milo Williams in the Tudor style. The accompanying article stated that "most of the examples given here are of the old English timbered work, or its modifications; a style particularly

1023 Jefferson Avenue. (Photo credit: Robert J. Cangelosi, Jr.)

satisfying and pleasing in its effects." In 1911 the same publication addressed the style by publicizing Sophie Wright School at Napoleon and Prytania (E.A. Christy), and describing the Louisiana Avenue Fire Station (2312 Louisiana) as "designed in the old English style of brick first story and half timbered and stucco on the second."[26]

Tudor Revival residences in Jefferson City from the same period include 4438 Carondelet (see Inventory); 5402 Claiborne Avenue; 5319 Dryades; 1028, 1910, and 2437 Jefferson Avenue (1916); and 1212 Valence.

SUMMARY

We see thus that New Orleans, following leads wholly foreign to its Creole vernacular culture, in a relatively short time absorbed and reproduced many of the world's architectural styles as its own. The growth of communication—through books, periodicals, and travel—brought these national and international trends to the Crescent City. Because of the rapid transmission of information, New Orleans architects were quick to mimic new styles, as the city embraced one trend after another, from the asymmetrical, pretty, and picturesque to the academic, square-massed, and rock-faced. By the turn of the twentieth century, New Orleans had yielded to a small, democratic suburban style devoid of historical precedents that came to symbolize the contemporary consumer-oriented American house.

New Orleans, however, as it always has, combined and reshaped the national currents to its own needs. Today, for example, "Gingerbread"—rather than Charles Eastlake—comes quickly to mind when one gazes at Jefferson City's charming rows of jigsaw-front shotguns. And St. Charles Avenue's many revival styles—those that sprang up so persistently, only to fade from the fashion scene—have blended with time into their homogeneous, oak-shrouded, semitropical environment.

One needs only a leisurely walk through the streets of Jefferson City to realize that discussing the philosophy of origination of any particular type of architecture fades in importance when compared to the charm of the *tout ensemble*.

ARCHITECTURAL STYLES LISTING

NEW ORLEANS BRACKETED

ADDRESS	OWNER	DATE	PRICE
726-28 Aline	James Bond A. Bensel, Jr., builder	May 20, 1886	$ 1,000
921 Aline	Mrs. Eliza Blohm John Blohm, builder	Jan. 29, 1887	$ 500
5113 Annunciation	J.W. Torrence	1914	
1101-03, 1105-07, 1109-11 Bordeaux	Frank Dameron	1899	
3506-11 Camp	William A. Mysing T.J. Casey, builder	July 28, 1884	$ 3,000
3619 Camp	William Stinson	Jan. 12, 1885	$ 750
4427 Camp	Miss. M. Mouledous J.M. de Fraites, builder	1915	
4435 Camp	Provident Bldg. & Loan Assn. A.P. Boh, builder	1914	
5201-03 Camp	Edward Lacivar	Mar. 26, 1884	$ 500
5304 Camp	Mrs. Emily Cragg	1895	$ 2,200
3711 Carondelet	F.C. Fazenda Louis Durel, builder	Oct. 8, 1886	$ 1,800
3621 Chestnut	Mrs. J.H.Mott	1886	
4613-15 Chestnut	Mrs. M. Folse O. Sharp, builder	ca. 1912	
3439 Constance	Wm. Ebert H. Bensel, builder	July 21, 1883	$ 2,600
3635-37 Constance	Mrs. Mary Ebert C. Winderberg, builder	Feb. 6, 1886	$ 1,600
4725-27, 4729-31, 4733-35, 4737-39 Constance	Messrs. McNulty & West	Apr. 30, 1886	$ 4,000
709 Constantinople	L. Sukno	1915	
1912-14, 1920-22, 1924-26, 1928-30 Constantinople	A. Thompson	ca. 1913	
3309-11, 3313-15 Dryades	Jacob Roelin	1896	$ 3,200
531-33 Dufossat	Wm. J. Reim	1914	
1019-21, 1023-25 Foucher	B. Maitre A. Leiber, builder	1893	$ 5,500
2201-03 Foucher	M. Stolzenthaler	ca. 1913	
2225-27 Foucher	E. Winter	1915	
706-08 Gen. Taylor	Mrs. C. Knight	1904	$ 2,500
3516-18 Laurel	Adam Bultman C. Hedid, builder	July 7, 1885	$ 1,800

3629-32 Laurel	H.J. Soland Geo. Donard, builder	1885	$ 1,200
4849-51 Laurel	Mrs. E. Pfefferle George E. Dickey & Son, builder	1897	$ 2,300
741-37 Louisiana	Herman H. Blayer	Mar. 3, 1886	$ 800
2233-35 Louisiana	J. Ciaccio	ca. 1912	
3634 Magazine	Mrs. Elizabeth Holderith	1895	$ 2,000
4228 Magazine	Baptiste Jung	1904	$ 3,500
5219 Magazine	Mrs. Mary Leibrook	1897	$ 2,350
4600-02, 4604-06, 4608-10, 4612-14 Magnolia	L. Rosenson	ca. 1911	
3423-25 Prytania	H. Nieso Seybold Bros., builder	1914	
3419-21 Prytania	Mrs. W.H. Dumestre Seybold Bros, builder	1914	
3427-43 Robertson (4 double shotguns)	C.T. Fletcher	1913	
3509-15 Saratoga	J. St. Maid	ca. 1912	
3614-16 Saratoga	J.J. Zollinger	1915	
2500-06 Soniat	Dr. J.G. Stuib	ca. 1914	
1922-24, 1926-28, 1930-32, 1934-36 Toledano	Leon Lavadon	1899	$ 4,500
5242-44 Valmont	Bernard H. Collins	Jan. 16, 1883	$ 1,400

From Sanborn maps, the following residences were built between 1893 and 1896:

912-14 Aline	1221 Constantinople
917 Aline	815-17 Delachaise
3925-27 Annunciation	714-16 Foucher
4210 Annunciation	730-32 Foucher
729-31 Antoine	3662-66 Laurel
730-32 Austerlitz	3725 Laurel
4116-18 Coliseum	3908-10, 3912-14 Laurel
3801-03 Constance	3932 Magazine
4022 Constance	

QUEEN ANNE

ADDRESS	OWNER	DATE	PRICE
4920 Camp	Mrs. Harry W. Wright	1899	$ 2,700
4803 Carondelet - 1706 Bordeaux	Herman Meader L.H. Lambert, architect	1891	$ 6,000
3509-11 & 3515 (now demolished) Chestnut	Louis Rice	1895	$ 9,600/3

3727 Coliseum	Mrs. A. Triss Moss Toledano & Rausch, architects	1897	
1514 Dufossat	Cullon W. Kay	1899	$ 2,300
1650-52, 1654-56, 1660, 1666-68 Dufossat	Julius Freyhan T. Carey, builder	1893	$13,800
1325 Gen. Pershing	Frank L. Gordon F. Reusch, Jr., builder	1892	$ 8,000
925-27 Jefferson	Mrs. C. Miller	1897	$ 4,000
1220 Jefferson	Mrs. P. Clark	1900	$ 2,000
1646 & 1648 Jefferson	L.H. Lambert	1886	$ 6,000
1654 Jefferson	Geo. Lynd A.A. Adams, builder	1890	$ 3,500
1737 Jefferson	George L. Gurley	1896	$ 3,300
1648 Joseph	Irma A. Moses Wm. Depass, architect	1896	
916 Leontine	Mrs. Anthony Alonzo	1895	$ 2,500
1240 Louisiana	Eugene Hornot	1893	$ 5,000
4917 Magazine	Frederick N. Miller	1895	$ 2,700
5005 Magazine	Mrs. Lulu Saxon	1895	
2134 Marengo	James B. Pike	1898	$ 3,000
1305 Milan	Mrs. Bernard J. Walle Thomas Booth, builder	1892	$ 4,000
1806 Milan	B. Meyer Kelly Bros., builder	1894	$ 4,360
1421 Napoleon	Emilien Perrin Toledano & Wogan, architects	1904	$12,500
1715 Napoleon	Junes Kranz	1898	$ 2,000
1719 Napoleon	Mrs. C.A. Beck	1898	$ 2,388
2013 Napoleon	Mrs. Henry F. Schaefer	1899	$ 3,800
2324 Napoleon	George B. Harrison	1904	$ 4,500
1923 Octavia	James S. Hastings	1902	$ 2,200
1717 Peniston	George Baquie	1895	$ 4,000
4032 Prytania	B.H. Flaspoller H. Tagnian, builder	1894	$ 5,900
4525 Prytania	Girault Farrar Charles A. Favrot, architect	1893	$ 8,000
920 Robert	Joseph F. Bogner	1915	$ 5,900
1034-36 Robert	S. Weiss	1895	$ 2,440
4917 St. Charles	Mrs. L. Mehle	1900	$ 3,800
1221 Soniat	Miss Annie Fell	1909	$ 3,000

EASTLAKE

ADDRESS	OWNER	DATE	PRICE
1104 Bordeaux	Louis J. Durr	1906	$ 2,400
4901 Camp	Charles F. Hardie	1895	$ 3,200
4603, 4607 & 4617-19 Coliseum	Julius Magner	1897	$ 4,800
5259-61 & 5265-69 Constance	Mrs. O. Carson	1896	$ 2,500
2018-20 Delachaise	J.A. Durr, owner/builder	ca. 1912	
2200-02 Delachaise	J.J. Sullivan, owner/ builder	ca. 1913	
4424-26 & 4428-30 Dryades (2 of 3)	Henry Staub	1895	$ 7,000
1917 Gen. Pershing	Norman Eustis	1895	$ 6,000
1922 Gen. Pershing	Mrs. L.B. Ogden	1895	$ 3,500

1515 Jefferson	Norton B. Robert	1898	$ 3,000
614 Jena	Rev. G.W. Toney Pine Grove Realty Co.	1913	
3908-10, 3912-14 Laurel	Mrs. L. Miller	1896	$ 2,000
2612-14 Magazine	James M. DeCoursey	1904	$ 2,585
5333-35 Magazine	Charles F. Skerker	1902	$ 2,400
1328 Octavia	Mrs. W. Gurley	1895	$ 2,000
1805 Upperline (now part of 1801)	Anthony April Abraham H. Moise, architect	1897	$ 2,225

From Sanborn insurance maps, the following Eastlake residences were built between 1893 and 1896:

1138-40 Amelia	4234 Chestnut
1220-22 Amelia	816 Foucher
805-07 Antonine	3646-48, 3650-52 & 3654-56 Laurel
1121-23 Antonine	3611 Prytania
3912-14 Carondelet	3932 Prytania

COLONIAL REVIVAL

ADDRESS	OWNER	DATE	PRICE
4116-18 Annunciation	Wm. Henry	1912	
4225-27 Annunciation	R.F. Gregory Chas. Pfister, builder	1915	
4229-31 Annunciation	R.J. Gregory A. Osborn, builder	ca. 1911	
5118-20 Annunciation	Mrs. J.C. Code	ca. 1913	
5301-03, 5305-07 Annunciation	Mrs. J.L. Pattzer Seybold Bros., builder	1914	
5627-29 Annunciation	E.M. Jaimes	ca. 1911	
919 Antonine	William T. Newton	1909	$ 3,200
810-12 Austerlitz	M. Zang J. Baehr, builder	1916	$ 2,000
4717-19 Baronne	A. Garrett	1909	$ 2,500
1718 Bordeaux	Herman Davis	1904	$ 4,915
1740 Bordeaux	Mrs. Lucretia, Mr. Horner	1904	$ 4,000
1117-19 Cadiz	J. Spielberg	ca. 1911	
1309 Cadiz	John Riess	ca. 1911	
3914-18 Camp	J.A. Langlois G.C. Bordenave, builder	ca. 1913	
4117-19 Camp	J.A. Patin J. Patin, builder	ca. 1911	
4904 Camp	A.D. Henriques	1895	$ 3,500
5504-06 Camp	P. Palmisane C.E. Newald, builder	ca. 1913	
4223 Carondelet	H.L. Burton, architect	1907	
4615 Carondelet	Lauren J. Bradley	1909	$ 4,600
3519-21 Chestnut	Mrs. L. Sontheim	1907	
4800-02, 4804-06 Chestnut	G.A. Thomas	1914	
5346 Chestnut	John L. Diasellis Sully, Burton & Stone, architects	1900	$ 2,500
4115 Coliseum	Alexander J. Parlange	1909	$ 2,878
5228-30 Constance	Hy W. Meyer	ca. 1912	
601-03 Constantinople	R.J. Nelson	ca. 1912	
3433 Dryades	Joseph Drego	1916	
5121 Dryades	Mrs. M. McGregor	ca. 1913	
1514 Dufossat	Cullon W. Kay	1899	$ 2,300

1520 Dufossat	Ed Cunningham	1899	
1917 Gen. Pershing	Willie Seago	1897	$ 4,000
2021 Gen. Pershing	Seymour J. Gonzales Frank P. Gravely, architect	1911	
2035 Gen. Pershing	Leopold Tassin Frank P. Gravely, architect	1909	
2105 Gen. Pershing	Edward J. Ross	1909	
2225 Gen. Pershing	M. Boyden J. Miriot, builder	ca. 1913	
2626-28 Gen. Pershing	J.H. DeBat Hartman & Toups, builders	1915	
714-16 Jefferson	C. Bungdall E. Mofhert, builder	ca. 1913	
925-27 Jefferson	Mrs. C. Miller	1897	$ 4,000
928 Jefferson	C.H. Lagan	1898	$ 3,000
1009 Jefferson	John E. McEnery	1897	$ 4,160
1016 Jefferson	Mrs. Chas. Raymond	1904	$ 3,000
1205 Jefferson	Mrs. John Charlton Charlton & Dannenmann, architects	1907	
1220 Jefferson	Mrs. P. Clark	1900	$ 2,000
1500 Jefferson	Henry Grabenheimer	1900	$ 7,300
1546 Jefferson	N. Riviere	1899	$ 5,189
1737 Jefferson	George L. Gurley	1896	$ 3,300
1900 Jefferson	Mrs. L.R. Hoover	1900	$ 2,500
1936 Jefferson	Albert J. Nelson	1902	$ 4,000
2032 Jefferson	S.L. & G.B. Hiller Geier Bros., builders	ca. 1913	
2236-38 Jefferson	Edwin J. Cooper	1909	$ 3,475
815-17 Jena	Mrs. L.S. Snow Seybold Bros, builders	ca. 1911	
1034-36 Jena	J.W. Lennox	ca. 1913	
2025 Jena	A.F. Legendre L. Bouse, Jr., builder	ca. 1913	
2508-10, 2512-14 Jena	M. Singer	1914	
1126 Joseph	Frank Leckert	1900	$ 2,300
1209 Joseph	Edward J. Heintz	1904	$ 3,000
1216-18 Joseph	J.F. Holmes Chas. Pfister, builder	1916	$ 2,500
3418-20 Laurel	C. Gitzinger P. Lagasse, builder	1914	
3960 Laurel	Mrs. J.P. Minne J.P. Kim, builder	1914	
3962 Laurel	Gottlieb Batt	ca. 1913	
4929 Laurel	Mrs. A.E. Beruer	ca. 1911	
5104-06 Laurel		1914	
5202-04 Laurel	Patrick McCarthy Seybold Bros, builders	ca. 1913	
2408-10 Louisiana	John Gordoun	1915	
2608-10 Louisiana	Jos. Schellkoffsky	ca. 1911	
4216-18, 4220-22 Loyola	L. Billet	1913	
4609-11 Loyola	Max Singer	1914	
3946-48, 3950-52 Magazine	Dixie Homestead Assoc. Louisiana Bldg. & Const Co.	ca. 1913	
612 Marengo	F.D. Costley	1916	
1730 Marengo	David Liberman	1904	$ 6,600
1812 Marengo	Mrs. Samuel Latte	1896	$ 5,900
1816 Marengo	Isidore Keiffer	1896	$ 5,200
1826 Marengo	Max Heller	1895	$ 6,000
1831 Marengo	Mrs. Henry Buddig Andry & Bendernagel, architects	1899	$ 6,740
2203 Marengo	Dr. Leonard Chamberlain	1906	$ 3,400
2231 Marengo	L. Roane Favrot & Livaudais, architects	1901	
2336-39 Marengo	Mary Burgogne H.L. Burton, architect	1906	
2525 Marengo	Joseph A. Watzki Redgley Bros., builders	1916	$ 3,900
1001 Milan	Mrs. M. Roy O'Keefe Geier Bros, builders	1914	
1704 Milan	B. Dilerno H.L. Burton, architect	1908	
2006 Milan	F.M. Milan Frank P. Gravely, architect	1904	$15,010
2009-11 Milan	Frederick R. Hottinger	1906	$ 4,480
2224 Milan	Pierce Butler	1906	$ 4,350
2824-26 Milan	W.H. Hortwell A.M. Usner, builder	ca. 1911	
832-34 Napoleon	J.W. Kelly Seybold Bros, builders	1914	$ 2,000
1715 Napoleon	Jules Kranz	1898	$ 2,000
1906 Napoleon	William E. Raw	1895	$ 3,485
1918 Napoleon	Reginold H. Carter	1906	$ 4,500
1926 Napoleon	Andrew Martinez	1906	$ 4,500
2004 Napoleon	W.B. Leonard Frank P. Gravely & Co., architects		
2203 Napoleon	Jefferson D. Hardin, Jr.	1906	$ 4,100
2302 Napoleon	C. Gordon Railey Favrot & Livaudais, architects	1905	$ 6,000
528-30 Octavia	W. Williams	1914	
1329 Octavia	C.H. Black Soule & MacDonnell, architects	1909	
1412 Octavia	J.F. Charlton	1900	$ 2,000
1923 Octavia	James S. Hastings	1902	$ 2,200
2335 Octavia	G.R. Gragara	1915	
1224 Peniston	Marie Cohen	1909	$ 3,000
1925 Peniston	Alfred P. Malochee	1909	$ 3,700
1938 Peniston	Warren J. Crane	1909	$ 3,400
2620-22 Peniston	Joseph S. Kelly	1909	$ 2,500
3423-25 Prytania	H. Nies Seybold Bros., builders	1014	
3419-21 Prytania	Mrs. W.H. Dumestre Seybold Bros., builders		
5213 Prytania	Charles H.C. Brown	1896	
5218-20 Prytania	Mrs. K. Glynn	1909	$ 3,000
5346 Prytania	Frank Dannermann Dannermann & Charlton, architects	1897	$ 2,500
1038 Robert	Miss Aman Troescher Emile Weil, architect	1909	$ 3,000
1629 Robert	H.A. Ferrandin Aug. Baclay, builder A.J. Nelson, architect	1916	$ 6,000

4437 St. Charles	Mrs. M. Monlezun Favrot & Livaudais, architects		
5603 St. Charles	T.H. McCarthy Soule & MacDonnell, architects	1903	$30,000
4520-22 Saratoga	R.T. Scott H. Walther, builder	1914	
1208-10 Valence	Mrs. L. Leonard F.W. Kickberg, builder	ca. 1912	
2520-22 Valence	John Untereiner J. Minox, builder	ca. 1911	
2708-10 Valence	L. Arnstead W.E. Robeson, builder	1914	
2424-26 Valmont	Dryades Homestead J.B. Veglia, builder	ca. 1913	

CRAFTSMAN

ADDRESS	OWNER	DATE	PRICE
3423-25 Annunciation	William Goelzenlenchter	1915	
1009-11 and 1013-15 Bellecastle	Jones & Roessle	1914	
4409 Carondelet	J.B. Harrison E.L. Markel, builder	1915	
4416-18 Constance	Mrs. J. Ventura J.M. Defraites, builder	1914	
5204 Constance	D. Grammel, Jr.	1916	$ 1,050
501-03 Dufossat	J. Schwabe	1916	$ 1,400
507-13, 519-21 Dufossat	Mrs. M. Decuir	1913	
2225-31 Gen. Pershing	J.A. Rodick	ca. 1913	
1721-23, 1725-27, 1733- 35, 1737-39 Gen. Taylor	G. Ciaccio Morris & Maitrejean, builders	ca. 1913	
2021 Gen. Taylor	D. A. Nelkin Francis MacDonnell, architect	1911	
2503 Gen. Taylor	Edmund Hughes E.F. Sporl, architect	ca. 1918	
2115 Jefferson	Irwin Fuerst Louis Preston, builder	1914	$ 4,000
2210-12 Jefferson	Union Homestead	1916	
2237-39 Jefferson	Security Bldg. Loan Assn. Jones & Roessle, builders	1915	
1803 Marengo	Christian Miller Weiss & Dreyfous, architects	1920	
2833 Napoleon	Weiss & Dreyfous, architects		
1905 Peniston	William O. Hudson	1909	$ 7,500
1934 Peniston	A. Veman Robert Spenser Soule, architect	1911	
2040 Peniston	H.D. Ogden H.L. Burton, architect		

2202 Peniston	M.L. Costley	1916	$ 2,500
2239 Peniston	W.R. Gilbert	1914	
2301 Peniston	A.J. Holzer	1917	$ 2,000
2328 Peniston	W.R. Gilbert	1914	
5204 Prytania	Isidore Jackson Francis J. MacDonnell, architect	1908	$ 5,000
5210 Prytania	A.D. Danziger Francis J. MacDonnell, architect	1909	
5527-29 Pitt	Savings & Homestead Assn. W.V. Landry	1913	
1800 Robert	Mrs. J. Weil	1915	
1806 Robert	Sol Weiss, architect	1916	
2000-02 Robert	Mrs. T. Reinach A.G. Bear, builder	1914	
2019-21, 2023-25 & 2027-29 Robert	Mrs. B.F. Abadie Max Singer, builder	1915	
4626 St. Charles	H. Jordan MacKenzie, architect		
4820-30 St. Charles	Victor Latour	1916	
5303-05 St. Charles		1917	
1818 Upperline	Peter Jung	1914	
937-39 Valence	Dr. J. Mullin M. Singer, builder	1914	
2401-03 Valence	J.J. Sullivan	1914	
2412-14 Valence	P. Johnson L. Aronson, builder	ca. 1913	
1311 Valmont	W.C. Moss L.F. Larsen, builder	ca. 1911	
1614-16 Valmont		1914	
2338 Valmont	Charles A. Thiery	1913	
2401-03 Valmont	D.R. Dickerson G.L. & J.D. Young, builders	ca. 1912	

PRAIRIE INFLUENCE

ADDRESS	OWNER	DATE	PRICE
1716-18 Dufossat	Mrs. W.B. Bloomfield W.W. Van Meter, builder	1915	
1901-03 Gen. Taylor	Dr. Russell Stone	1909	$ 3,500
2037 Jefferson	C.J. Sinnot J.C. Sinnot, builder	ca. 1912	
2323 Napoleon	Dr. R. Harrison E.L. Markel	1915	
2414 Octavia	C.A. Ramsey	1911	
2120-22 Peniston	Phoenix Bldg. & Homestead M. Koecke, builder	1914	
2418-20 Robert	J.B. Bastrow Henidas Pearie, builder	ca. 1913	
1634-36 Robert	O.B. Webb J.A. Newstadt, builder	1915	

ARCHITECTURAL INVENTORY

AMELIA

1017-19, 1023-25 AMELIA, bet. Magazine, Constance, bb. Antonine [Faubourg Delachaise]. These two identical, four-bay, double shotguns have oversized lattice-design brackets and stylized door and window trim. Henry Meyer, a carpenter, bought the two lots for $900 from Mme Aline Delachaise Dugué in 1873. Meyer probably built the cottages within a year, as Soards' 1874 *Directory* locates him on Amelia between Constance and Magazine.

LIST

1138-40 AMELIA, bet. Camp, Magazine, bb. Peniston [Faubourg St. Joseph]. This one-story double shotgun has a small gable over each entrance and a larger gable with a window in the center. Turned colonnettes, brackets, a turned-spindle frieze, and scale shingling animate the façade. The house was in existence in 1894, when Soards' *Directory* located Severin Schill and his wife, Sophie Kubler, there. The Schills sold the property for $2,700 in 1900.

LIST

1218 AMELIA, bet. Camp, Chestnut, bb. Peniston [Faubourg St. Joseph]. Originally a double, this four-bay, hipped-roof cottage has lost its gallery railing and has been converted to a single. Oversized brackets and elaborate cornices decorate the façade. Reeded pilasters, segmental heads, and multi-light sash accent the openings.

In November 1888, Eureka Homestead purchased the vacant property for $405 and resold it, with the present structure, to Eugene Hornot six months later for $4,000. Soards, however, does not list Hornot living at this address until 1891.

LIST

1220-22 AMELIA, bet. Camp, Chestnut, bb. Peniston [Faubourg St. Joseph]. Here is a house built as a one-story double shotgun during the 1890s and enlarged with a somewhat awkward camelback during the twentieth century. It was constructed after a succession of sales in the Charles D. Lee family. Its most interesting details are the turned colonnettes, spindle frieze, and circular bracket forms.

LIST

1419 AMELIA, bet. Prytania, Coliseum, bb. Antonine [Faubourg Delachaise]. John Pfieffer bought this property in 1863 when the lot extended to Coliseum Street. His succession sold and subdivided the lot in 1889, and this five-bay, center hall cottage was built shortly after that.

Large jigsaw brackets supporting the overhangs are prominent features of an otherwise simple façade that has unadorned cornices over segmental openings.

1422-24 AMELIA, bet. Perrier, Coliseum, bb. Peniston [Faubourg St. Joseph]. This unusual double camelback with double bays and a central projecting dormer probably dates from just after 1886 when William Mather Baker purchased the ground. Each half-hexagon bay has three corniced windows and a dentiled frieze. The large dormer, cantilevered over the entrance, forms a porch. The dormer may be an addition, but the bays are evident on an 1893 Sanborn insurance map.

Baker, a surveyor, may have built the double as rental property. According to Soards' 1891 *Directory*, he resided around the corner on Coliseum.

1628 AMELIA, bet. St. Charles, Carondelet, bb. Peniston [Faubourg St. Joseph]. This two-story, Italianate, galleried townhouse lacks a lower gallery railing, but the upper is in place. Cornices, paneled box columns, a well-detailed entablature, and a rear bay reflect building styles that continued into the 1870s in New Orleans.

The original owner was William M. Pinckard. Pinckard exchanged some lots in the square with John D. Rouse in 1872, and built the subject structure shortly after that. Gardner's 1873 *Directory* locates him on Amelia Street between Carondelet and St. Charles.

1641 AMELIA, cor. Carondelet, bb. St. Charles, Foucher [Faubourg Delachaise]. In 1868 New Orleans architect James Freret designed this handsome, two-story frame house with fluted Corinthian columns on both levels. It is one of three remaining houses in this area that can be attributed to him. Jefferson Parish builder Joseph H. Dorand constructed the house to face St. Charles at the corner of Amelia. The owner was Joseph Hernandez, a prominent businessman and civic leader and one-time president of the New Orleans and Carrollton Rail Road.

Henry Newman bought the house in 1894 and moved it to its present location before 1896. He

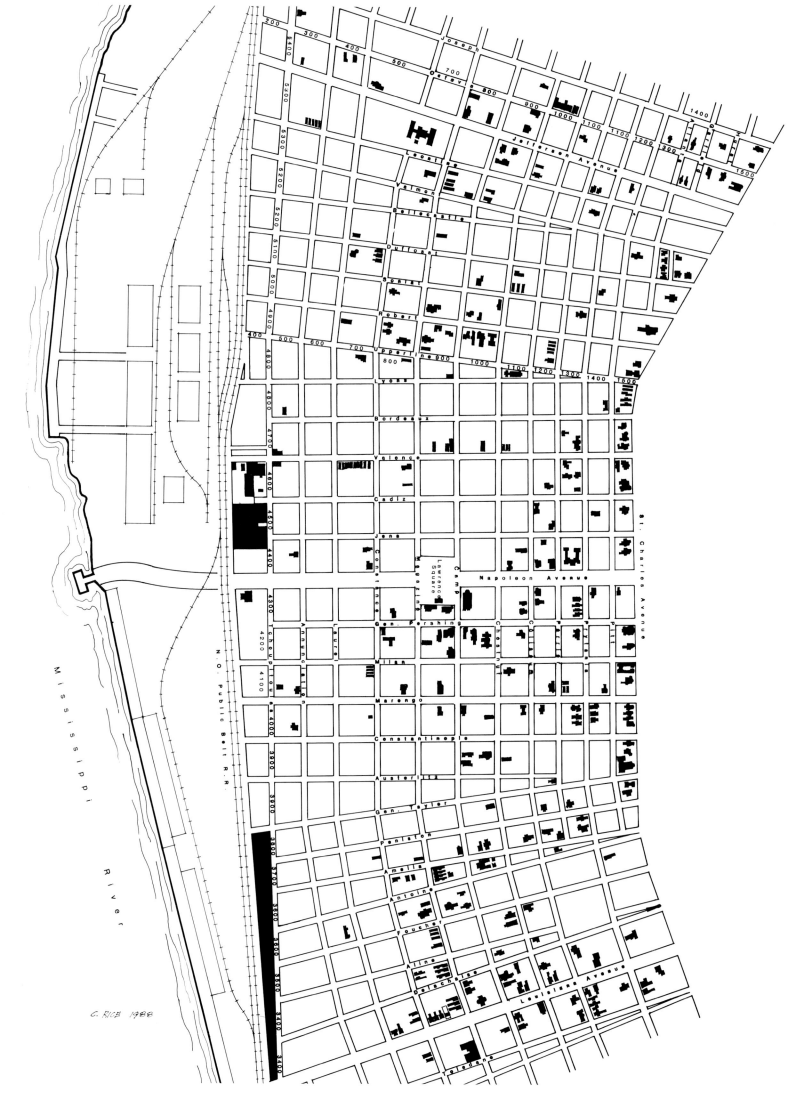

C. RICE 1988

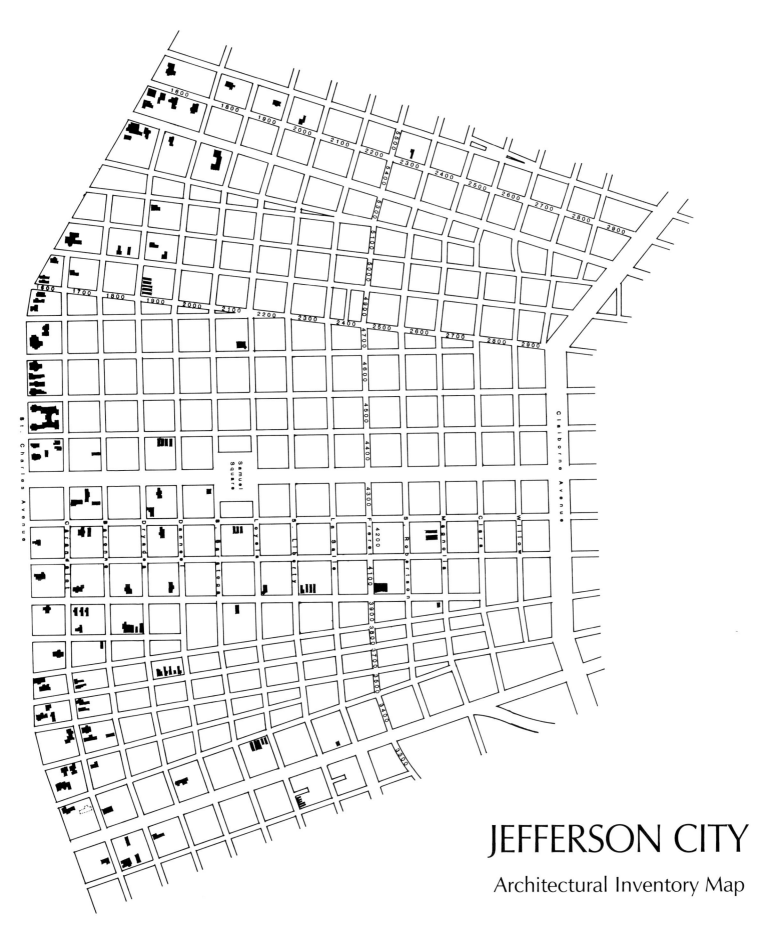

JEFFERSON CITY

Architectural Inventory Map

then built two Queen Anne style houses (now de-molished) on the St. Charles Avenue lot.

The 1868 contract price of $12,500 for this single-family dwelling included several ornate interior specifications such as sliding doors nine feet wide, eleven feet high, two inches thick and each half six-panelled. On the main floor, the doors were to have silver-plated hardware with white porcelain-like doorknobs. In the bathroom there was a fire-place with cypress mantel and a "cast iron bath tub with hot and cold water cock and shower arrange-ment complete. Also there shall be in the bath-room a patent water closet with mahogany seat and cover."

On the exterior, four paired central columns and pilasters framing the elegant door make an impres-sive entranceway. A tall central dormer adds height to the façade. Altogether, this is an important structure with fine architectural elements and an interesting history, well worth preserving.

ANNUNCIATION (Jersey)

4416-18 ANNUNCIATION, bet. Napoleon, Jena, bb. Tchoupitoulas [Faubourg West Bouligny]. This dou-ble cottage in Creole style with gable-ended roof, four room square interior plan, central chimney, and overhang is one of the earliest building types appearing in Jefferson City. The vertical board, bat-ten shutters are probably replacements, but the sturdy slate roof may be original.

Gardner's 1861 *Directory* lists a probable early owner, Mrs. B. Armbruster on Jersey near Napo-leon, Jefferson City.

ANTONINE (Antoine)

1126 ANTONINE, bet. Magazine, Camp, bb. Amelia [Faubourg Delachaise]. Here is a high, raised cot-tage, set on brick columns, and retired from the street. Spandrels with incised floral pattern and central pendant impart an Italianate feeling to the façade. Note the heavy cast-iron railing in a pattern common to the 1870s. A frame apron at the lower level and the lower enclosure probably resulted from twentieth century renovations.

Isom Davenport acquired the property from Louis Philippe Delachaise in 1861. Gardner's 1868 *Directory* lists Isham [*sic*] Davenport residing on Antoine [*sic*]. Rose Collins Davenport, Isom's wid-ow, may have built the present house soon after 1870. The property remained in the Davenport fam-ily until 1949.

BARONNE (Bacchus)

LIST

3321 BARONNE, bet. Toledano, Louisiana, bb. Dry-ades [Faubourg Plaisance]. Half of the facade of this hipped-roof cottage indicates how it might have looked with slender, square, chamfered colonnet-tes all the way across. Their simple brackets form arches which support a spindle frieze.

Louis Bovering (Bevering) acquired the lot in 1853, and when his son or grandson sold the prop-erty in 1896, the vendor agreed that the dairy and old cottage belonging to William Bevering be re-moved. The vendor "further [bound] himself not to allow any cattle to roam on the said adjoining lots." The present residence was built shortly after this 1896 sale. Harriet Kibbe, widow of Francis Gor-ton, is listed in Soards' 1898 *Directory* at this ad-dress. She had purchased the property in March of 1896.

LIST

3604-06 BARONNE, bet. Foucher, Amelia, bb. Caron-delet [Faubourg Delachaise]. This Eastlake double shotgun is typical of many built throughout the city. Fortunately, the structure has retained much of its original detailing, except for the wooden gal-

lery decking and steps. The triple-gabled façade was a popular technique of the 1890s, rendering the most important elevation as picturesque as possible.

The shotgun was built between 1893 and 1896, as indicated on Sanborn insurance maps of those years.

LIST

4316 BARONNE, bet. Napoleon, Gen. Pershing, bb. Carondelet [Faubourg West Bouligny]. In 1898 Long-imanus Soards, of Soards' *Directory* fame, assem-bled this property for development along with sev-eral other sites in the area. His residence was nearby at 1809 Napoleon (now demolished).

Soards probably built the present Queen Anne double shortly after his purchase. Its unusual mas-sing provides two front doors giving entry to the enclosed central bay. Soards' widow sold the prop-erty in 1919.

4420 BARONNE, bet. Napoleon, Jena, bb. Carondelet [Faubourg West Bouligny]. Paired gables, shingling, and asymmetrical massing contribute to a pictur-esque effect on this turn of the century Victorian town house. At the lower level, Ionic columns sup-port an upper gallery, suggesting the arrival of Co-lonial Revival tastes.

Charles Mazzoletti bought the thirty-foot lot in 1905 for $700 and mortgaged the property to Se-curity Building and Loan Association a year later for $5,000. This evidence suggests a building date of 1905. Mazzoletti owned the house for nine years, but never lived there.

BLANC PLACE

LIST

BLANC PLACE, bet. Valmont, Dufossat, bb. St. Charles, Atlanta. [Faubourg Avart]. Blanc Place is a quiet, one-block street that flows from Dufossat to Val-mont, bisecting an old double square between St. Charles and Atlanta. Its five conservative, eclectic-style homes reflect the ambience of their well-to-do builders. Most were built during the 1920s, after the Home for Destitute Orphan Boys, one-time occupant of the double square, closed. Developers sold the lots around 1920, with restrictions as to the "character, kind and cost of buildings to be erected." Those restrictions, although no longer legally binding, persist in fact today, since all of the original houses survive with the practical support of single-family zoning in a stable residential neighborhood.

Nos. 2, 4, 6, and 8 are one- and two-story homes set in well-cultivated gardens. No. 2, built for Robert Hayne Tarrant, and No. 6, built for Emile and Rosamonde Kuntz, are Mediterranean in style. Builder George Glover was the first owner of No. 8, a home with Georgian character. Splayed brick lintels and a brick entablature nicely cap the roofline of No. 9, built for Dr. Haidee Weeks Guthrie. Percy Kaufman built No. 4.

BORDEAUX

512 BORDEAUX, bet. Tchoupitoulas, Annunciation, bb. Lyons [Faubourg West Bouligny]. Although prevalent in New Orleans' older downtown neighborhoods, a stuccoed-brick Creole cottage is unusual in this area. The gable-sided structure has been re-roofed with galvanized metal, and has lost its central chimney and iron-supported overhang, but it is nevertheless a classic Creole cottage.

In 1864, Joseph Walshe sold the lot to Joseph Engelbrecht for $400. Gardner's 1868 *Directory* shows that a Joseph Engelbrecht, machinist at Lane Cotton Mills, and Joseph Engelbrecht, cabinet maker, both resided at that location. Perhaps they were father and son. Caroline Engelbrecht Appel sold the house to Philip Throunk in 1893. The cottage remained in the Throunk family until 1977.

LIST

1424 BORDEAUX, cor. Pitt, bb. Prytania, Lyons [Faubourg West Bouligny]. Here is a two-story, late Classic town house that seems to date from the era of Jefferson City. Joseph W. Davis, a grocer, purchased the land in 1867, probably built the house shortly thereafter, and was listed in Gardner's 1868 city *Directory* at "Pitt corner Bordeaux." In 1870 his listing was changed to "Bordeaux sw corner Pitt." The two-bay, double-galleried, narrow house with a two-story, river-side bay relates to the trend of 'façade architecture' common in nineteenth-century New Orleans neighborhoods.

1500 BORDEAUX, cor. Pitt, bb. Upperline, St. Charles [Faubourg West Bouligny]. This center hall, gable-sided American cottage originally stood at the corner of St. Charles and Bordeaux. It has undergone at least two decorative revisions since its construction during the 1850s. It is one of only a few documented antebellum houses in the Uptown area.

Jules Dolhonde acquired about half of the square in 1855 and built the house soon thereafter. Gardner's 1858 *Directory* locates him in Jefferson City. In 1866 Mrs. Burgess Bennett purchased the property and the Bennett family lived there until 1884. A

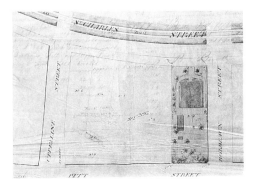

survey made for a Bennett family partition in 1887 indicates that the house had two dependencies, in addition to a cistern and a well.

The appearance of the house as seen in the old photograph probably dates from an updating completed after Mary Cahill Offner acquired the property in 1887. Note the polychromed painting, brackets, scrolls, panels, and dropped capitals. Mrs. Offner's tenure was brief, but the Edward Gauche

family lived in the house for almost forty years after her departure.

Pendleton Lehde bought the house in 1926, and soon afterwards had it moved to its present location. Following an interim owner, Clayton Nairne bought the house in 1959. The Nairne family resided there for nearly thirty years.

LIST

3311-13 CAMP, bet. Toledano, Louisiana, bb. Chestnut [Faubourg Plaisance]. Here is a two-story Eastlake style or "gingerbread" double, dating from after the turn of the twentieth century. James H. Maloney purchased four lots on this block in 1901 for $2,800. He probably built the three doubles 3301 to 3313 Camp as an investment before 1905. In 1909 he sold the package to F. Faessel for $4,000.

LIST

3314 CAMP, bet. Toledano, Louisiana, bb. Magazine [Faubourg Plaisance]. The original porch is missing on this typical hipped-roof shotgun, but the roofline, deep overhang, brackets, and other details are intact. It was perhaps built by carpenter-builder John Page, who purchased two lots on the block in 1878 and lived on Toledano in the same square. Page's succession sold the house to engineer Joseph Evans in 1887.

1629 BORDEAUX, bet. St. Charles, Carondelet, bb. Valence [Faubourg West Bouligny]. This unique house may be a great deal older than it first appears. It could be a mid-nineteenth century Gothic home with an enclosed front gallery added. Both title evidence and Sanborn insurance maps suggest that it was moved from 4717 St. Charles (at the corner of Valence) after 1901, when William Perry Brown bought the property to build the house now on that site.

An elaborate verge board attracts the eye to the side gable and rear bay. A cross gable with finial and pendant sits astride the main mass of the façade. Both Gothic and Mission details ornament the porch. The effect actually results from a successful melange of eclectic massing and detail.

In 1904 the Bordeaux Street property was sold to Oliver Dunn, who probably rebuilt it shortly after that.

CADIZ

1201 CADIZ, cor. Coliseum, bb. Jena, Perrier [Faubourg West Bouligny]. Individually listed in the National Register of Historic Places, this church was built in 1858 to serve a white congregation known as the Jefferson City Methodist Episcopal Church South. During the late 1860s, St. Peter African Methodist Episcopal Church was incorporated in Jefferson City. That congregation bought the building from the Methodists in 1877, and has owned it ever since.

The church structure was remodeled first in 1890, and later in 1924. It is an amalgam of elements that includes a shingled octagonal tower and geometrically patterned stained glass windows.

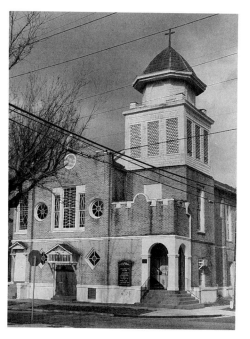

3427 CAMP, bet. Louisiana, Delachaise, bb. Chestnut [Faubourg Delachaise]. This extremely interesting and important Italianate cottage was owned by the family of its builder, Hugh Evans, for over a century. Evans, a designer-builder, purchased the Camp Street lot in 1863. Gardner's 1869 *Directory* lists him as "carpenter" residing on Camp near Delachaise. The property remained in his family's ownership until 1979.

The raised, three-bay cottage retains many of its original details. The most engaging features are the well-detailed porch and the ornamental chimney. The high gable roof permits an attic half-story, giving the cottage an imposing appearance for such a small structure.

In the side yard, an antique cistern, virtually intact, survives. Supported on a brick base with storage inside, this cistern is the only one we have observed in this area.

This part of Camp retains its brick sidewalks and open gutters.

3435 CAMP, cor. Delachaise, bb. Chestnut, Louisiana [Faubourg Delachaise]. This Italianate, center hall cottage was built in 1868 and has been well maintained through the years. Pilasters and a stilted segmental arch with keystone frame the recessed entrance. Full-length windows flank the doorway. The large central dormer has a double-hung window with a wide central mullion.

Adam Graner purchased four lots in this block in 1867. The following year, Gardner's city *Directory* located him on the corner of Delachaise and Camp. Graner, who variously described himself as "builder," "architect," "superintendent," and "carpenter," may have been the home's builder. He also owned the adjacent two-story house at 1221 Delachaise, using the Camp Street residence as rental property after 1870.

After Graner's time, the William Frank, Arthur Meyer, Abraham Burglass, Charles Janvier, Lily McCall Davis, and Daniel Johnson families owned the house.

3447 CAMP, cor. Delachaise, bb. Chestnut, Aline [Faubourg Delachaise]. Dating from the early 1860s,

this three-bay Italianate cottage has an unusual entablature that combines dentils, brackets, and modillions. As small as the front portion is, its shady gallery, garden setting, full-length windows, and recessed entrance lend the house elegance.

Jacob Born, an importer with Rice Brothers & Co., purchased the land from notary John French Coffey in 1861. He built the house, retaining the property until 1883. George Boning acquired it in 1885, and his family remained there until 1922. Elise Voss Vorhaben, William Darling, and Dr. Emile Naef were among subsequent owners.

3602 CAMP, cor. Foucher, bb. Antonine, Magazine [Faubourg Delachaise]. Here is a graceful Italianate shotgun in a shady garden setting. Decorative details include paneled columns, brackets, modillions, and a raised parapet.

Otto Thoman, a produce, wood, and coal dealer, bought this and three adjoining lots in 1876 from the estate of Ignatius Caulfield. Thoman had builder Hugh Evans construct the residence the following year.

3622 CAMP, bet. Foucher, Antonine, bb. Magazine [Faubourg Delachaise]. This house type, with a roof ridge parallel to the street, independently-roofed porch, and projecting side wing, was not generally found in nineteenth-century New Orleans. It is more typical of architecture in the South outside of New Orleans. The building nevertheless appears on Robinson's *Atlas* of the 1880s with generally the same form seen today. Records of notary Andrew Hero, Jr. demonstrate that Frederick Wing built a "one story frame house with outbuildings" on the

lot for Mrs. Annie G. Reynolds, wife of Allen A. Carman, in early 1876 for $1,500. Soards' 1878 and 1879 directories identify Allen A. Carman, "solicitor for the *Daily City Item*," on Camp between Foucher and Antonine. Wing himself must have liked his work, as he purchased the house in 1881.

3643 CAMP, bet. Antonine, Amelia, bb. Chestnut [Faubourg Delachaise]. Built as a fine residence for importer Henry Rice in 1866, this outstanding Italianate villa commands a strong presence in the neighborhood. The building is set far back from the street where it can be seen as a whole from each side. Its prominent gallery rests on six strong pillars and is bisected by a wide and steep staircase. Tall box columns support a heavy entablature beneath three large dormers.

In 1875 the City of New Orleans was able to purchase the house from the divorced wife of Henry Rice with funds bequeathed to the community by John David Fink (1786–1856). Fink had migrated to New Orleans in 1816 and acquired wealth in real estate. He left most of his estate to the City for the establishment of an asylum for Protestant widows and orphans. The City operated the Fink Home as an asylum for nearly one hundred years, adding two large rear wings as dormitories in 1891 at a cost of $15,000. By 1973, however, the institution could no longer comply with United States Health Department requirements and was closed.

Now in private ownership and completely restored with sensitivity and taste, the Rice home again enjoys family occupancy. It was marked by the Orleans Parish Landmarks Commission in 1962, and by the New Orleans Historic District Landmarks Commission in 1978. That year it was also listed in the National Register of Historic Places.

3937 CAMP, bet. Austerlitz, Constantinople, bb. Chestnut [Faubourg East Bouligny]. The picturesque massing of this raised cottage, its distinctive front and side gables, tall chimneys, high pyramidal roof, and an extraordinary balconied dormer, are all indicative of the Queen Anne style. Turned colonnettes connected by bracketed arches, decorative ridge tiles, and terra-cotta finials add interest to the structure.

Mutual Loan and Building Co. acquired the property in 1892 for $2,100, and probably built the structure. It appears on a Sanborn insurance map

of 1893. In 1896 it was sold to William Thomas Arney for $3,900. Soards' 1897 *Directory* locates Arney at this address.

In later years, Alfred Clyde Boswell, father of the famous Boswell Sisters, owned the house. He was there from 1918 to 1937 when the home passed to Martha Boswell. She retained it until 1949.

4029 CAMP (1001-03 Marengo), bet. Marengo, Constantinople, bb. Chestnut [Faubourg East Bouligny]. This gable-sided cottage was originally built as a double with the entrances on Marengo. The entrance is presently on Camp, but the most important aspect, nevertheless, continues to be Marengo Street. There, elaborate, lacy gallery details fashioned of pierced jigsaw work call attention to their erstwhile function as entrance decor.

Our interpretation of archival evidence relating to the history of this cottage, combined with an analysis of its architectural details, leads us to believe that it was moved to the present corner from an adjacent lot about 1893. The house may date from the late 1860s, as suggested by the modest size of its dentils and brackets; by the thick window mullions; and by the front drop siding, cast-

iron railing, and segmental openings. During the 1860s and 1870s, four twenty-nine foot lots occupied this quadrant of the square. Robinson's *Atlas* indicates that a double, probably gable-sided, cottage stood on the second and third of these lots. About 1893 the George W. and Joseph A. Moffett families arranged to subdivide the four smaller lots into three wider ones, and may have moved the double cottage to the corner at that time. They probably added the jigsaw gallery details then, and had the two 1890s-vintage cottages built next door.

George W. Moffett had acquired the property at a Sheriff's sale in 1869. Edwards' 1871 *Director* lists J.H. (probably Joseph A.) Moffett and A.W. Moffett as residing at Marengo between Camp and Chestnut.

3945 CAMP, bet. Austerlitz, Constantinople, bb. Chestnut [Faubourg East Bouligny]. This three-bay shotgun with an oversized dormer retains much authentic period detailing. The unusually tall spindle-swag frieze rests on jigsaw brackets springing from box columns with curious applied pilasters. The dormer is too large for the structure, but its three louvered openings and decorative details diminish the ponderous effect.

Dr. Gustave Walker mortgaged the property to the New Orleans German American Homestead and Building Association in 1897, after acquiring it in 1894. The house was built in the late 1890s, possibly for a member of Walker's family or as rental property. The doctor himself resided at 3420 Magazine.

4200 CAMP, cor. Milan, bb. Gen. Pershing, Magazine [Faubourg East Bouligny]. In September 1905 *Architectural Art and Its Allies* recorded construction of the New Orleans Evangelical Salem Church, now known as Salem's United Church of Christ. The architects of this brick Gothic structure were Diboll and Owen, the contractor and builder James A. Petty, and the price $16,000.

4842 CAMP, cor. Lyons, bb. Upperline, Magazine [Faubourg West Bouligny]. Small corner grocery stores are important reminders of the domestic culture of old New Orleans neighborhoods. This store-house has several traditional features: the commercial corner entrance into the store half of the structure, a side door leading to the living quarters, and a wraparound overhang providing respite from heat and rain.

Although Robinson's *Atlas* indicates there was a structure on this site during the 1870s, it was not until 1888 that the property quadrupled in value, suggesting construction of the present building. Soards' 1888 *Directory* lists Charles Curcia, grocer, at Lyons corner of Camp.

LIST

4930 CAMP, bet. Upperline, Robert, bb. Magazine [Faubourg Avart]. Here is a bayed shotgun with jigsaw trim in Eastlake style. Scalloping and an incised sunburst decorate the small projecting pediment over the entrance. Attractive stained glass panels fill the upper bay windows.

James Flynn, identified by Soards' 1889 *Directory* as being in the bagging and twine business, bought half of the square, still undeveloped, in 1881. In 1894 he sold the subject lot to Eveline S. Pritchard, widow of George S. Purves, who erected the present house. It remained in the Purves family for nearly fifty years.

4933 CAMP, bet. Upperline, Robert, bb. Chestnut [Faubourg Avart]. Here is a center hall, five-bay cottage with six paneled columns supporting the gallery roof. The large central dormer has paired windows with stilted segmental heads. The entrance is recessed, and half of the front door has a single pane of glass over a wood panel. Decorative pyramidal wooden ornaments accent the frieze of the dormer and gallery.

No early city directory listings have identified owners of the property at this location. Leonide Marie Castendyk, wife of August Freitag, purchased the property with her own funds in 1895. Soards' 1896 *Directory* shows that August Freitag, who had a "Homeopathic pharmacy and surgical instruments" business, resided at that address.

LIST

5007 CAMP, bet. Robert, Soniat, bb. Chestnut [Faubourg Avart]. This two-story, frame, Queen Anne dwelling has an independently-roofed wraparound porch with spindle railings, heavy turned colonnettes, and spandrel brackets. A small roof balcony

with turned railing and post punctuates the porch roofline above the entrance.

In a notarial act of July 13, 1892, Marcel Ducros, N.P., records that the "President of Eureka Homestead declares that the corporation has contracted or will contract with a responsible builder to erect a two story frame house and dependencies at a cost of not less than $3,550 with a view of ultimate transfer to William Rollins for $5,500." Rollins owned the property from 1892 to 1894, when it was transferred to Susan M. McCabe, wife of John K. Turley. Susan Turley's heirs inherited the property in 1928 and retained it until 1960.

5300-02 CAMP, cor. Valmont, bb. Leontine, Magazine [Rickerville]. John Joseph Hecker built a pair of identical, two-story Eastlake doubles on this square after purchasing the property in 1895. One is 5300-02 Camp and the other, on the diagonally opposite corner, is 5333-35 Magazine.

Slender colonnettes support spandrels surmounted by pierced friezes on both levels. Unusual second floor side galleries are virtually intact on each structure. Of Hecker's two investments, this double was probably rental property, as Soards' 1897 *Directory* lists his residence at 5333 Magazine.

5301 CAMP, cor. Valmont, bb. Chestnut, Leontine [Rickerville]. This late-nineteenth-century Queen Anne dwelling is individually listed in the National Register of Historic Places. The picturesque façade employs an irregular plan and mass accompanied by a variety of structural expressions and ornamentation including a multi-gabled roof, cutaway corners, an assortment of decorative brackets, a well-detailed wraparound porch, and a variety of window shapes.

Mrs. Annie E. Wilmuth, wife of Dr. Edmund P. Lowe, bought the property August 6, 1896, for $940. The *Daily Picayune* of September 1, 1897, re-

ports that Mrs. Annie Lowe obtained a building permit for a $3,000 two-story frame house in this square. Soards' *Directory* lists Dr. Edmund P. Lowe, a physician, as having his office and residence at 5301 Camp Street in 1898.

LIST

5315 CAMP, bet. Valmont, Leontine, bb. Chestnut [Rickerville]. Exuberant detailing, including fluted colonnettes on squared bases, fantastic jigsaw brackets painted to accentuate cutouts, a spindle frieze, and scalloped trim, adorns this three-bay shotgun. Dentils just below the scalloped trim and a Queen Anne gable window with console decorative motifs add interest and individuality.

In 1896 Gustave A. Roessle sold this property to the widow Anna Oser Stockton. The following year, Soards' *Directory* listed her at this address. It was probably she who built the residence, as it does not appear on Sanborn's *Insurance Maps* of 1896, the year of the purchase.

5349 CAMP, bet. Leontine, Jefferson, bb. Chestnut [Rickerville]. Complete with a high gable, diminutive turret, decorative ridge tiles, polychromatic slates, and a monumental chimney, this cottage is a modest version of the once-fashionable Queen Anne house. The present gable window, however, is not in keeping with the style of the whole.

Pasquale Palmissanno paid $1,450 for the unimproved property in 1897. Two years later, Soards' *Directory* lists his residence at 5349 Camp for the first time. The Palmissanno family retained ownership of the property until 1941.

A recent real estate transfer records a selling price of $255,000 for the property.

CARONDELET (Apollo)

LIST

3303 CARONDELET, cor. Toledano, bb. Louisiana, Baronne [Faubourg Plaisance]. A bold partial gallery with five fluted "Tower-of-the-Winds" columns and cast-iron railing dominates this Queen Anne dwelling. The downtown corner of the house has a spacious, three-story hexagonal tower culminating in a tent roof with a terra-cotta finial and ridge tiles. A large projecting attic gable is curiously balanced atop the second story bay. Dentils on the gallery frieze and modillions beneath the second floor soffit add scale to an otherwise clumsy structure.

Charles Shepard started to assemble this site in 1893. Three years later a Sanborn insurance map indicates this structure as "Being Built."

3314 CARONDELET, bet. Toledano, Louisiana, bb. St. Charles [Faubourg Plaisance]. Despite severe alterations, this wide, raised cottage with its graceful front gallery has retained some original classical elements. The iron fence and gate appear to be intact.

In June of 1867, Simon Newburger, who had owned the property for a little over a month, sold it to Mrs. Mary Georgie Keller, the wife of Gideon Folger, who probably built the house a short time later. Gardner's 1868 *Directory* lists G.L. Folger as residing on Carondelet near Toledano. He was a clerk at Folger & Co., "Dealers in Hardware, Cutlery and Iron etc." The Folger family occupied the home for nearly forty years until 1907.

DEMOLISHED

3418 CARONDELET, bet. Louisiana, Delachaise, bb. St. Charles [Faubourg Delachaise]. The distinctive two-story, double-galleried, late Italianate residence which once stood here was significant for its unusual dormer and side galleries. Unique tapered columns on pillars supported a heavy second level entablature with dentils and applied jigsaw motifs. First level squared, paneled columns, also on pil-

lars, combined with scroll-like brackets and jigsaw embellishment. Segmental second level bays had jigsaw motifs with pierced scalloped cornices. The recessed entrance was framed by pilasters which duplicated the columns on that level.

Richard and Mary Newman Herrick sold the property to George W. Sentell in 1887. The *Daily Picayune* of September 1, 1890, states that J.B. Chisolm built the house for Sentell that year.

The loss of this unique Italianate structure is irreparable. Both interior and exterior architectural details were of fine quality. In 1984 a neighboring drugstore chain unnecessarily destroyed the building to augment a large, unsightly parking lot and make room for a fast food outlet.

3419-21 CARONDELET, bet. Louisiana, Delachaise, bb. Baronne [Faubourg Delachaise]. A distinctive attic vent topped by an unusual finial distinguishes this typical late nineteenth-century shotgun double. Large jigsaw brackets support a heavy overhang with diminutive jigsaw decoration. Cornices with a modified sunburst pattern surmount the four openings and incorporate a dentil motif and bull's-eyes. The structure is quoined, and the framing around the openings is typical millwork of the last quarter of the nineteenth century. Scal-

loped sheet metal awnings protect the side windows. The small camelback appears to be a later addition.

Jean Rotge bought the property in 1877, but it is not until 1885 that Soards' *Directory* lists John Rotge, milkman, as residing on Carondelet between Louisiana Avenue and Delachaise. The structure is delineated on Robinson's *Atlas* (ca. 1875), but the owner is not recorded there.

LIST

3527 CARONDELET, bet. Delachaise, Foucher, bb. Baronne [Faubourg Delachaise]. This simple, three-bay cottage has four chamfered colonnettes, modest spandrel brackets, a metal roof ventilator, wood balusters, drop siding, and quoins.

Joseph Sitt completed his acquisition of the property in 1882 and lost no time building this cottage. He is listed in Soards' *Directory* of 1883 as a painter residing on Carondelet between Delachaise and Foucher. Sitt owned the property until 1913, when his heirs sold it at auction to Frank J. Matthew.

3611 CARONDELET, bet. Foucher, Amelia, bb. Baronne [Faubourg Delachaise]. Changes have been made in this early center hall, gable-sided cottage. The gallery, cornices, balustrade, overhang, brackets, and especially the false parapet have all been added. Today, the wraparound gallery is a distinctive feature.

William Judson, business manager of the *New Orleans Times*, bought the property in 1877, and is listed in Soards' 1878 *Directory* as residing at 813 Carondelet. No. 813 became No. 3611 when the house numbers were changed in 1895.

3627 CARONDELET, cor. Amelia, bb. Baronne, Foucher [Faubourg Delachaise]. Individually listed in the National Register of Historic Places and given the highest rating by the New Orleans Historic District Landmarks Commission, this exuberant structure was designed by architect Edward Gottheil. The *Daily Picayune* of September 1, 1868, describes the dwelling as a "Beautiful Swiss Villa" and further states: "The plan, we understand, was brought from Europe by Mr. Gottheil, our Commissioner to the Paris Exposition, who is giving his personal supervision to its construction."

The home was built for Cuthbert Bullitt, and originally faced St. Charles Avenue in the square

3805 CARONDELET, cor. Peniston, bb. Gen. Taylor, Baronne [Faubourg St. Joseph]. Deep jigsaw brackets support the hipped roof overhang of this five-bay, center hall, Italianate cottage. Four-over-six-light windows allow easy access to the gallery. Drop siding and quoins enhance the façade, although the sides are covered with a simple weatherboarding.

The house probably dates from 1886 when Samuel Carlisle paid the Eureka Homestead Society $5,000 for the property, a significant increase over the $825 that Eureka had paid for the land that same year. Soards' 1887 *Directory* indicates that Carlisle, a lawyer, resided at that location.

bounded by Carondelet, Peniston, and Gen. Taylor. In 1883 Simon Hernsheim moved the house to its present location to make way for his new mansion, now known as the Columns Hotel.

As John P. Coleman romanticized in the *New Orleans States* of May 11, 1924: "When built, it was an isolated mansion, standing alone in the midst of immense unoccupied and unimproved spaces. The Cuthbert Bullitt mansion was at that time the last house in [what later became] the 12th Ward, and there was nothing back of it in the shape of a habitable structure. The sidewalks in all that section were of wood, some of gunwales from the wrecks of old flatboats that brought produce down from Ohio. . . . Originally the building and grounds occupied the whole of the block."

Distinctive diamond-patterned lights frame the entrance. Pairs of four-light, double-hung windows with pediments flank the door. Above is a balcony with a double door and stepped sidelights under a peaked pediment similar to those on the front windows. Note the tiny decorative windows on either side. Huge brackets support the massive overhang. All railings feature distinctive flat, cutout balusters.

The Swiss Villa style became popular in America as part of the romantic "picturesque" movement of the mid-nineteenth century. Its most overarching feature consists of the wide projecting gable ornamented with a jigsaw verge board. In this example, that pattern is repeated over the windows.

3809-11 CARONDELET, bet. Peniston, Gen. Taylor, bb. Baronne [Faubourg St. Joseph]. The configuration of this structure on Robinson's *Atlas* indicates that it was built as a double. It has retained that identity. The shotgun camelback has distinctive recessed galleries on each side, beyond the entrance hall. Three large chimneys along the center roof ridge serve both units. Six simple, square columns support an entablature with pairs of brackets and modillions. Without close inspection, it is not easy to see the camelback portion far to the rear of the structure.

George Clammann bought the property in 1868 and probably built the double soon after that. It was likely rental property, as city directories do not list Clammann as having lived there. The Clammann family owned the double until 1882, when they sold it to John L. Sterry. The Sterry family retained the house until 1902.

LIST

3713 CARONDELET, bet. Amelia, Peniston, bb. Baronne [Faubourg St. Joseph]. Here is a five-bay, frame, raised cottage with certain gallery alterations and a deep rear wing. Archival research suggests the house was built in 1885 for Louis Durel; however, Soards' *Directory* does not list him here until 1888 (old No. 823 Carondelet).

One of the notable owners from 1890 to 1911 was Meloncy Soniat du Fossat, a lawyer and amateur historian who made an early effort to record and clarify the land use history of this area.

3723 CARONDELET, cor. Peniston, bb. Amelia, Baronne [Faubourg St. Joseph]. This five-bay, Italianate, center hall cottage was built at a cost of $5,000 in 1877 for Robert Walker Rayne. Rayne sold it before it was finished to Robert L. Moore. The builder was Frederick Wing, who was most active in the Garden District after the Civil War.

The dormer is probably not original to the dwelling, but other features are intact. These include the shuttered, pilastered entrance crowned by a high entablature, and notable etched glass in the transom and door. The cast-iron gallery railing and fence also appear to be original.

After eight interim owners, Walter J. Amoss bought the cottage in 1962. The Walter J. Amoss, Jr. family resides there at this writing.

3912-14 CARONDELET, bet. Gen. Taylor, Constantinople, bb. St. Charles [Faubourg East Bouligny]. This large two-story double is generally well preserved, but it suffers from the loss of its lower gallery decking. It retains slender colonnettes, curious C-scroll brackets, and a frieze of pierced jigsaw work, all fashionable details of the 1890s in the United States. The cross gable and pediment serve to accentuate the entrance bay.

In 1870 Henry Carleton Miller bought one-half of this square, which fronted on St. Charles as well as Carondelet. His St. Charles residence has been demolished, but his family preserved this house as rental property for fifty years. According to the *Daily Picayune*, it was built in 1895 for $7,500.

4105 CARONDELET, cor. Marengo, bb. Milan, Baronne [Faubourg East Bouligny]. Here is a large, frame, Queen Anne house with strong vertical emphasis. The asymmetrical massing plays against a shed-roof gallery.

Frederick W. Ober bought the property and adjoining lots in 1868. Soards' *Directory* lists him as living on Carondelet between Marengo and Milan in 1875. In 1891 he sold the property to George W. Wilson, a relative, who probably built the present house in 1902. The Ober-Wilson family owned this property for 100 years, from 1868 to 1968.

4319 CARONDELET, bet. Gen. Pershing, Napoleon, bb. Baronne [Faubourg East Bouligny]. Originally built as a branch of the United States Post Office, this Art Deco building was designed by architect Albert Theard during the 1930s. It is now the headquarters of the Junior League of New Orleans, Inc.

The highly stylized classical building seems slightly pretentious in an old-fashioned residential neighborhood. It is set on the banquette line in the middle of a block where other site lines are generally set back. It is also too large for its lot, begging for landscaping that could never fit. Its Art Deco features nevertheless make the building interesting and worthy preserving as a statement of its time.

The monumental bas-relief in the frieze was inspired by the Mayan studies of Tulane University's Middle American Research Institute. The American eagle is a symbol chosen for the United States government.

4003 CARONDELET, cor. Constantinople, bb. Marengo, Baronne [Faubourg East Bouligny]. Surrounded by huge oaks, this one-story frame cottage is in a most agreeable setting. Delicate colonnettes with jigsaw brackets support the independent gallery roof. The six-sided bay with its conical roof balances the massing of the paired gables. The five-light elliptical opening in the forward gable and the oval light in the rear gable have Colonial Revival overtones. Both gallery and gables were added to a simpler core.

A bronze plaque on the fence indicates that the Reverend and Mrs. Linus Parker built a dwelling here in 1877. Bishop Parker was an eloquent preacher, editor and beloved bishop of the Methodist Episcopal Church South. He died here on March 5, 1885. A later owner, William Henry Adams, had the front rebuilt in a picturesque style between 1893 and 1896. During the next fifty years there was a succession of five owners. The Alva J. Groth family has owned the cottage since 1946.

4432, 4438 (illustrated) CARONDELET, cor. Jena, bb. Napoleon, St. Charles [Faubourg West Bouligny]. Architect Thomas Sully built these two houses about 1905. He had purchased the land from Mrs. Edgar Bright that year, and retained ownership until 1917, without ever living in either house. He also built an identical residence on Carrollton Avenue near Willow (Poplar) at the same time. The early photograph of 4438, dates from a 1929 real estate advertisement when it was bought by Robert Motte. The home today belongs to Patricia Motte Segleau.

4432 Carondelet has been drastically altered, but 4438 is quite intact and still has its original color, slate roof, Craftsman-style porch, and Tudor Revival-style second story projection. These modest frame houses are typical of Sully's early twentieth century work.

4917 CARONDELET, bet. Upperline, Robert, bb. Baronne [Faubourg Avart]. This five-bay, gable-sided, center hall cottage is in simple Classical style. Six box columns support the gallery roof. Four six-over-nine, double-hung, slip-head windows flank an entrance door with "Greek keyhole" framing. From the side it appears that a dependency or addition was attached to the rear of the structure after its construction.

William Riggs, Jr. bought the property in 1885 for $400, and sold it two years later to Clarence, Ethan, and Whittaker Riggs for the same amount. The Riggses built the house shortly thereafter, as Soards' 1888 *Directory* shows the family living there. The Riggs were in the business of making cisterns.

CHESTNUT

3427 CHESTNUT, bet. Louisiana, Delachaise, bb. Coliseum [Faubourg Delachaise]. Louvered shutters partially enclose the gallery of this gable-sided, one-and-one-half story, center hall, American cottage with an unsympathetic twentieth century dormer. This method of enclosure is aesthetically successful, since it does not obscure architectural lines, and the materials are appropriate.

Cottages have occupied the 3400 block of Chestnut since soon after the Delachaise heirs sold the square in 1859. The present house was probably built in 1859 for Adam Gaiser, a partner in Robeson, Witherell & Co., dealers in hides. It was the Gaiser home for ten years. Following the Gaisers, the Baptiste Hector, Henry R. Requier, and Eugene Doherty families each owned the house for periods varying from five to thirty-five years. Later, the Reverend Louis Voss and his family lived there for fifty-three years.

3518-22 CHESTNUT, bet. Foucher, Aline, bb. Camp [Faubourg Delachaise]. A prominent roof overhang protects the exterior and adds interest to the profile of this two-story, galleried, frame double. The overhang functions as a returning cornice. Below it, heart and diamond cutouts, apparently ventilators, attract the eye. Trim box columns support the gallery on both levels.

Elisha Robinson's *Atlas of the City of New Orleans* (ca. 1875) clearly outlines the structure, listing Patrick Donnelly as the owner. Donnelly had bought the property at auction in July 1866. In 1875 he sold it to Miss Kate Bergin, but finally re-acquired it in 1886. He probably had the double built during the 1870s, but not until 1887 did Soards' *Directory* list his residence at 358 Chestnut, corresponding to the uptown half of the duplex.

3528 CHESTNUT, cor. Foucher, bb. Aline, Camp [Faubourg Delachaise]. This charming 1890s center hall, galleried, Victorian cottage has an overstated, but nevertheless pleasing, roofline. A large dormer seems to emerge from the gable and gallery apron, competing for prominence with the busy frieze and gallery rail. Open fretwork, chamfering, segmentation, drop siding, and a railing on the dormer combine to reduce the effect of mass on the façade. These solids and voids achieve visual success in the face of a dormer that might have overpowered the building.

In the rear is an open gallery with a railing identical to that on the front. A large side gable is decorated with shingles. Finials, decorative ridge tiles, a double iron gate, and a rear dependency add interest to the house.

Mrs. Julia Horstmann, widow of Francis Rickert, bought the property in 1890 for $2,950. The *Daily Picayune* of September 1, 1891, reports that a city building permit was issued to Mrs. Julia Horstmann, widow of F. Rickert, for a $4,500 cottage to be built by Otto Manake. By 1893 Soards' *Directory* indicates that the Rickert family lived at 360 Chestnut, the early address for this residence.

3531 CHESTNUT, cor. Foucher, bb. Aline, Coliseum [Faubourg Delachaise]. Designated a local historic landmark, this raised, center hall, villa-style cottage in old Faubourg Delachaise is a fine example of masonry Greek Revival architecture, unusual for the more uptown sections of Jefferson City, but less so for the faubourgs near the Garden District. All of its details are classically simple and placed symmetrically—the important plastered chimneys, dentil row, box columns, side-lights, and over-lights accenting the entrance. On the roof is an unusual decorative lightning rod. The hexagonal bay on the Aline Street side was an addition of 1883, according to documents in the papers of builder Hugh Evans.

Henry J. Seward, a New Orleans commission merchant, bought the property from Delachaise assigns in 1862. Gardner's 1866 *Directory*, the first published after 1861, lists Seward's residence in Jefferson City. The following year, Graham and Madden's *Crescent City Directory* located Seward more specifically on Chestnut, corner Foucher. Since there was little local building during the Civil War, it may be assumed that the house dates from 1866.

In 1874 Seward sold the property to Frederick J. Odendahl whose family retained it, sometimes with difficulty, for sixty-two years. The Samuel W. Ryniker family has owned the cottage since 1936.

LIST

3818-22 CHESTNUT, bet. Peniston, Gen. Taylor, bb. Camp [Faubourg St. Joseph]. The wheelwright's shop of John M. Freudenstein and family was located on this site in old Faubourg St. Joseph. They purchased the property in 1866 and retained it until the turn of the century. There was probably an earlier cottage on the site, facing Chestnut, with the shop in the rear and opening to Gen. Taylor Street.

The present double, frame, camelback is built in the style of the 1890s. Perhaps the Louis K. Frank family, who purchased the house in 1899 and retained in until 1948, enlarged it at one time.

3938 CHESTNUT, bet. Constantinople, Austerlitz, bb. Camp [Faubourg East Bouligny]. This Queen Anne cottage features a wraparound gallery and a wide-spreading shingled gable with Palladian style window and miniature balcony. It was built in 1896 for Mr. and Mrs. Walter L. McConnico. The following year the McConnicos sold it to Amelia Graham. Subsequent owners included Thomas W. Fitzwilliam and Frank Pumilia.

3939-41 CHESTNUT, bet. Constantinople, Austerlitz, bb. Coliseum [Faubourg East Bouligny]. Built about 1875, this gable-sided, double cottage may have been remodeled during the 1880s. The gallery is in a highly decorative Neo-Grec style not commonly found on gable-sided cottages.

Mrs. Maria Doriocourt, a teacher at St. Henry's School, purchased the land in 1873 and sold it to John Thuer in 1884. The Thuer family owned the cottage for nearly a century.

4020-22 CHESTNUT, bet. Constantinople, Marengo, bb. Camp [Faubourg East Bouligny]. The Jacob Heitman family has owned this classic, galleried, double Creole cottage for over 120 years. Edwards' 1873 *Annual Director* lists Heitman, a painter, on Chestnut in this square. Family tradition indicates that Heitman built the original rear portion in 1866, and the family added the front cottage later.

This house type is found in early nineteenth-century New Orleans neighborhoods throughout the city.

4216, 4224, 4230 CHESTNUT, bet. Gen. Pershing, Milan, bb. Camp [Faubourg East Bouligny]. Here are three Queen Anne cottages built in the 1890s. Two early local building and loan companies—the Eureka and Mutual—financed two of them. All three cottages have rooflines important to their designs, shaped by repeating triangular forms. Fish-scale and saw-toothed shingling were fashionable details when the cottages were built.

Mrs. Benjamin J. Simms and later Dr. Felix Gaudin were early owners of 4216. 4224 was initially the home of Mr. and Mrs. Thomas Henry Dwyer, a railroad depot master. 4230 was the George F. Cranmer residence.

4849 CHESTNUT, bb. Upperline, Lyons, Coliseum [Faubourg West Bouligny]. Originally built in 1894 as McDonogh Memorial School (later designated McDonogh No. 6), this sprawling three-story brick structure was designed by the firm of Duval-Favrot. The *Daily Picayune* of September 1, 1894, reported the construction of "a brick schoolhouse in the square bounded by Chestnut, Upperline, Lyon[s] and Coliseum. The City of New Orleans, owner. T. Carey builder $16,000." E.A. Christy, city architect, designed an addition in 1925.

Brick pilasters running the full height add vertical emphasis to the older section. On the Chestnut Street façade, they terminate in chimney tops that are integral to an impressive parapet. The building continues the tradition of ornamental and ambitious New Orleans brick schoolhouses built with McDonogh Fund monies and executed most ambitiously in the work of William A. Freret. The enclosed raised basement is an important feature of the interior and of the design. Visually, it gives the

5129 CHESTNUT, cor. Dufossat, bb. Soniat, Coliseum [Faubourg Avart]. Here is a gable-sided, center hall, American cottage with Italianate details. Applied moldings form panels on the box columns, and an openwork frieze attracts the eye. A low parapet, pairs of brackets, and well-spaced modillions on the entablature are common design elements of the Italianate style in New Orleans. A three-sided addition on the downtown side forms a quasi *porte cochere* with a very high gabled roof.

Mrs. Barbara Engert Letten purchased the land with four other lots at a sheriff's sale in 1878. Archival research indicates that during the 1880s a cottage of medium value may have been erected on the site. The property value plummeted during the early 1890s, until architect William R. Sims acquired the property in 1897. Perhaps Sims remodeled an earlier cottage, adding the frieze and other decorative elements.

schoolhouse a sense of importance. Inside, it encloses recreational space for rainy days.

Now individually listed in the National Register of Historic Places, the former school has been converted to residential use.

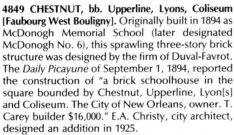

5347 CHESTNUT, cor. Leontine, bb. Jefferson, Coliseum [Rickerville]. In 1895 Mrs. Mary G. Decker had this two-story Queen Anne house constructed at a cost of $3,500, according to New Orleans city building permit records. Frederick S. Decker, her husband, was the chief clerk of the Southern Pacific Railroad's passenger department, according to Soards' 1896 *Directory*.

at 5426 Chestnut. A Sanborn insurance map of 1896 delineates a double numbered 5424 and 5426 Chestnut on the property. The double was probably demolished and the present structure built in 1907 when Pfaff obtained a $5,000 mortgage from Union Homestead.

5526 CHESTNUT, bet. Octavia, Joseph, bb. Camp [Rickerville]. This two-story, frame, Queen Anne house with a full-width, single-level gallery is known as Captain Cooley's house. It was built for LeVerrier Cooley in 1896. Captain Cooley was a famous steamboat man whose career spanned more than sixty-two years. The Orleans Parish Landmarks Commission has recognized the house.

5357 CHESTNUT, bet. Jefferson, Leontine, bb. Coliseum [Rickerville]. Distinctive spindle brackets and a frieze embellish this attractive early twentieth-century side hall residence. Deep brackets beneath the overhang draw the eye up to the gable and its Queen Anne window.

Mrs. Elizabeth Roberts Mullen bought the property for $500 in 1903. Soards' 1904 *Directory* lists her as residing at that address, but she sold the property the same year for $5,000.

3311, 3317, 3325 COLISEUM, bet. Toledano, Louisiana, bb. Prytania [Faubourg Plaisance]. These three Italianate cottages have been altered, but there are similarities that indicate they were all built around the same time. Robinson's *Atlas* delineates their shapes without indicating ownership. Thomas Pickles purchased the three lots in 1868 from Thomas Booth. Two years later he contracted to build, for Jefferson Davis van Benthuysen, a one-story frame cottage on Coliseum Street between Toledano and Louisiana. This is now 3317 Coliseum.

3311 was for many years the property of Algernon Badger, who purchased it in 1879 from George Baldy. Prominent public health activist Dr. Joseph Holt later owned it, toward the end of his life.

3325 Coliseum was the home of the John E. King family during the 1880s.

5432 CHESTNUT, cor. Octavia, bb. Jefferson, Camp [Rickerville]. Rambling and spacious, this early twentieth-century raised cottage shows the Craftsman Style influence on the Colonial Revival. A comfortable gallery moves horizontally across two-thirds of the façade, then wraps around the downtown side. The house has the appearance of a raised bungalow, but is substantially larger.

Will Pfaff, who bought the property in 1897 for $600, is listed in Soards' 1898 *Directory* as residing

COLISEUM (PLAQUEMINE)

3303 COLISEUM, cor. Toledano, bb. Louisiana, Prytania [Faubourg Plaisance]. James Freret was the architect for this two-and-one-half-story, late Greek Revival town house—surely one of Jefferson City's finest examples of its type. Four applique box columns support the galleries and a heavy entablature with appropriate brackets and dentils. A rosette-studded doorway framed by an elevated arch attracts the eye. This and the two pentagonal bays are the home's most distinguishing features.

The structure was built in 1869 for Thomas Pickles, of Pickles and Albert Druggists, for $5,000. Edwards' 1870 *Annual Director* locates Pickles at the Coliseum corner of Toledano, but he remained at that address for only one year. In 1871 Pickles sold the property to lawyer Edward Palfrey, and several prominent owners followed in succession. The Davis Lee Jahncke, Jr. family has owned the house since 1980.

3704 COLISEUM, cor. Amelia, bb. Peniston, Chestnut [Faubourg St. Joseph]. Blueprints for this one-and-one-half-story, frame cottage with balconied dormer have been found in the papers of Hugh Evans, nineteenth-century New Orleans builder. The oversized dormer with its amalgam of jigsaw elements dominating the façade is original, but plans show that the gallery railing was originally identical to that of the balcony. The house also lacks its original curved brackets which once sprang from the colonnettes. There is evidence that the back portion of the house was a later addition.

Evans built the cottage for R.J. Whann in the late 1880s. Soards' 1890 *Directory* lists Whann as residing on Coliseum, between Amelia and Peniston.

3715 COLISEUM, bet. Amelia, Peniston, bb. Perrier [Faubourg St. Joseph]. An oversized balconied dormer punctuates the façade of this cottage. There are two structures of the type in this square, and another at 3528 Chestnut. The house has a camelback supporting a visually prominent plastered chimney. The rear portion and a side bay provide needed space to an essentially one-room-wide cottage in an aesthetically successful manner.

Built for John H.H. Taylor after 1887, the house has lost some of its original ornamentation. It probably once more closely resembled 3704 Coliseum than it does presently.

4304 COLISEUM and 4312 COLISEUM, bet. Gen. Pershing, Napoleon, bb. Chestnut [Faubourg West Bouligny]. These two homes occupy five lots that were once the site of 4312 Coliseum (at bottom)

alone. That house, a center hall American cottage with attractive, but not original, French doors and columns, was built during the late 1850s for Charles Lagroue. Lagroue purchased the five-lot site from the City of New Orleans in 1858. Gardner's 1860 *Directory* locates him on Plaquemine (Coliseum) near Berlin (Gen. Pershing) in Jefferson City. When built, the house was closer to Gen. Pershing than it is today, as Robinson's *Atlas* of 1883 illustrates. Today front and rear galleries, a separate kitchen, and a rear stable survive intact.

In 1872, after several interim owners, James H. Hoyle sold the house, minus its yard, to Sylvester Parmelee. The Parmelee family retained the house until 1899. Meanwhile, the Hoyle family in 1879 sold the yard to former British Consul George Salkeld in 1884. Salkeld's daughter, Fannie Salkeld Freret, sold the land in 1889 to Widow Elizabeth Bird Moore, who probably had the corner house (4304 Coliseum, at top) built by 1890. Soards' 1890 *Directory* locates Edward A. Bird, a student and perhaps Widow Moore's brother, at Coliseum and Berlin. Tax assessments on the site increased from $1,000 to $4,000 that year.

One outstanding variant of the house style is the wide, flat-arch bay over the doorway. The home preserves its upper gallery pedestals, but it is unlikely that their iron railing, although attractive, is original. At that date, one would expect a wooden balustrade.

4311 COLISEUM, bet. Gen. Pershing, Napoleon, bb. Perrier [Faubourg West Bouligny]. 4311 Coliseum exhibits all the characteristic details of a galleried, post-Civil War cottage—and does so with some refinement. Reflecting the style of the 1880s in New Orleans are its well-molded capitals and multi-bracketed cornice, but both title and *Directory* research suggest that the house was built earlier than 1880 for Jules Auguste Honore Lagroue, probably in 1869.

When first built, the home faced Gen. Pershing (Berlin) on a three-lot site, slightly removed from the corner of Berlin and Coliseum. Robinson's *Atlas*, compiled during the 1870s, identifies it there. The house remained on Berlin during the ownerships of Lagroue and, following him, Elias R. May, Delia McCaleb Colwell, Josephine Jacob St. Pasteur, and Michael Glaser.

In 1914 Glaser sold the property to the Robert P. Hyams Coal Company, which at the beginning of World War I moved the house off Berlin to Coliseum, on the rear of the lots it formerly occupied. The company then sold off the Gen. Pershing portion of the lots. In 1922 it transferred ownership of the house, now on Coliseum Street, to Nellie Hyams Cooper. The Hyams family retained control until 1936. Among subsequent owners have been Lucinda W. Garaudy, Wiltz LeBoeuf, and the family of Nadia de la Houssaye St. Paul.

4422 COLISEUM, bet. Napoleon, Jena, bb. Chestnut [Faubourg West Bouligny]. Designated as a local historic landmark, this striking cottage has had a succession of prominent owners. It was evidently built for Theodule Martin in 1869. Maurice Glaudin, tax collector of Jefferson Parish, acquired it through a sheriff's sale in 1874—probably much to Martin's frustration.

The three-bay frame cottage has an unusually large central dormer, possibly added. Its recessed doorway has a segmental transom and pilasters supporting a heavy entablature. Storm doors fold back into a reveal.

The Louis Fruchter family restored the cottage after acquiring it in 1949. Mr. and Mrs. Peter Howard have been the owners since 1981.

5429 COLISEUM, bet. Jefferson, Octavia, bb. Perrier [Rickerville]. The comfort and grace of a raised house, with deep, covered gallery continuing through a curved bay and returning down the side which it shelters, evokes an era of long evening hours spent out of doors. Built after the turn of the century, this home combines a wide expanse of turned spindling and balusters with gables and a conical roof to maintain a plastic dynamism on its façade.

John W. Huggett, who purchased two lots from Omer Villere in 1904, was evidently the first owner. He retained the house until 1923, when he sold it to Thomas F. Hall. The Hall family remained there forty-five years.

CONSTANCE (Live Oak)

3312-14 CONSTANCE, bet. Louisiana, Toledano, bb. Laurel [Faubourg Plaisance]. Here is a rural Creole cottage with a double-pitch, gable-sided roof incorporating the gallery. This type of house may be found throughout the early quarters of New Orleans. It continued to be built through the 1860s. The floor plan consists of four square rooms, about fifteen by fifteen feet, without a hall. In the rear are two smaller rooms called *cabinets*, which flank a recessed porch called a *cabinet* gallery. Back-to-back fireplaces serving the front rooms share a common chimney, which pierces the roof

in the center. Another serves the rear. Contrast this outline with that of the adjacent shotgun, one room wide, with succeeding chimneys lined up in a row.

Although Robinson's *Atlas* does not show this structure, notarial research reveals that it may have been built before the Civil War. Peter Wahl sold this lot, with buildings and improvements, to Michael Wahl in 1862 for $350. The property appears in the succession of Michael Wahl in 1917.

LIST

3318 CONSTANCE, bet. Louisiana, Toledano, bb. Laurel [Faubourg Plaisance]. Now a single-family dwelling, this structure was originally a four-bay, double shotgun in the Greek Revival style. Surrounding both the present entrance door and the former entrance door are "Greek keyhole" designs. Note the decorative scalloped verge board on the overhang.

On June 21, 1869, Peter Wahl bought the property at an auction of the succession of John Fresch. By 1870 Edwards' *Annual Director* indicates that Peter Wahl resided on Constance, near Louisiana. Edwards' publication of the following year reveals that Wahl was a dairyman located on Constance, between Toledano and Louisiana.

LIST

3418 CONSTANCE, bet. Louisiana, Delachaise, bb. Laurel [Faubourg Delachaise]. Note the distinctive recessed side gallery of this ca. 1870 shotgun with heavy Italianate entablature. Gallery supports have been remodeled in California bungalow style. This shotgun was probably built by Mrs. Sarah Mosely Rea prior to 1874.

LIST

3422-24 CONSTANCE, bet. Louisiana, Delachaise, bb. Laurel [Faubourg Delachaise]. Once a single-family dwelling, this late 1890s Eastlake style residence has a well-detailed porch and gable. It was built for Henry Dannenfelser between 1896 and 1909. Dannenfelser had purchased the land from Mrs. Sarah Mosely Rea in 1874. His family owned it for over thirty-five years.

3455, 3461 CONSTANCE, bet. Delachaise, Aline, bb. Magazine [Faubourg Delachaise]. These two, originally identical, Italianate camelbacks have engaging arched gallery bays formed by spandrels between box columns. Above each column is a pair of brackets with dentils between them. Parapets top each entablature. Segmental-head, double-hung windows, six-over-nine, have simple cornices, as do the segmental recessed entrances. The camelback areas are hardly discernible from the street.

Henry Bensel bought the corner lot (now the location of 3461) in 1871, and Leonhart Bensel bought the adjacent property at the same time.

Soards' 1874 *Directory* records that Henry Bensel, carpenter, resided on Constance, northeast corner Aline. In 1876 Soards' lists Henry Bensel as a "builder." One supposes that he built these homes, using popular carpenters' pattern books.

3619 CONSTANCE, bet. Antonine, Foucher, bb. Magazine [Faubourg Delachaise]. A side wing rendered in miniature of the main structure is a curious adjunct to this hipped-roof, single shotgun. Oversized brackets support the roof overhang which is decorated with a "fleur de lis" verge board. The shuttered openings have segmental heads under simple cornices, and the original iron fencing and decorative gate are intact.

On October 25, 1879, Louis Lambert bought the property for about $900, selling it eight years later for $7,500. Soards' 1887 *Directory* lists Lambert as a civil engineer residing at 677 Constance, the early number for this structure. Robinson's *Atlas* shows a narrow building on this lot without indicating an owner. A building permit for a frame, slate-roofed addition to cost $700, with H. Fredericks as builder, was issued January 1885.

3657-59 CONSTANCE, cor Amelia, bb. Magazine, Antonine [Faubourg Delachaise]. In September 1873 Jacob Welsch acquired this property as bare land from Theodore Grever. Grever had bought the real estate a few months before from Mrs. Aline Delachaise Dugué de Livaudais. Soards' *Directory* first mentions Catharine, widow of Jacob Welsch, residing at Constance, northeast corner Amelia in 1876. Robinson's *Atlas* (ca. 1875) depicts a structure at this location but does not give further identification.

The gable-sided cottage belongs to a general type that is found throughout Creole New Orleans. Five box columns support the roof overhang

which incorporates the gallery. The doors appear to be original, and the windows are double-hung, six-over-six.

LIST

3718-20 CONSTANCE, bet. Amelia, Peniston, bb. Laurel [Faubourg St. Joseph]. A highly decorative frieze and cornices embellish this Eastlake style double shotgun.

The house probably dates from 1900, when Teutonia Loan and Building Co. loaned $2,500 to Robert B. Beck.

4124-26, 4128-30, 4132-34, 4136-38 CONSTANCE, bet. Marengo, Milan, bb. Laurel [Faubourg East Bouligny]. These four identical double shotguns are fairly typical of investment property built in late nineteenth-century New Orleans. Louis Paysse bought the property in 1885 and probably built the

structures soon after that, as they appear on a Sanborn insurance map of 1887.

All have hipped roofs, segmental openings and cornices decorated with a scallop line. Wooden box steps and porch railings are missing.

4012-14 CONSTANCE, bet. Constantinople, Marengo, bb. Laurel [Faubourg East Bouligny]. Just one room deep, this cottage is of a type that served Jefferson City butchers, tanners, and laborers before the Civil War. The building type is related to, but not developed into, a Creole cottage. It lacks a commodious overhang, *cabinets*, and separate living and bedrooms. A rear building, once separate, is now attached.

Robinson's *Atlas* indicates the structure, but does not give the owner's name. Jacob Hoeffner acquired the property in 1866 from Laurent Millaudon and owned it until 1869. Gardner's 1867 *Directory* lists Hoeffner as a butcher residing on the corner of Live Oak (Constance) and Constantinople.

4219 CONSTANCE, bet. Gen. Pershing, Milan, bb. Magazine [Faubourg East Bouligny]. This unusual structure was built during the mid-1870s for religious purposes, which no doubt explains its style. Crossed timbers, a decorative verge board, and a hammer-arch suggest and animate a semi-Gothic façade. However, oversized plantings and an inappropriate fence obscure the front today and detract from the intended three-dimensional effect of the timbers and the decorative beams which give the façade lateral support.

Napoleon Joseph Perché, Archbishop of New Orleans from 1870 to 1883, sold lots 25 and 26 on this square to the Germany-based Society of Sisters of Christian Charity in 1874 for $5,500. The sisters probably built immediately, as the structure shows on Robinson's *Atlas* (compiled about 1875). An 1887 Sanborn insurance map identifies the building as belonging to the Sisters, who owned it until 1939 when they sold it to the congregation of nearby St. Henry's Roman Catholic Church for $15,000. St. Henry's used it as a rectory until 1987.

Recently the Archdiocese has selected the building to house *Stella Maris*, a longtime Archdiocesan service for sailors in maritime commerce who need a wholesome center where they can relax, attend church services, find company, and make calls home in a quiet atmosphere. After over a century, the building continues in charitable service to New Orleans.

4424 CONSTANCE, bet. Napoleon, Jena, bb. Laurel [Faubourg West Bouligny]. Here is a Queen Anne camelback featuring a conical roof porch bay. Note the spindle frieze, with knots in a wave pattern, repeated in the balustrade. The highly decorative porch is just one element in a series of asymmetrical massings here.

The house dates from about 1904 and was probably built for Edmond Woods, who lived there until 1921.

4868 CONSTANCE, cor. Upperline, bb. Lyons, Laurel [Faubourg West Bouligny]. Long confused with the similar but now demolished Avart Plantation House, which once stood in an adjacent square but was across the dividing line between Faubourgs Avart and West Bouligny, this distinguished galleried manor house was actually built in 1853 for Samuel L. Ewing, a New Orleans commission merchant (a commodities middleman). Ewing assembled twelve lots on the square during the early 1850s. Cohen's 1853 *Directory* locates him in Jefferson City, and

Gardner's 1860 *Directory* later pinpoints him living on Upperline in Jefferson City. In March of 1866 Ewing sold the twelve lots with buildings and improvements for $9,000. A Sanborn insurance map of 1896 (above) clearly illustrates both Ewing's and Avart's galleried houses standing contemporaneously.

True to the style of the 1850s, the Greek Revival building has a simple colonnade and plain entablature on which the only decoration is a course of dentils. The gallery wraps around three sides ending at the rear with a service wing. Four six-over-nine-paned, double-hung windows offer light from the front gallery to the hall-less interior. In Creole fashion, the gallery bays relate only casually, or not at all, to the window spacing. One of the windows, perhaps not original, functions as a doorway.

Inside, monumental ceiling heights, wide flooring, sophisticated window surrounds and pilastered mantels give evidence that this is one of the

finest extant homes of those built during the days of Jefferson City, certainly one of the first in West Bouligny.

The New Orleans Historic District Landmarks Commission has appropriately designated the structure a local historic landmark.

LIST

4929-31, 4935-37 CONSTANCE, bet. Robert, Upperline, bb. Magazine [Faubourg Avart]. This square contains a number of pleasing Victorian shotguns and camelbacks. 4929-31 and 4935-37 Constance are identical camelbacks built in 1896. The owner of the latter has found in the attic a plaster remnant bearing the date 1896 and the name Terence Smith. The *Daily Picayune* of September 1, 1897, reported the construction of two frame doubles for Terence Smith by Marsel and Smith, builders, at a cost of $4,000.

LIST

5027 CONSTANCE, cor. Soniat, bb. Robert, Magazine [Faubourg Avart]. The *Daily Picayune* of September 1, 1895, reported the construction of this house for John A. Harris, who had inherited the land that year. It is a comfortable Queen Anne structure with deep porches, picturesque balcony, decorative gables, and textural shingling.

Soards' directories of 1904 and 1906 inform us that Thomas H. Wilson, a pilot, moved from 4920 Constance to 5027 Constance about 1905 after his purchase of the subject property in September 1904.

CONSTANTINOPLE

1735 CONSTANTINOPLE, cor. Baronne, bb. Carondelet, Gen. Taylor [Faubourg East Bouligny]. Many New Orleanians will recall watching moving pictures in this building, once the Fine Arts Theater, built in 1917 on the site of an earlier theater, the Pastime. Since its closing about twenty years ago, the structure has been adaptively used, first as a church and presently as a warehouse for a liquor store. The present owner has repaired the exterior and accented the decorative detailing.

The *Times-Picayune* of July 1, 1917, reported that the Fine Arts Theater was to be built on the site of the Pastime Theater according to plans "drawn by M.H. Goldstein, the architect, . . . considered to be as beautiful as anything in New Orleans in the way of a motion picture theater. . . . The exterior will be an Italian loggia with its columns and façades finished in stucco, equipped with approximately 800 opera chairs, a most modern ventilating system, the latest motor-driven projectors, gold fibre screen, and in the way of conveniences, they will have a beautiful ladies' rest room, free running ice water, telephone service and other accessories. Twenty-two 16 inch oscillating fans will also be installed."

5124-26, 5128-30, 5132 CONSTANCE, bet. Soniat, Dufossat, bb. Laurel [Faubourg Avart]. This block contains a row of two identical double shotguns beside a single shotgun, all connoting the peculiar charm of a New Orleans vernacular street scene. All have the same elaborate jigsaw brackets supporting hipped-roof overhangs. Segmental bays with simple cornices sound an interesting repetitive theme. The cottages appear on an 1896 Sanborn insurance map, and may have been built in 1890 by William Markel, an entrepreneur active in the old Faubourg Avart.

LIST

1816, 1820-22, 1824-26, 1830, 1832-34 CONSTANTINOPLE, bet. Baronne, Dryades, bb. Marengo [Faubourg East Bouligny]. This was originally a row of four shotgun doubles next to a single shotgun at 1816 Constantinople. Two of the doubles have been converted to singles, a sign of upgrading in this relatively unstable neighborhood. 1824-26 and 1830, on the third and fourth lots from the corner of Dryades, were originally identical. They were built in 1892 by Elias Williams, who obtained a $2,700 mortgage from Mutual Loan & Building Co. that year. They are shallower in plan than 1832-34, which was built in 1900 by Joseph and Ann Howard as a camelback. Four of the cottages originally had side galleries toward the rear. All of the structures once had detached service buildings. 1816, which seems to be raised unusually high, was built that way, according to a Sanborn insurance map of 1896.

DANNEEL STREET (S. Rampart)

5527 DANNEEL, bet. Octavia, Joseph, bb. Saratoga (St. Patrick) [Rickerville.] This raised, center hall, hipped-roof, frame cottage is a handsome accent in its neighborhood. At this writing, the Roland S. Byron family has owned and beautifully maintained it for over fifty years. The house and a rear stable once occupied fully half of the square. Frank or Francis Schaub bought the whole square in 1888, but was not until 1895 that Soards' *Directory* listed him as residing there.

The house has some simple Classic style details, mixed with some Italianate. Its slip-head windows were designed to give easy access to the gallery. Elevation and setback give the structure an imposing appearance.

DELACHAISE

1221 DELACHAISE, bet. Camp, Chestnut, bb. Louisiana [Faubourg Delachaise]. Built ca. 1870, this late Classic style house originally had double frame galleries. The bracketed cornice with parapet is original.

Adam Graner, a builder, purchased the land in 1866. The following year he built a center hall cottage facing Camp (see 3435 Camp). About 1870 he built the subject house as his residence and leased out 3435 Camp. Graner and his wife Catherine recorded wills in 1871 from their Delachaise Street home. Noted previously (3435 Camp), Gardner's city *Directory* had located Adam Graner at the cor-

ner of Delachaise and Camp in 1868, probably in the other house.

In 1886 the Delachaise house passed to the Walter Henry Cook family, who retained it until 1906 when Frank Rawlins purchased it. In 1910 Walthall and Louise Moragas Zigler purchased the home and owned it until her death in 1986. The brick column replacement occurred during their ownership. The present owner has begun gallery restoration.

1401 DELACHAISE, cor. Coliseum, bb. Louisiana, Prytania [Faubourg Delachaise]. Somerville-Kearney House. Individually listed in the National Register of Historic Places, this large, asymmetrical raised Queen Anne cottage displays many interesting elements of its style. Monumental chimneys with corbelled tops punctuate the gabled roof ends. This type chimney is common to English forms, but infrequently used in New Orleans. A large cross gable and a dormer with fish-scale shingling accent the roofline. Turned colonnettes with small brackets contribute to the picturesque effect.

Walter Byers Somerville, an associate justice of the Louisiana Supreme Court, built the structure in 1890. His family occupied it for thirty years.

LIST

2121-23, 2125-27, 2129-31, 2133-35, 2137-39 DE-LACHAISE, bet. S. Saratoga, Loyola, bb. Louisiana [Faubourg Delachaise]. This is a long shotgun row that is substantially unaltered. Distinctive scroll-shaped jigsaw work in the gables gives life to the modest façades. The houses were evidently built as rental property during the ownership of Anthony J. Winter, who purchased the land in 1895 and whose family retained ownership of the row for over seventy years.

DRYADES

LIST

3423 DRYADES, bet. Delachaise, Louisiana, bb. Danneel [Faubourg Delachaise]. In 1861 Pierre A. Delachaise sold this square to Williamson Terry. Terry and other subsequent investors developed only a few residences there during the nineteenth century because the area was partially industrial. Rosetta Gravel Paving Co., Barber Asphalt Paving Co., American Sash Door and Blind Factory, McArdle & Sinclair Manufacturing Company, and Woodside Dairy were among the businesses in this lake or "woods" part of old Faubourg Delachaise.

Before the turn of the twentieth century, Ruddock Cypress Company's lumber, coal, and wood yards occupied the Louisiana Avenue side of the square containing the 3400 block of Dryades. There were also two railroad spurs that entered from Louisiana.

The present house at 3423 Dryades is a turn of the century bayed cottage, probably built by William S. Fassman.

LIST

4901-03, 4905-07, 4909-11, 4915, 4917-19 DRYADES, bet. Upperline, Robert, bb. Danneel [Faubourg Avart]. This interesting block contains a row of five 1890s and turn of the century shotgun doubles. Thomas Tomeny developed the pair of identical cottages at 4905-07 and 4909-11 (second and third from Upperline) in 1895. Later he added the corner cottage at 4901-03. 4915 Dryades is a single shotgun, ca. 1900. 4917-19 was probably built in 1893 and first owned by Angeline Bienvenu, widow of George Buyatt, who sold to Baptiste Dejean in 1899. The Dejean family held this cottage and the one next door for over sixty years.

This streetscape is typical of turn of the century Uptown working class housing, often referred to as "tenements" in local building permits of the time. 4907 is the most intact, retaining its wooden porch railing and buttresses.

5027 DRYADES, cor. Soniat, bb. Robert, Danneel [Faubourg Avart]. Popularly known as the Soniat-Dufossat Plantation House, this raised suburban house is neither a plantation house, nor was it built for the Soniat family. During the early nineteenth century, the land belonged to the François-Robert Avart family. In 1849 Mme Amélie Delassize Avart donated it, with several other undeveloped squares,

to her daughter Louise Almaïs, wife of Valmont Soniat Dufossat. In 1851 Louise sold the bare land to William O. Denègre for $1,000.

Denègre sold the square to Henry M. Robinson in 1854 for $2,200, with buildings mentioned. Four years later Charles A. Rondeau, a developer, sued Robinson and forced the house into a sheriff's sale, where Charles Patterson bought it. Patterson owned the house through most of the Civil War, but sold it in the summer of 1864 to James Madison Wells, then Lt. Governor of Louisiana under Michael Hahn. The following year, Wells succeeded Hahn as governor and made this house his residence during his two-year term and for eight years thereafter. Gardner's 1866 city *Directory* lists Wells, Governor of Louisiana, as residing at Soniat, corner Dryades, Jefferson City. Robinson's *Atlas*

clearly defines the house with its outbuildings, and J.M. Wells as the owner.

Set in a lush garden and raised on brick pillars, the house today still has a romantic antebellum appeal. Its pillared gallery overlooks the garden and contains four full-length shuttered windows designed for access and free flow of air. The basement level entrance, leading to the *rez-de-chaussée*, may be original, although the main living quarters were on the upper level, or *premier étage*.

William Denègre, the presumed builder, was a prominent banker and descendant of St. Domingue refugees of the French Revolution. Mrs. Lillian Lewis Rainey purchased the house in 1948. Members of her family have owned and occupied it for nearly forty years.

DUFOSSAT

1550 DUFOSSAT, cor. Blanc Place, bb. St. Charles, Valmont [Faubourg Avart]. The firm of prominent New Orleans architect Moise Goldstein designed this pristine Mediterranean style house for the Leopold Feibleman family in 1922. In 1943 James K. Feibleman sold it to Ralph Nicholson for $42,000. It recently sold for over $1 million.

The original exterior was a rose-hued textured stucco, ornamented by a contrasting plaster trim. The window boxes and cast stone balustrade form part of the Mediterranean scheme, blending well with the barrel tile roof.

FOUCHER

830 FOUCHER, cor. Laurel, bb. Annunciation, Antonine [Faubourg Delachaise]. On the site of Dugué's Brick Yards, formerly Delachaise Brickworks, and now hidden behind a high hedge, this frame Queen Anne cottage was once quite picturesque. A striking pyramidal roof with a well-detailed dormer and decorative chimney, a curved wrap-around gallery with fanciful turned balusters, and a spindle frieze give the house the charm evident in the vintage photograph. On the side facing the generous yard, a circular "spoked" window seems to admit colored light to the parlor. It is, however, actually a blind window behind a chimney. The camelback, an unusual configuration on an asymmetrically massed cottage, is scarcely visible from the street.

On March 10, 1892, John Hasselbeck sold three lots on this block to Michael Lambour, Jr. for $1,800. "Solid Columns of Bricks and Mortar" in the *Daily Picayune* of 1892 reports the construction that year by B.J. Schiender of three one-story frame dwellings for M. Lambour, Jr. for $6,000. Soards' 1893 *Directory* informs that Michael Lambour, Jr. owned the large corner house, while Frank Lambour and Michael Lambour lived in the adjacent structures.

LIST

1631-33, 1637 FOUCHER, bet. St. Charles, Carondelet, bb. Delachaise [Faubourg Delachaise]. Benjamin Morgan Harrod, who achieved distinction as chief of the Board of State Engineers in Louisiana after the Civil War, and later as New Orleans City Architect, probably designed this pair of Queen Anne residences. Built about 1885, they are fairly early examples of the style in New Orleans.

Henry B. Richardson, who succeeded Harrod as chief of the Board of State Engineers, purchased the lot at 1631-33 in 1885. This was his residence and that of his wife Anna T. Howard, daughter of Louisiana lottery king Charles T. Howard.

GEN. PERSHING (Berlin)

812 GEN. PERSHING, cor. Constance, bb. Magazine, Milan [Faubourg East Bouligny]. A bronze plaque on St. Henry's Catholic Church reads as follows: "The Vincentian Fathers of the Parent Parish of St. Stephen initiated St. Henry's to meet the spiritual needs of the growing German population of the City of Jefferson during Reconstruction days. The First United States Convent of the Congregation of

the Sisters of Christian Charity founded in Germany by Mother Pauling Mallinckrodt opened St. Henry's in 1873. . . . In 1909 a fire destroyed the School and damaged the Church which was replaced by present brick structure in 1925. Father Ludolph Richen appointed pastor in 1890. Served St. Henry's till his death in 1937 setting the record for one of the longest New Orleans pastorates."

The architectural firm of Diboll and Owen designed the church built in 1925 with Lionel Favret as contractor. The design combines a Lombard-Romanesque core with "decorative brick" style bonding and Mission-style tiling for embellishment.

925 GEN. PERSHING, bet. Camp, Magazine, bb. Milan [Faubourg East Bouligny]. This two-story brick structure was for many years the Jefferson City and Sixth District Jail. Today, it has been considerably altered. It has lost its second floor balcony, its full-length balcony windows have been narrowed and shortened; lower level bays have suffered the same infill treatment, and now contain an inappropriate reel shutter and iron door. The modern

shutters do not fit the openings. The most intact feature is the brick parapet with sawtooth row at the cornice line.

On August 6, 1860, Faubourg Bouligny agent Joachim Kohn sold the property to Samuel H. Cor-

ey for $650. A few days later, Corey sold the same piece of land for $11 more to the City of Jefferson, represented by Mayor John T. Michel. Evidently the building was erected shortly after that and designated as the jail.

The structure continued in use as a jail and Recorder's Court after Jefferson City's annexation to New Orleans in 1870 and until 1900. The city then sold the building to Philip Throunk. Within a few months of his purchase, Throunk sold the property to Frank Von der Haar in 1933, and it has remained in that family for over fifty years.

The nearby intersection of Gen. Pershing and Camp was the civic center of Jefferson City. Next door was the courthouse, and in the immediate neighborhood were the market house, fire houses, churches, and lawyers' offices.

929 GEN. PERSHING, cor. Camp, bb. Magazine, Milan [Faubourg East Bouligny]. Adjacent to the former Jefferson City Jail is a severely altered building that was originally the courthouse of Jefferson City. David Simpson and his wife, Eliza Walsh, sold the property in 1862 for $850 to Jean Michel, who likely built the structure shortly thereafter. Evidently Michel controlled the property, as it appears in his succession of 1883.

1013, 1017 GEN. PERSHING, bet. Camp, Chestnut, bb. Milan [Faubourg East Bouligny]. These bayed cottages re-interpret a similar theme. The house on the right was built between 1893 and 1896 to complement its neighbor at left, which seems to be a few years older. Both cottages have porches with slender chamfered pillars supporting a spindle frieze, and bays with "clipped" corners. The cottage numbered 1013 has a front gabled roof with fish-scale shingling surrounding a small window, while 1017, at left, has a hipped roof, slightly altering the visual theme.

William Murray, cistern maker, bought the two lots in November 1891. 1017 appears on a Sanborn insurance map of 1893 without its neighbor; 1013 first appears on an 1896 Sanborn map. Soards' *Directory* of 1895 lists Murray as residing at 1013 Berlin. That property remained in the Murray family over sixty years.

1131 GEN. PERSHING, cor. Coliseum, bb. Chestnut, Milan [Faubourg East Bouligny]. This one-and-one-half-story, center hall, Greek Revival cottage seems to date from the 1850s. Its square post-and-lintel openings, box columns, butt-joint façade treatment, and cornice moldings reflect the simplicity of the antebellum period. The entablature, however, seems to date from the 1870s. The high roofline, added central dormer with six-over-six lights, and paired gable windows allow for well-ventilated living quarters upstairs.

Marcelen Florian Michel, the elder brother of Jefferson City Mayor John T. Michel, purchased six lots on this square at auction in 1864. He sold them for a substantial sum the following year. After an interim owner, Laura Garfield, the widow of Mortimer M. Reynolds, bought the property in 1866. The first city directory listing for her appears in 1879 when Soards' locates her, perhaps in error, on Coliseum between Berlin and Milan, on this square.

1325 GEN. PERSHING, cor. Prytania, bb. Perrier, Milan [Faubourg East Bouligny]. Prominently located at the downtown river corner of Gen. Pershing and Prytania, this multi-gabled Queen Anne cottage with ample side yard imparts a feeling of roomy comfort. Outstanding features include varied types

of random shingling, chimneys with brick belt courses, and terra-cotta ridge tiles with ball-shaped finials.

In the September 1892 *Daily Picayuner*, "Solid Columns of Brick and Mortar" reports that F. Reusch, Jr. built a one-story, frame, slated cottage for F.L. Gordon in that square that year for $8,000. Gordon was in the cooperage business and president of New Orleans Stave and Heading Co., Ltd.

1717, 1725 GEN. PERSHING, bet. Baronne, Carondelet, bb. Milan [Faubourg East Bouligny]. This pair of bayed builder's cottages is among several examples noted that show the Craftsman influence on the Colonial Revival. Wood-sheathed end pillars with mitered joints, narrow weatherboards, brick-corbelled stair buttresses, and Tudor style windows are Craftsman in inspiration. At the same time, the use of columns *in antis*, the modified Ionic capitals, the gooseneck railing, the wreath,

and the cartouche show a taste for the Colonial Revival.

M. Buddick and John Legier, Jr., a lawyer, bought the property in 1902 for $1,500. Published building permit records for that year show that $6,000 was to be spent for two frame dwellings on that block. Soards' 1903 *Directory* lists Legier at 1717 Berlin.

1902 GEN. PERSHING, cor. Dryades, bb. Danneel, Napoleon [Faubourg East Bouligny]. At first view this one-story frame cottage appears to be very small, but a closer inspection reveals an amalgam of additions. It contains numerous Queen Anne elements including the entrance door, the curious turned colonnettes, a protruding bay with Queen Anne

windows, a porch bay with pyramid roof, and fish-scale shingling in the gable.

William T. Coats, whose business was safes, bought the land in 1893 and financed the house through Eureka Homestead the following year. He retained the house until his death in 1914, after which heirs sold it to Gus and Michel Pelias in 1916. Today the Coats Safe and Lock Company is still in business, and the Pelias family still owns 1902 Gen. Pershing.

1925 GEN. PERSHING, bet. Dryades, Danneel, bb. Milan [Faubourg East Bouligny]. Prior to the turn of the twentieth century, the David C. McCan family, owners of a prosperous iron foundry and cooperage, held a great deal of property in this neighborhood. McCan built many residential structures on and around Berlin Street before 1893, although the street was still not paved as late as 1896. McCan at one time owned six two-story Queen Anne dwellings on Berlin, probably designed by architect William C. Fulham. Fulham also designed a house, identical to 1925 Gen. Pershing, at 1921 Napoleon. Of these houses, 1925 Gen. Pershing is the most intact example. Very large and distinctive pierced-work jigsaw brackets, springing from turned colonnettes on both levels, form fanciful arches. Sturdy spindle railings cross the gallery. The front gable is pierced with two central windows surrounded by fish-scale shingling.

David McCan died in 1893, whereupon his heirs declined to continue operating the foundry and cooperage or to maintain the family home, a mansion on St. Charles Avenue. They partitioned the estate in 1903 and dispersed McCan's investments on Jena, St. Charles, Berlin, Napoleon, Carondelet, Foucher, and Milan streets.

2119-21, 2123-25, 2127-29 GEN. PERSHING, bet. Loyola, St. Saratoga, bb. Milan [Faubourg East Bouligny]. These three double camelbacks are designed in Craftsman-Colonial Revival style. This hybrid style, popular during the first two decades of the twentieth century, features wood sheathing on columns and a series of elements known as Tudor Revival, which echo uses common in sixteenth and seventeenth century England. The diamond-patterned windows and decorative half-timber work in the gables are obvious examples of the Tudor style. All of these elements combine with a garlanded frieze and fluted, modified Ionic columns to follow the recommendations of Gustav Stickley's publication, the *Craftsman*, which as early as 1902 began to influence the appearance of otherwise Colonial Revival cottages in New Orleans.

Alphonse Denis acquired ten lots on this square in 1898, and in 1904 sold them to Charles Denis. Charles sold nine of the lots to Arthur Denis, his real estate partner, in 1906. They probably built these doubles on speculation soon thereafter.

persisted since the nineteenth century, the house cannot possibly be one of Hurst's dependencies unless it was moved from Hurstville. It is located in Rickerville, a faubourg adjacent to Hurstville, in a square bounded by Octavia and Joseph streets.

During the era of Jefferson City, Joseph Street was the upriver boundary of Rickerville and the downriver boundary of Hurstville. When Rickerville was partitioned in 1849, this square became the property of the City Bank of New Orleans, which sold it that year to Augustus W. Walker and W.B. Partee for $5,918. In 1855 Walker and a partner sold the property to Williamson Terry for $6,000. The square measured 280 feet on St. Charles by over 550 feet on Octavia and 628 feet on Joseph. No building was mentioned in the 1855 sale, but Cohen's 1856 *Directory* locates Williamson Terry, trader, dwelling in Rickerville. Quite possibly the house dates to the 1850s and was built by Terry. In 1858 Terry sold the property to Charles Singleton, who retained it until 1873. In 1876 Dr. T.G. Richardson, et al., sold it to Miss Fannie Freret, acting for architect William A. Freret, who owned the house until 1901 and resided there.

It is assumed that Freret added the twin mansard towers, brackets, cast iron crestings, and gallery— all of which bear the stamp of the flamboyant style of Freret's architectural office. This addition created a highly unusual specimen out of what was basically a simple, four-bay, gable-sided, rural cottage.

In 1906 the Alden McClellan family sold the house to Napoleon S. Hoskins, whose family kept it until the mid-1970s. Hoskins's daughter, Frances Hoskins Daniels, reminisced late in life that her mother remembered the home facing St. Charles Avenue, set far back on the lot beyond an elliptical, tree-bordered drive. Robinson's *Atlas* shows that during the 1870s the square extended from the Avenue to what is now Garfield, and that Hurst Street had not yet been cut through, substantiating the Hoskins' family recollection.

JEFFERSON AVENUE (Peters Avenue)

LIST

508 JEFFERSON, bet. Annunciation, Tchoupitoulas, bb. Octavia [Rickerville]. This is a "box house" of a type commonly found in poorer sections of New Orleans. Its chief characteristics are a hall-less, two-room wide, one-room deep floor plan, with a clipped eave, asymmetrical roof.

Insurance maps indicate that there was no house on this lot as late as 1909, suggesting that the cottage may have been moved there. Joseph Adam and his family owned this property from 1887 until 1972.

900 JEFFERSON, cor. Magazine, bb. Camp, Octavia [Rickerville]. Massive in size and completely covering the lot, this building dominates its corner. It demonstrates the penultimate stage of corner store-house development as observed within the limits of Jefferson City. Corner store-houses began quite modestly as one-story Creole cottages with wraparound walkways, one or two rooms behind the store, and a rear entrance. Later they were larger as shotguns, and then even larger as two-story buildings.

HURST STREET (Freret Place)

5520 HURST, bet. Joseph, Octavia, bb. Garfield (Jennet) [Rickerville]. Popularly known as the overseer's cottage to the Cornelius Hurst Plantation, this house sits on land Hurst never owned. Although one hesitates to discount oral tradition that has

Although the date of the present structure is late for Queen Anne, its two-story turret with decorative slate roof, gables with varied openings, brackets supporting the roof overhang, and an abundant use of garland and ribbon motifs are all elements of the style. On the lake side of the first level, a curved porch with spindle railing forms the entrance to the upper living quarters. The building originally had a covered, wraparound walkway and gallery supported by columns. The full-length windows on the Jefferson elevation led to this gallery.

Edward Walsdorf bought the property in 1899, and by 1900 was living there, according to Soards' *Directory*. In 1901 Soards' indicated that Walsdorf's Drug Store and residence were both at that address. Walsdorf sold the property in 1923, but it has continued in use as a drug store and home.

936-38 JEFFERSON, bet. Magazine, Camp, bb. Octavia [Rickerville]. Centered, recessed, twin entrances are distinctive features of this camelback double built in 1895. Mrs. Amelia Sievers, wife of James Reid, bought the land in 1895 and sold it with the house in 1927 to Emma Roubillac Hotz and her husband, Frank J. Hotz.

The structure has an attractive spindle frieze and a front gable with striking patterns. Galleries shade both sides of the camelback. Note the elaborate detailing of the doors and windows.

LIST

1009 JEFFERSON, cor. Camp, bb. Leontine, Chestnut [Rickerville]. Built in 1897, this Colonial Revival cottage is an early example of the simplified mode of its style. It departs in spirit from the busy detail of the Queen Anne to embrace cleaner, simpler

lines, while retaining some of the asymmetrical massing of the Queen Anne style. John McEnery purchased the property from Julia Goll Hecker for $2,600 in 1896 and had the house built for $4,160 the next year. The McEnery family retained the house until 1942.

This Jefferson Avenue neighborhood has continued to increase in quality since the construction of this building. The house sold recently for $415,000, an increase of nearly one thousand percent on the entire property.

LIST

1017 JEFFERSON, bet. Chestnut, Camp, bb. Leontine [Rickerville]. Mrs. William H. Krone had this two-story Queen Anne dwelling built for $2,600 in 1898. She held it only two years, selling to attorney Kossuth V. Richard in 1900. Later it was the William H. Fitzpatrick family home for thirty-five years.

1036 JEFFERSON, cor. Chestnut, bb. Camp, Octavia [Rickerville]. Occupying a prominent site on the corner of Jefferson and Chestnut is this large Queen Anne cottage with a massive cross gable forming a spacious half-story. A pedimented entrance punctuates the expansive gallery. A recessed porch in the gable has been screened, but has retained its turned balustrade, similar to that of the lower gallery.

Walter Edwin Payne built the house in the late 1890s. Before construction, Payne removed an earlier structure on the lot to an adjacent square at 922 Octavia (since demolished). He had purchased the earlier house with half of the square from business magnate Charles P. McCan at a public sale in 1884. The property has remained in the Payne family for over one hundred years.

LIST

1423 JEFFERSON, cor. Pitt, bb. Prytania, Leontine [Rickerville]. This century old shotgun has been redone without having lost its essential character. The entrance has been moved to the lake side of the house, but the segmental bays with their simple cornices and square pillars, the spindle railing, the quoining, and the raised motifs on the entablature maintain the integrity of the façade.

According to the September 1, 1885, *Daily Picayune*, Mrs. E.C. Bouligny built a frame house on

Peters Avenue (Jefferson) between Pitt and Prytania that year. The following year, Soards' *Directory* listed James G. Bouligny (husband of Ernestine Bouligny) residing on Peters, corner Pitt. The Boulignys sold to Joseph Bassich in 1892, and the house remained in the Bassich family until 1928. At that time it was bought by Edward Hathaway, noted Tulane professor of biology, who owned it for over fifty years.

LIST

1540, 1546 JEFFERSON, bet. Garfield, Atlanta, bb. Octavia [Rickerville]. Here are two Colonial Revival houses built just prior to the turn of the twentieth century. Nicholas Riviere, secretary of the St. Charles Rail Road Company, built 1546 in 1899 for $5,189, according to the September 1, *Daily Picayune*. Two years earlier, J. Numa Roussel, a physician, built 1540 at a cost of $3,510.

LIST

1621 JEFFERSON, bet. St. Charles, Dryades, bb. Valmont [Rickerville]. This is another of the large single-family dwellings that has been moved from St. Charles Avenue. It was moved to Jefferson Avenue during the 1930s.

It is likely that John W. Dwyer, who bought one-third of the square in 1880, replaced an existing house with the present one. Decorative elements such as shingling and jigsaw work are typical of the late 1880s and early 1890s. The *Daily Picayune* of September 1, 1890, cites a building permit for a "frame, slated dwelling, in square bounded by St. Charles and Peters avenues and Octavia and Jeannette [*sic*, Dryades] streets; J.W. Dwyer, owner; John McNally, builder, $9000." The Dwyer family held the property until 1932 when it was sold to R.P. Farnsworth & Co. Farnsworth moved the house to Jefferson Avenue in order to build the Art Moderne apartment building now on the corner of St. Charles and Jefferson.

1701-05 JEFFERSON, cor. Dryades, bb. Danneel, Valmont [Rickerville]. This massive two-story, Queen Anne structure was built as a single-family residence. The unusually steep roof contains a high pedimented dormer, along with projecting and engaged gables. Note the polychromed fish-scale

shingles in the apron between the first and second levels.

Samuel Henderson, Jr. purchased the square in November 1894 for $20,000. A few months later he sold this choice corner lot to James W. Kinabrew for $3,500. The *Daily Picayune* of September 1, 1895, records that Kinabrew had built that year a two-story dwelling for $3,000. Soards' 1896 *Directory* lists James W. Kinabrew as residing at this address. The property remained in the possession of descendants of the Kinabrew family until 1975.

1831 JEFFERSON, cor. Saratoga, bb. Danneel, Dufossat [Rickerville]. Isidore Newman Manual Training School was the gift of philanthropist Isidore Newman and his family to the orphans of the Jewish Children's Home. Its purpose was to provide an education and vocational training for those children so that they could be self-supporting. From its initial school year in 1904, the school was nonsectarian and welcomed private students. Until 1946 when it was incorporated as an independent, non-profit institution, it was owned and operated by the Jewish Children's Home. The Newman family continued to support the school financially for many years.

Pictured is an early photograph of the original building, which is still in use. Favrot & Livaudais designed it in 1903 for the Association for the Relief of Jewish Widows and Orphans. The campus has undergone many additions and substantial expansion until, except for one privately-owned lot on the corner of Jefferson and Danneel, it now extends from Jefferson to Dufossat and from Danneel to Loyola.

From Isidore Newman's early philanthropic effort, Newman School has developed into an outstanding college preparatory institution with classes from kindergarten through high school.

JENA

1215 JENA, bet. Perrier, Coliseum, bb. Napoleon [Faubourg West Bouligny]. This four-bay cottage is

an extremely simple structure with pairs of brackets and modillions on the entablature as the only decorative features. Five plain box columns support the roof overhang.

James Bateman Dunn, an architect, probably built this Classic style cottage shortly after he bought the property in 1886 for $500. Soards' 1887 *Directory* lists him as residing at 217 Jena (old number), the house next door. A later owner was Timothy Brophy, whom Soards' *Directory* of 1898 locates at the subject address. The property remained in the Brophy family until 1942.

1222 JENA, cor. Perrier, bb. Coliseum, Cadiz [Faubourg West Bouligny]. Although this center hall, Classic style American cottage follows an architectural tradition that antedates the Civil War, an 1869 sale of the property describes a "vacant lot of ground." That year Mrs. Margaret Brosnahan, widow of Edmond Sheehan, purchased the lot for $2,000, signing with an "X." Edwards' 1872 *Directory* lists her as residing at Jena, corner Perrier. She lost the property several years later as the result of a suit filed by George Brandt, no doubt a creditor, who took over the house in 1880 and sold it to Frederic Sholtz Neustaatl that year.

LAUREL

4933-35 LAUREL, bet. Upperline, Robert, bb. Constance [Faubourg Avart]. Distinctively turned colonnettes and a dormer with recessed balcony are characteristic of the turn of the century style of this double shotgun. It stands on a square that once

contained the Avart plantation. The land was first subdivided during the 1890s.

Valentine Wehrman, an engineer at Lane Cotton Mills, bought the subject property in December 1902. Soards' 1904 *Directory* lists him as living there. As late as 1920, the Avart house still dominated the square. It was demolished soon after that, however, making way for the bungalows down the block from this house.

1923-25, 1927-29, 1931-33, 1935-37 JENA, bet. Danneel, Dryades, bb. Napoleon [Faubourg West Bouligny]. A colorful row of double shotguns illustrates the characteristic uniformity of modest back street developers' housing, which sometimes involves interesting minor variations. A single shift in bracket style could mean that one of the cottages

was built later than the others. Documentary evidence—the September 1, 1899, issue of the *Daily Picayune*—indicates that Thomas Gillane built three frame cottages for $3,600 that year. Gillane had purchased the land on this block for $1,350 in 1897.

5127 LAUREL, bet. Soniat, Dufossat, bb. Constance [Faubourg Avart]. Title research and a dramatic increase in price from $800 in 1890 to $2,777.78 in 1891 indicate that this late Victorian bayed cottage was built in the first half of 1891. William Markel, a carpenter, used unusual brackets and chamfered colonnettes along with diamond shingling to make this residence fashionable and saleable.

Theodore Clapp Stewart, treasurer of the Grand Opera House at 919 Canal, bought the property in June of 1891. Soards' 1892 *Directory* lists him at 715 Laurel, corresponding to this address.

5203-05 LAUREL, cor. Dufossat, bb. Bellecastle, Constance [Faubourg Avart]. This severely altered but salvageable antebellum cottage has had its gallery flooring removed. The present inappropriate paired columns with brick bases are unsightly. Both columns and flooring should be restored by analogy to other antebellum galleried house types.

This may have once been the home of Drauzin Berthaud, a Jefferson City carpenter, who bought the land in 1854. Gardner's 1858, 1859, and 1860 directories list him as residing in Jefferson City, and in 1861 Gardner's locates him at this corner. The present house type suggests a building date at least as early as Berthaud's ownership.

5401 LAUREL, cor. Jefferson, bb. Octavia, Constance [Rickerville]. An ingenious combination of prefabricated jigsaw details has produced an original design here. The apron roof scheme, intersected by a gable, combines with a lateral projection roofed with a single pitch.

Frederick Minning and his wife Catherine Hauck Minning bought the land in 1891 and sold it with the house in 1893. Soards' 1892 *Directory* lists them as living "on Laurel nw cor. Peters Av."

LEONTINE

LIST

500 BLOCK LEONTINE, bet. Annunciation, Tchoupitoulas, bb. Jefferson [Rickerville]. These five double, early twentieth-century shotguns were built as rental property for Dr. Davis Lipscomb Watson prior to 1909. They are typical "tenements" or rental property of the late nineteenth and early twentieth centuries.

LIST

1304 & 1310 LEONTINE, bet. Prytania, Perrier, bb. Jefferson [Rickerville]. Architect-builders Frank Dannermann and John Charlton built this pair of two-story Queen Anne singles as speculative investments. 1304 Leontine dates to 1896; 1310 to about 1899.

LOUISIANA AVENUE (Grande Route Wiltz, Grande Cours Wiltz)

904 LOUISIANA, cor. Laurel, bb. Constance, Delachaise [Faubourg Plaisance]. This Classic style American cottage stands on the main thoroughfare of old Faubourg Plaisance. Here was located the heart of Jefferson City's slaughtering and cattle brokerage industry. Clement Wilkins, a stock dealer, purchased the land from a Delachaise heir in 1853, and evidently built the subject house soon afterwards. Kerr's 1856 *Directory* lists Wilkins as residing on "Louisiana Avenue bet. Laurel, Live Oak." Wilkins lived in the home until his death in 1873.

This kind of cast-iron railing pattern, along with restrained detailing and "Tower of the Winds" capitals were used frequently during the 1850s. The latter were more common in the prosperous adjacent City of Lafayette than they were in Jefferson City, except for Faubourg Plaisance.

912-14 LOUISIANA, bet. Laurel, Constance, bb. Delachaise [Faubourg Plaisance]. Here is a large, gable-sided double built as rental property during the early 1880s on a lot owned by the same family for over sixty-five years. Joseph Gitzinger, owner of a feed store near the Faubourg Plaisance stock landing during the 1860s and 1870s, purchased this lot before 1876. Gitzinger sold, then later repurchased it, and the cottage was still in the family when Charles Gitzinger died in 1919. The following year Elizabeth Gitzinger Brandt donated it to her son, Charles F. Brandt. Mrs. Emma Barth Brandt re-

ceived the house from Charles Brandt's succession in 1928, and in 1941 sold it to Patrick J. Walsh.

This cottage type was built in New Orleans from the 1870s until the 1890s. If the present house dates from the mid-1870s, its Queen Anne details such as the dormer windows, jigsaw brackets, and gallery rail have resulted from an 1890s updating. Alternatively, the entire house could date from the 1890s. It does appear on an 1893 Sanborn insurance map.

1030 LOUISIANA, bet. Magazine, Constance, bb. Delachaise [Faubourg Plaisance]. Now an antique center, this complex of buildings was originally Christian Schopp's livery stables and undertaking establishment. Because of the coincident capital needs of each line, livery stabling and undertaking were allied businesses during the nineteenth century. Christian Schopp, who advertised "coffins of all descriptions constantly on hand" and "carriages to hire," had a business at one time with Dr. P. Rub, on Chippewa between Toledano and Louisiana. He also received income from the City of

Jefferson by employing his livery equipment between funerals as an ambulance service, "howling" (hauling) the sick to Charity Hospital in New Orleans.

In 1868 and 1869 Schopp purchased property on this block to build the present structures. He had the three-story building built, along with the adjacent two-story narrow stable along one side of the

rear, and another shed across the back. These service buildings framed a courtyard which Schopp probably used as a martialing area until he had it filled in with a two-story, addition in place by 1893.

Robinson's *Atlas* of the 1870s shows a livery stable on the second lot from the corner of Louisiana and Magazine. A Sanborn insurance map of 1893 indicates that Schopp had expanded his buildings by then to cover the entire property, and had a gallery in front of the present three-story building. Schopp died in 1902, and his heirs sold the property to Isaac Sontheimer, who later operated his own undertaking establishment there.

1010-14, 1016-18, 1020-22 LOUISIANA, bet. Magazine, Constance, bb. Delachaise [Faubourg Plaisance]. These three, originally identical, galleried double shotguns were built in 1869 for Joseph Kohn, nephew of Faubourg Bouligny developer Samuel Kohn. Notary Eusebe Bouny's Acts of June 23, 1869, record the building contract. Faehnle and Kuntz were builders for the "three double attic dwellings" that were to cost a total of $11,200. These cottages are some of the earliest fully documented shotguns we have observed.

The specifications called for, among other things, the steps to be cypress "painted in imitation of granite." The front door was to be "grained in imitation of oak." The numbers of the houses were to be painted and gilded on the glass front door

"headlights" (transoms). The builders were to engage a bell hanger to provide and fix "bells with best springs and copper wires from the front gates to the kitchen buildings" [since lost].

The original columns have been replaced and dormers have been added to 1016-18. The present box columns support an entablature embellished with pairs of brackets and modillions appropriate to the period of the 1860s.

Kohn owned the properties until his death in 1883. His succession then sold to Michael Irwin. In 1905 Irwin sold 1020-22 to Isaac Sontheimer, who owned the property until 1921 while developing Isaac Sontheimer & Son, Undertakers, at 1030 Louisiana.

1124 LOUISIANA, bet. Magazine, Camp, bb. Delachaise [Faubourg Plaisance].

Elegant spacious family residence on Louisiana Avenue. Elegant two story frame dwelling with ten foot gallery and iron railing in front, large hall, two parlors with rear gallery, library, dressing rooms with Egyptian marble mantels. Two story frame kitchen, separate storehouse with two large rooms, wood and coal house, stables, two cisterns, patent pumps, yard paved, brick banquette and shade trees. Situated on

1216 LOUISIANA, bet. Chestnut, Camp, bb. Delachaise [Faubourg Plaisance]. Successive remodelings have altered the original form of this house beyond recognition. A splendid ca. 1890 illustration depicts this house when first built by William P. Nicholls about 1885. Nicholls, who was assistant cashier of the State National Bank, had bought the

the finest avenue in or near the city. Accessible by the Magazine and Louisiana Avenue lines of City Railroad near the Upper Market, in a pleasant, well improved neighborhood, it cannot fail to commend itself to all in search of a comfortable residence, with large improved grounds.

So ran a *Picayune* insert of April 1867. The advertisement was for the succession of James Alexander, who had acquired the property in 1856. The house probably dates to the Civil War decade, judging from the character of the bay, the Corinthian over modified Doric columns, and the bracket-and-dentil cornice motif. Alexander's first mention in a New Orleans *Directory* at that address, moreover, was in 1866.

Camp and Chestnut," may have been the original owner.

An undated floor plan in the papers of builder Hugh Evans at the Historic New Orleans Collection reveals that the John C[alhoun] Bachs, who owned the property from 1882 to 1889, had the rear wing added, perhaps to attach the early kitchen.

1205 LOUISIANA, cor. Camp, bb. Chestnut, Toledano [Faubourg Plaisance]. Now converted to institutional use, this center hall, Garden District type mansion was originally the home of Charles W. Wilson, a New Orleans builder. Wilson purchased the land in 1859, and by 1861 was living there with his large family and servants. His family remained at the site until 1875. A century later, the New Orleans Catholic Archdiocese converted the building into Louise Day Care Center for Children, after using it as a convent for the School Sisters of Notre Dame. These sisters have staffed Our Lady of Good Counsel Parish School for over fifty years.

The building has excellent detailing, including a fine cast-iron railing, bracket column capitals, and highly ornamental brackets at cornice level.

land in 1884. In 1885 Soards' *Directory* canvassers located him at 180 Louisiana in 1885, equivalent to the present designation.

A second, early twentieth-century photograph documents the first major alteration to the front. The camelback had been enlarged and brought forward to form a full second floor, a new dormer had been added, and a new projecting gallery had been built. Since that renovation, another room has been added over the new gallery, and an enclosed side porch has been appended.

Original remaining elements include the front door and windows, dropped siding, pendants, and possibly the stilted arches. Original interior elements are well preserved.

The house was purchased by Cathrine Louise Casey Irwin in 1912, and has remained in possession of her heirs for over seventy-five years.

1224 LOUISIANA, bet. Chestnut, Camp, bb. Delachaise [Faubourg Plaisance]. The four-room, center hall plan of this house follows a familiar scheme, although there are relatively few similar examples of the raised cottage of its approximate date in this area.

Louis Gabb, a Jefferson City butcher located by Gardner's 1869 *Directory* on "Louisiana between

1231 LOUISIANA, cor. Chestnut, bb. Camp, Toledano [Faubourg Plaisance]. Thomas H. Carter was the architect and Thomas Cary the builder for the church of Our Lady of Good Counsel Parish. Parishioners and neighborhood businessmen, under the leadership of Father J.F. Lambert, collected funds to build the church at a time when the Archdiocese was unable to help them financially. Their new building, begun in August 1890 to replace a smaller adjacent church, was dedicated in 1894 and finally cost $30,000.

The building's style reflects both traditional values and values contemporary to its time. The craftsmanship of the brick masonry exterior continues a nationally-followed tradition of mid-nineteenth century institutional architecture. The building's freely gothicized style, however, is in the romantic manner of the 1890s. An asymmetrically placed tower with Gothic arches visually counters the steep pinnacle at the right. The tower has lost its original steeple, and the decorative entrance porches are later additions. On the interior, the eye is drawn to the lofty columned nave, complemented by a series of stained glass windows installed during the 1920s.

1312 LOUISIANA, bet. Chestnut, Coliseum, bb. Delachaise [Faubourg Plaisance]. Originally this was the home of James Brison Woods, a nineteenth-century wholesale grocer, steamboat and commission agent, and president of Home Insurance Co., who purchased the land in 1869. Woods built the Italianate house before 1872 when Edwards' *Directory* listed him there. In 1900 Woods had additions

made, possibly rebuilding the porch with Tudor arches and paired columns. The cost, as reported in the *Daily Picayune* September 1, 1900, was a relatively substantial $2,900.

This design is one that more accurately reflects the national character of Italianate than that usually seen in New Orleans. The site plan, on the other hand, was originally laid out in typical Garden District fashion, four houses to a square, each occupying a quadrant.

1322-24 LOUISIANA, bet. Chestnut, Coliseum, bb. Delachaise [Faubourg Plaisance]. Here is a transitional turn of the century Colonial Revival house, still showing some of the asymmetry and picturesque qualities of the preceding Queen Anne style. Its many marks of the Colonial Revival include wreaths, fluted columns on bases, and modified Ionic capitals.

In 1899 Simon Haspel bought the side yard of 1328 Louisiana, corner Coliseum (a house since demolished), and built this house. Haspel died in 1921, leaving the property to David M. Haspel, et al. The heirs immediately sold their interest to Emile Mayer and his wife Dora Haspel, who retained the property until 1926.

1331 LOUISIANA, cor. Coliseum, bb. Chestnut, Toledano [Faubourg Plaisance]. Situated far back on the lot, this classic cottage is attractive for its setting and simplicity. It has had some alterations, however. French doors have replaced original full-length front windows. A massive central dormer accents the hipped roof.

Henry Chapotin bought the property in 1858, but was not listed on this corner in a local directory until 1871. Soards' 1876 *Directory* informs us that Chapotin was general bookkeeper for the Bank of America, and states accurately that his residence was on Louisiana, southeast corner of Coliseum. Robinson's *Atlas* also identifies the house that decade, designating the owner as "Hy. Chapotam."

Among the numerous owners have been Thomas Pickles (1876-1881), the Livaudais-John Bendernagel family (1881-1906), and the Abraham Pailet family (1926-1946). John Canaday, artist, art critic and director of Newcomb Art School, owned the house for a few years until 1953, selling to Peter and Doris Hansen, the present owners.

1403 LOUISIANA, cor. Coliseum, bb. Prytania, Toledano [Faubourg Plaisance]. This imposing Classic style, double-galleried side hall town house probably dates from the 1860s. Miss Georgine Pritchard purchased the land from Henry A. LeSassier, a family member, in 1868. Miss Pritchard owned the house for over thirty-five years until her death in 1906. At that time, R.P. LeSassier et al., inherited the house and sold it to Dr. James Belden. Dr. Belden died in 1920, whereupon Dr. Webster W. Belden inherited his estate.

The lower gallery capitals are common to twentieth-century usage and, with the front door, are undoubtedly replacements. The upper gallery railing is probably original.

1413 LOUISIANA, bet. Prytania, Coliseum, bb. Toledano [Faubourg Plaisance]. Originally built as a double and now converted into a number of apartments, this two-story house has been well maintained and retains its elegant Italianate detailing. Side galleries with cast-iron railings on the second level are unusual for most Jefferson City buildings, but not for Faubourg Plaisance, which relates architecturally to its neighboring buildings in the Garden District.

Edward Beebe acquired this property in 1872 and had the double dwelling built that year. Henry Bensel was the builder. Edwards' 1873 *Annual Director* provides evidence that Mr. Beebe did not live long to enjoy his new home. It lists his widow residing on Louisiana between Prytania and Coliseum in 1873.

1424 LOUISIANA, bet. Coliseum, Prytania, bb. Delachaise [Faubourg Plaisance]. This fine raised brick Italianate villa is presumed to have originally been the Eugene Schmitt home. Schmitt acquired the large lot in two purchases of 1865 and 1867, probably with an earlier house. Schmitt likely built the house in 1870, as he is first listed at this address in an 1871 city *Directory*. The property remained in his family until 1909, when it was sold to Jules Monroe. Monroe's heirs still own it.

Italianate details include the fine segmentally arched window heads, paneled box columns and gallery ceiling, entablature with paired brackets and dentils, bold baluster turnings, and arched-head door panels and sidelights.

1525 LOUISIANA, bet. St. Charles, Prytania, bb. Toledano [Faubourg Plaisance]. Perhaps the most widely recognized house remaining from the days of Jefferson City, this raised villa was the home of New Orleans cotton press owner, sheriff, and legislator James Peter Freret. Freret purchased six bare lots extending through the square from Louisiana to Toledano at an 1854 auction. Jefferson City

Council minutes mention that Freret was building a house on Louisiana Avenue in 1857. Gardner's 1860 *Directory* listed him on Louisiana near St. Charles in Jefferson City.

Freret was one of three brothers who inherited a cotton press business from their father James Freret (1772-1834). The oldest brother, William, was mayor of New Orleans from 1840 to 1844, and lived nearby during the 1850s. The third brother, John, co-managed the cotton press and died in 1852, leaving a family of fifteen.

James Freret and his wife Livie D'Arensbourg also had a large family of seventeen children. The oldest son was the noted architect James P. Freret, who studied Beaux Arts architecture at a Paris atelier in the early 1860s. He returned home during the Civil War to serve as a Confederate army engineer. In later years, he applied his Parisian training to the design of quite a few buildings in New Orleans.

In 1876 Mrs. Livie Freret, now widowed, bought out the children's interest in her husband's estate. At that time it was heavily mortgaged, as the family was trying to hold on to Willow Grove Plantation in St. John the Baptist Parish. The widow died that same year, and the children finally had to sell their home in 1880.

In 1909 food wholesaler and New Orleans Railroad Company president Hugh McCloskey purchased the house, along with most of this square. He made this home a gift to his son and daughter-in-law, Harry and Adele Merihl McCloskey. At the same time, he built 1520 and 1524 Toledano on the same square as wedding gifts to his daughters Hughetta McCloskey Evans and Corinne McCloskey Maunsell.

After several years, Mrs. Harry McCloskey persuaded her husband to sell the Louisiana Avenue home in order that she might live on St. Charles Avenue. The McCloskeys sold to Mrs. Genevieve Clark Thomson, who re-sold in 1925 to Alfred Bultman, Jr., owner of Bultman's Mortuary next door. In 1965 Mrs. Muriel Bultman Francis, philanthropist and art collector, inherited the house and lived there until her death in 1986. Her heirs still occupy the home.

The house originally had side and rear galleries. These were enclosed sometime after 1896. The main floor being the raised portion, one presumes that the house is also missing its central stairway. Archival documents refer to it as a "raised cottage on a brick basement," which it actually is.

LIST

1717-19 LOUISIANA, bet. Carondelet, Baronne, bb. Toledano [Faubourg Plaisance]. This simple double cottage, almost devoid of decorative features, is prototypical of New Orleans' modest nineteenth-century galleried dwellings. The porch, however, is missing a column, and the roofline its chimney. James Westaway and his brother-in-law Arthur Bouden acquired the land in 1852 and may have built the house then. Gardner's 1867 *Directory* lists Mrs. James (Jane) Westaway on Louisiana Avenue between Apollo (Carondelet) and Bacchus (Baronne).

LIST

2312 LOUISIANA, bet. S. Liberty, LaSalle, bb. Delachaise [Faubourg Plaisance]. 2312 is a Tudor style fire station designed by city architect Edward A. Christy during the Martin Behrman era in 1910.

LOYOLA

LIST

3301-03, 3305-07, 3309-11, 3313-15, 3317-19 LOYOLA [Faubourg Plaisance]. Here are five, four-bayed shotguns that form an attractive row. Various roof forms, jigsaw brackets, shingling, verge boards, and pendants provide the interest and dynamism that typifies a late nineteenth-century New Orleans street scene.

LIST

5526 LOYOLA (St. David), bet. Octavia, Joseph, bb. S. Saratoga (St. Patrick) [Rickerville]. Here is a large, boldly detailed dwelling, built in 1907 by Frederick W. Sutter of Sutter Van Horn Ltd. A series of owners held the Rickerville land in speculation for fifty years before the house was constructed. Ionic columns, Palladian type windows, brackets, jigsaw work, and terra-cotta tiles contribute an animated effect to this façade.

MAGAZINE

3300 MAGAZINE, cor. Toledano, bb. Louisiana, Constance [Faubourg Plaisance]. This property in old Faubourg Plaisance remained in the Delachaise family until 1892, when it was sold to Charles Wirth. Wirth built the present double, brick com-

mercial building that year, and moved his business, Charles Wirth Grocery Co., Ltd., into the corner half of the structure. He rented the remainder as two shops. Wirth's family retained possession of the property until 1959.

3308, 3310, 3312 MAGAZINE, bet. Louisiana, Toledano, bb. Constance [Faubourg Plaisance]. Charles Wirth built this row of three, two-story structures for $5,000 in 1894. Although altered, the buildings retain their well-detailed cornices, parapets and segmental second floor windows. Large gabled dormers, a cast-iron gallery, and the original ground floor sash have been lost.

LIST

3420 MAGAZINE, bet. Louisiana, Delachaise, bb. Constance [Faubourg Plaisance]. Dr. Gustave Walker built this two-story frame residence, which reflects the style of the 1870s. Dr. Walker purchased the land in 1867. Although he is not listed at that location until 1887 in Soards' *Directory*, the structure does appear on Robinson's 1870s-era *Atlas*. The property remained in the Walker family for seventy-three years.

A deep, bracketed overhang sheltering a one-story gallery characterizes this style. A fine heavy iron fence and cast-iron railing at the lower level remain, although an unsympathetic metal railing has replaced the original second floor wooden railing.

A stucco cornice with two parapets and nine original segmentally arched openings define the façade. The building has lost its original stucco covering and sidewalk awning. In the rear is a two-story portion.

LIST

3424, 3426 MAGAZINE, bet. Louisiana, Delachaise, bb. Constance [Faubourg Plaisance]. These matching shotguns have heavy, classic style entablatures, imparting an overly ambitious effect to essentially modest structures. Christopher Ullman, a prosperous Jefferson City tailor, probably built them during the late 1860s. During the twentieth century the Castanado family owned the cottages for many years.

3433, 3439 MAGAZINE, bet. Louisiana, Delachaise, bb. Camp [Faubourg Plaisance]. Originally identical, these two important double American cottages

with classical detailing were probably built as rental property shortly after 1869. Louis Gabb bought the three lots for $4,000 that year. Edwards' 1871 *Director* lists Gabb as a butcher working at the 9th Street Market and living in one of the buildings. Gabb sold the three lots with buildings and improvements for $14,000 in 1871.

During the post-Civil War era, members of Jefferson City's most prominent cattle brokerage firm, McQuoid, Mehle & Co., traded the land back and forth. When the residences were auctioned

for the succession of James McQuoid in the spring 1884, *Picayune* advertisements described "a well built double tenement frame slated cottage residence on each lot . . . containing in each double tenement halls and some 12 or 14 rooms with gas and gas fixtures throughout, wash houses, sheds, cisterns, etc., the whole in very nice order and repair."

Graceful symmetry imparts a sense of serenity to the façades. On each side are paired windows, brackets, and gateways framing the paired doorways. An inappropriate dormer on 3433, should, however, be removed or be properly spaced and redesigned.

3442, 3446 MAGAZINE, bet. Delachaise, Aline, bb. Constance [Faubourg Delachaise]. Peaked entry bays on independently-roofed front porches distinguish these camelbacks from more modest dwellings. Building permits cited in the *Daily Picayune* of 1892 list them as two, one-story, frame, slated cottages built for J.H. Keller by C.H. Girding for $5,000.

3452 MAGAZINE, bet. Delachaise, Aline, bb. Constance [Faubourg Delachaise]. J.H. Keller must have liked the two cottages constructed for him by C.H. Girding on the same block with this shotgun. The *Daily Picayune* of September 1, 1899, reports that Keller had another single, frame cottage built for $2,870 seven years after completing his first investment. Although similar to the earlier cottages, the subject structure is not identical, nor is it a camelback.

3516-20 MAGAZINE, bet. Foucher, Aline, bb. Constance [Faubourg Delachaise]. Now adaptively used as architects' offices, this four-bay, double shotgun camelback retains its original iron fencing with double entrance gates. Its chief ornament is a stepped parapet over a well-detailed entablature with paired brackets, modillions, raised panels, and spandrel arches between the columns. The slate roof, chimneys and service building are intact. The façade is nearly identical to William Bell's design No. 27 in *Roberts & Company's Design Catalogue*, published in 1880.

Reinhart Maitre, a partner with Delachaise Nurseries on Magazine and Foucher, bought the property in 1867 and probably built this structure by 1871 when Edwards' *Annual Director* locates his residence on Magazine Street, between Aline and Foucher. The Maitre family retained the property until 1901, when the widow Maitre sold it to William B. Bear.

3508 MAGAZINE, bet. Aline, Foucher, bb. Constance [Faubourg Delachaise]. Unusual decorative details, including a semi-turret with a pointed, multi-colored slate shingled roof, distinguish this two-story Queen Anne style residence.

Louis Luderbach acquired the property in December of 1885 for $1,525. Soards' 1889 *Directory* lists him as a plumber residing at 966 Magazine, a number that corresponds to the present address.

3522-24, 3528-30 MAGAZINE, cor. Foucher, bb. Constance, Aline [Faubourg Delachaise]. This pair of beautifully detailed, double-shotgun camelbacks add great distinction to an interesting Magazine Street block. They cost Jefferson City nurseryman Reinhart Maitre $5,500 when he had them built in 1893, according to an account in the *Times-Democrat* of September 1 that year. The shingling, jigsaw decorative elements, and porch railing as seen at 3528-30 were high fashion at that time.

3606 MAGAZINE, cor. Foucher, bb. Antonine, Constance [Faubourg Delachaise]. Originally a single-family dwelling, this two-story structure is now adaptively used as offices. It is a good example of property that has been renovated to the advantage of the owner and of the neighborhood.

Paul Tricou bought two lots nearest the corner of Magazine and Foucher in 1873, and probably built the subject house in 1881 after he bought a third adjacent lot. Soards' 1881 *Directory* lists Tricou at 980 Magazine, the early number.

Henry Schulze, a sugar broker, bought "three lots with buildings" in 1885, and can be found in Soards' 1887 *Directory* at the same address. During 1892 Shulze made $4,000 worth of additions and alterations to the house, probably adding the roof pediment, pierced-work frieze, brackets, and other detailing. N. Blank was the contractor.

3607 MAGAZINE, cor. Foucher, bb. Antonine, Camp [Faubourg Delachaise]. Neo-Grec details are unusual design accents of this large, originally single-family dwelling, which was once topped by a decorative cupola. At this writing, it is scheduled to be adaptively used as a "home decorating store" for the hardware store across Foucher.

Alfred William Cockerton, cashier in the state treasurer's office, bought the property at an auction in March 1881. Cockerton built the house shortly after that, and is located there in Soards' 1883 *Directory*.

3612-14 MAGAZINE, bet. Foucher, Antonine, bb. Constance [Faubourg Delachaise]. Originally a double shotgun, this four-bay structure was the property of the Peter Dorr family for over sixty years

after they purchased it from the Delachaise heirs in 1871.

The large entablature with paired brackets, modillions, and raised parapet dominates the façade, modifying an otherwise simple, classic style structure that is typical of the 1870s.

3641, 3645, 3649, 3653 MAGAZINE, bet. Antonine, Amelia, bb. Camp [Faubourg Delachaise]. Two matched pairs form this row of shotguns. Their cornice and parapet treatment is consistent, indicating that the cottages may have been identical until numbers 3645 and 3641 underwent updatings during the 1890s. Robinson's *Atlas*, compiled during the 1870s, clearly delineates five shotgun-type houses on these and an adjacent lot. Louis P. Delachaise owned the property from 1865—the time of a partition among the Delachaise heirs—until 1887, when he bequeathed it to his cousin Philip Thompson. Delachaise had probably built the cottages as rental property during the 1870s.

LIST

3700 MAGAZINE, cor. Amelia, bb. Peniston, Constance [Faubourg St. Joseph]. A two-story, frame, corner store-house with a wraparound wooden gallery supported by turned colonnettes is another example of a corner neighborhood business. A grocery was located at this intersection in 1871 when Edwards *Annual Director* listed William H. Harrison as living and selling groceries here. The present structure was not built until after 1909.

4100 MAGAZINE, bet. Constance, Milan, bb. Marengo [Faubourg East Bouligny]. Here is a successful example of adaptive reuse. Now a restaurant, this former firehouse dates from 1884. The architect was James Freret and the builder Albert Thiesen. It housed the volunteer fire company, Home Hook and Ladder No. 1, which was organized from a disbanding company of Jefferson City National Guards, as a bucket and axe brigade in 1858. Home Hook and Ladder paid Thiesen $4,700 for the building, but owned it only briefly. On January 7, 1890, the Company transferred to the City of New Orleans the building and lot for $6,000, a truck "complete and in good order" for $1,200, two horses at $200 each, and harness for two horses complete for $50.

A contemporary Magazine-side entrance has now replaced the original entrance on Marengo, but the latter façade is of the greatest interest. The two-level structure has lost its original rustication, and the engine entrance has been glassed and incorporated with a segmental transom. A belt course delineates the first and second levels. Four shuttered openings, central pilasters, and a heavy entablature with brackets and dentils give interest to the upper level.

4215 MAGAZINE, bet. Gen. Pershing, Milan, bb. Camp [Faubourg East Bouligny]. On the lake side of Magazine, between Gen. Pershing and Milan, is a severely altered brick building that once housed the Pioneer Fire Engine Company #1. Jefferson City residents organized this company on March

31, 1853, when they determined to no longer be dependent on New Orleans fire companies for protection. By 1895 Engine Company #15 was also housed at this address.

The Jefferson City Firemen's Charitable Association was organized February 9, 1858, with Jefferson City political leader John T. Michel as president. Michel was also president of Home Hook and Ladder #1, nearby on Marengo near Magazine (see 4100 Magazine).

tion in homes. The street-side gallery millwork here is typical of the 1890s. Sanborn insurance maps of 1896 were the first to delineate the cottage.

4319 MAGAZINE, bet. Napoleon, Gen. Pershing, bb. Camp [Faubourg East Bouligny] SECOND DISTRICT POLICE STATION. Municipal buildings of the nineteenth century, unlike many modern city buildings, generally have a graceful appearance that enhances the cityscape. Not quite an architectural landmark, the Second District Police Station, designed by City Engineer A.C. Bell, has a sturdy character that imparts its role as a citadel of the police.

The building's cornerstone states that it was built in 1899 during the adminstration of Mayor Walter C. Flower. A renovation of the 1960s included the glazing that fills the old carriage entry. This and adjacent squares have housed Jefferson City and New Orleans municipal buildings since the 1850s.

The traditional office of city surveyor—filled notably by Jacques Tanesse and the Pilié family in New Orleans and by William H. Williams in Jefferson City—had given way to a city engineer's office in 1896 as the surveyor's duties became too numerous for the office to handle.

4610 MAGAZINE, bet. Valence, Cadiz, bb. Constance [Faubourg West Bouligny]. This small, hipped-roof shotgun has a distinctive side gallery entered through a lattice door. Many of the original side galleries on shotguns like this one have been enclosed now that there is less need for cross ventila-

4636 MAGAZINE, cor. Valence, bb. Cadiz, Constance [Faubourg West Bouligny]. Valence Street Baptist Church is one of the few public buildings in Jefferson City designed by architect Thomas Sully. Contractor M.L. Costley built the massive wood structure in 1885 for $6,000, as reported in the *Daily Picayune* on September 1 of that year. The structure was called Mission Baptist Church.

The church's design combines traditional ecclesiastical massing with Victorian detailing.

LIST

4866 MAGAZINE, cor. Upperline, bb. Lyons, Constance [Faubourg West Bouligny]. This corner store is set up to the banquette and has a wraparound covered walkway. Originally, the corner half of the structure was commercial and the downtown half residential. The building dates from 1891, when Mutual Building and Homestead Association financed and built it for Mrs. Sophia Jaeger Dannemann at a cost of $2,600.

4901-03 MAGAZINE, cor. Upperline, bb. Robert, Camp [Faubourg Avart]. Fine decorative jigsaw elements distinguish this two-story double as a product of the 1890s. The side galleries on the second level are also highly ornamental. Alphonse Billiet purchased the property in 1893 for $775. He owned it until 1901, when he sold for $3,500, strongly suggesting that the house was built between the 1893 purchase date and 1896, when it appeared on a Sanborn insurance map.

LIST

4904 MAGAZINE, cor. Upperline, bb. Robert, Constance [Faubourg Avart]. Now adaptively used as a specialty shop, this three-bay frame cottage has an unusual side-rear bay with both an entrance and a double-hung window. Jigsaw brackets spring from the four square columns on the front gallery, forming arches with small keystone motifs. Segmental bays on both galleries form a simple outline beneath restrained bracket-and-dentil cornice decorations.

The property was held in speculation until Mrs. Charles F. Hardie purchased it from William Markel in 1888. Mrs. Hardie probably built the house soon afterward with a $2,500 loan from Eureka Homestead. Soards' 1890 *City Directory* lists C. F. Hardie, seaman, at 1276 Magazine, which corresponds to the present number. By 1891 he is designated as a captain.

to the *Daily Picayune*. The Saxon family retained it for fifty years. It is a comfortable, rambling cottage with a shady porch, many large gables, and several bays.

LIST

5221-23 MAGAZINE, bet. Dufossat, Bellecastle, bb. Camp [Faubourg Avart]. Narrow side balconies and detailed fretwork add interest to this large Victorian double, although it is now missing a column. John J. Hecker, an area property owner, purchased this lot in 1893 and soon built the structure as rental property. An 1896 Sanborn insurance map outlines it, but incorrectly designates it as a single-story house. The *Daily Picayune* of September 1, 1895, reported that Hecker had obtained a building permit for a two-story dwelling on Magazine Street between Bellecastle and Dufossat to cost $2,250.

5315-17, 5319-21, 5323-25, 5324-26 MAGAZINE, bet. Valmont, Leontine, bb. Camp [Rickerville]. The row of three, hipped-roof, double shotguns on the lake side of this block was probably built during the early 1890s, shortly after John E. Breaux, Sr. acquired the land in 1891. Soards' 1896 *Directory*

reports that Breaux, a lawyer, lived at 5323 Magazine. The houses remained in the Breaux family until 1954.

The severely altered shotgun across the street at 5324-26 Magazine was probably identical to the other three. It was built in 1894 for Jackson Bokenfahr, who Soards' 1896 *Directory* identifies as a commission merchant, residing at that address.

4919-21 MAGAZINE, bet. Upperline, Robert, bb. Camp [Faubourg Avart]. This large, two-story double is the one remaining of an identical pair built during the late 1880s or early 1890s at this site and at the adjacent corner of Robert Street. An 1896 Sanborn map clearly outlines the two structures. Although not the first buildings to stand on this corner of old Faubourg Avart (see 919 Robert), they were probably built by the Thomas Markey-George McCloskey family, who acquired the lots in 1874. As rental property, the house remained in the McCloskey family for fifty years.

Unusual decorative motifs and gallery design mark this as a building of continuing appeal. It features scalloping at the eave line, distinctive spherical courses under the overhangs, a frieze of attached "platelets," an unusual cast-iron railing, and highly-trimmed, paired box columns.

5005 MAGAZINE, cor. Robert, bb. Soniat, Camp [Faubourg Avart]. Rescued from demolition in 1983, this Queen Anne residence is now adaptively used as landscape architects' offices. It was built for Walter and Lulu Saxon in 1895 for $6,000, according

5256 MAGAZINE, cor. Valmont, bb. Bellecastle, Constance [Faubourg Avart]. Long thought to have been built by Judge John Henry Ilsley in 1874, this late Classic structure was actually built in 1883 in a *retardataire* style. Property owner Dennis McRedmond in 1883 had builder Patrick Burns completely dismantle two earlier buildings on the site and reuse the serviceable bricks, lumber, and windows to build an eight-room, center hall home with two "kitchen rooms" in a rear wing. The front galleries, now enclosed, originally had cast-iron railings.

The commodious sixteen-by-eighteen-foot rooms and the deep galleries have lent themselves well to the current use as an art school and gallery.

5333-35 MAGAZINE, cor. Leontine, bb. Valmont, Camp [Rickerville]. This two-story, Eastlake style double is nearly identical to 5300 Camp at the opposite corner of this square, and to 5221-23 Magazine in the next block. As reported in the *Daily Picayune* of September 1, 1896, John Joseph Hecker had 5333-35 Magazine built for $2,200 that year. By 1897, according to Soards' *Directory*, Hecker was living there on the downtown side.

Both sides of the structure have second level galleries, and both lower and upper front gallery partitions have been retained.

5453 MAGAZINE, bet. Leontine, Jefferson, bb. Laurel [Rickerville]. Once a towering three-story brick Italianate orphan asylum, the Poydras Home, now for elderly ladies, today has but one level, and a re-roofed portico.

Built in 1857 on two prominent squares of old Rickerville from designs of the noted architect Lewis E. Reynolds, it was the most important building in the neighborhood in its time. The institution was, even then, one of the oldest charitable establishments in New Orleans, having been founded in 1816. Julien Poydras, a bachelor philanthropist and first president of the Louisiana Territorial Council, donated his home at the corner of St. Charles and Julia for the first building. The Home remained downtown until its new building was finished in Jefferson City.

An article in the *Daily Picayune* of February 14, 1858, states that the site in Rickerville, 800 by 400 feet, was purchased for $150,000. This was probably the site of the master house and buildings of the old Beale-Ricker plantation. The article continued:

It is a most charming spot. The grounds are shaded by the spreading branches of the Louisiana live oak, while a scattered growth of other native trees add to its rustic beauty. On this property a spacious and truly magnificent building has been erected and on the 1st of February last the orphans took possession of its spacious apartments. . . . The Poydras Asylum is . . . in dimensions one hundred by two hundred feet and three stories in height. . . . The side porticoes are one hundred feet long and fifteen feet broad, and recessed into the sides of the building. . . . The style of architecture of the exterior of the building is Roman Corinthian as modified adapted to domestic purposes, and more generally known as the Palladian style. . . .

The whole arrangements are with the highest regard to comfort, and the establishment, for neatness, vastness, massiveness and beauty, will find no equal in the South.

Much credit is due to Mr. Reynolds, of 31 Camp street, who designed and built this edifice, that reflects credit upon the liberality and the taste of the lady patronesses of the institution.

HNOC Acc. No. 1951.41.17

The building cost $75,000, and is yet almost entirely unfurnished, except with what is absolutely necessary for present comfort.

The institution continued to function as a home for orphan girls until 1959 when the board of managers, considering the declining enrollment, determined to change the Home's use to a residence for elderly ladies. The two upper floors were demolished at that time.

Crescent City Illustrated by Edwin L. Jewell featured an illustration of the old three-story building in 1873.

MAGNOLIA (Victor, Acadia or Arcadia)

LIST

4216-18, 4220 MAGNOLIA, bet. Gen. Pershing, Milan, bb. S. Robertson [Faubourg East Bouligny]. 4216-18, a double, galleried Eastlake shotgun, is typical of New Orleans cottages of the 1890s. The building has detailing similar to the two-story dwelling next door at 4220. Both structures were built by Richard Hooper in 1892 or 1893, when the property assessment nearly doubled.

Originally a single-family residence, 4220 Magnolia is a tall two-story, two-bay structure now being adaptively used as an architect-planner's office. The first and second level galleries have spindle railings and round colonnettes scored in the middle. Sunburst brackets support spindle friezes with square jigsaw motifs at the end of each frieze.

MARENGO

526 MARENGO, cor. Annunciation, bb. Milan, Tchoupitoulas [Faubourg East Bouligny]. This fine center hall, gable-sided American cottage with front and rear galleries, was built for prosperous Jefferson City butcher Christian W. Gogreve soon after the Civil War. Gogreve purchased five lots forming the corner of this square in 1866, the year of his marriage to Anna Maria Adelheid Ossing of Hanover, Germany. Gogreve's butchering establishment at the time was on Levee (Tchoupitoulas) in this square, probably at the corner of Milan. He and his wife had completed their new home at Marengo and Jersey (Annunciation) by 1870 when Edwards' *Annual Director* located them on Jersey,

northwest corner Marengo. In 1872 the listing was corrected to read Marengo, southwest corner Jersey.

Gogreve retained the house until 1890, the year after his wife's death. After two interim owners, William and Emma Couret Henry purchased the house in 1893 and lived there for thirty years. Henry, president of Sixth District Building & Loan Association and a custom house broker, owned the house when George W. Engelhardt's *Book of the Chamber of Commerce and Industry in Louisiana* featured it 1903. Another prominent owner was New Orleans historian Dr. Isabel French, during the 1940s.

824 MARENGO. *See 4100 MAGAZINE.*

919 MARENGO, bet. Magazine, Camp, bb. Constantinople [Faubourg East Bouligny]. Here is a raised cottage with three bays and a heavy Classic style portico. The heavy entablature, with small dentils and brackets, resting on box columns dominates the front. It minimizes and obliterates all formal

aspects of the roof and sides. This is a characteristic of 1860s Anglo style architecture in New Orleans.

Archival evidence indicates that Albert Blanchard, identified by Gardner's city directory as chief engineer for the Canal and Claiborne Street Railway, built the house about 1866.

926-28 MARENGO, bet. Magazine, Camp, bb. Milan [Faubourg East Bouligny]. This is, for the neighborhood, an early Creole cottage. It is a four-bayed double, with two center entrances flanked by full-length, shuttered windows. The two large dormers with double-hung windows were no doubt later additions.

Stanislas Veret, a butcher, bought the property in 1853. Cohen's 1854 *Directory* indicates that he lived on Marengo near Camp in Jefferson City.

1001-03 MARENGO. *See 4029 CAMP.*

1129-31 MARENGO, cor. Coliseum, bb. Chestnut, Constantinople [Faubourg East Bouligny]. Four small projecting gables augment this hipped-roof Eastlake double. The house has a unique gallery rail of interlocking spindles, as well as a spindle frieze, pierced-work brackets, and heavy composite colonnettes. John E. Richard probably built it during 1891-1892. He owned it for exactly one year before

selling to William O. Seymour in 1892 for $4,000. Soards' 1893 *Directory* lists Seymour at 125 Marengo, which corresponds to the present address.

LIST

1213 MARENGO, bet. Coliseum, Perrier, bb. Constantinople [Faubourg East Bouligny]. Built in 1906, this Flemish-bond brick Colonial Revival style house with an Ionic portico demonstrates an early twentieth century reaction to Victorian picturesque asymmetry in architecture.

Johnston Armstrong, an attorney, purchased the lot with an earlier building for $2,000 in 1906. He sold it for $15,000 in 1919. Later owners include Dr. Charles J. Bloom and Dr. Charles Chaissaignac.

1224 MARENGO, cor. Perrier, bb. Milan, Coliseum [Faubourg East Bouligny]. Decidedly Queen Anne in style, this massive structure dominates the area. The large turret with decorative slate and terra cotta accents does not detract from, but rather augments the recessed dormer with small balcony. Stained glass, shingling, massive brackets, and various jigsaw elements are hallmarks of the 1880s.

LIST

1302-04, 1310-12 MARENGO, bet. Perrier, Prytania, bb. Milan [Faubourg East Bouligny]. Here are two of three large, identical Eastlake doubles in this square. The other is 4117-19 Perrier. Although all have been altered, 1310-12 retains much of its original appearance, having lost only its first floor wooden gallery rail. Slender colonnettes support interesting brackets that form paired arches over the entrances. Short spindle friezes cross the galleries.

This was one of the many squares in old East Bouligny inherited by the Kohn family from Samuel Kohn. Miss Marie Amelie Kohn received the land in an 1854 partition and, as the widow of Armand Heine, sold it to Daniel H. Kernaghan nearly forty years later. Laurence Fabacher, the next purchaser, bought sixteen vacant lots in 1891 and built the doubles in 1894. Fabacher also developed six houses facing Prytania in the same square which came to be known as Fabacher Row.

LIST

1420-26 MARENGO, bet. Pitt, Prytania, bb. Milan [Faubourg East Bouligny]. A well-renovated four-family dwelling built during the early 1890s for developer Anna Pottharst Flaspoller. *See 4013-15 Prytania.*

Christian Hanson, a cotton broker, bought the property in 1887. In 1888 Soards' *Directory* listed the Hanson residence at Marengo, southwest corner Perrier. Hanson sold the property to Auguste Schmedtje of Schleswig-Holstein, Germany in 1912. Schmedtje was manager of Anheuser-Busch operations in New Orleans. The house remained in the Schmedtje family for over seventy-five years.

LIST

1619-21 MARENGO, bet. St. Charles, Carondelet, bb. Constantinople [Faubourg East Bouligny]. This large Queen Anne style structure was briefly the home of architect Thomas Sully, who resided there in 1886, as recorded in Soards' *Directory*. Sully bought the property in 1884 and retained possession until 1898.

The gable may have once had a recessed balcony—a Sully trademark. The enclosed portion of the gallery is probably original, as it appears on an 1893 Sanborn insurance map.

1703, 1711-13, 1715-17 MARENGO, bet. Carondelet, Baronne, bb. Constantinople [Faubourg East Bouligny]. These three comfortable, identical homes seem to reflect the essence of the late nineteenth-century American family residence. They are sited on deep lots with diminishing setback, an unusual arrangement—perhaps a design consideration. Inviting curved porches, shingled surface texture, and asymmetrical massings give each house picturesque appeal.

Thomas Sully purchased the land from Leonhard Naef in 1891 and had it surveyed for building in January 1892. The houses were evidently one of Sully's building investments with his wife, Mary E. Rocchi.

1828 MARENGO, bet. Baronne, Dryades, bb. Milan [Faubourg East Bouligny]. Unusual plaster or wood swags under the overhang and above the columns are distinguishing features of this home. It is a large frame two-story, built for Rabbi Max Heller in 1895. As reported in the *Daily Picayune* of September 1 that year, Toledano and Reusch designed and built the house at a cost of $6,000. Curiously, Isidore Hernsheim owned the property from May 4, 1895, to February of 1898 when he sold it to Rabbi Heller. Heller was rabbi of Temple Sinai from 1887 to 1929.

1934 MARENGO, cor. Danneel, bb. Dryades, Milan [Faubourg East Bouligny]. Here is a massive shingled Tudor style house built in 1904 for Otto Walther from designs of H. Jordan MacKenzie of MacKenzie and Goldstein. Walther sold the house in 1922. A later owner was Frederick Wahlig, who bought the home in 1931. In recent years, the New Orleans Historic District Landmarks Commission designated it a local landmark, known as the Walther-Wahlig House.

LIST

2117 MARENGO, bet. Loyola, S. Saratoga, bb. Gen. Taylor [Faubourg East Bouligny]. Actually a shotgun, this large cottage is decorated ambitiously in the so-called Eastlake style. Its front gables are stepped to effect the asymmetrical massing characteristic of the style. The forward gable is shingled and has a sunburst motif. The rear gable features a triangular sunburst. Quoins, pendants, brackets, scallops, and spindles orchestrate a romantic effect on the façade. The cottage was probably built for Hiram A. Sutton in 1899.

2200-06 MARENGO, cor. Loyola, bb. Liberty, Milan [Faubourg East Bouligny]. For many years this massive Queen Anne style structure on the uptown-lake corner of Marengo and Loyola was a neighborhood grocery store with family living quarters above. It represents the penultimate stage of an interesting architectural evolution from the old Creole cottage corner store-house, through the shotgun store-house, through the Queen Anne as here, to an ambitious turn of the century store-house like the drugstore at 900 Jefferson. A picturesque wraparound walkway on the subject house,

set on turned colonnettes, and with a spindle frieze (now lacking a roof) seems to represent the height of corner store-house hospitality.

Henry Alfred Zahn acquired the property in 1901 and likely built the structure soon after, as he can be found in Soards' 1902 *Directory* at the S. Franklin (Loyola) side of the house as Zahn Grocer, 2143 S. Franklin. The business continued as Zahn Brothers Grocery and Market until the succession of Sidney Zahn in 1962.

2300-02 MARENGO, cor. S. Liberty, bb. LaSalle, Milan [Faubourg East Bouligny]. Like its neighbor at Marengo and Loyola, this corner store-house is larger and more commodious than its predecessor types in old New Orleans neighborhoods. It has a very sophisticated, elaborate wraparound walkway, complete with a spindle frieze and cast-iron railing (a replacement). The house is basically a two-bay, two-story shotgun, and may have been raised just after the turn of the century.

The structure may have been built about 1895, and enlarged after Charles Mazzoletti bought the property in 1902. Soards' 1903 *Directory* lists Mazzoletti's business as a dry goods store at 2300 Marengo. Rudolph M. Jung, Henry Baumann, Leopold Levy, and St. Cyr Belou were subsequent owners.

LIST

2304-06, 2308-10, 2312-14 MARENGO, bet. S. Liberty, LaSalle, bb. Milan [Faubourg East Bouligny]. These three identical Colonial Revival double shotguns, all altered to some degree, have Tuscan columns supporting gable roofs. 2314, decorated with garlands and modillions, is the most intact. Records indicate that the cottages were built in 1905.

LIST

2500-02, 2504-06, 2508-10, 2512-14, 2516-18 MARENGO, bet. Freret, S. Robertson, bb. Milan [Faubourg East Bouligny]. This row of five double shotguns—perhaps originally six—was built about 1903. Their jigsaw brackets, pendants, shingled gables, and apron overhangs create a distinctive New Orleans street scene on the lake side of the East Bouligny suburb.

LIST

2639-41 MARENGO, cor. Magnolia, bb. S. Robertson, Gen. Taylor [Faubourg East Bouligny]. A wide, five-bay galleried Eastlake cottage occupies this corner lot. Felix Quirm purchased the property in 1904 for $800. Two years later he sold it to Dr. Edmond U. Bourg for $5,000, an indication that Quirm built the cottage. Bourg was residing there by 1907.

MILAN

1111 MILAN, cor. Chestnut, bb. Coliseum, Marengo [Faubourg East Bouligny]. MCDONOGH NO. 7. One of the original nineteen schools built with a $700,000 bequest left to the city by John McDonogh, this school opened for classes in the fall of 1877. The three-story Gothic style structure with unusual brickwork has had alterations, principally from an 1890 enlargement and a 1920 renovation, but the building retains its striking elegance. A brick in the front wall has an upside-down, roughly carved date of July 29/76—possibly when construction was started. William A. Freret was the architect; J. C. Kiddell the builder. *(See 923 Napoleon for a similar McDonogh school designed by Freret.)*

According to a written history left by the late Miss Augusta Littlejohn, principal from 1920 to 1949, that was published in the *Times-Picayune* May 9, 1976, the school was built on the site of an old racetrack known as Crescent Green. Woods separated the school from the railroad running

from New Orleans to Carrollton, she said, and boys in the upper grades escorted their teachers to the stop.

The elementary school observed its centennial of continuous use in the fall of 1977 with a celebration. More than a decade into its second century, McDonogh No. 7 still succeeds as an educational structure.

NAPOLEON

419 NAPOLEON, cor. Tchoupitoulas, bb. S. Water, Gen. Pershing [Faubourg East Bouligny]. Thomas Sully was the architect for this one-story brick powerhouse constructed in 1892 for the New Orleans and Carrollton Rail Road Company. On September 1 of that year, the *Times-Democrat* reported that Muir and Fromherz were to build it at a cost of $15,000.

The subtle design of shallow blind arches, recessed base panels, and suggested pilasters continues a tradition of decorative brickwork frequently employed on nineteenth-century industrial buildings.

This facility once drew water for steam generation from the Mississippi River and from three artesian wells. It had four engines of 400 horsepower running turbines in the section behind the blind arch wing. Three auxiliary water tanks, once set behind the building, have been removed. The facility is now a training school for Regional Transit Authority drivers.

738 NAPOLEON, cor. Constance, bb. Laurel, Jena [Faubourg West Bouligny]. One of the early structures in the area is this one-story, five-bay, center hall cottage. The doorway is recessed with sidelights and transom. The very large dormer with applied jigsaw work dominates the façade.

Alfred Bouligny sold lots 9 and 10 on this square to John Bourdet in 1856. By 1858 Gardner & Wharton's *Directory* was listing Bourdet on Napoleon, corner Live Oak (Constance) in Jefferson City.

If this is the house built by Bourdet, it may have undergone alterations at the instance of Henry Michel, the subsequent owner from 1881 to 1912.

913 NAPOLEON at Lawrence Square, bet. Camp, Magazine, bb. Gen. Pershing [Faubourg East Bouligny]. NAPOLEON AVENUE BRANCH LIBRARY. The Napoleon Avenue Branch is one of the few still-operating New Orleans libraries of those built through an endowment of New York steel magnate-philanthropist Andrew Carnegie. In 1903 Carnegie pledged $250,000 for new library buildings in New Orleans. Two years later, the library board chose Favrot and Livaudais to design this one.

Although fundamentally Italian Renaissance in style, the building demonstrates influences contemporary to its time. It is listed in the National Register of Historic Places.

923 NAPOLEON, bet. Magazine, Camp, bb. Gen. Pershing [Faubourg East Bouligny]. Designed by William A. Freret and built in 1875 as McDonogh No. 6, this brick building was one of the first public schools "for colored children" in New Orleans. The Gothic styling highlighted by masonry buttresses distinguishes this and 1111 Milan from other William A. Freret designs. A feature common to the numerous Freret school designs is the ground floor open play area, now enclosed.

In 1925 the School Board renamed McDonogh No. 6 to honor Joseph Gustave Kohn, agent and nephew of Bouligny developer Samuel Kohn. The school then became a girls' commercial high school. In 1960 the Conservative Hebrew congregation Tik-

vat Shalom purchased it. In 1977 the building became St. George's Episcopal School.

The present St. George's has an entrance portico in a style that contrasts with the building, added during the twentieth century.

The New Orleans Historic District Landmarks Commission has designated the building a local landmark.

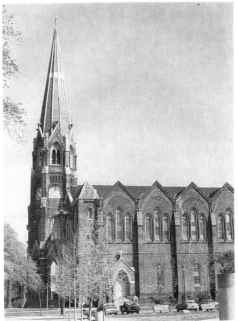

1025 NAPOLEON, cor. Camp, bb. Chestnut, Gen. Pershing [Faubourg West Bouligny]. ST. STEPHEN'S CHURCH. Ranked as one of the most impressive religious buildings in this area, St. Stephen's took nearly twenty years to complete, receiving its foundations in 1868 and its cornerstone in 1871. Because of the parish's poor financial condition, the church was not ready for its first Mass until 1887. The original architect was Thomas W. Carter, and the builder was Thomas O'Neil. Carter, who came to New Orleans from England in 1870, later de-

signed Our Lady of Good Counsel Church on Louisiana Avenue. The spire of St. Stephen's, the highest of any New Orleans church, was an addition in 1905–1908 by the architectural firm of Favrot and Livaudais.

Father Angelo Gandolfo of the Vincentian Fathers founded St. Stephen's Parish in 1849. In 1851

the fathers built a small chapel which was later moved to Chestnut and Gen. Pershing, and demolished in 1960. Collections for the present church began in 1858. Those first donations did not develop into the reality of this church for thirty years.

St. Stephen's Church has been designated a local landmark by the New Orleans Historic District Landmarks Commission.

1106 NAPOLEON, bet. Chestnut, Coliseum, bb. Jena [Faubourg West Bouligny]. A missing center column modifies the façade of this frame, Italianate double shotgun, which may have once had a wooden partition dividing the front porch.

It was once the residence of Jefferson City Mayor John T. Michel, who took office in 1860. Michel bought the property in 1857, and three years later Gardner's *Directory* listed his residence on Napoleon near Plaquemines (Coliseum). Towards the end of 1871 Michel sold the property, but in 1874 his son Jean Michel re-acquired it at a public sale. After Jean Michel's death in 1882, a *Times-Democrat* ad read:

> Handsome Cottage forming corner of Napoleon and Chestnut #190. Double cottage adjoining the above and fronting Napoleon Avenue. Handsome double frame cottage, slate roofed, retired from the street, eight rooms, front and side galleries, kitchen adjoining the house of four rooms, sheds, two cisterns, privies etc., the whole divided into two tenements and rented at $38.00 per month.

Note the interesting open side galleries.

LIST

1201 NAPOLEON, cor. Coliseum, bb. Perrier, Gen. Pershing [Faubourg East Bouligny]. Henry Hyman, a "ship broker," bought four lots on the corner of Napoleon and Coliseum in 1890. According to the *Daily Picayune* in 1895, Hyman had a two-story dwelling built for $3,400 that year. A house next door already existed at that time on two of the four lots, according to Sanborn's *Insurance Maps* of 1893. Mrs. Clara Hamer Hyman inherited 1201 Napoleon in 1935.

An earlier structure on the site, owned before 1866 by Hugh McCloskey and after that by Dr. John R. Walker, was probably demolished during the early 1890s.

1204 NAPOLEON, cor. Coliseum, bb. Perrier, Jena [Faubourg West Bouligny]. A comparison of Robinson's *Atlas* and Sanborn's 1893 *Insurance Maps* indicates that the left side bay of this residence was added. Perhaps the gallery detailing is also a modification of an earlier porch style, made at the time of the bay addition. 1890s insurance maps show two rear wings connected by a porch; however, this porch has been totally enclosed.

Intrusive fencing and a subdued paint scheme have altered the picturesque effect seen in the early photograph. The cast-iron railings of the fence and the upper gallery are, however, both appropriate forms.

The Justus Francke family, who apparently built the house about 1870, owned the property from 1870 until 1884. In 1905 John T. Michel, prominent politician, Louisiana secretary of state, and son of the former mayor of Jefferson City, purchased the home. His heirs sold it during the 1920s.

1224-26 NAPOLEON, cor. Perrier, bb. Jena, Coliseum [Faubourg West Bouligny]. Antonio Scolari, who had a variety store on Magazine Street between Napoleon and Berlin, purchased this property in 1868. Graham and Madden's *Directory* of 1870 lists his residence on this corner. At that time the cottage was probably a recently-built three-room deep, double shotgun. A later owner may have added the room on the Coliseum side before 1893. The gallery arches formed by spandrels with applied jigsaw decor, as well as the fleur de lis frieze, were probably also added, during the 1890s.

Jean Baptiste Trapolin bought the home in 1885. It appears in his widow's succession of 1937.

1314 NAPOLEON, bb. Prytania, Perrier, Jena [Faubourg West Bouligny]. ST. ELIZABETH'S CHILDREN'S HOME. St. Elizabeth's Children's Home is a conspicuous Uptown landmark in the French Second Empire style. Both the building and its mother institution have rather complicated histories. The Society of the Daughters of Charity of St. Vincent de Paul acquired the land in 1862 and is still the nominal owner, although Associated Catholic Charities now administers the Home.

The first structure on the site was a two-story building which the Daughters built in 1826 at Jena and Prytania for St. Joseph's Academy, a girls' boarding grammar and high school. About 1865 the central block of the structure of today replaced it. In 1870 the order moved its orphans' work training center from Magazine and Josephine to this location. At that time St. Joseph's Academy was discontinued and its pupils relocated to the nearby St. Vincent's Academy at Jena and Camp, now St. Stephen's Parochial School. The former St. Joseph's building was renamed St. Elizabeth's in honor of Elizabeth Mercer, daughter of benefactor Dr. William N. Mercer.

Thomas Mulligan, a native of Donegal County, Ireland, designed and built the central mass of the building, dominated by its two-level Corinthian porches, cast-iron hood moldings, and convex mansard roof. Local nineteenth-century journalists referred to Mulligan as "a modest, unobtrusive, skillful artisan," but he was actually a master builder of many fine religious and institutional buildings in the city.

In 1883 Albert Diettel designed and Albert Thiesen built the Home's right-hand, L-shaped wing along Prytania at a cost of $10,000, according to the *Daily Picayune* of September 1 that year. The corresponding addition on the Perrier Street side dates from the following year at a matching cost. A carriage house, demolished in recent years, once stood at Jena Street.

The most intact interior feature today is the chapel, which occupies the length of the Prytania wing on the second floor between the corner pavilions. Its central exterior feature, a neo-baroque curvilinear gable form, oculus window, and wrought-iron cross, is virtually a Diettel signature. The handsome interior, about a hundred feet long, has a heavy plaster cornice and ceiling medallions, and patterned windows in colored glass.

LIST

1401 NAPOLEON, cor. Prytania, bb. Pitt, Gen. Pershing [Faubourg East Bouligny]. This large Edwardian period residence showing some influence of the Beaux Arts features a very fine beveled glass doorway and unusual oversized decorative brackets on the columns.

It was evidently built for Valentine Franz, who bought the lot in 1909. Its presence on both Napoleon and Prytania contributes stability to an important intersection.

1501 NAPOLEON, cor. Pitt, bb. St. Charles, Gen. Pershing [Faubourg East Bouligny]. Originally built as a fire station housing the 34th Engine Co., this structure has recently been converted into a private residence. Edward A. Christy was the architect when it was built in 1917. It reflects the "Craftsman" movement of its period.

In 1983 the New Orleans Historic District Landmarks Commission designated the building a local landmark.

LIST

1727 NAPOLEON, bet. Carondelet, Baronne, bb. Gen. Pershing [Faubourg East Bouligny]. Longimanus Soards, publisher of a well-known New Orleans city directory, built this two-story frame residence as rental property about 1898. A more complete discussion of its Neo-Grec Style is given in the essay, "Architectural Styles," appearing earlier in this volume.

LIST

1921 NAPOLEON, bet. Dryades, Danneel, bb. Gen. Pershing [Faubourg East Bouligny]. William C. Fulham, an architect-builder who resided on Milan Street, built this house as an investment. The *Daily Picayune* reported on September 1, 1895, that this was one of two dwellings he built in this square at a total cost of $6,250. Unfortunately, Fulham lost his investment in a sheriff's sale of 1898.

Six houses on Gen. Pershing on or near this square are almost identical to this one. All were evidently the work of Fulham, who designed the other buildings for business magnate David C. McCan.

2037 NAPOLEON, cor. S. Saratoga, bb. Danneel, Gen. Pershing [Faubourg East Bouligny]. This curious but striking residence may be atypical in this area, but there is ample logic in its concept of large, double, pagoda-like overhangs, which provide protection from the sun and rain of our climate.

On August 31, 1904, the *Daily States* pointed out that the unique structure was also a curiosity in its day:

> Among the numerous frame residences erected during the past twelve months, that of Raoul Vallon, designed by Frank P. Gravely & Co., Limited, located at Napoleon avenue and Saratoga street, is one of the most costly, and by far the most unique and picturesque in design. While the architects executed the actual design it was along the line of the ideas suggested by Mr. Vallon. In design the building bears a close resemblance to the Japanese architecture, the eaves of the roof and the gallery sheds having the pagoda-like upturn at the corners, and the general appearance otherwise being much after the appearance of Japanese or Chinese structures. It is said, also,

that the building is being fitted throughout in Japanese furniture, draperies, etc.This beautiful and novel dwelling cost to complete $15,000 or more. It has the distinction of being the only one of the kind in the city, there is not another residence in this section which is even a near approach to it in appearance.

The Vallon family owned the house until 1925.

OCTAVIA

LIST

415, 419-21 OCTAVIA, bet. Annunciation, Laurel, bb. Jefferson [Rickerville]. In 1887 Christian Thomas purchased this entire square, holding it until 1901 when he sold to other speculators, who in turn resold for development. Metropolitan Building Company evidently built the double 419-21 Octavia in 1903. The adjacent house with rear wing (No. 415) was the home of the John Bives family for nearly forty years. Soards' *Directory* first listed Bives at that address in 1905.

1000 block OCTAVIA, bet. Chestnut, Coliseum, bb. Joseph [Rickerville]. Eight varied but compatible shotguns all contribute their own special effects to the charm of this Uptown street scene. Their construction dates span the decade between 1895 and 1904. The two pairs and four individual designs—some with galleries, others with apron overhangs supported by brackets or columns—recombine the builders' vocabulary of modest but pleasing details.

Amanda Clark built the house at the corner of Octavia and Chestnut (1000-02) between 1901 and 1904. Adjacent to it are three homes built in 1895; of these, 1004-06 and 1008-10 are a pair built by Emile Leonval. Next to them is 1012-14, unique on

the block, designed and built by W.C. Williams and Brother, architects, for Sixth District Building and Loan Company. Sixth District and other savings and loans indeed provided the impetus for design, construction, and financing for quite a few shotguns in this area.

Next door to 1012-14 is a pair that are similar but not identical. Both have bracketed apron overhangs under gable windows, but 1016-18 dates from before 1896 while 1020-22 dates from 1903. Security Building and Loan financed this latter house (third from the Coliseum corner) for Christian Schmidt.

Finally, there is a pair of ca. 1904 cottages at the corner of Coliseum. These are the most recent on the block, having replaced a large story-and-one-half house with a stable in the rear that straddled both lots until after the turn of the twentieth century.

LIST

1320 OCTAVIA, bet. Atlanta, Pitt, bb. Joseph [Rickerville]. This is an Eastlake style house of the mid-1890s—so called because of its spindle work, columns and spandrels. (For a discussion of Eastlake, see the article on "Architectural Styles of Jefferson City.")

Hewes T. Gurley purchased the bare lot in 1892 from Cosmopolitan Building and Loan for $1,600, and in 1895 sold the property to Mrs. Marie Wright Gurley for $4,000. A Sanborn insurance map of 1896 outlines the house with its gallery and two rear bays.

LIST

1404 OCTAVIA, cor. Atlanta, bb. Joseph, Garfield [Rickerville]. Here is a large, comfortable, late nineteenth-century home with several offsets and porches and some Colonial Revival detailing. Robert Jarvis Wood, manager of Gulf Bag Co., Ltd., purchased the lot in 1896, and evidently built the house the following year. Soards' *Directory* listed his residence there in 1898. Wood sold the property in 1909 to Francis Hewitt Buckner.

LIST

1435 OCTAVIA, bet. St. Charles, Garfield, bb. Jefferson [Rickerville]. Queen Anne detailing is evident in this dwelling built in 1896 for Mrs. Corinne Catlett Christian, as reported in the *Daily Picayune* of September 1 that year. Samuel Snodgrass bought the property in 1899, and in 1912 hired William L. Kiefe to enlarge the house to its present size.

1539-41 OCTAVIA, bet. St. Charles, Garfield, bb. Jefferson [Rickerville]. As unlikely as it seems, this massive Queen Anne structure was moved to its present site from its original St. Charles Avenue location. Thomas Sully designed it in 1887 for Benedetto Onorato, an auctioneer and real estate agent. On the interior were doors and paneling of highly polished oak and cypress. A wide "living hall" with a broad stairway opened to a large parlor that connected by sliding doors to an octagonal-shaped dining room large enough to seat thirty persons. Six bedrooms, also finished in polished woods, had built-in linen closets. Bathrooms, electric bells, and kitchen facilities were of the most up-to-date form.

One can more readily perceive the appeal of Sully's exterior design by imagining the front without the present oversized concrete and slate stairs,

enclosed left side bay, or asbestos siding. A porch originally projected to the right. The house was raised somewhat in order to accommodate an additional floor.

In spite of its alterations, the structure retains many stylish features of the 1880s—gables, dormers, shingling, terra-cotta ridge tiles and finials, and a prominent turret.

A real estate advertisement in the September 1, 1891, *Daily Picayune* describes the property as

Occupying nearly a half square of ground [and] filled with the rarest and most costly foreign and domestic plants, shrubs, and flowers, the collection being one of the finest and largest in the UNITED STATES, having been specially imported [by Onorato] with the

native earth. . . . Seven large hothouses and one large propagating house are fully equipped with machinery and appurtenances of modern character, thus making it the most complete nursery in the south. In addition there are several ponds, containing several thousand gold and silver fishes of rare quality.

The property once measured 140 feet on St. Charles by 350 feet on Octavia. On the grounds, in addition to the several hothouses, were a two-story stable with coachman's quarters, and a cow barn. These were located at the rear of the lot presently occupied by the three-family complex on St. Charles and Octavia.

1631 OCTAVIA, bet. St. Charles, Danneel, bb. Jefferson [Rickerville]. Once the only residence on this square and surrounded by dependencies with a garden overlooking St. Charles, this circa 1857 mansion has suffered not only the loss of its premiere location on the Avenue, but the drastic removal of its original columns, upper gallery and central dormer. Column replacements are out of proportion to the height of the façade, and the once full-length upper level windows seem to miss the gallery onto which they once opened. All of its losses evidently occurred after World War II.

Robinson's *Atlas* sites the structure when it faced St. Charles and dominated the square. At that time Peter R. Fell, an agent with the Imperial Fire Insur-

ance Company of London, owned the property. Fell had purchased the house from O.H. Karstendieck in 1870 for $22,500, the price of the entire square. Karstendieck had in turn acquired the property from the heirs of William Laurens in 1866 for a comparable value of $20,000. Gardner's 1861 *Directory* locates W. Laurens at St. Charles, corner Peters (Jefferson), the equivalent location. As early as 1857, Mygatt's *Directory* had located him in Jefferson City, suggesting the early actual date of this house, which is possibly the oldest in Rickerville.

Peter Fell lost his house to post-war taxes in 1874. The following year he re-acquired the property, but could not hold it. John L. Byrne then purchased it in 1878. During Byrne's sixteen-year ownership, the New Orleans Conservatory of Music and School of Languages occupied the house and grounds as a boarding and day school for music students. An early print illustrates the building at that time, set behind an arched cast-iron gateway. Six correctly-styled, double-level columns with simple caps supported an architrave quite similar to the present one. A large dormer divided an iron cresting at the roofline.

In 1891 John M. Bonner paid $18,000 for the property and subdivided the land for the first time. The house was moved to 1631 Octavia after 1907 to make way for the Octavia Apartments. Today the home, although altered, is still imposing and boasts a fine interior.

LIST

1637 OCTAVIA, bet. Danneel, St. Charles, bb. Jefferson [Rickerville]. This small frame residence has undergone some alterations from its original form. Commercial Homestead Association evidently built it between 1890 and 1892, when the property value increased from $900 to $3,200.

Washington Hands bought the house in 1893 for $4,600. Soards' 1894 *Directory* lists him "on Octavia between St. Charles and Dryades."

1661 OCTAVIA, bet. Danneel, St. Charles, bb. Jefferson [Rickerville]. A feeling of comfort and adaptation to climatic conditions is apparent in this spacious one-and-one-half-story cottage built in 1894, as reported in the September 1 *Daily Picayune* of that year. F.H. Hoffman was the builder for owner Patrick Thompson, and the price was $6,000.

LIST

2020 OCTAVIA, bet. Loyola, S. Liberty, bb. Joseph [Rickerville]. The lake side of St. Charles Avenue in old Rickerville contains few pre-1890 structures, as the entire faubourg lagged behind the develop-

ment of other parts of Jefferson City. Even in the other faubourgs, early residential areas generally clustered on the river side of St. Charles. The entire square bounded by Octavia, Joseph, S. Liberty, and Loyola was still practically bare of construction as late as 1909.

This Tudor Revival adaptation of half-timber construction was originally the home of Eldon S. Lazarus, who employed architect Leon Weiss of the firm of Keenan and Weiss to design it about 1910. The product was one of Weiss's early designs. Lazarus had purchased the land in the spring of that year. At this writing, his family still owns the property.

LIST

2318 OCTAVIA, bet. Freret, S. Robertson, bb. Joseph [Rickerville]. As late as 1909, only four houses stood on this square. The present shotgun was evidently built about 1906 for Samuel and Rose Gysie Marshall, who financed their home through Metropolitan Building Company. Soards' 1908 *Directory* located Marshall, a "pattern maker," at this address.

PENISTON

1210-12 PENISTON, bet. Coliseum, Perrier, bb. Gen. Taylor [Faubourg St. Joseph]. John Thuer bought this property in 1883 and probably built the structure for rental income shortly after that. No record of his having lived there has been located, but the building remained in the hands of his family until 1936.

The segmentally arched gallery and cast-iron railing yield an attractive pattern of light and shadow. Six bays, with doors at each end, remind us that the house was originally a double. It appears on a Sanborn insurance map of 1893 with recessed side galleries, which have since been enclosed.

1300 PENISTON, cor. Perrier, bb. Prytania, Gen. Taylor [Faubourg St. Joseph]. A Peniston Street address denies the original orientation of this cottage toward Perrier Street. Robinson's *Atlas* delineates the building with a Perrier address, no doubt without the conical tower, rounded dormer, projecting porch gable, stained glass, friezes, and other Queen Anne details. These were probably added during the ownership of the descendants of pre-

sumed builder Eugene May, between 1890 and 1913.

The Peniston address appears on a Sanborn insurance map as early as 1896, indicating that the cutaway side gateway may have been added by then. Robinson's *Atlas* shows the side wing and basic floor plan as they lay soon after Miss Victoria Richards (later Mrs. Eugene May) completed her purchase of four lots on this block over a period of nine years beginning in 1866. The original house could even date to mid-nineteenth century, as the fine Perrier-side doorway details suggest. Gardner's city *Directory* lists Eugene May simply as a Jefferson City bookkeeper in 1861, but in 1868 locates him on "Ferrier [*sic*] bet. Peniston and Gen. Taylor."

1615 PENISTON, bet. St. Charles, Carondelet, bb. Amelia [Faubourg St. Joseph]. This Tudor Revival structure was originally the St. Charles Avenue home of Samuel Worms, a Canal Street merchant who sold fancy goods and notions. It is one of seven extant houses in this area identified as having been removed from the Avenue. When built during the 1890s, it replaced an 1876 dwelling designed by architect Charles Hillger that had stood on St. Charles at the corner of Peniston. Some time after 1931, this house was in turn replaced by a brick apartment building, and was moved from 3723 St. Charles to Peniston Street.

Because of its dominant front and side gables, the building still retains a nineteenth-century flavor. It shows, however, some alterations that have diminished its intended Tudor Revival effect. The principal changes are nevertheless in detailing rather in than massing.

The early photograph shows the home's original diamond-paned leaded glass windows in the front and side gables, which have now been replaced by jalousie-style ones. A cast-iron railing has been

added where there was none before at the lower level; however, the upper railing seems to be substantially original. All of the window sashes were originally double-hung; their casement-style replacements are a strong reminder of the World War I era. Finally, the once single-family residence has now been divided into a number of apartments.

LIST

1900 block PENISTON, bet. Danneel, Dryades, bb. Amelia, Gen. Taylor [Faubourg St. Joseph]. Jefferson City's sparsely developed squares lakeward of Carondelet lay generally unsubdivided until after the turn of the twentieth century. As late as 1910, groups of speculators were still holding large blocks of land in this area under corporate names such as Financial Improvement Co., Mississippi Valley Co., New Orleans Real Estate Mortgage and Security Co., and Carrollton Land Co. Drainage improvements on this side of St. Charles Avenue finally spurred development about that time.

The four nearly identical two-story builders' houses flanking the 1900 block of Peniston date from about 1910. Some were built with the help of the German American Homestead.

PERRIER

3900-02 PERRIER, bet. Gen. Taylor, Austerlitz, bb. Coliseum [Faubourg East Bouligny]. This modest Creole cottage is one of the oldest building types in New Orleans faubourgs. It was probably not built, however, until 1885, when Mary Louise Kennedy

Genella acquired the property. Two years later it appeared on a Sanborn insurance map.

The house is typical of the kind of low income rental property that one may see around the corners on Gen. Taylor and Coliseum streets. This type of house continued to be built into the twentieth century.

LIST

4117-19 PERRIER, bet. Marengo, Milan, bb. Prytania [Faubourg East Bouligny]. *See 1302-04, 1310-12 Marengo.*

4602 PERRIER, cor. Cadiz, bb. Valence, Coliseum [Faubourg West Bouligny]. The building contract for this frame camelback, dated April 6, 1889, called for a one-story, frame cottage to be built by William Markel for Louis Barthelemy at a cost of $2,397.40 (Benjamin Ory, N.P., New Orleans Notarial Archives). The specifications included wooden ventilators in the kitchen, pantry and rear hall, two cisterns, and papered hall, parlors, and dining room.

In view of the building contract, one might conclude that the camelback was a later addition, an idea further verified by a Sanborn insurance map of 1896

4619 PERRIER, bet. Cadiz, Valence, bb. Prytania [Faubourg West Bouligny]. This one story frame, three-bay shotgun originally faced Valence, as shown on Robinson's *Atlas*. Sanborn insurance maps of 1896 and 1909 reflect the early change in location. Daniel Weidner bought the whole square in 1865 when it was still used agriculturally. At the

time of his purchase from James D. Dameron, Weidner agreed to allow "the present cultivator of the square . . . sufficient time to gather and remove from said premises his present crop, say until the first day of February next 1866." By 1873, however, Weidner had built a home on the square, as Soards' *Directory* found him on Valence between Prytania and Perrier that year.

This is a typical Italianate cottage of the post-Civil War period, with segmental bays, plain, squared pillars, modillions, dentils, and a raised paneled parapet. It remained in the hands of the Weidner-Buck-Henriques family for over 100 years.

LIST

4636 PERRIER, cor. Valence, bb. Cadiz, Coliseum [Faubourg West Bouligny]. A complete post-1945 remodeling of this large, one-story cottage included relocating the original entrance, which was on Valence Street, as shown on an 1896 Sanborn insurance map. Edward C. Barthelemy bought the whole square in 1880. Soards' *City Directory* of 1885 listed him as a sugar refiner residing at Valence, southeast corner Perrier.

4721 PERRIER, bet. Valence, Bordeaux, bb. Prytania [Faubourg West Bouligny]. This lovely story-and-one-half, center hall cottage with Classical detailing once faced Valence, and may once have faced Prytania in the same square. It has an attractive entrance, with a many-paneled door and a circular light transom. Distinctive spandrels form lowered arches between the six gallery columns, while metal ventilators and end chimneys punctuate the roof ridge.

Charles Pascoe, a builder, probably constructed the cottage about 1870. He or Annie L. Pascoe owned half of the square fronting on Perrier for about twenty years, Annie Pascoe finally selling to Charles Buck in 1893. The home remained in the Buck-Henriques family until 1939, when Sally Dart acquired it and had architect Richard Koch plan an extensive renovation. In 1947 Miss Dart sold to the Paul Blanchard family, who retained the cottage for thirty years.

LIST

4904-06 PERRIER, bet. Upperline, Robert, bb. Coliseum [Faubourg Avart]. Walter C. Flower, mayor of New Orleans from 1896-1900, purchased this lot in 1893 and probably built the two-story, double-galleried Eastlake home here soon afterwards. His family owned the property for twenty-four years, but actually resided at 1805 Coliseum.

LIST

4920-22, 4924-26, 4928-30, 4932-34 PERRIER, bet. Upperline, Robert, bb. Coliseum [Faubourg Avart]. In the 4900 block of Perrier is a row of four double shotguns that were once identical. Front-gabled, with deep brackets supporting the generous overhangs, the cottages reflect the modest style of the 1890s rental market. They appear on an 1896 Sanborn insurance map, and were probably built by architect Albert Toledano or his partner Ferdinand Reusch, Jr.

PITT

5219 PITT, bet. Dufossat, Valmont, bb. Atlanta [Faubourg Avart]. Striking spacial play accents this extraordinary eclectic two-and-one-half-story house. Probably built by Leonard Chattock in 1902, it has a combination of historically disparate but interesting details. Today the house is well maintained with all of its original elements.

Purchased by Louis N. Till in 1919, the house has remained in his family to the present time—nearly seventy years.

PRYTANIA

3307 PRYTANIA, bet. Toledano, Louisiana, bb. St. Charles [Faubourg Plaisance]. Originally Italianate and reflecting the style of the 1870s, this two-story frame house has been altered and embellished with 1890s-style Eastlake ornament, or "gingerbread" in common parlance. Jigsaw work, lattice brackets, spindle friezes and railings, and a pair of elaborately detailed gables, were added to the house.

Mrs. Elizabeth Delachaise Dugué sold the unimproved lot with other property on the square to

banker James Peter Freret in 1856. Twenty years later, a judgment in the case of "Herminie Freret vs. Heirs of James P. Freret" put Mrs. Livie d'Arensbourg Freret, James's widow, in possession. This judgment mentions of a two-story frame dwelling with shingled roof on the site. Mrs. Freret had died by November 1876, when her twelve surviving children sold the real estate to Anna M. Fell Baker, wife of Page Baker, editor and manager of the *Times-Democrat*. Soards' *Directory* indicates that the Bakers lived there in 1879. The Baker family made the alterations mentioned above, retaining the house through 1914, when Hugh McCloskey purchased it, along with three-quarters of the square. The house has remained in the hands of McCloskey's descendants for over seventy years.

3313 PRYTANIA, bet. Toledano, Louisiana, bb. St. Charles [Faubourg Plaisance]. This large, galleried, modified Greek Revival house was meticulously restored from a deplorable state in 1977. The gallery features fluted Corinthian columns *in antis* on each level. Segmental window heads, a cast-iron railing, and a heavy entablature with raised parapet reflect the tastes of the post-Civil War era.

With the adjoining lot, this land was part of James P. Freret's purchase from the heirs of Philippe Delachaise in 1856. Freret built a home on

this square in 1859 (see 1525 Louisiana), and subsequently built this house and the adjoining one at 3307 Prytania, probably during the late 1860s.

In 1871 the Freret heirs sold this property to James Edward Reade for $4,000. Edwards' 1872 *Directory* locates Reade on Prytania between Louisiana and Toledano.

LIST

3324-26 PRYTANIA, bet. Toledano, Louisiana, bb. Coliseum [Faubourg Plaisance]. Neglect and gallery enclosures have diminished the value of this once-good example of the Queen Anne single family home. It stands on what was originally the side yard of a large mansion on the corner of Prytania and Louisiana.

In 1878 merchant William Palfrey invested $2,000 in this lot, selling it in 1883 to John R. Fell. Fell retained it as land until 1890, when he sold to Charles S. Rice for $4,000. According to the September 1, 1891, *Daily Picayune*, a two-story frame, slated building was soon to be built at a cost of $7,000 for Charles Price [sic] in that square by builder John B. Chisolm. Soards' *Directory* located Rice there the following year.

LIST

3431 PRYTANIA, bet. Louisiana, Delachaise, bb. St. Charles [Faubourg Plaisance]. This is a Classic style shotgun of a kind that could date any time from the Civil War decade to the middle 1880s. Archival evidence strongly suggests that the cottage was built in 1885 for George E. Pitcher, who is listed in Soards' 1886 *Directory* at this location, then 463 Prytania.

The house has a "Greek keyhole" doorway and a gallery with a heavy cornice over wooden columns, standard but time-tested decorative elements.

LIST

3621 PRYTANIA, bet. Foucher, Antonine, bb. St. Charles [Faubourg Delachaise]. A deep, bracketed overhang with scalloped verge board dominates the façade of this mid-1880s shotgun. Helen Davenport Bouligny and her husband Gustave bought the property in 1884, and by 1886 were in Soards' *Directory* on Prytania, between Antonine and Foucher.

3706 PRYTANIA, cor. Amelia, bb. Peniston, Perrier [Faubourg St. Joseph]. This recently renovated cottage in the Queen Anne style aptly reflects mid-1880s architecture. Its multi-gabled, dormered roof, the projecting bay, diamond-patterned windows heavy chamfered columns, and "egg crate"

segmental spandrels with keystone motif and pendant are stylistically typical of that era.

The *Daily Picayune* of September 1886 reported that William O. Hart, a prominent lawyer, built this structure for $5,000 during that year. The home remained in the Hart family over sixty years.

LIST

3726 PRYTANIA, cor. Peniston, bb. Amelia, Perrier [Faubourg St. Joseph]. This two-story galleried home was built as a single-family residence for Benjamin and Georgine White Crump after they bought the property in 1886. Soards' 1890 *Directory* lists them at this location, where they resided for over thirty years while raising a family of six. Mr. Crump, a cotton broker, migrated to New Orleans from Pass Christian, Mississippi. His wife was the daughter of prominent merchant Maunsell White.

4013-15, 4025-27 PRYTANIA, bet. Constantinople, Marengo, bb. Pitt [Faubourg East Bouligny]. This pair of doubles illustrates the use of similar stock building parts recombined in various reversed schemes. We see their design philosophy again at 5022-24 Prytania, 3912-14 Carondelet, 1302-04 and 1310-12 Marengo, 1420-22-24-26 Marengo, 4117-19 Perrier, and 1322-24-26-28 Jefferson. All of these dwellings feature an animated gallery design while suggesting the builder's frequently repeated procedures in assembling segmental frames, scored and chamfered columns, quoins, and pierced-work friezes at various levels. As a type, the commodious house provided ample living space for an expanding population through the overall arrangement of scale, plan, and the massing of a doubled, two-story, galleried building with halls and attic spaces.

The Anna Pottharst Flaspoller family built several of these units at different times during the 1890s. 4013-15 Prytania or 4025-37 Prytania appeared in the year's construction list of the 1890 *Daily Picayune*.

LIST

4016-18, 4020 PRYTANIA, bet. Marengo, Constantinople, bb. Perrier [Faubourg East Bouligny]. This pair of Queen Anne houses, built for Mrs. B.H. Flaspoller in 1899, were once identical. Their design anticipated the arrival in New Orleans of the Colonial Revival period of American architectural history, which occurred during the first decade of the twentieth century. During that time, designers discarded the worn taste for picturesque Victorian asymmetry to seek a more balanced effect. At 4016-18, a massive triangular gable outlined with horizontal and raking cornices dominates the façade. In it is a Palladian window which, like the gable, is centrally balanced. At the upper level beneath the pediment, a gallery, now half enclosed, crosses the façade in a straight line that repeats the horizontal of the main cornice. At the lower level, a shallow portico projects exactly at midpoint.

The houses were two of several major investments on Prytania by the Bernard-Anna Pottharst Flaspoller family.

4032 PRYTANIA, cor. Marengo, bb. Perrier, Constantinople [Faubourg East Bouligny]. Dominating the downtown river corner of Prytania and Marengo is a Queen Anne mansion that is one of New Orleans' finest examples of any late nineteenth-century style. Its dominant feature within a symphony of distinctive elements is the corner turret, which crowns a double-galleried circular bay. Other period elements include a magnificent leaded-glass door, a range of textures, random massing, stock woodwork, and a complex roof of gables, dormers, tower, and patterned slates.

Bernard H. Flaspoller acquired the lot in 1868 and may have lived there in an earlier home. The present house, however, dates from 1893. The 1892 building contract states that Antoine Lagmann, builder, was to remove the existing house, outhouse, cistern, and appurtenances to a new lot created from the rear of the site on Marengo to be completed prior to March 1, 1893, at a cost of $1,800. Lagmann was then to build a two-story

frame house for Mrs. Flaspoller, to be completed prior to July 1, 1893, for $13,445. As several listings on this block indicate, Mrs. Flaspoller was a major developer in this area. In 1919 her heirs sold the family home to Jacob and Leopold Klein. Later in the twentieth century, Mrs. Marie Straub Bussey and the Frank Giarranto family were longtime owners of the mansion.

Today the once proud home has been divided into apartments, while the exterior languishes for paint and repair.

4035 PRYTANIA, cor. Marengo, bb. Constantinople, Pitt [Faubourg East Bouligny]. This story-and-one-half center hall cottage combines a number of interesting features to achieve a pleasing effect. A large central gable with ocular fitted with dropped siding first attracts the eye. Beneath its pediment is the full-width front porch, articulated with varying roof arrangements and a pierced-work, scored frieze. Chamfered box columns are so designed to separate all surfaces into small, picturesque parts.

Here again is a house built on Prytania for Mrs. B.H. Flaspoller, who had purchased the lot in 1887. Three years later the *Times-Democrat* reported the construction by A. Leake, builder, of a "two story frame slated dwelling for Mrs. B.H. Flaspoller in square bounded by Prytania, Constantinople, Marengo and Pitt" for $15,000.

The house was destined for August Flaspoller, a son, whose home then faced his mother's. This arrangement evidently lasted until 1910. During the 1920s Mrs. Alice Smith Martin purchased the house, and it remained in her family until 1964.

LIST

4300-02, 4306-08, 4310, 4316 PRYTANIA, cor. Gen. Pershing, bb. Napoleon, Perrier [Faubourg East Bouligny]. People's Homestead Association built these four originally identical single-family residences about 1889. Two have been altered, while the third, 4310, appears to be the most intact. The houses were all designed with a small porch having a mansard-type roof over the entrance. The two that have lost this feature to an enclosure have forfeited the most distinguishing aspect of their façades.

LIST

4525 PRYTANIA, bet. Jena, Cadiz, bb. Pitt [Faubourg West Bouligny]. Here is a very large Queen Anne residence set back comfortably on a spacious lot.

The *Daily Picayune* of September 1, 1893, attributed construction to Charles A. Farrot (possibly Favrot), builder, for Gerault Farrar for $8,000. Soards' 1894 *Directory* lists Gerault Farrar at 625 Prytania, the early number. In 1898 the house was sold to Marie Adele Tassin, and later was the residence of the William J. Montgomery family for many years.

4602 PRYTANIA, cor. Cadiz, bb. Valence, Perrier [Faubourg West Bouligny]. This Classic style single shotgun reflects a simple dignity. It was built before the era of fancy jigsaw work that embellished so many later shotguns. Its five box columns support a simple hipped roof overhang.

Alfred Baker purchased the property—possibly with the house—from Daniel Weidner in 1873. In 1875 Soards' *Directory* listed him as a carpenter residing on Prytania, southwest corner of Cadiz. Soards' 1878 *Directory* upgraded Baker to "builder." The Baker family retained ownership until 1896, when Andrew McDermott purchased the property. McDermott's heirs owned the house until 1923. At that time Horace Upton bought the property, and his heirs are still in possession at this writing.

4624 PRYTANIA, bet. Cadiz, Valence, bb. Perrier [Faubourg West Bouligny]. This one-and-one-half-story, five-bay, center hall frame cottage in late Classic style originally faced Valence. It was turned on its original lot and removed from the corner of Valence and Prytania to its present location during the 1930s. The cottage may date to the late 1860s. It was the wedding gift of Charles F. Buck, onetime New Orleans city attorney, to his bride, Mary Weidner, according to Buck family tradition. Ornate side dormers towards the rear of the house were probably additions to the original house.

In 1865 Mrs. Buck's parents, Mrs. and Mrs. Daniel Weidner, purchased the entire square from

J.D. Dameron. At some later date, they donated the corner lot to their daughter and her husband. The widowed Mrs. Weidner, Margaretha Fischer, was living in the home at the time of her death in 1885. By then, the Bucks had moved across the street to a new William Fitzner-designed home (see 1320 Valence). The smaller cottage that is now facing Prytania remained in the Weidner-Buck-Henriques family until 1954, when Margaret Henriques Jahncke sold it to Bamboo Realty Co.

5022-24-26-28 PRYTANIA, bet. Soniat, Robert, bb. Perrier [Faubourg Avart]. Although individually listed in the National Register of Historic Places, this building is actually prototypical of several other large galleried doubles in the Jefferson City region. Refer to 4013-15 and 4025-27 Prytania for a description of style characteristics and related structures.

The present house was one of the several late nineteenth-century neighborhood investments of Mary Louise Kennedy, wife of Charles Genella, who bought this property in 1889 at public auction. She had the subject structure built shortly thereafter.

5117 PRYTANIA, bet. Soniat, Dufossat, bb. Pitt [Faubourg Avart]. In 1893 Julius Freyhan, president of Lane Cotton Mills, bought four lots in this square and soon built a row of three similar two-story dwellings. Freyhan completed the houses

with unusual woodwork details before 1896. Since other Freyhan-built row housing exists in the area, and since Freyhan's residence was at 5223 St. Charles, we assume that the subject residences were designed as rental property, possibly for upper-level mill employees with large families.

5308 PRYTANIA, bet. Valmont, Leontine, bb. Perrier [Rickerville]. This massive two-and-one-half-story Colonial Revival house dominates the square, even though the land around it has been sold and other structures now surround it. The house was constructed at the turn of the present century for a member of the Flaspoller family, who were given to having large homes built on spacious corner lots. The property originally extended to Valmont. As late as 1909 this was the only house on the square.

Eight fluted Corinthian columns support the curving gallery at the first level. The second and third levels combine on the façade to form a giant Palladian arch. The mansion was designed to present a prominent mass on a large site. Its lateral gables, massive chimneys, and gallery curve contribute to this effect.

August Flaspoller acquired the property in 1899 and had the house completed by the end of 1900. The cost, as reported in the *Daily Picayune* September 1, 1900, was $10,750. Soards' 1901 *Directory* listed August H. Flaspoller at this location.

ROBERT

919 ROBERT, bet. Camp, Magazine, bb. Upperline [Faubourg Avart]. Although its three oversized dormers may be additions to the original, this Classic style frame cottage is witness to many of the local architectural fashions of the pre-Civil War era. Four corniced and shuttered openings, box columns supporting the entablature, cast-iron gallery railings, and an impressive entrance are hallmarks of the antebellum American cottage. The house is one of a few remaining residences of its era in Jefferson City.

The cottage originally faced Magazine. As early as 1860, Gardner's *Directory* listed Mrs. Carolina Harmon, the presumed builder, on "Magazine near Upperline, Jefferson City." Mrs. Harmon had acquired the property in 1857 from Richard Harrison. In 1866 when she sold the property to Thomas Waterman, the act of sale referred to a "one story frame dwelling raised on brick columns with attached galleries front and rear and back buildings." Ten years later, Robinson's *Atlas* showed the house facing Magazine. Some time later, however, perhaps close to the end of the nineteenth century, it was moved to Robert Street to accommodate the building of two duplex structures facing Magazine, one now demolished (see 4919-21 Magazine). All three structures show clearly on an 1896 Sanborn insurance map.

LIST

1020 ROBERT, bet. Camp, Chestnut, bb. Soniat [Faubourg Avart]. This side-gallery shotgun with a spindle frieze, pierced-work arched spandrels, and apron overhang was built sometime between 1896 and 1909. It replaced an earlier structure when a larger lot was subdivided.

LIST

1021 ROBERT, bet. Camp, Chestnut, bb. Upperline [Faubourg Avart]. Here is a good example of the late nineteenth-century bayed cottage. The projecting bay in this case substitutes for a front gallery, and only a recessed portico shelters the doorway.

Miss Josephine Gregory bought the lot in 1894 and erected the structure prior to 1896 as a private grammar school, of which she was the principal.

1029 ROBERT, bet. Camp, Chestnut, bb. Upperline [Faubourg Avart]. Shuttered and in need of repair, this large bayed cottage with center hall, projecting pediment, and bayed dormer is a prime candidate for renovation. The steep hipped roof lighted by

the dormer allows for a spacious half-story upstairs.

Anna Oser Stockton, who purchased the property in 1894 for $1,225 and sold it a year later for $5,000, was probably the first owner of the house.

1041-43 ROBERT, cor. Chestnut, bb. Camp, Upperline [Faubourg Avart]. Unusual because of its size, this double camelback has six bays with doorways at either end. Decorative cornices have central fan motifs, while deep jigsaw brackets with pendants support the apron overhang. Alternating rows of rectangular and sawtooth shingles, along with a triple window, decorate the gable. The full-width front porch is probably not in its original form.

Chalmette Homestead Association may have built the structure between 1887 and 1889, as it bought the property in 1887 for $900 and sold it two years later for $2,600. The buyer, William B. Daniel, evidently used it as rental property. City directories locate his residence around the corner on Chestnut. Mrs. Emma Elizabeth Gamard, widow of Adrien Guillemet, bought the property in 1893. Soards' 1896 *Directory* lists her residence at 1043 Robert.

1680 ROBERT, bet. Baronne, Dryades, bb. Soniat [Faubourg Avart]. Here is a little-noticed but important center hall cottage that was standing in old Faubourg Avart during the heyday of Jefferson City. The house once faced Baronne Street, set back on a generous 125 x 151 foot lot. The square was one of a dozen that Madame François Robert Avart donated in 1849 to her daughter Almaïs, wife of Martin Valmont Soniat Dufossat. About ten years later, investor Edward Buisson sold it to John M. Bateman.

As early as 1867, Gardner's city *Directory* listed Bateman's daughter Sally Ann and her husband

Robert Sanders at Bacchus (Baronne), corner Robert, Jefferson City. Mrs. Sanders and her sister, Katie L. Bateman Woods, held on to the house through the Civil War, Reconstruction, tax sales, and mortgages until 1921. Curiously, Sanborn insurance maps of 1896 and 1909 indicate that the residence was a double, perhaps because both the Sanders and the Woods lived there.

The family may have added a new gallery during the 1880s or early 1890s when the house was moved from Baronne to its present alignment facing Robert. Heavy octagonal columns, scalloped flat arches, and a spindle frieze decorate this gallery. Note that the house is well raised, with an interesting, high-pitched roof behind the gallery.

LIST

1692 ROBERT, bet. Baronne, Dryades, bb. Soniat [Faubourg Avart]. Situated on part of the property that John M. Bateman bought in 1858, this two-story house is typical of the architectural style of the late 1890s and early 1900s in New Orleans. In 1895 Alonzo Robert, chief clerk of the U.S. Engineers Office, bought an adjacent corner house, which included this site. Ten years later, Robert sold his side yard to Antonio Vienna. Since Soards' 1906 *Directory* lists Vienna's residence on Jackson Avenue, and since a Sanborn insurance map of 1909 shows 1692 Robert as a double, the subject address was likely rental property. Probably neither Robert nor Vienna ever lived there. Soards' *Directory* of 1909 lists Vienna's residence as 1698 Robert.

LIST

1726 ROBERT, bet. Dryades, Danneel, bb. Soniat [Faubourg Avart]. Here is a raised stucco bungalow dating from 1912 that combines various eclectic details. The balcony rail and arch are "Venetian Gothic," and the door Art Nouveau. According to Soards' *Directory*, Mrs. Adeline Levy Weiss lived here in 1912.

ST. CHARLES (Cours des Nayades, Nayades)

3437-39 ST. CHARLES, cor. Delachaise, bb. Louisiana, Carondelet [Faubourg Plaisance]. A central, engaged tower dominates the façade of this Queen Anne residence. In 1890 the *Daily Picayune* reported its construction by J.B. Chisholm for George W. Sentell at a cost of $5,000. Soards' *Directory* listed

Sentell at 859 St. Charles (old number) the following year.

This is one of the few nineteenth-century buildings still standing on the Avenue between Toledano and Marengo, and the only one in a three-block stretch from Louisiana Avenue to Amelia.

3442 ST. CHARLES, at Aline, Delachaise, bb. Prytania [Faubourg Delachaise]. The striking little building on the triangle of land between Aline and Delahaise generates much visual interest. It style falls into a narrow phase of early twentieth century American architecture that combines the Spanish Mission style and Art Nouveau. The building's galvanized metallic, bell-shaped roofline and curved walls reflect the latter movement, while the stucco exterior and rear parapets reflect the Mission style as practiced in California at the turn of the century. Both of these styles were very progressive in their day, the former constantly evolving and the latter nearly precedent-free.

The structure was built in 1904 as a florist shop known as Avenue Floral Company. The tapering front portion housed the office, while the hothouse section was to its rear.

3513 ST. CHARLES, cor. Delachaise, bb. Foucher, Carondelet [Faubourg Delachaise]. Well-concealed behind thick hedges, this large brick Louisiana Colonial Revival dwelling was the work of Richard

Koch of Armstrong and Koch in 1932. The house was built for Harry T. Howard, whose heirs owned it until 1987. Mr. Howard had an earlier family home on the site demolished to make way for the present building.

Louisiana Colonial was the trademark design of architect Richard Koch. The style actually echoes the era of the 1830s and 1840s in Louisiana, but was called Colonial nevertheless. The dormers with their curved muntins are quite similar to those of numerous nineteenth-century Vieux Carré cottages and town houses. Koch used this pattern to reconstruct the dormers of Oak Alley Plantation in St. James Parish.

Koch also designed the plantings for the house and planned the screening that shields it so well from the street. In the rear is a formal garden which is an important component of the setting.

LIST

3607 ST. CHARLES, cor. Foucher, bb. Amelia, Carondelet [Faubourg Delachaise]. Site of Isidore Newman house (1890), now demolished.

3711 ST. CHARLES, cor. Amelia, bb. Peniston, Carondelet [Faubourg St. Joseph]. Here is one of the earliest surviving of Jefferson City area homes on St. Charles Avenue. It is Italianate in style, and dates to the 1870s. The double gallery diminishes its scale, and is actually the most forward of a series of widening and receding planes. The design shows an ambivalent mixture of classical symmetry and offsetting bays. It anticipates the arrival to exteriors of the irregular massing that resulted from free-flowing late nineteenth-century interior floor plans.

Robinson's *Atlas* suggests that John D. Rouse built this house some time after 1871, when he purchased the entire square. By 1876 all but one large lot in the square had been developed. Robert

J. Harp purchased 3711 St. Charles in 1876, but went bankrupt a few years later. James R. Mitchell, a creditor, sold the house to Mary Nevins Kirkpatrick in 1881.

3804 ST. CHARLES, cor. Peniston, bb. Gen. Taylor, Pitt [Faubourg St. Joseph]. Architect Henry Hobson Richardson was a native Louisianian who during the 1880s popularized throughout America a variation of the heavy, Romanesque Revival style seen in this building. Richardson died before his design ideas became popular in New Orleans, as the Isidore Newman house, begun in 1890, was the first local residence to be built in the style. 3804 St. Charles, built in 1905 for Mrs. Fannie Kiefer Newman, widow of Newman's brother Charles, is a late example of Richardson's concept of heavy stone massing. It is, however, smaller and less richly ornamented than was the Isidore Newman home.

The house is of rock-faced quarry stone laid in alternating, narrow and wide bands. It is actually a stone veneer building framed in wood. The building contract cost was $30,000.

3811 ST. CHARLES, bet. Peniston, Gen. Taylor, bb. Carondelet [Faubourg St. Joseph]. Individually listed in the National Register of Historic Places, this imposing structure was built for cigar magnate Simon Hernsheim in 1883. In September of 1883 the *Daily Picayune* reported Hernsheim's new home would "equal if not surpass any residence on the street. Mr. Hernsheim will, in the course of a few weeks, leave his orders for a plan and specifications. The cost of the new building, it is believed, will not fall short of $40,000." Architect Thomas Sully, rather than Mr. Hernsheim, actually planned the design

referred to in the paper. A year after its first report, the *Daily Picayune* added that "Mr. Simon Hernsheim's new residence on St. Charles Avenue between General Taylor and Peniston streets, will be completed by January 1, and will be one of the finest dwellings in the city. It is being built by Mr. Sully. It is two storied, with an attic. The interior will be very handsome, and will be finished in hard wood."

Although this house is one of Sully's earliest extant designs and may still be attributed to him, extensive exterior changes were made after a 1915

hurricane hit New Orleans. An early photograph given the present owner by a great-granddaughter of Simon Hernsheim demonstrates these alterations.

After Hernsheim's death, Clementia Hubbard Norman, wife of John R. Norman, acquired the property in 1900. She sold it in 1914 to Hubbard Moylen Feild, whose family retained the house until 1953. During that time, it was run as a boarding house. Richard Baumbach subsequently purchased the structure and operated it as the Columns Hotel, still essentially a boarding house. The present owner, Mrs. Claire Creppel, has restored the interior and operates the Columns as a hotel.

LIST

3820 ST. CHARLES, bet. Gen. Taylor, Peniston, bb. Pitt [Faubourg St. Joseph]. PLAZA COURT Plaza Court is an early apartment complex built in 1917 at a cost of about $60,000, as reported in the *Times-Picayune* of September 2 that year. Nathan Kohlman was the architect, with G.E. and E.E. Reiman Co., builders, for the Klein brothers, owners.

3823 ST. CHARLES, cor. Gen. Taylor, bb. Peniston, Carondelet [Faubourg St. Joseph]. Built on land once part of the Simon Hernsheim property, Emlah Court was the first "co-op" to be built in New Orleans. Diboll, Owen & Goldstein designed the building in 1913, not long after a Beaux Arts design by Collins Diboll and Allison Owen won a competition for the New Orleans Public Library at Lee Circle.

Emlah Court's sophistication suggests the tastes of Eastern Seaboard style Beaux Arts buildings,

which were popular around the nation by 1913. Each floor contains a single, spacious, three-bedroom apartment. Prominent residents have been John Legier, Jr., Meyer Lemann, Herman Aron, Isidore Hechinger, and Martha G. Robinson.

3900 ST. CHARLES, cor. Gen. Taylor, bb. Constantinople, Pitt [Faubourg East Bouligny]. Rayne Memorial Methodist Church, begun in 1875 by James Cox for a Methodist Episcopal congregation, was the design of German-born architect Charles Lewis Hillger. Hillger frequently combined Gothic and Romanesque styles in designing local Protestant churches after the Civil War. Rayne Memorial, however, is purely Gothic Revival, from the tower to the pointed windows.

Hillger's designs for German congregations established his reputation as a leading church architect. After he designed Zion Evangelical Church at

1924 St. Charles Avenue in 1871 and Jackson Avenue German Protestant Church in 1872, he received contracts from several non-German congregations. Hillger had also designed buildings such as St. Vincent's Seminary (on Napoleon) and St. Joseph's Asylum (at Laurel and Josephine) for Catholic congregations while in partnership with William Drews.

Robert Walker Rayne purchased the site of Rayne Memorial in 1873 and gave it to the congregation of St. Charles Avenue Methodist Episcopal Church South in 1875. He then made a substantial contribution to the nearly $17,000 cost of constructing the church in 1875 to memorialize his son William, who had been killed in the Civil War.

3924 ST. CHARLES, bet. Gen. Taylor, Constantinople, bb. Pitt [Faubourg East Bouligny]. Originally built in the Colonial Revival style, this house has a Queen Anne style element—the tower—added at a later date. Generally, the taste for Colonial Revival followed a decline in rather than a rekindling of interest in the Queen Anne style. That pattern is repeated in this building.

The earliest photograph (above) shows the building as it appeared in 1892 when first built—less busy and picturesque than it later became, but still

having an asymmetrically placed porch and multiple projections. An intermediate photograph (above) reveals a tower addition, which has created a decided Queen Anne effect. The Georgian "pineapple" window is lost to the tower, the porch pro-

jection eliminated, and a central Palladian window is less prominent in the design. Today's illustration (above) documents a few slighter changes—loss of the "goose neck" balcony railing and elongated piers upstairs; wood-buttressed stairs changed to brick; and the loss of balcony railings over the bays. Still there is a fine and well-preserved Colonial-Queen Anne mixture that accurately reflects the tastes of its time, if in reverse of the usual chronological evolution.

The house was built for George F. Lapeyre, a prominent local attorney, by Louis A. Ganter, architect and builder. Hinderer's Iron Works made the fence, and Sumner Building and Supply furnished the mantels, grates, terra cotta, and white glass. Lapeyre had the tower added about 1900. His family continued to own the home until 1983.

3926 ST. CHARLES, bet. Gen. Taylor, Constantinople, bb. Pitt [Faubourg East Bouligny]. This 1887 Queen Anne structure is known as the Grant-Black House for its builder, William Grant of New York, and for his daughter Virginia, Mrs. Alexander Black. It is individually listed in the National Register of His-

toric Places. Grant was a lawyer and the law partner of St. Charles Avenue resident John Rouse from 1876 until 1919.

According to the *Times-Democrat* of September 5, 1887, architects Muir and Fromherz of New Orleans designed the building. They achieved a picturesque effect through the use of contrasting textures of shingles and weatherboards combined with broken rhythms in the colonnettes. Even today, contrasting paint colors could enhance the patterns of light and shadow that animate the façade, diminishing the impression of mass.

4010 ST. CHARLES, bet. Marengo, Constantinople, bb. Pitt [Faubourg East Bouligny]. This is one of quite a few houses that New Orleans architect Thomas Sully designed and used as his own residence. It was originally built of unpainted brick at the first level and of natural-finish shingling above. The *Daily Picayune* of September 1, 1886, reported that Sully's two-story, frame building on St. Charles would cost $4,000 to construct.

In 1895 Sully and his wife Mary Eugenia Rocchi were separated in property, and she received the house. She sold it in 1907 to Mr. and Mrs. Aron

Peiser, whose daughter Stella Peiser Sherick received it in 1930.

The early photograph illustrates the house when Sully owned it and the flared brick columns supported a front porch with a projecting side deck. The porch railing, shutters, and a more verdant garden supplied a needed softening to the façade. In comparison to Sully's other residences, this house is a more modest, but delightfully sophisticated creation.

4020 ST. CHARLES, bet. Marengo, Constantinople, bb. Pitt [Faubourg East Bouligny]. 4020 St. Charles is a two-story Queen Anne with elaborate applied jigsaw work on the gable and frieze. It was probably built in 1887, but its present appearance belies that date. The Queen Anne style colored glass windows, stylized box columns, jigsaw work, and brackets belong to a slightly later era than the 1880s, and were probably added after construction.

The house was built for Charles W. Mackie, who purchased the bare lot in 1886. A presumed remodeling of the 1890s, perhaps by the Simon Haspel family (1894-1899) or by subsequent owner Samuel Lowenberg (1899-1908), seems to have effected the changes to Mackie's original house. Sanborn insurance maps of 1893 and 1896 tell us that the front gallery originally had a projection on the right side, part of a scheme to emphasize the slightly recessed doorway. In addition, the gallery did not return down the side as it does today, although a porch wrapped the downtown side bay. The present gallery, which has lost its railing at the first level, was in place by 1909. The other changes were no doubt also completed by that date.

4026 ST. CHARLES, bet. Marengo, Constantinople, bet. Pitt [Faubourg East Bouligny]. Here is a mid-1880s residence that has undergone changes so drastic as to encourage one to doubt that it is the same house depicted in the early C. Milo Williams photograph, which documents the original design. The entire front gallery, with all of its columns and a brand new architectural style, was added twenty years after construction. A two-story Queen Anne tower, with conical roof and curved gallery, was completely removed. These were not unmanageable changes, but is hard to believe the roof was actually reframed to provide for a fashionable pedimented front gable. The front was also widened

with an entire room which now projects to the side where there was once a recess. This is one of several instances wherein we have observed a clear disillusionment with the Queen Anne style within a decade or two of its origin.

Mrs. Blanche Paul Lorenzen, widow of William Lorenzen, was evidently the first owner. She purchased the land in 1881 and was listed in Soards' 1885 *Directory* at 1006 St. Charles, the old number

here. In 1891 her estate sold the house to Dr. Otto Joachim, a founder of the Eye, Ear, Nose and Throat Hospital. Dr. Joachim employed architects Favrot and Livaudais to make the changes that rendered a turreted house into a galleried one. In 1904 he sold to Emma Dechamps Mallard, widow of Prudent Mallard; her heirs sold in 1913 to brewer Valentine Merz. The Merz family lived at this prominent address until 1935.

4036 ST. CHARLES, cor. Marengo, bb. Constantinople, Pitt [Faubourg East Bouligny]. Few important structural changes have been made to this large frame residence, but gallery screening on both levels diminishes the façade's Colonial Revival appeal. The screening obscures the free-standing nature of the gallery and detracts from the intended prominence of the central pediment.

The house was built for $12,500 in 1902 for the

widow Maline Godchaux Lehmann and her seven children, according to the *New Orleans States*. Emile Weil, who was fluent in many architectural styles of the early twentieth century, designed this house along with the two immediately to its rear

facing Marengo, all in Colonial Revival style. The latter were the homes of Gus Mayer and Isidore Kohlmeyer.

In 1913 Mrs. Nettie Lehmann, wife of Abraham Frank, and her co-heirs sold the St. Charles house to Charles Godchaux. Later the Eduardo Mendez and Emile Hymel families owned the house for a number of years.

4114 ST. CHARLES, bet. Marengo, Milan, bb. Pitt [Faubourg East Bouligny]. Sully and Toledano were architects for this grand Queen Anne house, which shows some influence of the American Shingle Style without really conforming to it. Shingles do clad the house, but it retains the picturesque massing of the Queen Anne. It lacks the simple controlling roofline which characterizes the true Shingle Style building as popularized by architects such as McKim, Mead, and White in Eastern Seaboard houses.

Although the home has lost a widow's walk, a *porte-cochere*, and a few decorative ridge tiles, its exterior is generally true to the original form. The blue and white tile course relates to other Sully and Toledano homes in this block, including the Mrs. John P. Richardson and Henry Abraham homes (now demolished) formerly at 4109 and

4132 St. Charles. The building is also strikingly similar to the John S. Wallis home in Pass Christian, Mississippi, also designed by Sully and Toledano. The carriage house (now 4115 Pitt Street) serves as a private residence.

John S. Wallis, president of the Louisiana Sugar Refining Company, commissioned the house for his daughter, Mrs. L.E. Griffin, in 1885. Four years later it was finished. In 1896 Mrs. Griffin sold it to Edgar H. Bright, whose succession sold it in 1923.

ornament the windows. The site arrangement around a garden is designed as a departure from the more monolithic high-rise block apartment building type.

While one regrets the Avenue's loss of a fine single-family mansion to an apartment complex, this example underscores the difficult economics of maintaining oversized residences. Many of the Queen Annes that do remain on the Avenue have been converted to multi-family use. The phenomenon of increasing density on St. Charles is, in any case, a recurring one. At the turn of the twentieth century, many mansions occupied entire squares facing St. Charles, and a number of the large homes that stand today replaced them between 1900 and 1910.

LIST

4206 ST. CHARLES, bet. Milan, Gen. Pershing, bb. Pitt [Faubourg East Bouligny]. This altered, relatively simple Queen Anne house was built for Brown Ayers in 1888. Ayers sold it to Rosa Marks Lowenberg in 1911, and the house remained in the Lowenberg-Finegold family until 1960. Reconstruction of the front porch would restore the integrity of this building.

4125 ST. CHARLES, bet. Marengo, Milan, bb. Carondelet [Faubourg East Bouligny]. Alterations and front yard clutter seriously detract from the once proud appearance of this 1891 Sully-designed Queen Anne house. The early photograph shows the building before the era of its decline. It hardly needs noting that the front-yard shed evolved later, and that enclosures obscure the once-lovely, comfortable front gallery. On the left is an awkwardly added side room. Baluster railings and the fine old iron fence are missing. Unattractive awnings cover the windows.

L.C. LeCorgne was the builder for Henry and Julius Picard. The construction cost was $12,000, as noted in the *Daily Picayune* of September 1, 1891. The second owner was Moise Waldhorn, whose family owned the house from 1902 to 1919.

This is an example of disregard for the integrity of St. Charles Avenue and for a once fine home.

Historic districting can prevent such inappropriate alterations, but not after the fact. The New Orleans Historic District Landmarks Commission unfortunately also lacks jurisdiction over front yard clutter.

4132 ST. CHARLES, cor. Milan, bb. Marengo, Pitt [Faubourg East Bouligny]. A 1930s vintage "garden apartment" complex now occupies the corner of St. Charles and Marengo where the 1890 Henry Abraham mansion once stood. The early house was a massive, three-story, masonry Queen Anne. Sully and Toledano designed it in 1890, and L.C. LeCorgne built it for $19,500.

The present apartment building shows some influence of European Modernism. The corner windows indicate an interior framework that renders the exterior a "skin." A few scant Art Deco details

4217 ST. CHARLES, bet. Milan, Gen. Pershing, bb. Carondelet [Faubourg East Bouligny]. Although no longer a single-family dwelling, this ornate Queen Anne has survived the years amazingly intact. As the early photograph demonstrates, the blank, siding-covered wall to the left of the stairs, the cantilevered upstairs side projection, and the enclosed porch bay were there in 1900 just as they are

now. The primary change has been the porch, now open, but once screened.

The house was built for Abraham Ermann shortly after he purchased the property in 1890. Soards' 1891 *Directory* lists him as a commission merchant residing at 1039 St. Charles, corresponding to the current number.

4238 ST. CHARLES, cor. Gen. Pershing, bb. Pitt, Milan [Faubourg East Bouligny]. Emile Weil was the architect for the "new" Touro Synagogue when it was constructed in 1908 at a cost of $100,000. Weil won a design competition for the synagogue in 1907. That year, *Architectural Art and Its Allies* published his drawings, along with those of his competitors. Weil chose a Byzantine style for the structure,

using brick and polychromatic terra-cotta throughout, even on the dome.

An addition on Gen. Pershing has an unusual Moorish entranceway with three arches inside of a larger arch. This addition repeats the ornament of the main synagogue.

The Touro Synagogue congregation was formed from an amalgam of two earlier groups— Shangarei Chesed (Gates of Mercy), founded by German-Jewish settlers in 1828, and Nefutzot Yehuda (Dispersed of Judah), a Spanish-Portuguese congregation that was organized a decade later. When the two congregations formally

NEW TOURO SYNAGOG—EMILE WEIL, ARCHITECT.

merged in 1881, they adopted the present name for Judah Touro, the famous philanthropist and community leader, who had been generous in his support of both early synagogues.

At the present writing, a chapel addition designed by local architects Lyons & Hudson is on the drawing board. The building, designed as a "miniature jewel-box" reflection of the larger structure, will occupy two lots on St. Charles adjacent to the synagogue. The congregation has demolished a once-fine turn of the century residence and a not-so-fine 1950s-era apartment building to make way for the addition.

4417 ST. CHARLES, bet. Napoleon, Jena, bb. Carondelet [Faubourg West Bouligny]. Sully, Burton and Stone designed this Renaissance Revival house for Alfred Hiller in 1896. Quarried stone covers the entire exterior. A belt course separates the rusticated stones of the first level from the smooth stones of the second. The front gallery, which has lost a railing, retains Ionic columns. Large carved

stone modillions support the roof overhang. At this writing, the house has undergone a recent renovation, but shed dormers across the attic level and on the side continue to disfigure the third story.

Alfred Hiller acquired the land in 1895 and built the structure for $16,000, as reported in the *Daily Picayune* of September 1, 1896.

LIST

4428-32, 4436 ST. CHARLES, bet. Napoleon, Jena, bb. Pitt [Faubourg West Bouligny]. Here is an identical pair of turn of the century residences, perhaps the two mentioned in a *Daily Picayune* article of 1900 as being constructed from designs by architect Samuel G. De l'Isle. The houses replaced a story-and-one-half galleried American town house. The heirs of David C. McCan partitioned ownership of the property in 1903.

4433 ST. CHARLES, bet. Napoleon, Jena, bb. Carondelet [Faubourg West Bouligny]. Emile Weil was the architect for this half-timbered and gabled residence in "English Suburban" style, now known as Tudor Revival. The house was built for Jacob K. Newman in 1909 at a cost of about $20,000. Pressed brick, half-timbering, and stucco in the gables pro-

vide contrasting textures on the exterior. Multiple planes in the dormers and gables break up the line of the roof. An distinctive belt coursing begins with the window sills and continues around the uptown side.

The front portico has been slightly, but quite noticeably, altered by enclosure of the space between the large brick piers. As the early photograph shows, this detail was designed to accommodate a large planter.

4521 ST. CHARLES, bb. Jena, Cadiz, Carondelet [Faubourg West Bouligny]. This house of the Academy of the Sacred Heart is known as The Rosary. It was founded in 1887 by the Society of the Sacred Heart, an international Catholic teaching order established in France in 1800 by Madeleine Sophie Barat, who was canonized in 1926.

The Rosary's first home on St. Charles was a villa-style, galleried, house built in 1847 by John Calhoun, a real estate auctioneer, speculator, and pol-

itician. In 1851 the two-square estate became the final home of Samuel J. Peters, New Orleans businessman par excellence, who died there in 1855. Peters co-developed the 2nd Municipality of New Orleans, now the Central Business District, and was instrumental in founding the New Orleans Public School and Public Library systems, along with the first St. Charles Hotel. When Peters moved to Jefferson City with his family in 1851, they added two buildings flanking Calhoun's central structure. The present fountain was in place at that time.

After Peters' death, his son-in-law Jules Blanc offered the estate at auction. Three owners later, the Society purchased the complex from St. Charles Hotel owner Robert E. Rivers in 1887.

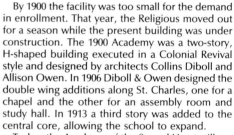

4534 ST. CHARLES, cor. Cadiz, bb. Jena, Pitt [Faubourg West Bouligny]. New Orleans architect Frank P. Gravely designed this ashlar mansion in 1906 for William Mason Smith, president of the New Orleans Cotton Exchange. The building's design seeks to express both the wealth of the family that commissioned it, and the stability of the society to which they belonged. Its architecture seems to share the monumentality of Henry Hobson Richardson's Romanesque Revival, because of the Byzantine leafwork capitals and hewn-stone construction. The latter is, nevertheless, veneer over a wooden frame, and laid in alternate courses of

By 1900 the facility was too small for the demand in enrollment. That year, the Religious moved out for a season while the present building was under construction. The 1900 Academy was a two-story, H-shaped building executed in a Colonial Revival style and designed by architects Collins Diboll and Allison Owen. In 1906 Diboll & Owen designed the double wing additions along St. Charles, one for a chapel and the other for an assembly room and study hall. In 1913 a third story was added to the central core, allowing the school to expand.

Today, the Academy of the Sacred Heart still occupies the two full squares from St. Charles back to Baronne, and has added three buildings on the rear square.

rusticated and smooth stone facing, unlike the pattern of Richardsonian houses. Richardson's influence was evident in the St. Charles Avenue homes of Isidore and Charles Newman, Harris Hyman, and William Perry Brown. The present house lacks their French Gothic dormers, Syrian arches, and steep vertical gables, all hallmarks of the Richardsonian style. This house more aptly relates to the Mediterranean style because of its expansive tile roof and deep overhang.

William Mason Smith purchased the 75-foot-wide lot on which the house sits from Isaac and

Samuel Delgado in 1901. In 1923 he purchased from C.D. Rodick an adjacent lot where S.D. Moody's Italianate town house once stood alone on the block. This addition widened the Smith property to the generous 150 by 200-foot dimensions that it has today. Mr. Smith and his wife, prominent patrons of the arts in New Orleans, both died in 1936. Their heirs retained the property until 1948, when they sold it to Harry T. Howard, Jr. The Howard family resided there until its sale in 1987.

4600 ST. CHARLES, cor. Cadiz, bb. Valence, Pitt [Faubourg West Bouligny]. The congregation of St. George's Church, organized in 1874, used as its first church a building at St. Charles and Valence. The present Gothic Revival building was erected in 1899, and the first service held on February 4, 1900.

The muscular, somewhat ungainly tower block and gabled sanctuary wall are set a little too close to the street. Their mass, however, provides the streetscape a needed balance to the bulk of the apartment house next door, which bullishly overpowers its lot.

A parent congregation to St. George's called Emmanuel Episcopal was organized in 1859. Another congregation, St. Mark's Episcopal, was founded in 1871 and met in a building at the uptown-river corner of St. Charles and Valence. In 1874 Emmanuel and St. Mark's, both closely related and both deeply in debt, merged. The combined congregation, now known as St. George's Episcopal, used the former St. Mark's building at Valence and St. Charles for a time and later moved it to Napoleon and Pitt, next to the former firehouse. In 1879 St. George's purchased property at St. Charles and Cadiz and moved the frame structure to its third location. In 1883 a fire badly damaged it, but the congregation, nevertheless, had it repaired and moved it to its final location at Cadiz and Pitt in 1892. It functioned as the main church building until 1899, when it was converted into an auxiliary to the present church.

4605 ST. CHARLES, cor. Cadiz, bb. Valence, Carondelet [Faubourg West Bouligny]. Here is a town house that features a double-level gallery abutting a semi-hexagonal bay. It is one of the oldest houses along this stretch of the Avenue, dating from the 1870s. Maria Tibbetts, widow of George Ruleff, purchased the land in 1869. Robinson's *Atlas*, compiled about 1875, indicates that the house was standing by the mid-1870s. Mrs. Ruleff owned it until 1877, when she sold to John T. Randolph. Soards' 1879 *Directory* locates Randolph on St.

Charles, northwest corner of Cadiz. Later owners included the Lagarde and O'Sullivan families, and Dr. Saint Mark Fortier.

Although a side addition and enclosures have widened the façade, the spindly, paired box columns and brackets authentically reflect the style of their period. Segmentally-arched window heads are also a hallmark of the 1870s decade. The doorway has an elaborate elliptical arch with transom and sidelights.

4613 ST. CHARLES, bet. Cadiz, Valence, bb. Carondelet [Faubourg West Bouligny]. "The handsome raised cottage of Mr. E. Eisenhauer on St. Charles Avenue, has been erected during the year, Diettel and Son being the architects," reported the September 1, 1884, *Daily Picayune*. Edward Eisenhauer had purchased land on this block in 1883. The house remained in his family until 1917.

A Sanborn insurance map of 1896 reveals that the house was originally a galleried shotgun with an uptown-side bay, about four rooms deep and having three exterior dependencies, including a hothouse. By 1909 the Eisenhauers had added a stable and henhouse, connected to a story-and-one-half service building in the rear. Various owners eventually incorporated the dependencies, until the floor plan became quite deep.

The Neo-Grec façade has segmented arches with raised ornaments applied to the box columns. The pediment covers only two of the three gallery bays.

In 1917 The Eisenhauer family sold the house to Peter Copland. Subsequently, the Morris Sherman, James Henriques, and Bernard Mason families owned it. The Jack Scheinuks have owned the house since 1970.

4621 ST. CHARLES, bet. Valence, Cadiz, bb. Carondelet [Faubourg West Bouligny]. Here is another example of a St. Charles Avenue home moved from its original location. This one, unlike several others, remained on the Avenue. It originally stood on the corner of St. Charles and Valence, where its neighbor at 4631 St. Charles now stands.

In 1896 Christian L. Keppler, a druggist, purchased the subject house with its generous yard of five lots. Soon afterward, he built the neighboring home for himself and moved this one fifty-five feet towards downtown.

An earlier cottage and stables stood on the property as early as 1860, when John Keelty put the five lots up for auction. Keelty had purchased the bare ground at St. Charles and Valence in 1858, and evidently built a home there soon afterwards. During the Civil War he may have reacquired the property, but it ended up by 1864 in a sheriff's sale. At that time James Madison Wells, one of several "carpetbagger" politicians who moved in on Jefferson City's St. Charles Avenue values with post-war gains, purchased it. In 1867 Wells sold the house to Felix and Eulalie Charleville Voisin, and the Voisins settled there until 1885. That year, the Voisin estate sold the property to Joseph E. Leon Joubert de Villamarest in a transaction that described a two-story frame residence. Thus the present house had replaced the earlier cottage by the mid-1880s.

The present gallery design, with its round arches, spindle frieze, bosses, and spandrel brackets, was probably added during the nineties when the house was moved.

In addition to Voisin and Keppler, other pre-World War I owners have been Benjamin O.L. Rayne, Richard Jones, Henry F. Dart, Gladys Keppler Hereford, Samuel J. Hart, and Stella Carroll Nichols.

4630 ST. CHARLES, cor. Valence, bb. Cadiz, Pitt [Faubourg West Bouligny]. An early photograph of this rock-faced, ashlar house with its Renaissance porch shows that few changes have been made to the original Emile Weil design of 1906. Leonard Krower, a Canal Street jeweler, purchased the land in 1904 from Jane E. Oothout and retained the property until his death in 1914. Krower's heirs kept the house until 1929, when they sold to Thomas C. Anderson, the notorious saloon keeper and self-proclaimed mayor of Storyville. Anderson died in 1933, after which his widow, Gertrude Hoffmire Anderson, retained ownership until 1955, when she sold to the Consul General of Belgium, who retained the house until 1970.

4631 ST. CHARLES, cor. Valence, bb. Carondelet, Cadiz [Faubourg West Bouligny]. This elegant Colonial Revival residence is another example of the work of architect Frank P. Gravely. Gravely used the curved porch, corner pilasters with applied cutouts, and two-story gallery on this and other designs for 22 Audubon Place, 2006 Milan, and 1524 Seventh Street. The present house was built for druggist Christian L. Keppler in 1896. The widow's walk has been removed, and the interior has been converted into a double. The exterior has been well maintained.

The early photograph illustrates the structure when it was fairly new and young fan palms dotted the yard. Rush-bottomed rockers and a ceiling fan on the porch bay evoke the unhurried lifestyle of the period. Today a pair of stately oaks shades the garden.

Seven years after its completion, Keppler sold the house to Simon Hirsch, president of J.C. Morris, Ltd. The Hirsch family lived there until 1924. The subsequent owner, Charles Ziegler, leased the house to the Japanese Consulate from 1938 to 1941. At that time a room was added on the downtown side. This part of the façade was originally recessed and had a large Palladian window. In 1947 the Spanish Consulate leased the building. The present owners, Dr. and Mrs. John Ernst III, purchased the house in 1972.

The Colonial Revival style began to gain favor in the early 1870s, and was given momentum by the Centennial Exhibition in Philadelphia in 1876. At first the style was related to the Queen Anne, being very picturesque, but by the twentieth century it had begun to use a scholarly approach, and featured symmetrical massings. 4631 St. Charles obviously reflects the early stages of the style.

4706 ST. CHARLES, cor. Valence, bb. Bordeaux, Pitt [Faubourg West Bouligny]. Incredibly, the house at the uptown-river corner of St. Charles and Valence originally appeared as shown in the early photograph. This is one of quite a few Avenue homes whose owners have responded to the urge to completely obliterate an earlier style by a massive "updating." When built in 1887 it was the residence of Mrs. Cornelia B. Neville Graham and her daughter, Mrs. Gracie M. Graham, wife of Edward Yorke Ames. Mrs. Graham had purchased the vacant lot left by the removal of St. Mark's Episcopal Church (later St. George's) in 1874. A *Times-Democrat* notice of 1887 pinpoints the construction date of the Graham-Ames house.

Louis H. Lambert was architect for the original Queen Anne house with its tower, arched gal-

lery, tall gables, and romantic oriel (at right in the photograph). The latter was an engaged, turreted bay where a family might arrange a comfortable reading nook or place the *de rigeur* harp. The practiced eye can easily see that the present exterior smothers an older house.

Mrs. Graham and the Ameses evidently lived in the house only two years, from 1887 to 1889 when the mother died. The daughter then sold to Edward Feibleman, whose family retained the home until 1920. Following an intervening owner, Samuel Gainsburgh bought the house, and in 1922 mortgaged it for $25,000 to Security Building and Loan. Perhaps at that time he made the "Spanish" modifications.

4717 ST. CHARLES, cor. Valence, bb. Carondelet, Bordeaux [Faubourg West Bouligny]. The *Daily States* of August 31, 1904 praised this Richardsonian Romanesque mansion as "by far the most elegant and expensive among the new residences" of New Orleans. It was built for "the bull cotton king, W.P. Brown," as the newspaper called him. The *States* went on to say

> This splendid structure, which was designed by Favrot and Livaudais, is entirely of stone and brick, two and a half stories in Romanesque style of architecture. It is to be heated throughout with hot air, each bedroom is to have an individual bath, the lighting is to be both electric and gas and electric call signal service is to be installed throughout. When completed it will be one of the finest most thoroughly modern residences in the city and will cost upwards of $30,000. The residence, it is declared by many who know, will be as near in approach to a palace in so far as arrangement, construction and finish of building are concerned in the United States.

The William Perry Brown family retained the home until Mrs. Will Gibbons sold it in 1979 for $500,000. The subsequent owners completely renovated the house and had the large murals restored.

4718 ST. CHARLES, bet. Valence, Bordeaux, bb. Pitt [Faubourg West Bouligny]. Here is another St. Charles Avenue home that has gone through a remarkable metamorphosis. It was standing as early as 1869 when John F.H. Grace, flour dealer, lived there. Columbus Allen, owner of Brook Rice Mill, followed Grace at this location in 1871. In 1880 Columbus H. Allen, et al. sold the property to Samuel Brook, perhaps a relative; Brook resold to Allen the following year. In 1885 Allen sold the house to William N. Grunewald, whose family remained there until 1919.

During the Grunewald era the house received a

"Queen Anne" updating with new features including a tower with pyramidal roof and a large central gable (at center in the early 4706 St. Charles photograph). Later in its history, the house underwent yet another striking change at a time when people began to feel an outright revulsion for the busyness and picturesque irregularity of Queen Anne architecture. Today one hesitates to assign the house a particular stylistic designation; however, its raised basement, story-and-one-half right side, and two-story left side are original.

4730 ST. CHARLES, cor. Bordeaux, bb. Valence, Pitt [Faubourg West Bouligny]. In the segment of St. Charles Avenue between Cadiz and Robert is a cluster of Italianate houses that lend a distinct flavor to the stretch. Frame construction, asymmetrical massing, segmental openings, quoins, and heavy modillions characterize their style. The house at 4730 St. Charles has an elaborate front door with chamfered pilasters and a flattened archway. The carriage house was relocated about thirty years ago. The home essentially retains its original Italianate appeal.

C. Frentz, builder, constructed the house at a cost of $6,000 in 1884 for Mrs. Alfred D. DePass. Daniel DePass, cashier (treasurer) at Schmidt & Ziegler, wholesale grocers and importers of wines and liquors, actually owned the land from 1882 until 1898. At that time he sold to Valentine Merz, a prominent brewer who had founded Merz's Steam Brewery during the mid-nineteenth century. Merz later became president of the New Orleans Brewing Co., a holding company for several smaller breweries. The home remained in the Merz family until 1953 when Dr. Harrison Wynne bought it. The shifting of the carriage house axis occurred soon thereafter.

This square has had an interesting sequence of owners. Prudent Mallard, the well-known cabinetmaker, owned the whole square right after the Civil War. Ownership turned over frequently during the next few years, suggesting quite a bit of speculation. Reconstruction figures Michael Hahn, Louisiana governor, and Henry Clay Dibble, infamous city judge, acquired ownership during the depths of Reconstruction in the early 1870s.

4801 ST. CHARLES, cor. Bordeaux, bb. Upperline, Carondelet [Faubourg West Bouligny]. Individually listed in the National Register of Historic Places, this is one of the few surviving Second Empire style houses on the Avenue. Ironically, it was not built

as a Second Empire house, but was originally a double-galleried, late Greek Revival, set well back from the street.

Both the house and the property have had a long, full history. Laurent Millaudon, co-developer of Bouligny, sold the entire square to Daniel C. Aldrich, a merchant in western produce, in 1866. Four months later, Aldrich sold half of the square to Thomas Brown Wright. The following month, Aldrich's wife Susan acquired the property from Wright, with the notation that she herself had made improvements.

In 1867 Gardner's *Directory* located D.C. Aldrich at the St. Charles-Bordeaux corner. Toward the end of 1869 Susan Aldrich sold the property to Silas Daily and Joseph J. Alston, who purchased it "for speculation" in Silas Daily's name. A. Wallace Hunter bought from the speculators six months later and retained the property for nearly two years, selling it to George Walker, who was forced to relinquish it

back to Hunter a month later. In 1874 the Widows and Orphans General Relief Association, Independent Order of Odd Fellows of the State of Louisiana, acquired the property and held it for eleven years.

Joseph Hernandez, president of both the Jefferson City Gas Light Co. and the New Orleans & Carrollton Rail Road Co., purchased the house in 1885. According to city surveyor records, he received a permit in May of that year for J.J. Kelly to do a frame slate addition for $3,000. At this time Hernandez added the stair tower and third story, defined on the exterior by the slate mansard roof. After his death, Hernandez's heirs sold in 1895 to Mary Louise Genella, whose heirs sold eight years later to Walter Catesby Jones and William Edward Walls.

In 1903 William Walls opened Rugby Academy, a private school for boys, in the enlarged house. Rugby, in its day, attracted some of the city's most prominent families as patrons, but in time both the school and the building declined. A new brick addition in the front yard was good for the school, but spoiled the street scene, making Rugby less attractive. The school closed in the mid-1970s because of dwindling enrollment. At that time, the main house was threatened with demolition. In 1977 architect Lee Connell and partners devised a plan to save and renovate the house by demolishing the brick addition, moving the house forward, and building three residences facing Bordeaux in the rear.

The flamboyant Second Empire details are among the most successful examples of the style in New Orleans. The four-story stair tower reinterprets a vocabulary of keystone motifs and pilasters under a steep dormered roof. The structure's third floor, defined by the concave slate mansard, added a great deal of space to the home. Today, after a turbulent century and a quarter, this landmark is one of the Avenue's proudest.

1903 and has remained the McFetridge home ever since. The early photograph could guide a restoration of 4814. The spindle friezes and stilted arches are original. The owner could easily remove the screened porch and its framing, especially the horizontal siding, and rebuild the balustrade and wooden stairs. The cast-iron fence with its heavy gateposts, however, would be more difficult to replace today. 4812 has lost a great deal more than its former twin. Most of the fenestration is intact, but the gallery has been significantly altered.

4812, 4814 ST. CHARLES, bet. Bordeaux, Upperline, bb. Pitt [Faubourg West Bouligny]. These two, originally identical, two-story frame dwellings were built by Mary Louise Kennedy Genella shortly after she acquired the property in 1885. Both structures have been drastically altered, but an old photograph illustrates their original appearance. Mrs. Genella, "separate in property" from her husband Charles, was an energetic lady who enhanced her income by dealing in real estate ranging from large two-story family dwellings to modest frame cottages and row houses (see Genella's Row, 4841-43 and 4845-47 Coliseum).

4812 and 4814 St. Charles were originally rental property, but 4812 was sold to John McFetridge in

4822, 4828, 4834 ST. CHARLES, bet. Bordeaux, Upperline, bb. Pitt [Faubourg West Bouligny]. Notarial evidence suggests that Burgess Bennett built three identical structures at this location during the 1870s. Of the three visible on Robinson's *Atlas*, 4828, the middle house, no longer stands, as Victor Latour, an owner-builder, replaced it in 1917. 4834 still stands, although it was extensively remodeled after 1910 when Mrs. Henry Hausmann bought it from Burgess Bennett's daughter, Fannie Bennett Harris.

4822 remains as the most representative of the three original buildings, although its bracketed and arched motifs seem somewhat incompatible with the Italianate character of the façade. They could have been added by Capt. and Mrs. Louis Delahoussaye, who purchased the property in 1887, or they may possibly be original.

4827, 4831-33 ST. CHARLES, bet. Bordeaux, Upperline, bb. Carondelet [Faubourg West Bouligny]. Originally identical, and hidden behind trees and shrubbery, one of these two structures has been severely altered. The *Daily Picayune* of September 1, 1884, noted "Mr. Sully has designs for two Queen Anne cottages corner of St. Charles Avenue and Upperline streets to be built for Mrs. Brownlee and Col. J.W. Coleman, respectively at a cost of $5,000." A year later the same paper reported:

> Mr. J. Walker Coleman, of the Illinois Central Railroad, having concluded to have a home built that should combine elegance with comfort, selected Mr. H. Wellman to do the work, he having agreed to do it for $8,000. The site of the new building, which was completed last fall, is on St. Charles Avenue, between Upperline and Bordeaux streets. It is a two-story frame dwelling and is complete in all its appointments. Adjoining Mr. Coleman's house Mrs. Isabelle Brownly built a house similar in every respect, which was also completed by Mr. Wellman, the contract price being the same as the other, $8,000.

These two homes represent the beginning of Thomas Sully's New Orleans career. He arrived here in 1882 at the age of twenty-seven, after working in New York and in Austin, Texas. Compared to his later, grander mansions on St. Charles, the houses are cautious, tentative, and use a combination of stock elements. Locally they would be among the earliest references to the Queen Anne style.

4900 ST. CHARLES, cor. Upperline, bb. Robert, Pitt [Faubourg Avart]. CASA GRANDE APARTMENTS. An article in the *Daily States* August 31, 1908, describes "A splendid apartment house . . . designed by MacKenzie and Biggs . . . the property of A. Aschaffenburg. It is in Spanish renaissance . . . and is the only building of its kind in the United States which is built entirely of reinforced concrete. . . . It contains twenty-six apartments lighted by both

gas and electricity and heated by steam. . . . When completed this distinctive marker of the advancement of New Orleans will have cost upward of $100,000."

Unfortunately, the reinforced concrete building lost many of its original details during a mid-1930s renovation. These lost elements reflected not only the Spanish Renaissance, but the Viennese Art Nouveau (Secessionist) which MacKenzie advocated. The apartment house was renovated and converted to condominiums in 1985.

4901, 4905 ST. CHARLES, cor. Upperline, bet. Robert, Carondelet [Faubourg Avart]. Situated on the gentle curve of the Avenue and shaded by large magnolia trees, this pair of late nineteenth-century houses blend Italianate and Eastlake detailing. 4901 retains its original projecting center bay balcony. Its decorative elements appear to be original, except for the steps. Both houses have been well maintained through the years, and have escaped "updating" for a century, perhaps because the Italianate style has stood the test of time and usability.

Mary Louise Kennedy Genella acquired the property in 1885 from the heirs of Burgess Bennett. She completed the houses four years later, as a

substantial increase in property assessment shows. James J. Conway purchased 4901 in 1893; the home remained in his family until 1915. Frances Gasquet purchased 4905 the same year, and her heirs retained it until 1924.

4920 ST. CHARLES, bet. Upperline, Robert, bb. Pitt [Faubourg Avart]. Architectural writers of the early twentieth century frequently referred to imposing columned houses such as this one as Southern Colonial. The style is also closely allied with the Renaissance Revival, but Colonial Revival—not "plantation style"—most aptly fits the theme.

The "colossal" order of Corinthian columns, set on small piers, paired at the corners, and with well-balanced "entasis" or center swelling to convince the eye of perfect proportions, dominates the façade. The side elevations retains its original marquee, supported both by chains on brackets.

Herman Fichtenberg bought the entire square from the Society of the Daughters of Charity of St. Vincent De Paul in 1906. There, for a few years, the Daughters occupied a large raised home with many outbuildings, all of which had occupied the entire square for many years. In 1900-1901 the Rosary Academy of the Sacred Heart leased this property from the Daughters for a school season, while the Religious of the Sacred Heart were having a new academy built at 4521 St. Charles.

Fichtenberg evidently subdivided the square after 1906, and sold this lot in 1911 to Ephriam Rosenberg. Rosenberg had the imposing structure built that year according to a design by Emile Weil. In 1913 he sold the property to John Dantzler, who sold it to Norman Mayer in 1925. After Mayer's death, Dr. Donovan Browne purchased the home in 1940, and resided there for twenty-nine years, selling in 1969 to the William Becks, present owners.

4941 ST. CHARLES, cor. Robert, bb. Upperline, Carondelet [Faubourg Avart]. Here is a variation on the twentieth century Colonial Revival style. The *Daily States* reported that architects Robert S. Soule and F.J. MacDonnell designed this home for Henry Flaspoller in 1905. "[It] is two stories and an attic in height, of pressed brick and Colonial style with tile roof," reported the *States*. "It is fitted throughout with hot air heating and has both gas and electric lighting. Cost about $17,000." Combined gas-electric lighting, although quite dangerous, continued in use as late as 1920.

The front portico, originally had a small balcony. Today it has a post-construction upper level enclosure. A large glassed-roof conservatory lends grace and elegance to the uptown side façade. When built, the masonry was not painted, but left in its original "light star" shade of brick, which probably blended well with the red tile roof.

Architect MacDonnell considered his site plan for the house a creative solution to the problem of placing a large house on a small lot. He accomplished this with an indirect approach defined by a walkway curving around a raised terrace planting. Today boxwood outlines this walkway. The subtly-curved, laterally-oriented front stairs are part of this scheme.

Three years after building the house, Flaspoller sold it to William Bofinger. The next owner, Hubbard Moylan Feild, acquired the house in 1914, and

his family retained it until 1943. Two interim owners followed until James Viavant bought the property in 1947. The Viavant family has owned it for over forty years.

5005 ST. CHARLES, cor. Robert, bb. Soniat, Baronne [Faubourg Avart]. The Orleans Club, a New Orleans landmark, is one of the two oldest Jefferson City houses extant on St. Charles Avenue. William Lewis Wynn acquired the property from George C. Lawrason in 1859. Tradition has it that Wynn built the house as a gift to his only child Ann Elizabeth Wynn Garner. While the *Daily Picayune* of September 1868 attributed construction to Wynn's son-in-law, perhaps Mr. Wynn paid the bills. "On the corner of Robert and St. Charles," said the *Picayune*, "Col. George Garner is putting up an elegant brick residence two and a half stories high with bay windows, which will be a decided ornament to the locality."

John J. Gidiere acquired the house from the Garner family in 1882, but lost it in 1885 in a creditors' suit. The *Picayune* referred once again to the house as it went up for auction. "AN ELEGANT MANSION . . . with a Double Square of Ground, Charmingly Arranged in Garden and Lawn, with Orchard and Shade Trees." The Home Insurance Co. purchased the house at this auction and after a succession of owners, Mrs. Lillian Keener Lyons Clarke, widow of Lewis Strong Clarke, acquired the property in 1906 for $55,000. A year later, Mrs. Clarke made exterior and interior alterations, designed by Emile Weil at a cost of $32,000.

The home remained a private residence until 1925, when a group of three hundred women met to form a club dedicated to women's interests. In the spring of that year, they purchased the old Garner home for $62,500, inviting Mrs. Lucy Edelin Carter Green, Ann and George Garner's daughter, to participate as honorary life member. Since the first meeting of 1925, the Orleans Club has continued to fulfill its stated purpose of promoting both the dignity of women's interests and the study of art, music, and literature.

5010 ST. CHARLES, cor. Robert, bb. Soniat, Pitt [Faubourg Avart]. Edward Sporl designed this large Tudor residence for the Joseph Vaccaro family in 1909. Vaccaro was founder of Standard Fruit and Steamship Company, which pioneered the business of importing bananas to the United States from Central America.

Pegged half-timbering on the upper floor, picturesque roof massing, elaborate chimneys with

decorative chimney pots, and diamond-paned gable windows are typical elements of the Tudor style. The leaderheads on downspouts are exceptionally fine and well detailed.

The Vaccaro family retained ownership of the home for nearly fifty years.

5120 ST. CHARLES, bet. Soniat, Dufossat, bb. Atlanta [Faubourg Avart] Individually listed in the National Register of Historic Places, this imposing mansion, built as a private home in 1907, is now the Milton H. Latter Memorial branch of the New Orleans Public Library. It was designed by Favrot and Livaudais for Marks Isaacs, a prominent Canal Street merchant, and his wife. After Isaacs's death in 1912 the house was sold to "Lumber King" Frank B. Williams. Williams's son Harry, a pioneer aviator married to popular film actress Marguerite Clark of New Orleans, inherited it. The couple lived there until 1936, when Harry Williams was killed in a plane crash. Marguerite Clark remained in the house a year or so before moving to New York, where she died in 1940.

The mansion's next owner was racetrack owner Robert S. Eddy. In 1947 Mr. and Mrs. Harry Latter bought the house and gave it to the City of New Orleans to be used as a public library memorializing their son Milton, who was killed on Okinawa during World War II.

Old photographs indicate that there has been very little exterior alterations to the house. The original solid wood railing on the second level has been changed to wrought iron segments between stone piers.

Recently, the City effected a careful restoration to the interior, with substantial assistance from the Latter heirs.

LIST

5200 ST. CHARLES, cor. Dufossat, bb. Valmont, Blanc [Faubourg Avart]. Built in 1925 for Mrs. Clara Vatter Garic on property she purchased from the Society for the Relief of Destitute Orphan Boys, this house has had only three owners. In 1949 John Ramoneda bought the residence. It remained in the Ramoneda family until 1972 when Paul Rosenblum, who retains ownership at this writing, bought it.

LIST

5342 ST. CHARLES, cor. Jefferson, bb. Leontine, Atlanta [Rickerville]. Thomas Sully, whose conspicuous residences line St. Charles Avenue, also designed several institutions, including the Jewish Widows and Orphans Home built at this site in 1887. Its original Renaissance style was prevalent locally in public brick structures of the 1880s.

During the nineteenth century, New Orleans' numerous yellow fever epidemics contributed to the need for local orphanages. During the mid-twentieth century, however, a diminishing custom to house orphans in groups eventually rendered this imposing structure obsolete. In 1961 it was demolished and replaced by a smaller, more efficient Jewish Community Center designed by architects Curtis and Davis.

5345 ST. CHARLES, bet. Jefferson, Valmont, bb. Dryades [Rickerville]. The central cartouche and marquee successfully add a note of importance to the entrance of this sophisticated Mediterranean style Avenue home built in 1910. *Architectural Art and its Allies* illustrated the house when it was quite new and standing next to an open space.

Andry and Bendernagel designed the home for John Legier, Jr., a wealthy banker and president of the American Bank and Trust Co. For over sixty years it has been the home of the Hebert-Scheuermann family and their heirs.

5355 ST. CHARLES, cor. Jefferson, bb. Valmont, Dryades [Rickerville]. Weiss, Dreyfous & Seiferth, known for their modernist designs, were architects for this relatively rare example of European modernism in Louisiana. A conscious avoidance of detail and historic precedent characterizes the approach. The white painted brick patterns and incised horizontal and vertical bands create a subtle textural play of light and shadow. Wraparound

corner windows are expressive of the non-structural, outward skin of the building. In this scheme, exterior walls are not load-bearing, and a concrete or steel interior framework would support the structure.

R.P. Farnsworth & Co. built the structure as investment property in 1932. This is the third building known to occupy this site (see 1621 Jefferson).

5411 ST. CHARLES, bet. Jefferson, Octavia, bb. Danneel [Rickerville]. Allison Owen of Diboll, Owen & Goldstein, architects, designed this Mediterranean style residence built for Capt. James B. Sinnott in 1906. At that time, sections between the second level gallery pillars were of wood. Today, as the early photograph indicates, these have given way to wrought-iron elements employing the monogram of Crawford Ellis, who bought the house in 1918. The home remained in the Ellis family for fifty years. For the past twenty years, Maurice Hartson III and his family have owned the property.

5414 ST. CHARLES, bet. Jefferson, Octavia, bb. Atlanta [Rickerville]. Photographer-artist Capt. Edward J. Souby had this unusual raised camelback built in 1882 at a cost of $1,800. It uses a standard New Orleans house façade, but with an appended octagon and considerable distinction in detail. It is the oldest home along this stretch of the Avenue.

In 1887 the Soubys lost the residence to the sheriff, who sold it to William S. Benedict. Benedict shortly sold to Mrs. James A. Pierce, and in 1894 developer Albert Aschaffenburg acquired the property as his family residence. During fourteen years of residence in the neighborhood, Aschaffenburg developed the nearby Octavia and Casa Grande apartments on St. Charles Avenue.

Subsequent prominent owners of 5414 have included the Joseph P. Henican and Lester Gumbel families. The present owners, Mr. and Mrs. Victor Ray Rose, have extensively renovated and embellished the property.

5421 ST. CHARLES, cor. Octavia, bb. Jefferson, Danneel [Rickerville]. Albert Aschaffenburg's Octavia Apartment Company built this early twentieth century Favrot & Livaudais-designed complex in 1907. Aschaffenburg paid a premium for the location— nearly $20,000—a sum that included the residence now at 1631 Octavia, which he moved from the St. Charles Avenue site. For seventy years the Octavia succeeded as a low-profile but attractive apartment address, and during the 1970s became one of New Orleans' first condominiums.

5504 ST. CHARLES, cor. Octavia, bb. Hurst, Joseph [Rickerville]. The firm of Favrot and Livaudais designed this Colonial Revival residence built for Mr. and Mrs. Jacob H. Abraham at the turn of the twentieth century. The Abrahams acquired the bare lot in 1900, and by 1902 were in Soards' *Directory* at this address.

The gambreled house is faced with rough stucco and has unusually detailed quoins. The entrance porch employs a Georgian motif on the second level railing. Terraces flanking the porch have heavy concrete railings, somewhat incongruous

with the otherwise-refined colonial detail. Plain glass double outer doors protect elaborate leaded glass doors that open onto a large stair hall illuminated by stained glass windows. The base of the iron fence is early pre-cast concrete block.

This was the Walter Cleveland family residence for nearly thirty years (1918-1946). For fifteen years after that it was a much-neglected rooming house, finally rescued and renovated in 1961 by Dr. and Mrs. Frank Oser, the present owners.

5534 ST. CHARLES, cor. Joseph, bb. Octavia, Hurst [Rickerville]. The *Daily Picayune* of September 1, 1896, reported that John B. Cefalu had built this Queen Anne dwelling for $6,100 during the previous twelve months. Cefalu was president of the Columbia Cocoanut Dessicating Co., Ltd. and of the New Orleans Fruit Dealers Exchange. Cefalu sold the house in 1907 to Mrs. Julia Mayer, wife of Albert Wachenheim, who engaged Emile Weil as the architect for a two-story addition. The Wachenheim family owned the house for sixty-one years.

The building has a variety of window and gallery designs. The stained glass windows on the stairs have palm tree motifs. Two small stained glass windows over a sunburst pattern, flanked by two large windows, illuminate the bowed front bay. The front porch has modified paired Corinthian columns on small pedestals, a typical Queen Anne detail.

5531 ST. CHARLES, cor. Joseph, bb. Octavia, Danneel [Rickerville]. This Beaux Arts Renaissance styled residence is noteworthy for its fine architectural character and imposing siting on the Avenue. Emanuel V. Benjamin, proprietor of the Maginnis Cotton Mills, had the house built in 1916 according to the design of architect Emile Weil. The building permit for the house, as reported in *Building Review*, states that the house was to cost $30,000, an exceptionally large amount for its day. M. Federico's $2,265 contract for the houses's tile work exceeded the cost of entire houses built simultaneously along Audubon Boulevard.

Although considered Renaissance Revival when built, the two-and-one-half-story stone veneer residence actually combines details from various architectural periods and even demonstrates regional influence with the employment of iron railings and french doors. The usage of paired columns, as seen on the porch, is a design approach common to many Beaux Arts designs.

Benjamin's heirs sold the house in 1943 to Paul Maloney, Jr. Maloney owned it until 1951 when he sold to Mr. and Mrs. J. Edgar Monroe, the present owners.

SONIAT

1008 SONIAT, cor. Camp, bb. Dufossat, Chestnut [Faubourg Avart]. This story-and-one-half, center hall American cottage in an open setting suggests the era of Jefferson city in its late corporate days. At that time the Uptown neighborhood was just developing, and the house was fairly isolated. With

its rear service wing, stable, and outbuildings, the cottage once occupied half of the square.

William Brehm of Liverpool, England, had sold the property to Mrs. Georgiana Carter, wife of Edward Bower, in 1866. It was not, however, until the early 1870s that the Bowers built the present house. Soards' 1874 *Directory* listed Edw. Bower, chief clerk in the mayor's office, as residing there. Bower's heirs retained the property until 1922.

Architecturally, the cottage is simple and Classic in style. Transom and sidelights augment the panel door. The pilaster-framed entrance and the large central dormer with paired windows are features used consistently on New Orleans' nineteenth-century center hall cottages.

1041 SONIAT, cor. Chestnut, bb. Camp, bb. Robert [Faubourg Avart]. Here is a two-story single that is older than its current appearance suggests. William Linsey Jackson purchased the land from an auction held by Mme F.R. Avart in 1853, paying $1,200 for six lots, which made up a quarter of the square.

171

Graham and Madden's 1867 *Directory* located W.L. Jackson's widow residing at this intersection. Robinson's *Atlas* later identified the structure exactly at this site. Jackson had probably built it during the 1850s.

In 1881 Mrs. Cecile Le Blanc Asbury purchased the house, and retained it until her death. Her heirs sold in 1929 to Charles Roth. Mrs. Asbury undoubtedly replaced the front door and had the gallery remodeled in the style of the 1880s. Its oak leaf pattern cast-iron railing, however, seems original.

TCHOUPITOULAS (Levee, New Levee)

3400 TCHOUPITOULAS, from Louisiana to Gen. Taylor [Faubourgs Plaisance to St. Joseph]. The site of this half-mile-long, early twentieth century warehouse was once part of the industrial sector of Jefferson City. The Louisiana Ice Manufacturing Company was located on Tchoupitoulas between Delachaise and Foucher, directly across the street from the Delachaise Baseball Park. The park itself was the site of the old Delachaise Plantation house, which was next door to the century-old Delachaise Brick Works.

In 1898 the Illinois Central Railroad had a "frame shed" built along the river and Tchoupitoulas between Louisiana and Peniston. This $15,000 structure was, perhaps, a predecessor of the present warehouse which, from its poured concrete roof, pillars, and foundation, appears to date from the first decade of the twentieth century. At the rear, metal-clad doors opened up to freight bays, alongside which railway freight cars rolled up for cargo

handling. On the street side, wagons or trucks backed up to the freight aprons for pick up and distribution of merchandise.

The visual impact of this seemingly endless building is dramatic, if exhausting. To one viewer, the long wall is simmilar to the floodwall, "a necessary evil," somewhat overpowering, and only slightly more articulated. To another, the wall is a fascinating rhythm of forms and a reminder of the better architecture of earlier American industry, and a relic of the vibrant turn of the century New Orleans economy.

Structurally, the building demonstrates an interesting use of reinforced concrete, one of the first such uses in New Orleans. Designed for modest, animal-drawn wagons or small delivery trucks rather than eighteen-wheelers, the building today crowds the street, and the trucks that back up to it block traffic, automobiles, and other trucks, creating severe traffic problems.

1102-04, 1108-10, 1114-16 SONIAT, cor. Chestnut, bb. Dufossat, Coliseum [Faubourg Avart]. This unusual trio of camelback doubles with Mooresque elements and jigsaw detailing were probably built during the 1890s for Emma Dannermann Wilde. Mrs. Wilde purchased the land with earlier buildings in 1894, and retained the properties until 1920. 1114-16 has been drastically altered. A devastating fire recently destroyed 1108-10.

4109 TCHOUPITOULAS, bet. Marengo, Milan, bb. Annunciation [Faubourg East Bouligny]. One of the oldest structures in this area, this five-bay, center hall American cottage is a survivor of the era when Tchoupitoulas was a busy and valuable Jefferson City thoroughfare. Butcher Frederick William Fullmer purchased the land from Bouligny developer Samuel Kohn in two sales of 1850 and 1853. At that time the property extended from the present

house site to the corner of Marengo. Fullmer built his home off the corner about 1850. Cohen's city directories of both 1851 and 1854 list him residing at that location.

Architecturally, the house is Greek Revival in style, reflecting the date of Fullmer's purchase. The "Greek keyhole" doorway is intact, and the door

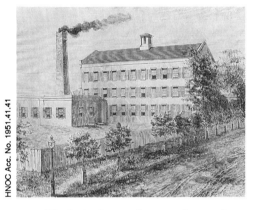

HNOC Acc. No. 1951.41.41

4608 TCHOUPITOULAS, bet. Napoleon, Valence, bb. S. Water [Faubourg West Bouligny]. Known for many years as Lane Cotton Mills, this complex of buildings played an important role in the economics and sociology of New Orleans and Jefferson City. For over a century this was the site of a cotton manufactory which grew from modest beginnings with a single building and lot to a whole complex of buildings sprawling over nearly three squares and two street beds.

The business was born in 1856 when George W. Hynson, John Bentham Leefe, Samuel S. Green, and others incorporated the New Orleans Manufacturing Company. Their goal was to make rope according to a new and more efficient manufacturing process for which they had purchased the Louisiana patent rights.

Architect George Purves designed the company's first factory building, a three-story red brick mill with attached octagonal smokestack at Tchoupi-

itself is particularly worthy of note. After more than 135 years, Fullmer's heirs still own the house and report that they have never made alterations to the interior except to modernize the plumbing and electricity.

toulas and Valence streets. Behind it were a small picker's house and two other small service buildings. Mill No. 1, which was typical of many in the Northeast, is depicted in Edwin L. Jewell's *Crescent City Illustrated.*

By 1858 New Orleans Manufacturing Company had failed and the following year Lafayette N. Lane purchased it. Ironically, although Lane's name is associated with the complex, his tenure there was brief—only three years. The property was confiscated by Federal troops for the United States Treasury Department, and Lane's name does not appear in mill records after the Civil War. Another seizure and sale appear in the notarial records, and then in 1872 Henry Abraham, cotton broker and civic leader, bought the factory with Emanuel and Mayer Lehman of New York and an era of expansion began. Now styled Lehman, Abraham, and Company, the mill continued to make rope, cotton yarn, and cordage, and expanded its land holdings to include the entire square along Tchoupitoulas from Valence to Cadiz. It operated an additional rope works in the neighborhood, at Valence and Annunciation. Across the street from this facility, the company built a block of employee housing which survives today as a row of modest shotguns (see 701-741 Valence).

In 1881 the company engaged architect William Fitzner to build a second, more ambitious mill house (still standing) at the immediate corner of Tchoupitoulas and Valence. Of four stories and brick, the new mill had Italianate style segmental arch openings, stepped brick cornices, and a distinctive elevator tower with ocular at the downtown end. Weaving was done on the first and second floors, carding on the third, and spinning on the fourth. This building became known as Mill No. 2.

In the spring of 1885, Abraham and his partners re-incorporated as the Lane Mills, with Maurice Stern as secretary. The following year, twenty-four year old Sigmund Odenheimer joined the business as plant superintendent. He would rise to president and guide the mills for fifty years.

Builders Koch and O'Neill constructed a three-story addition in 1893. This building, Mill No. 3, still stands at the Cadiz side of the square. Its design, by architect Diedrich Einseidel, generally follows that of the second mill building, and repeats its segmental-head windows and tall pilasters, but confines the cornice detail to a simple dentil row. Painted dark red and in fairly good condition, the building has new window sash in front, but remains close to its original appearance in the rear.

Lane Mills at the turn of the twentieth century was a major national producer of denim, cottonade, ticking, and cotton rope, with over 800 employees. The company was soon expanding again and purchased land in the adjoining square downriver, along with the bed of Jena Street. Here, in 1903 it added a large row of two-story buildings, along with a spacious addition in the rear of the 1893 Einseidel building. These warehouse structures, designed by Favrot and Livaudais and still standing, are of a light-colored brick, but their design relates to the earlier buildings through the use of the segmental arch and the two-story pilaster. Within the interior work spaces, foot-square wood piers support the framing. These were among the last of their type to be used, as the concrete pier soon replaced them for heavy building construction.

In 1905 the company re-incorporated to merge with Maginnis Cotton Mills at Annunciation and Calliope. By 1910, after a major bond issue, another name change, a damaging lawsuit, and a partition with Maginnis, the company reorganized as Lane Cotton Mills again, with Sigmund Odenheimer continuing as president. Eventually the company acquired property in the third square downriver, to Napoleon Avenue, and in 1932 had Favrot and Livaudais add a building there.

M. Lowenstein and Sons, Inc. of New York purchased the entire complex in 1948, and over the following decade, the company invested over $2.5 million improving the plant and its equipment. By the mid-1950s employment had risen to 1,400, but these employees were unionized, a sign of the competitive problems that would soon put Lane Cotton Mills out of business permanently.

Today, Mill No. 2 (1891), Mill No. 3 (1893), and the 1903 and 1932 Favrot and Livaudais buildings, the little office building, several brick storage sheds, and a row of warehouses along Front Street remain standing. United China and Glass Company owns the site. Palfrey-Rodd-Pursell Printing Company, a leaseholder of Mill No. 3 and its addition, manufactures its products using four generations of presses that include the most advanced machinery. Louisiana Variety Wholesale and several other companies have occupied various parts of the site since the 1950s.

New Orleans Manufacturing Company's original 1856 mill has been demolished, but its foundation and smokestack base are obvious. Iron bollards, an old hand pump, brick retaining walls, and a rectangular elevation mark the site.

Lane Cotton Mills was once one of New Orleans' premiere businesses. As late as the 1950s it provided as many as 1,400 jobs in important value-added manufacturing. Its architect-designed buildings of old Louisiana brick add interest to the city, and are reminders of of the one-time vigor of the cotton, railroading, and shipping industries of New Orleans. Cotton fabrics were rapidly losing ground to synthetics during the mid-1950s when unions were strong, and Lane went out of business. Unfortunately, Lane Cotton Mills, after surviving a century, did not survive to share today's renewed prosperity for cotton fabrics.

4637-39 TCHOUPITOULAS, cor. Valence, bb. Annunciation, Cadiz [Faubourg West Bouligny]. This plastered brick Creole cottage dates from the heyday of Faubourg West Bouligny. It once housed a business owned by Jefferson City Mayor François Jacques Laizer, who purchased the building from Pierre A. Bienvenu in 1855. Bienvenu had purchased the property from the succession of John Bellow in 1852, and probably built the structure soon after that. In 1868 Laizer sold to Joseph John Watermeier, a grocer and baker. Like Brand and Company's across the street, Watermeier's business no doubt flourished as the nearby Lane Cotton Mills increased its work force after the Civil War. The Watermeier family retained the property until 1891. After that year, grocer Peter Siren and his family owned the property until 1946. Siren had another business across the street (see 4701 Valence) until 1924.

Neglect and casual revisions to the exterior have eroded the building's integrity, but the wall and roof shape are intact. This house type is relatively rare among the extant building stock of uptown New Orleans.

4701 TCHOUPITOULAS, cor. Valence, bb. Bordeaux, Annunciation [Faubourg West Bouligny]. This important pair of antebellum corner stores was built as a grocery-residence and adjacent store, and continued in that kind of use until the mid-twentieth century. The original builders were brothers Charles W. and John Brand, grocers, of C.W. Brand & Company, who exchanged ownership of the properties in 1860. At that time, the buildings were already standing, and Gardner's 1860 *Directory* located Brand & Company at New Levee, corner Valence. During the Civil War, Frank Leidenheimer, a Jefferson City grocer, bought the two buildings from Charles Brand. In 1867 Gardner's located him in turn at this corner.

Today the buildings, with their pleasing segmental arch lintels, gallery on cast-iron colonnettes, and shuttered, full-length openings, remind us of the Jefferson City's bustling commercial era. Brand's and Leidenheimer's businesses no doubt flourished from the patronage of workers at Lane Cotton Mills and the old Justice's Court, both just across Tchoupitoulas.

The buildings are somewhat modest in scale and severe in style, but well-proportioned and built according to the excellent standards of brick masonry in their time. The service wings, not evident in the photograph, create a pleasant rear courtyard.

In 1882 Leidenheimer sold the buildings to Jeremiah Lyons. Peter Throunk, Peter Siren, and Charles K. Felder were successive owners who continued to operate the grocery business there until Felder's heirs sold to Margaret Henderson in 1974. After the sale to Mrs. Henderson, Rosie Wilson, doing business as Gammon Enterprises, purchased the structures for $50,000 and made a sizable investment to renovate the buildings and develop the property into a modern jazz club and restaurant. Gammon, Inc. installed an elaborate Art Deco style interior and provided restaurant seating in the now glass-enclosed courtyard. During its brief heyday, Rosie's club featured such prominent artists as Bobby Short, Chuck Mangione, and Fats Domino. Unfortunately, Rosie's did not survive. At this writing, the buildings house Omni Attractions/Productions, with residences upstairs.

5521 TCHOUPITOULAS, bet. Octavia, Joseph, bb. Annunciation [Rickerville]. Tchoupitoulas Street is still residential Uptown, but many of its extant homes are in a deteriorated condition. An exception is this large, center hall gabled cottage with Eastlake detailing. The well-maintained home has a dominant cross gable, with decorative shingling, a charming spindle frieze, and a turned baluster railing.

Robinson's *Atlas*, compiled about 1875, shows a house on this lot. It was, perhaps, the home of

Frederick Probst, a steamboat captain who purchased the ground with buildings in 1868 from Joseph Wittmann. Wittmann had a house there as early as 1866. Edwards' *Annual Director* locates Probst in Rickerville on Tchoupitoulas between Octavia and Joseph in 1870.

In 1881 Barbara Klinger Kern purchased the house with four adjacent lots. She retained the property until 1910. During this interval, Mrs. Kern either built or rebuilt the present house. Its gallery is predominantly mid-1890s in style, while its dropped siding reflects a usage common in New Orleans from the 1870s through 1900. The home's general envelope and chimneys, however, suggest an earlier house.

TOLEDANO

1330 TOLEDANO, cor. Coliseum, bb. Chestnut, Louisiana [Faubourg Plaisance]. The most salient feature of the center hall American cottage at Toledano and Coliseum is a large central dormer with bifurcated "Venetian" lights. This dormer style was popular in New Orleans during the 1870s and '80s. The home's columned gallery and entrance with narrow sidelights, on the other hand, is a feature that can be found on nineteenth-century New Orleans homes built over a half century, from about 1830 to 1880.

Henry Chapotin, owner of a house on the same square as this but facing Louisiana Avenue, sold this land to Jonathan Clarke Osborn in 1870. Osborn was probably the builder of the present house in 1870 or '71. Edwards' *Directory* located him there as early as 1872. Osborn died in 1879, leaving the property jointly to his sister, Elizabeth Kelly, and to several members of the Barrett family, who were out-of-state residents.

In 1901 Fischer Lumber and Manufacturing Co., Ltd. filed suit to recover the cost of paving on the side of the house, forcing the property into a sheriff's sale. There photographer George François Mugnier purchased it. In 1939 Mugnier's heirs sold it to Marielle M. Cleveland.

1720 TOLEDANO, bet. Carondelet, Baronne, bb. Louisiana [Faubourg Plaisance]. The most precise definition of a Creole cottage refers to a gable-sided building, usually having four square rooms, no hall, and two rear *cabinets* flanking a loggia (see *New Orleans Architecture Vol. IV*, pp. 41–54). In highly urbanized neighborhoods such as the Vieux Carré or Faubourg Marigny, the Creole cottage is generally set at the sidewalk. In more rural neighborhoods, we have observed full galleried cottages set well back from the street that still qualify as Creole cottage house types.

A notarial act of Antoine Doriocourt, August 25, 1858, mentions this quite modest, more rural type of Creole cottage. The French text reports that Carmelite Landry gave the house to her daughter Alexandrine Mouchon, widow of Benjamin McKenny, now married to Paul Esteben [*sic*], as part of her dowry. Gardner's 1861 *Directory* lists Paul Mouchon, trader, residing on Toledano near Carondelet. The 1868–1869 edition lists Paul Esteban residing on Toledano between Carondelet and Baronne, and also having a butcher shop on Baronne in the same square.

A New Orleans Notarial Archives watercolor drawing of November 16, 1880, by Deputy City Surveyor Louis H. Pilié also identifies the cottage. This illustration is a rare indication of the character of Jefferson City not long after its incorporation into the City of New Orleans.

The original french doors of the house as seen on the drawing have now disappeared, and the door heads are awkwardly lower. The house has also undergone veneering of synthetic siding and a corrugated metal roof addition.

VALENCE

701-03 To 739-41 VALENCE, bet. Constance, Laurel, bb. Cadiz [Faubourg West Bouligny]. This twenty-unit row of ten shotgun doubles on Valence near Tchoupitoulas was built as employee housing for Lehmann, Abraham Co. (Lane Cotton Mills) in 1882 for $7,500. The doubles were originally all identical, but most have suffered unsympathetic alterations. They are generally unadorned, with a simple scalloped fascia as the sole decoration. In their simplicity, the houses are historically important as reminders of generally decent nineteenth-century industrial workers' housing.

LIST

916-18 VALENCE, bet. Magazine, Camp, bb. Bordeaux [Faubourg West Bouligny]. Patrick Gilmartin, a carpenter and cistern maker, purchased this narrow "shotgun-sized" lot in 1885, probably with an earlier building. In 1900 Mary and P.K. Gilmartin completed a mortgage with Louisiana Homestead Association, possibly to finance construction of the present cottage. The home remained in the Gilmartin family until after 1942.

Spindle friezes and jigsaw work were generally a fully developed motif by the mid-1890s, but they continued in use until past 1900, as evidenced here. Sanborn insurance maps of 1896 do not show the structure, but it does appear on Sanborn's 1909 edition.

932-34 VALENCE, bet. Magazine, Camp, bb. Bordeaux [Faubourg West Bouligny]. Here is a galleried Creole cottage dating from the days of old West Bouligny. It was built as a double toward the late 1850s, probably by Philip E. or Daniel T. Walden, who traded ownership of the property in 1858 and 1860. Gardner's *Directory* of 1861 cites Philip Walden as living on Valence, corner Camp, Jefferson City. Notarial records of the time identify the house as a tenement, or rental property.

In 1869 the home went through a public auction, when it was advertised as a "double, one-story and attic cottage with slate roof, raised on about six feet pillars, with front gallery, four rooms, two cabinets, and rear gallery, two finished rooms in the attic, a kitchen of two rooms, cistern and shed."

Late nineteenth-century maps present inconsistent evidence about the rear service building. There was clearly a separate kitchen in 1869, but it is not readily observable on Robinson's *Atlas*, compiled about 1875. An 1896 Sanborn insurance map indicates that the house had been moved forward on the lot by that year, and had two rear service wings, somewhat narrower than the present ones. New front doors, dropped siding, cornices, and window lights may have been added during that decade. The rear continued its evolution after the turn of the century, perhaps through an extension of the service buildings.

After a succession of three owners, John Callaghan bought the property in 1913, and heirs of the Callaghan-Burch family retain ownership at this writing.

938 VALENCE, cor. Camp, bb. Magazine, Bordeaux [Faubourg West Bouligny]. An interesting complex of building and roof forms, constructed successively some time after 1871, are related visually to the adjacent, multiple-roofed cottage at 932-34. By the time Robinson's *Atlas* was completed, a structure was illustrated on that site. Sanborn insurance maps indicate that the rear two-story element (4706 Camp) was built between 1896 and 1909, when it had a gallery over the sidewalk.

Thomas Callaghan acquired the property in 1899 and this corner structure was known as Callaghan's for many years. It was probably built about 1871 by Mrs. Catherine O'Brian, who purchased it from Daniel O'Brian in 1870 and sold it to Jane O'Brian in 1871 with a price escalation from $500 to $1,500. Now Benny's Bar, the property is still owned by heirs of Thomas Callaghan.

LIST

1028 VALENCE, bet. Chestnut, Camp, bb. Bordeaux [Faubourg West Bouligny]. Trinity Methodist Church, a 1912 modified Gothic structure, succeeds a wood-frame church built for a congregation in place as early as 1866. James G. Simpson sold the land to the Missionary Society of the Methodist Episcopal Church of New York, a black congregation, in 1866. By the 1890s the church on the site had a fifty-foot tower.

After the turn of the twentieth century, the congregation, by then known as Jefferson Methodist Episcopal Church, evidently failed. In 1912 the property was sold to a reorganized group led by Albert L. Vitter, and the church was rededicated.

LIST

1100-02, 1104-06, 1108-10 VALENCE, cor. Chestnut, bb. Coliseum, Bordeaux [Faubourg West Bouligny]. These three double camelbacks were identical when they were built in 1896. William Weidner sold the lots to his daughter, Mary A. Weidner, wife of Charles Buck, in 1889. A building permit was issued to Charles F. Buck in 1896 to build three doubles and one single cottage for $7,000.

1320 VALENCE, cor. Prytania, bb. Perrier, Bordeaux [Faubourg West Bouligny]. This beautifully kept home, now quite simple in outline, has undergone several remodelings since its construction as an elaborate asymmetrical Victorian mansion in 1883. It was built by "O. Mansky" from plans by William Fitzner, an architect known for his Italianate designs. When the house was first built, the *Daily Picayune* described it as being "one and two stories high, and very ornamental as well as commodious," with front and side bays and galleries. This important hint about the massing suggests the asymmetry of the original house—a form that Sanborn insurance maps of later years would verify.

The home was originally the residence of Mr. and Mrs. Charles F. Buck. Mrs. Mary Ann Weidner Buck purchased one-half of the square in 1875. After building the house, Mr. Buck made substantial mortgages on the property from Mutual Building and Homestead Association in both 1890 and 1892, probably to build the three two-story bayed houses at 4716, 4730, and 4736 Prytania, once the Buck's back yard.

After the deaths of Mr. and Mrs. Buck, Dr. Curtis Tyrone, one of the founders of Ochsner Clinic, purchased the home in 1939, and had Paul Charbonnet, builder, make substantial renovations. In 1958 New Orleans antique dealer Henry Stern purchased the house from Dr. Tyrone and made further renovations. Today the original form is not evident, but the house is interestingly detailed without, and has elegant architectural elements within.

1503 VALENCE, cor. Pitt, bb. St. Charles, Cadiz [Faubourg West Bouligny]. Individually listed in the National Register of Historic Places, this late-Classic villa style house was once a boarding and day school for young ladies. Elizabeth Ann Mills, wife of James E. Tewell, bought the "property and appurtenances" in 1869 for $2,200. Robinson's *Atlas* (compiled about 1875) designates "Valence Institute" on the property. Since Valence Institute's publication, *Echo*, of August 1, 1884, marks the "7th Annual Commencement Exercises," the school must have been in existence as early as 1877. Mr. Tewell, once "collector of customs," became a professor at the school. Said the *Echo*

As a BOARDING SCHOOL, the location of the Institute is in every way desirable. It is sufficiently remote from the centre of the city to be free from its distractions, yet has two lines of street cars within two hundred feet, on ei-

ther of which Canal street may be reached within thirty minutes. Its situation, on the most elevated portion of the city, gives to it an atmosphere untainted by influences prejudicial to health. Parents should take these facts into consideration in selecting a Boarding School for their children. Another fact should have an important bearing in the selection, the pleasant walking distance of the Institute from the Park where the WORLD'S INDUSTRIAL AND COTTON CENTENNIAL EXPOSITION will be held. The Principal designs making that grand depository of useful information an adjunct to the Scholastic Course of the Coming Session.

The house was built sometime between 1869 and 1876. Mrs. Tewell owned it until 1899, when she sold to Johnston Armstrong. Subsequent owners have been John M. Burgoyne, R.L. Wilson, Alfred LeBlanc, Admiral A.S. Merrill, Harry McCall, Jr., and Moise Steeg, Jr.

VALENCE STREET SUBSTATION, Corner Valence and Loyola, bb. Cadiz, S. Liberty [Faubourg West Bouligny]. In 1909 the New Orleans Railway and Light Co. built this small but striking brick substation to provide electric power for St. Charles Avenue streetcars. Its walls and window heads are decorated with interesting brick moldings, while decorative ceramic insulators ornament the tower-like accent over the entry. The simple, efficient building stands as a reminder that industrial structures may be significant contributors to, rather than detractors from, the street scene.

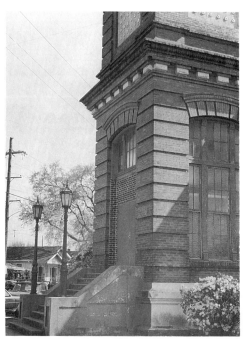

NOTES

THE FOUNDING FAMILIES AND POLITICAL ECONOMY, 1850–1870

1. *Acts*, State of Louisiana, May 27, 1946.

2. *Borough of Freeport v. Paul Lacroix and Lewis Ackerman*, filed 3rd Judicial District Court for the Parish of Jefferson (hereafter 3JDC) Dec. 7, 1846, New Orleans Public Library (hereafter N.O.P.L.); appealed to Louisiana State Supreme Court (hereafter LSSC) No. 473 (1848 Unreported Cases), University of New Orleans (hereafter U.N.O.), Earl K. Long Library, Archives and Manuscripts Department.

3. *Ibid.*

4. *Ibid.*

5. Gardner and Wharton's *New Orleans Directory*, 1858, p. 898; Gardner's *New Orleans Directory*, 1865, pp. 70–71, and 1868, pp. 31–59, 72; Ruth Koons Hollis, "Jefferson City 1851–1870: New Orleans' Urban Growth and Reconstruction Politics," graduate thesis, University of New Orleans, 1983, p. 12; Records of the City of Jefferson, "Item 1: Names and addresses of business people in the City of Jefferson," *passim*, City Archives, N.O.P.L.

6. *Live Stock Dealers and Butchers' Assn. of New Orleans v. Crescent City Live Stock Landing and Slaughter House Company*, December 7, 1883, filed July 22, 1869, N.O.P.L., appealed LSSC 2506, U.N.O.

7. *Inbau, Aycock & Co. v. Crescent City Live Stock Landing and Slaughter House Company*, 7th District Court (hereafter 7DC) for the Parish of Orleans, No. 1537, filed June 18, 1869, N.O.P.L., appealed to LSSC 2504, U.N.O; Gardner's *New Orleans Directory*, 1867–68.

8. "Plan of the City of Jefferson, 1860," by William H. Williams, Plan Book 64, fo. 41, New Orleans Notarial Archives (hereafter N.O.N.A.); Hollis, "Jefferson City," p. 12.

9. Donatien Augustin, *A General Digest of the Ordinances and Resolutions of the Corporation of New Orleans* (New Orleans, 1831), p. 349; John Calhoun, comp., *Digest of the Ordinances and Resolutions of the Second Municipality of New Orleans* (New Orleans, 1840), p. 71; F.R. Southmayd, *Digest of the Ordinances of the Second Municipality and of the General Council of the City of New Orleans Applicable Thereto* (New Orleans, 1848), p. 135.

10. Minutes of the [Jefferson City] Board of Aldermen, Vol. 1, September 1, 1857, October 8, 1857, N.O.P.L.; Hollis, "Jefferson City," p. 21; Ronald M. Labbé, "New Light on the Slaughterhouse Monopoly Act of 1869," in Edward F. Haas, ed., *Louisiana's Legal Heritage*, p. 151.

11. For particular examples, see Inventory section.

12. City directories of 1853–1868 list Michel as Jefferson City comptroller, alderman, mayor and fire company president, and Jefferson Parish Justice of the Peace and Parish Recorder. Second and Third Judicial District Court records, Louisiana Division, N.O.P.L., record his activities as a private attorney. Notarial records, particularly P.E. Davis, 1864–1866, record his contracting activities as mayor.

13. Minutes, Board of Aldermen, Vol. 1, September 2, 1857, October 8, 1857, January 12, 1858, January 16, 1859; for example of market lease, see P.E. Davis, notary, December 30, 1864, N.O.N.A.

14. "An Act to Incorporate the City of Jefferson," No. 93, 1850, *Acts Passed by the 3rd Legislature of the State of Louisiana at their Session Held and Begun in the Town of Baton Rouge on the 1st Day of January 1850*, p. 35; "Mayor's Message" [John T. Michel] in Minutes, Board of Alderman, Vol. 1, June 21, 1859, p. 233, N.O.P.L.

15. "Act to Incorporate City of Jefferson," Sections 12, 13, 18, 19, 23–24; Minutes, Board of Aldermen, Vols. 1–4, *passim*.

16. "An Act to Incorporate the Town of Carrollton," Act 91, Louisiana State Legislature, 1845; "An Act to Consolidate the City of New Orleans, and Provide for the Government and Administration of its Affairs," *Acts of the State of Louisiana*, 1852, p. 42; amendments to Charter of City of Jefferson, *Acts*, March 4, 1852, April 29, 1853, March 18, 1856, March 15, 1859.

17. "Act to Incorporate City of Jefferson," Section 3.

18. Hollis, "Jefferson City," p. 13.

19. *Ibid.*, p. 14.

20. *Acts*, State of Louisiana, March 26, 1870; Act 118, 1869; Labbé, "Slaughterhouse Monopoly Act," pp. 144–48; *Crescent City Livestock Landing and Slaughter House Company v. City of New Orleans*, 5DC No. 10,494, filed January 26, 1880, N.O.P.L., appealed to LSSC 7996, U.N.O.

21. Albert Robichaux, Jr., comp., trans., ed., *Louisiana Census and Militia Lists, Vol. I: 1770–1789*, p. 20.

22. Winston DeVille, *Colonial Louisiana Marriage Contracts, Vol. 3: Pointe Coupee*, p. 80; Jack D.L. Holmes, *Honor and Fidelity: The Louisiana Infantry Regiment and the Louisiana Militia Companies, 1766–1821*, p. 165.

23. Michel de Armas, notary, April 22, 1811, N.O.N.A.

24. P. Pedesclaux, notary, May 12, 1811, N.O.N.A.

25. Michel de Armas, notary, April 12, 1814, N.O.N.A.

26. *Robert and Benjamin Fox v. François-Robert Avart*, 1st Judicial District Court for the Parish of Orleans (hereafter 1JDC), No. 7034, filed April 14, 1826, N.O.P.L.

27. The François Avart townhouse was at the corner of Condé (Chartres) and Hospital (Gov. Nicholls). See L.T. Caire, notary, May 1, 1838, N.O.N.A.

28. *New Orleans and Carrollton Rail Road v. Jean Louis Drouet, Jerome Toledano, and Robert Avart*, Orleans Parish Court No. 8582, filed December 18, 1835, N.O.P.L., appealed to LSSC 2883, U.N.O.

29. F.E.D. Livaudais, notary, June 9, 1838, March 19, 1838, Jefferson Parish notarial records; L.T. Caire, notary, May 1, 1838, N.O.N.A.

30. Correspondence file, December 17, 1800, Archives, Archdiocese of New Orleans, Archbishop Antoine Blanc Memorial, New Orleans.

31. T. Guyol, notary, November 19, 1849, N.O.N.A.; C.C. Ladreyere, notary, February 28, 1855, N.O.N.A.; F.E.D. Livaudais, notary, June 9, 1838, Jefferson Parish; "Succession of Thomas Peniston," 2DC No. 20,128, appealed to LSSC 747, U.N.O.

32. Several court cases of the 1820 begin to mention the "Widow Avart," for instance 1JDC 3114, filed April 20, 1820, N.O.P.L., and 1JDC 6164, filed May 3, 1824, N.O.P.L.; later, see LSSC 747, "Succession of Peniston," U.N.O.; for Madame Avart, see for example A. Chiapella, notary, December 13, 1854, N.O.N.A., and *New Orleans Bee*, March 25, 1855.

33. C. Boudousquie, notary, June 28, 1842, December 30, 1847, November 1, 1849, N.O.N.A.; G. Duplantier, notary, August 20, 1856, October 25, 1856, N.O.N.A.; Plan Book 6, fo. 7, N.O.N.A.; W.V. Miller, notary, May 11, 1922, N.O.N.A.; New Orleans Conveyance Office Book 368, fo. 308, October 13, 1924.

34. The auction was on March 30, 1853; see C.C. Ladreyere, notary, Vol. 4, No. 47 (April 1853), N.O.N.A.

35. A. Chiapella, notary, December 13, 1854, N.O.N.A.; G. Duplantier, notary, August 20, 1856, N.O.N.A.; S. Magner, notary, October 3, 1866, N.O.N.A.; *Louisiana Courier*, August 15, 1858.

36. Henry C. Bezou, ed., comp., *Jefferson Parish Historical Markers*, p. 17.

37. *Borough of Freeport v. Lacroix and Ackerman*; T. Guyol, notary, November 19, 1841, N.O.N.A.; G. Duplantier, notary, May 1, 1855, May 14, 1855, N.O.N.A.; Antoine Doriocourt, notary, April 8, 1852, N.O.N.A.

38. C. Boudousquie, notary, June 28, 1842, November 1, 1849, N.O.N.A.; Guy Duplantier, notary, May 1, 1856, May 14, 1856, August 20, 1856, November 22, 1856, N.O.N.A.

39. J. Cuvillier, notary, November 30, 1864, March 16, 1865, N.O.N.A.; Antoine Doriocourt, notary, December 16, 1868, March 31, 1868, April 16, 1870, April 12, 1872, N.O.N.A.

40. "Succession of Peniston"; *New Orleans Picayune*, October 21, 1881; 2DC 3207, filed December 2, 1867, N.O.P.L., appealed to LSSC 1645, U.N.O.

41. "Succession of Martin Valmont Soniat," 2DC 39,992, December 26, 1877, N.O.P.L.; "Succession Louise Avart Soniat," 2DC, August 7, 1878, N.O.P.L.; Antoine Doriocourt, notary, April 12, 1872, N.O.N.A.; C.T. Soniat, notary, April 26, 1884, N.O.N.A.; M.C. Soniat, notary, May 7, 1890, N.O.N.A.

42. Antoine Doriocourt, notary, December 28, 1870, N.O.N.A.; Dr. and Mrs. Theodore-Louis Soniat, telephone interview with author, December 15, 1987, New Orleans; Dr. and Mrs. L. Sidney Soniat, telephone interview with author, February 1, 1988, New Orleans; Soniat family genealogy, 1320–1948, in possession of Dr. and Mrs. Theodore L. Soniat; *New Orleans Times-Picayune*, February 12, 1924, December 1, 1936.

43. P. Pedesclaux, notary, May 12, 1810, N.O.N.A.

44. Holmes, *Honor and Fidelity*, p. 165.

45. L.T. Caire, notary, March 22, 1833, N.O.N.A.; LSSC 1645, 1646, (June 1869) and 747, "Succession of Peniston," U.N.O.

46. *New Orleans Bee*, March 6, 1847; "Succession of Mrs. Thomas Peniston," 2DC 3207, filed June 12, 1867, N.O.P.L., appealed to LSSC 1645, U.N.O., reported 19 *La. Ann.* 277 and 21 *La. Ann.* 440.

47. Marriage contract, H.B. Cenas, notary, January 2, 1856, N.O.N.A.

48. "Succession of Peniston"; *New Orleans Daily Picayune*, December 3, 1863.

49. "Succession of Thomas Peniston."

50. *Ibid.*

51. "Succession Mrs. Thomas Peniston."

52. *New Orleans Daily Picayune*, December 14, 1899, October 21, 1881; see also Obituary file, N.O.P.L.

53. Alcée Fortier, *Louisiana: Compromising Sketches of Parishes, Towns . . .*, p. 194.

54. Talmadge Butler and M.F. Martin, *Louisiana Successions, Vol. 1: St. Landry Parish, 1807–1865*, pp. 114, 191, 903; *Louisiana Courier*, September 25, 1818; *New Orleans Bee*, May 14, 1839; *Margaret Chretien v. P.A. Delachaise*, 1JDC, filed August 2, 1824, N.O.P.L.

55. *Widow Combe and Derbon, fils, & Co. v. P.A. Delachaise*, 1JDC 1904, N.O.P.L.

56. Michel de Armas, notary, July 21, 1820, N.O.N.A.; T. Seghers, notary, June 21, 1838, N.O.N.A.

57. C. Pollack, notary, February 14, 1832, N.O.N.A.

58. *John F. Miller v. P.A. Delachaise and F.X. Martin*, 1JDC 5614, N.O.P.L.

59. *P.A. Delachaise v. Norbert Fox, et al.*, 1JDC 5876, filed January 27, 1824, N.O.P.L.; see also *P.A. Delachaise v. B. Silva*, 1JDC 7360, 7364, N.O.P.L.

60. Marriage contract, M. Lafitte, notary, April 13, 1822, N.O.N.A.; T. Seghers, notary, October 14, 1828, N.O.N.A.

61. G.R. Stringer, notary, May 18, 1822, N.O.N.A.

62. P. Pedesclaux, notary, July 3, 1822, N.O.N.A.; M. Lafitte, notary, October 6, 1823, N.O.N.A.

63. C. Pollack, notary, February 14, 1831, N.O.N.A.

64. F. de Armas, notary, February 13, 1828, N.O.N.A.; Jefferson Parish Book 3, fo. 156–58; M. Lafitte, notary, February 12, 1824, March 18, 1824, N.O.N.A.

65. T. Seghers, notary, June 21–July 9, 1838, N.O.N.A.

66. *Ibid.*

67. T. Guyol, notary, April 20, 1855, N.O.N.A.

68. *New Orleans Commercial Bulletin*, November 6, 1861.

69. Minutes, Board of Aldermen, Vol. 1, March 16, 1858, April 6, 1858, N.O.P.L.

70. Marriage contract, F. Grima, notary, October 24, 1840, N.O.N.A.

71. T. Guyol, notary, April 20, 1855, October 12, 1891, N.O.N.A.; "Plan of City of Jefferson"; S. Magner, notary, October 5, 1866, April 18, 1867, April 1868, N.O.N.A.; J.C. Wenck, notary, October 14, 1891, N.O.N.A.

72. T. Guyol, notary, April 20, 1855, N.O.N.A.

73. J.F. Coffee, notary, January 9, 1862, February 27, 1862, N.O.N.A.

74. Labbé, "Slaughterhouse Monopoly Act," p. 153.

75. Jas. Fahey, notary, February 23, 1885, N.O.N.A.; "Succession of Philip Delachaise," Civil District Court No. 20,224 and Will Book 23, fo. 148, N.O.P.L.

76. Jas. Fahey, notary, January 7, 1888, N.O.N.A.; see also Obituary file, N.O.P.L.

77. P. Pedesclaux, notary, April 29, 1818, N.O.N.A.

78. *Augustin Macarty, Test. Executor J.B. Soubie v. Widow Beale, et al.*, 1JDC 3968, filed May 4, 1821, N.O.P.L.

79. *Ibid.*

80. *Ibid.*; *Chloe Delancey et al. v. Celeste Beale, et al.*, 1JDC 3737–38, filed March 4, 1830, N.O.P.L., appealed to LSSC 1958, U.N.O.

81. *Delancey v. Beale.*

82. *Ibid.*; Michel de Armas, notary, April 27, 1819, N.O.N.A.

83. *Widow Thomas Beale v. Delancey, et al.*, reported 6 *Mart*, NS 640 (April 1828).

84. *Nathaniel Chamberlain v. Celeste Beale*, 1JDC 9113, filed November 2, 1830, N.O.P.L.; T. Seghers, notary, March 19, 1831, N.O.N.A.

85. Guillermo Náñez Falcón, ed., and Connie G. Griffith, trans., *The Favrot Papers*, pp. 153–54.

86. *Lakin and Wife and Guttierez and Wife v. Samuel Ricker and John H. Pearson*, 4DC 6738, filed July 7, 1853, N.O.P.L., appealed to LSSC 425, U.N.O.; record contained in *J.M. Butchert v. Samuel Ricker, Jr.*, Parish Court for Jefferson Nos. 883–94, filed April 24, 1854, appealed to 3JDC 197, appealed to LSSC 4251, U.N.O.

87. Falcon, ed., *Favrot Papers*, pp. 153–54; *Lakin and Guttierez v. Ricker and Pearson.*

88. *Lakin and Guttierez v. Ricker and Pearson.*

89. *City Bank of New Orleans v. Daniel T. Walden*, 1JDC 21,366, filed May 11, 1842, N.O.P.L., appealed to LSSC 5978, U.N.O.; *James Beale, et al. v. D.T. Walden*, 11 Rob. 67.

90. W.Y. Lewis, notary, March 17, 1846, March 19, 1846, in L.R. Kenny, notary, March 7, 1849, N.O.N.A.

91. *Lakin and Guttierez v. Ricker and Pearson*; *J.H. Pearson & Co. v. Samuel Ricker and G.H. Pearson*, 4DC 100, filed September 2, 1846, N.O.P.L.

92. *Pearson v. Ricker and Pearson.*

93. L.R. Kenny, notary, April 27, 1849, N.O.N.A. (Act of Partition pursuant to *Minors Ricker v. City Bank et al.*, 3JDC 676).

94. *Ibid.*; *Celeste Josephine Beale v. Samuel Ricker, Jr.*, LSSC 2355, filed November 14, 1851, U.N.O., reported 7 *La. Ann.* 667; *Lakin and Guttierez v. Ricker and Pearson*; *Butchert v. Ricker.*

95. *Celeste Josephine Beale v. Ricker.*

96. *Lakin and Guttierez v. Ricker and Pearson.*

97. *Ibid.*

98. *Ibid.*

99. *Ibid.*; *Pearson v. Ricker and Pearson*; *Ernest Samuel Ricker v. J.J. Guttierez*, 2DC 32,214, N.O.P.L.

100. Gardner's *New Orleans Directory*, 1867–1868.

101. L.T. Caire, notary, April 7, 1829, N.O.N.A.

102. L.T. Caire, notary, April 19, 1831, N.O.N.A.

103. *Louis Bouligny v. His Creditors*, 1JDC 11,895, field December 3, 1834, N.O.P.L., appealed to LSSC 4221, U.N.O.

104. L.T. Caire, notary, May 26, 1834, N.O.N.A.

105. Cohen's *New Orleans Directory*, 1853; the plantation property was located on the west bank of the Mississippi River south of Marrero, and known as Estelle and Front Place Plantations.

106. *Laurent Millaudon v. New Orleans and Carrollton Rail Road*, and *New Orleans and Carrollton Rail Road v. Laurent Millaudon*, filed April 3, 1841, 3 *Rob.* 488. Millaudon had heirs who inherited much of his property. They included Benjamin L., Henry Clement, Marie, Lizzie, Madeleine, Genvieve, and Constantine C. Millaudon, and Jeanne H. Gardaune.

107. Kohn's partner in this venture was H. Labruere. Bertram Wallace Korn, *The Early Jews of New Orleans*, pp. 119–20.

108. In addition to his Bouligny properties, Kohn owned about thirty lots with stores in the Vieux Carré and central business district. He also invested in Bank of Louisiana, Union Bank, and New Orleans and Carrollton Rail Road stock. In 1829 he became president of the New Orleans Navigation Company after a *coup d'état* by stockholders who wished to sell the business to the state. L.T. Caire, notary, December 31, 1840, N.O.N.A.; A. Mazureau, notary, January-April 1854, N.O.N.A.

109. *Borough Freeport v. Lacroix and Ackerman.*

110. *Saint Stephen's Parish 125th Anniversary, 1849–1974*, pp. 15–17.

111. The auction was on May 11, 1854, with sales recorded in A. Mazureau, notary, Vol. 118, Acts 180–240, N.O.N.A.

112. P.E. Davis, notary, December 30, 1864, February 10, 1865, N.O.N.A.; S. Magner, notary, December 27, 1867, N.O.N.A.

113. Minutes, Board of Aldermen, Vol. 1, November 16, 1858, p. 149, N.O.P.L.; Gardner's *New Orleans Directory*, 1868, p. 72, and 1870, p. 800.

114. "Index to Ledgers of Property Seized in New Orleans," RG 366, Bk. 44, pp. 2–367, 384–425, National Archives, Washington, D.C.; "Confederate Hearings, Investigations of the Navy Department," p. 573, in "Official Records of the War of the Rebellion," Series III, Vol. 1, U.S. Navy Department, Washington, D.C.

115. Hollis, "Jefferson City," pp. 34–42; *State of Louisiana v. John L. Kreider*, 21 *La. Ann.* 482.

116. Hollis, "Jefferson City," pp. 45–45.

117. *Ibid.*, pp. 48–53.

118. *Ibid.*, pp. 54–57.

119. "List of Acts and Resolutions Passed by the General Assembly of Louisiana, Sessions of 1869 and 1870, With the Dates of Their Promulgation," *Acts*, Louisiana, 1870, pp. 4–17.

120. Act 118, passed March 8, 1869.

121. *Ibid.*; *Butchers' Benevolent Assn. v. Slaughter House Company*; *Inbau, Aycock v. Slaughter House Co.*; *Bertinet, et al. v. Crescent City Live Stock Landing and Slaughter House Company*, LSSC 3917, U.N.O., reported 28 *La. Ann.* 210; *Crescent City Live Stock Landing and Slaughter House Company v. Butchers' Benevolent Assn. of New Orleans*, filed June 8, 1869, 5DC 585, N.O.P.L., appealed to LSSC 2509, U.N.O.; *State ex rel. Belden v. Fagan, et al.*, filed 5DC 809, transferred to 8DC 122, N.O.P.L., appealed to LSSC 2508, U.N.O., reported 22 *La. Ann.* 545, 77 US (10 Wall) 273; *Wilson, Fagan & Co. v. Crescent City Live Stock Landing and Slaughter House Company*, filed June 2, 1869 7DC 1544, N.O.P.L.; Labbé, "Slaughterhouse Monopoly Act," pp. 155–57.

122. Labbé, "Slaughterhouse Monopoly Act," pp. 156–57.

123. *Insurance Maps of New Orleans, Louisiana* (New York: Sanborn Insurance Co., 1903).

SURVEYORS AND SURVEYING

1. Albert A. Fossier, M.D., *New Orleans—The Glamour Period.*

2. "Jefferson City Surveyor's Office Correspondence Book: 1866–1870."

3. "Specifications, Surveyor's Office: February 10, 1869–April 3, 1873."

4. Henry P. Dart III, "The Arpent," *Loyola Law Review* 13.

5. "Contract between E.W. Foster, Surveyor General of the United States for the District of Louisiana, and William Ross and Valerien Sulakowski," June 7, 1871, Louisiana State Land Office, Baton Rouge, La.

6. Edmond R. Kiely, Ph.D., *Surveying Instruments: Their History.*

7. "Spanish Land Laws of Louisiana," *Louisiana Historical Quarterly* 2 (4).

8. Andrew Ellicott, *The Journal of Andrew Ellicott* (Philadelphia, 1802).

9. *New Orleans Times-Picayune*, December 24, 1911; May 3, 1936.

10. "Jefferson Parish Survey Book, Vol. 2, May 20, 1857," Historic New Orleans Collection.

11. *New Orleans Bee*, May 31, 1874.

12. "Barthelemy Lafon Contract Record Book," February 17, 1805. Contract with Joseph Pilié from Santo Domingo to work in Lafon's geographer's office for two years at a salary of sixteen dollars per month plus food and lodging. English translation in files of Samuel Wilson, Jr.

13. Leonard V. Huber, *Jackson Square Through the Years* (New Orleans: Laborde Printing, 1982).

14. Act before Paul Emile Théard, notary, December 1, 1856, New Orleans Notarial Archives (hereafter N.O.N.A.).

15. *New Orleans Times-Democrat*, April 24, 1886.

16. *New Orleans Daily Picayune*, January 23, 1912; *New Orleans Daily States*, January 22, 1912.

17. Edmond A. d'Hémécourt, great-grandson of Allou d'Hémécourt.

18. Act before Antoine Doriocourt, notary, September 7, 1859, N.O.N.A.

19. Act before Theodore Guyol, notary, January 21, 1847, N.O.N.A.

20. Ordinance No. 14,669, Commmission Council Series, December 14, 1937.

21. *New Orleans Times-Picayune*, July 22, 1973.

22. Louisiana State Land Office, Baton Rouge.

23. Col. Francis C. Kajencki, "The Louisiana Tiger," *Louisiana History* 15 (1).

24. *New Orleans Daily Picayune* and *New Orleans Times*, June 20, 1873.

25. *New Orleans Daily True Delta*, October 29, 1865.

26. *Louisiana Historical Quarterly* 22 (1).

27. *New Orleans Times*, July 12, 1865.

28. "Field Book No. 9, Fees of Parish Surveyor," January 22, 1856, p. 22.

ARCHITECTURAL STYLES

1. H. Hanley Parker, "New Orleans Architecture, As Others See It," *Architectural Art*, January 1908, pp. 1– 2.

2. Hilary Irvin and Robert Cangelosi, Jr., "Uptown New Orleans," pp. 1, 44–46.

3. *New Orleans Daily Picayune*, September 1, 1884, p. 2.

4. *New Orleans Daily States*, August 31, 1902, p. 32.

5. Talbot Hamlin, *American Spirit in Architecture* (New Haven, Conn., 1926), p. 263.

6. *New Orleans Daily Picayune*, September 1, 1886, p. 2.

7. *New Orleans Times-Democrat*, 1893.

8. *New Orleans Daily Picayune*, July 29, 1888, p. 8.

9. Louis H. Gibson, *The Convenient House* (New York, 1889), p. 105.

10. *New Orleans Daily Picayune*, September 1, 1896, p. 14.

11. C.M. Price, "Sincerity in Architecture," *Building Review*, January 23, 1915.

12. Only two architects in New Orleans demonstrated Art Nouveau tendencies—H.J. MacKenzie and Morgan Hite; MacKenzie was more experienced in the style.

13. *New Orleans Daily States*, August 31, 1908.

14. *New Orleans Daily Picayune*, September 1, 1896, p. 14.

15. *New Orleans Daily States*, August 31, 1905, p. 41.

16. Gustav Stickley, *Craftsman Homes*, p. 16.

17. *Ibid.*

18. *Ibid.*, pp. 9, 129, 133.

19. *New Orleans Morning Star*, April 1907, p. 23.

20. Frank Lloyd Wright, *Architect's Journal* (London, 1936), reprinted in *Natural House* (New York, 1954), p. 27.

21. Frank Lloyd Wright, "In the Cause of Architecture," *Architectural Record*, March 1908, pp. 154, 157.

22. Frank Lloyd Wright, "Modern Architecture," 1931; reprinted in *Frank Lloyd Wright, Writings and Buildings* (New York, 1960), p. 42.

23. Morgan Hite, "Bungalow," *Architectural Art and Its Allies*, August 1911, pp. 5–7; idem, "The Influence of Wood in Architecture," *Building Review*, June 1918, p. 23.

24. Stickley, *Craftsman Homes*, p. 32.

25. *New Orleans Daily States*, August 31, 1908.

26. *Architectural Art*, June 1909, p. 19; December 1911, pp. 9, 11; March 19, 1911, p. 21.

PLATE 16.

Atlas of the City of New Orleans—1883, portion of plate 16 (Upperline to Joseph, River to Perrier). Elisha Robinson. (Courtesy The Historic New Orleans Collection, Museum/ Research Center, Acc. No. 1952.8.18.)

BIBLIOGRAPHY

BOOKS, NEWSPAPERS, ARTICLES

Aladdin Company. *Aladdin Homes Catalog No. 31.* 1919. Reprint. Watkins Glen, N.Y.: American Life Foundation, 1985.

American Institute of Architects, New Orleans Chapter. *A Guide to New Orleans Architecture.* 1974. Reprint. New Orleans, 1981.

Andrews, W. *Architecture, Ambition, and Americans.* New York: Harper and Brothers, 1947.

Augustin, Donatien. *A General Digest of the Ordinances and Resolutions of the Corporation of New Orleans.* New Orleans, 1831.

Badger, Daniel D. *Illustrations of Iron Architecture Made by the Architectural Iron Works of the City of New York.* 1865. Reprint. New York: Dover Publications, 1981.

Barber, George F. *George F. Barber's The Cottage Souvenir No. 2.* Reprint. Watkins Glen, N.Y.: American Life Books, 1982.

Baudier, Roger. *The Southern Plumber.* November 1930–April 1932.

Bell, Wm. C. *Illustrated Catalogue of Mouldings, Architectural and Ornamental Woodwork.* New Orleans: Roberts & Co., 1880.

Benjamin, Asher. *The American Builder's Companion.* 1827. Reprint. New York: Dover Publications, 1969.

Berg, Donald J., ed. *Houses and Cottages.* 1893. Reprint. Rockville Centre, N.Y.: Antiquity Reprints, 1983.

———,ed. *How to Build, Furnish and Decorate.* Reprint. Rockville Centre, N.Y.: Antiquity Reprints, 1983.

———, ed. *Modern American Dwellings.* 1897. Reprint. Rockville Centre, N.Y.: Antiquity Reprints, 1984.

———, ed. *Shoppell's Modern Houses.* 1887. Reprint. Rockville Centre, N.Y.: Antiquity Reprints, 1983.

Bezou, Henry C., comp., ed. *Jefferson Parish Historical Markers.* Monograph X, Jefferson Parish Historical Series. Harahan, La.: Jefferson Parish Historical Commission, 1987.

Bicknell, A.J. and Company. *Bicknell's Village Builder and Supplement.* 5th ed. 1878. Reprinted as *Bicknell's Victorian Buildings.* New York: Dover Publications, 1979.

Brooklyn Museum. *The American Renaissance, 1876–1917.* New York: Pantheon Books, 1979.

Brooks, Allen H. *Prairie School Architecture Studies from "The Western Architect".* New York: Van Nostrand Reinhold, 1983.

———. *The Prairie School.* New York: W.W. Norton, 1976.

Bruns, Mrs. Thomas Nelson Carter. *Louisiana Portraits.* New Orleans: Historical Activities Committee, National Society of the Colonial Dames of America in the State of Louisiana, 1975.

Butler, Talmadge, and Martin M.F. *Louisiana Successions, Vol. 1: St. Landry Parish, 1807–1865.* Fort Worth, Tex., 1968.

Byne, Arthur, and Byne, Mildred. *Spanish Architecture of the Sixteenth Century.* New York: Knickerbocker Press, 1917.

Calhoun, John, comp. *A Digest of the Ordinances and Resolutions of the Second Municipality of New Orleans.* New Orleans, 1840.

Christovich, Mary Louise; Evans, Sally Kittredge; and Toledano, Roulhac. *New Orleans Architecture, Vol. V: The Esplanade Ridge.* Gretna, La.: Pelican Publishing Co., 1977.

Clark, Robert Judson, ed. *The Arts and Crafts Movement in America, 1876–1916.* Princeton, N.J.: Princeton University Press, 1972.

Coleman, John. "Historic Houses of New Orleans." *New Orleans States,* October 28, 1922–December 12, 1925.

Coleman, William, comp. *Historical Sketch Book and Guide to New Orleans.* New York, 1885.

Collection of Dr. I.M. Cline. Catalog of sale January 17–18, 1927, Samuel T. Freeman & Co., Auctioneers.

Comstock, William. *Modern Architectural Designs and Details.* 1881. Reprint. Watkins Glen, N.Y.: American Life Foundation, 1979.

Craig, James P. *New Orleans: Illustrated in Photo Etching.* 1890.

Craig, Lois. *The Federal Presence.* Cambridge, Mass.: M.I.T. Press, 1984.

Cummins & Jeansonne, ed. *A Guide to the History of Louisiana.* Greenwood Press, 1982.

Curl, Donald W. *Mizner's Florida.* Cambridge, Mass.: M.I.T. Press, 1984.

Current, William R., and Current, Karen. *Greene & Greene: Architects in the Residential Style.* Dobbs Ferry, N.Y.: Morgan and Morgan, 1977.

Davey, Peter. *Architecture of the Arts and Crafts Movement.* New York: Rizzoli, 1980.

Delery, Simone de la Souchère. *Napoleon's Soldiers in America.* Gretna, La.: Pelican Publishing Co., 1972.

DeVille, Winston. *Colonial Louisiana Marriage Contracts.* Vol. 3. Point Coupee, La.

Downing, Andrew Jackson. *The Architecture of Country Houses.* 1850. Reprint. New York: Dover Publications, 1969.

———. *Cottage Residences.* 5th ed., 1873. Reprinted as *Victorian Cottage Residences.* New York: Dover Publications, 1981.

Eastlake, Charles L. *Hints on Household Taste*. 1878. Reprint. New York: Dover Publications, 1969.

Eberlein, Harold. *Villas of Florence and Tuscany*. Philadelphia, 1922.

Edgell, G.H. *The American Architecture of Today*. New York: Charles Scribner's Sons, 1928.

Editorial Committee, Architects Emergency Committee. *Great Georgian Houses of America*. New York: Kalkhoff Press, 1933.

Engelhardt, George W. *The City of New Orleans: The Book of the Chamber of Commerce and Industry of Louisiana*. New Orleans, 1894.

——. *New Orleans, Louisiana, The Crescent City: The Book of the Picayune also of the Public Bodies and Business Interests of the Place*. New Orleans, 1903–04.

Falcón, Guillermo Náñez, ed., and Griffith, Connie G., transc. *The Favrot Papers*. Vol. XV, 1823–1839. Transcriptions of Manuscript Collections of Louisiana [series] No. 1. New Orleans: Tulane University, 1982.

Fortier, Alcée. *Louisiana: Compromising Sketches of Parishes, Towns . . .* Vol. 1. Century Historical Association, 1914.

French, Leigh, Jr. *Colonial Interiors*. New York: 1923.

Gallier, James. *The Autobiography of James Gallier, Architect*. Paris, 1864. Reprint. Introduction by Samuel Wilson, Jr. New York: DaCapo Press, 1973.

Girouard, Mark. *Sweetness and Light: The Queen Anne Movement, 1860– 1900*. New Haven, Conn.: Yale University Press, 1984.

Gordon-Van Tine Co. *Architectural Details*. 1915. Reprint. Watkins Glen, N.Y.: American Life Foundation, 1985.

Gorin, Abbye A. *A Guide to Photographic Collections in New Orleans*. ed. Marie E. Windell. University of New Orleans, 1987.

Gowans, Alan. *The Comfortable House*. Cambridge, Mass.: MIT Press, 1986.

Guilbeau, L.L. *The St. Charles Street Car or the New Orleans & Carrollton Rail Road*. Guilbeau, 1975.

Hamer, Collin B. Jr. "Records of the City of Jefferson (1850–1870) in the City Archives Department of the New Orleans Public Library." *Louisiana History* 17:1 (Winter 1976).

Hennick, Louis C., and Charlton, E. Harper. *The Streetcars of New Orleans*. Gretna, La.: Pelican Publishing Co., 1975.

Hines, Thomas S. *Burnham of Chicago: Architect and Planner*. Chicago, University of Chicago Press, 1979.

Hitchcock, Henry-Russell. *The Architecture of H.H. Richardson and his Times*. New York: Museum of Modern Art, 1936. rev. ed. Cambridge, Mass.: M.I.T. Press, 1966.

——. *Architecture: Nineteenth and Twentieth Century*, 4th ed. New York: Penguin Books, 1977.

Hollis, Ruth Koons. "Jefferson City, 1851–1870: New Orleans' Urban Growth and Reconstruction Politics." Graduate thesis, University of New Orleans, 1983.

Holly, Henry Hudson. *Country Seats*. 1863. Reprint. Watkins Glen, N.Y.: Library of Victorian Culture, 1977.

——. *Modern Dwellings in Town and Country*. 1878. Reprint. Watkins Glen, N.Y.: Library of Victorian Culture, 1977.

Holmes, Jack D.L. *Honor and Fidelity: The Louisiana Infantry Regiment and the Louisiana Militia Companies, 1766–1821*. Louisiana Collection Series of Books and Documents. Birmingham, 1955.

Huber, Leonard V. *Jackson Square Through the Years*. New Orleans: Laborde Printing, 1982.

——. *Landmarks of New Orleans*. New Orleans: Laborde Printing, 1984.

——. *New Orleans: A Pictorial History*. New York: Crown Publishers, 1971.

Hussey, E.C. *Home Building*. 1875. Reprint. Watkins Glen, N.Y.: American Life Foundation, 1976.

Irvin, Hilary, and Cangelosi, Robert, Jr. "Uptown New Orleans." Report for the Uptown National Register District for the Preservation Resource Center, n.d.

Irvin, Hilary S. "The Impact of German Immigration on New Orleans Architecture." *Louisiana History*. Fall 1986.

Jewell, Edwin L. *Crescent City Illustrated*. New Orleans, 1873.

Jordy, William H. *American Buildings and Their Architects*. Garden City, N.Y.: Anchor Books, 1976.

Kaufmann, Edgar, and Raebuin, Ben. *Frank Lloyd Wright: Writings and Buildings*. New York: Times Mirror, 1960.

Keenan and Weiss, Architects. Brochure, ca. 1910.

Kidney, Walter C. *The Architecture of Choice*. New York: George Braziller, 1974.

Kimball, Fiske. *Domestic Architecture of the American Colonies and of the Early Republic*. New York: Charles Scribner's Sons, 1922.

King, Anthony D. *The Bungalow: The Production of a Global Culture*. London: Routledge and Kegan Paul, 1984.

Korn, Bertram Wallace. *The Early Jews of New Orleans*. Waltham, Mass.: American Jewish Historical Society, 1969.

Koyl, George S. *Index to a Catalog of Original and Measured Drawings of Buildings of USA to Dec. 31, 1917*. Koyl, 1969.

Labbé, Ronald M. "New Light on the Slaughterhouse Monopoly Act of 1869." In *Louisiana's Legal Heritage*, edited by Edward F. Haas, pp. 143–62. Studies in Louisiana Culture Series, Louisiana State Museum. Pensacola, 1983.

Lafever, Minard. *The Modern Builders Guide*. 1833. Reprint. New York: Dover Publications, 1969.

Lancaster, Clay. *The American Bungalow, 1880–1930*. New York: Abbeville Press, 1985.

Lemann, Bernard. *Historic Sites Inventory, New Orleans*. Rader and Associates for the Regional Planning Commission, 1969.

Lewis, Arnold. *American Country Houses of the Gilded Age Sheldon's "Artistic Country Seats")*. New York: Dover Publications, 1982.

Lewis, Pierce F. *New Orleans: The Making of an Urban Landscape*. Cambridge, Mass: Ballinger Publishing, 1976.

Lockwood, Charles. *Bricks and Brownstones*. New York: McGraw-Hill Book Co., 1972.

Louisiana Motorist 2, No. 7 (July 1921).

Louisiana Today. comp. James O. Jones Co. Louisiana Society, 1939.

Lowell, Guy. *More Small Italian Villas and Farmhouses*. New York, 1920.

Maass, John. *The Victorian Home in America*. New York: Hawthorn Books, 1972.

Makinson, Randall L. *Greene & Greene: Architecture as a Fine Art*. Salt Lake City: Peregrine Smith, 1977.

McAlester, Virginia, and McAlester, Lee. *A Field Guide to American Houses*. New York: Alfred A. Knopf, 1984.

McCoy, Esther. *Five California Architects*. New York: Praeger Publishers, 1975.

Metropolitan Museum of Art, New York. *In Pursuit of Beauty: Americans and the Aesthetic Movement*. New York: Rizzoli, 1986.

Modern American Houses. 1913. Reprinted as *Country and Suburban Homes of the Prairie School Period*. New York: Dover Publications, 1982.

A Monograph of the Works of McKim, Mead and White, 1879–1915. New York: Arno Press, 1977.

Mumford, Lewis. *The Brown Decades*. New York: Dover Publications, 1971.

Newcomb, Rexford. *Mediterranean Domestic Architecture in the United States*. Cleveland: J.H. Jansen, 1928.

——. *The Spanish House in America*. Philadelphia: J.B. Lippincott, 1927.

New Orleans & Carrollton Railroad, Light and Power Co. *Around the St. Charles Belt*. New Orleans, ca. 1906.

Ochsner, Jeffrey Karl. *H.H. Richardson's Complete Architectural Works*. Cambridge, Mass.: M.I.T. Press, 1984.

O'Conner, Thomas, ed. *History of the Fire Department of New Orleans*. New Orleans, 1895.

O'Gorman, James F. *Henry Hobson Richardson and His Office*. Cambridge, Mass.: M.I.T. Press, 1974.

Orleans Manufacturing and Lumber Co. *Cypress Sash, Doors, and Blinds*. Chicago: Rand McNally & Co., 1893.

Rhoads, William B. *The Colonial Revival*. New York: Garland Publishing, 1977.

Richtor, Henry. *Standard History of New Orleans*. Chicago: Lewis Publishing Co., 1900.

Robichaux, Albert J., comp., trans., ed. *Louisiana Census and Militia Lists, 1770–1798*. Harvey, La., 1973.

Rossi, Aldo. *Architecture of the City*. American ed., 1982.

Roth, Leland M. *McKim, Mead and White, Architects*. New York: Harper and Row, 1985.

Saxon, Lyle. *Fabulous New Orleans*. New York: D. Appleton-Century Co., 1935. Reprint. Gretna, La.: Pelican Publishing Co., 1988.

Scully, Vincent J. Jr. *The Shingle Style*. New Haven, Conn.: Yale University Press, 1973.

Seale, William. *The Tasteful Interlude*. Nashville, Tenn.: Association for State and Local History, 1981.

Shoppell, R.W., et al. *Turn of the Century Houses, Cottages and Villas*. New York: Dover Publications, 1983.

Sloan, Samuel. *City and Suburban Architect*. Philadelphia, Pa., 1859.

——. *The Model Architect*. 2 vols. 1852. Reprinted as *Sloan's Victorian Buildings*. New York: Dover Publications, 1980.

Soniat, Meloncy C. "The Faubourgs Forming the Upper Section of the City of New Orleans." *Louisiana Historical Quarterly* 20 (January 1937).

Southmayd, F.R. *Digest of the Ordinances of the Second Municipality and of the General Council of the City of New Orleans Applicable Thereto*. New Orleans, 1848.

Spencer, Brian A., ed. *The Prairie School Tradition*. New York: Whitney Library of Design, 1979.

Stein, Susan R., ed. *The Architecture of Richard Morris Hunt*. Chicago: University of Chicago Press, 1986.

Steegman, John. *Victorian Taste*. Cambridge, Mass.: M.I.T. Press, 1971.

Stevens, John, and Cobb, Albert. *Examples of American Domestic Architecture*. New York, 1889.

Stevens, Patricia Land, et al. *Louisiana's Architectural and Archaeological Legacies*. Natchitoches, La.: Northwestern Univ. Press, 1982.

Stevenson, Katherine, and Jandl, H. Ward. *Houses by Mail*. Washington, D.C.: Preservation Press, 1986.

Stickley. Gustav. *Craftsman Homes*. 1909. Reprint. New York: Dover Publications, 1979.

——. *More Craftsman Homes*. 1912. Reprint. New York: Dover Publications, 1982.

Storrer, William Allen. *The Architecture of Frank Lloyd Wright*. Cambridge, Mass.: M.I.T. Press, 1982.

Swanson, Betsy. *Historic Jefferson Parish: From Shore to Shore*. Gretna, La.: Pelican Publishing Co., 1975.

Tallmadge, T.E. *The Story of Architecture in America*. New York: W.W. Norton & Co., 1927.

Toledano, Roulhac; Evans, Sally Kittredge; and Christovich, Mary Louise. *New Orleans Architecture Vol. IV: The Creole Faubourgs*. Gretna, La.: Pelican Publishing Co., 1974.

Tuthill, Wm. B. *Interiors and Interior Details*. 1881. Reprinted as *Late Victorian Interiors and Interior Details*. Watkins Glen, N.Y.: American Life Books, 1984.

Universal Design Book. 1904. Reprinted as *The Victorian Design Book*. Ottawa, Canada: Lee Valley Tools, 1984.

Van Rensselaer, Mariana Griswold. *Henry Hobson Richardson and His Works*. 1888. Reprint. New York: Dover Publications, 1969.

Vaux, Calvert. *Villas and Cottages*. 1873. Reprint. New York: Dover Publications, 1970.

Waldhorn, Judith L. *A Gift to the Streets*. San Francisco: Antelope Island Press, 1976.

Waldo, J. Curtis. *Illustrated Visitors' Guide to New Orleans*. New Orleans: L. Graham, Printer, 1879.

Waldo, Rudolph H. *Notarial Archives of Orleans Parish*, New Orleans, 1946.

——. *Notarial Archives of Orleans Parish: Plan Books*. New Orleans, 1946.

Weil, Emile; Benson, H.A.; and Bendernagel, Albert. *Illustrations of Selected Work of Emile Weil, Architect, New Orleans, La., 1900–1928*. New Orleans, n.d.

Weitze, Karen J. *California's Mission Revival*. Los Angeles: Hennessey and Ingalls, 1984.

Whiffen, Marcus. *American Architecture Since 1780*. Cambridge, Mass.: M.I.T Press, 1974.

—— and Koeper, Frederick. *American Architecture*. 2 vols. Cambridge, Mass.: M.I.T. Press, 1983.

Whittlesey, Austin. *The Renaissance Architecture of Central and Northern Spain*.

Williams, William. "History of Carrollton." *Louisiana Historical Quarterly* 22 (January 1939).

Wilson, Samuel Jr., ed. *Impressions Respecting New Orleans by Benjamin Henry Bonval Latrobe*. New York: Columbia University Press, 1951.

——. *The Vieux Carré, New Orleans: Its Plan, Its Growth, Its Architecture*. New Orleans: Historic District Demonstration Study, Bureau of Governmental Research, 1969.

——, and Huber, Leonard V. *The Cabildo on Jackson Square*. New Orleans: Friends of the Cabildo, 1970. Reprint. Gretna, La.: Pelican Publishing Co., 1988

———, and Huber, Leonard V. *Baroness Pontalba's Buildings: Their Site and the Remarkable Woman Who Built Them.* New Orleans: Louisiana Landmarks Society and Friends of the Cabildo, 1964.

Wilson, Samuel Jr. and Lemann, Bernard. *New Orleans Architecture Vol. I: The Lower Garden District.* Gretna, La.: Pelican Publishing Co., 1971.

Winkler, Gail Caskey, and Moss, Roger W. *Victorian Interior Decoration.* New York: Henry Holt, 1986.

Woodward, George E. *Woodward's Architecture and Rural Art.* 2 vols. 1867, 1868. Reprint (2 vols. in 1) as *Woodward's Victorian Architecture and Rural Art.* Watkins Glen, N.Y.: American Life Foundation, 1978.

———. *Woodward's National Architect,* Vol. 2. New York: Geo. E. Woodward, 1869.

———, and Thompson, Edward G. *Woodward's National Architect, Vol. 1.* New York: Geo E. Woodward, 1869.

PERIODICALS

The American Architect and Building News
Architect's and Builder's Magazine
Architectural Art and Its Allies
The Architectural Forum
Architectural Record
Architectural Review
Architecture
Architecture and Its Allied Arts
Better Homes and Gardens
Brickbuilders
The Builder's Journal
Building Review
Building Trade News
The Bungalow Magazine
The Craftsman
Carpentry and Building
Century Magazine
Harper's
House Beautiful
House and Garden
Inland Architect
Journal of the Society of Architectural Historians, Philadelphia
Ladies Home Journal
The Old House Journal
The Western Architect
White Pine Series

NEWSPAPERS

Louisiana Courier
New Orleans Bee
New Orleans Commercial Bulletin
New Orleans Daily Picayune
New Orleans Daily True Delta
New Orleans Daily States
New Orleans Item
New Orleans States
New Orleans Times
New Orleans Times-Picayune
New Orleans Times-Picayune/New Orleans States Magazine
Preservation Press and Preservation in Print, Preservation Resource Center of New Orleans

NEW ORLEANS CITY DIRECTORIES

Tulane University, Howard-Tilton Memorial Library, Louisiana Division:
Cohen Company. *New Orleans Directory.* New Orleans, 1853–1855.
———. *New Orleans and Southern Directory.* New Orleans, 1856.
Edwards Company. *Annual Director.* New Orleans, 1870–1871, 1873.
———. *Annual Directory.* New Orleans, 1872.
Gardner Company. *New Orleans Directory.* New Orleans, 1859–1861, 1866–1869, 1873.
Gardner and Wharton. *New Orleans Directory.* New Orleans, 1858.
Graham and Madden. *Crescent City Directory.* New Orleans, 1867, 1869, 1870.
Kerr. *General Advertiser and Crescent City Directory.* New Orleans, 1856.
Mygatt & Company. *New Orleans Directory.* New Orleans, 1857–1858.
Soards' Directory Company. *City Directory of New Orleans.* New Orleans, 1874–1912.
———. *Soards' Elite Book of New Orleans.* New Orleans, [n.d., ca. 1907].
Tulane University, Howard-Tilton Memorial Library, Rare Books & Manuscripts Section:
Cohen Company. *New Orleans and Lafayette Directory.* New Orleans, 1849–1852.
Gibson Company. *Guide and Directory of the State of Louisiana and the Cities of New Orleans and Lafayette.* New Orleans, 1838.
Michel Company. *New Orleans Annual and Commercial Register.* New Orleans. 1834, 1840, 1841, 1843, 1846.
Paxton, J.M. *New Orleans Directory and Register.* New Orleans, 1822.
Percy Company. *New Orleans City Directory, 1832.* New Orleans, 1832.
Pitts and Clark. *New Orleans Directory for 1842.* New Orleans, 1842.

MAPS AND SURVEYS

Casey, Edgar. "Plan of Choice Property, Sixth District." Danziger & Tessier, n.d.
"City of New Orleans and Suburbs." Theo Pohlmann, 1883.
"Gray's Map of Louisiana." 1878.
The Historic New Orleans Collection, Museum/Research Center:
—*Insurance Maps of New Orleans, Louisiana.* New York: Sanborn-Perris Map Co., 1887, 1893, 1896, 1909.
—"New Orleans and Its Environs." F.B. Ogden, 1829.
—"Norman's Chart of Lower Mississippi River." A. Persac, 1858.
—"Plan of the City of New Orleans." L. Pessou and B. Simon, 1855.
—Robinson, Elisha. *Atlas of the City of New Orleans, Louisiana.* New York, 1883.
—"Plan of New Orleans and Environs." W. Walter, pub. A. Bronsema, 1855.
—"Topographical Map of New Orleans and Its Vicinity, 1834." Charles F. Zimpel.
Koch and Wilson Architects. "Map of the City and Environs of New Orleans." Maurice Harrison, 1845

Lawyers' Title Insurance Co.
—"Plan of the City of Jefferson." H.C. Brown, 1867.
—"Copy of Plan of 224 Lots in Suburb of Delachaise, City of Jefferson, to be Sold at Auction Thursday, March 25th, 1852 by Alfred Bouligny, Auctioneer."
—"Sale of 98 Lots of Ground, Faubourg Avart, City of Jefferson." 1859.
Louisiana State Land Office, Baton Rouge. Township Plats T12, T13S, R11E.
New Orleans City Hall, Property Management Office. Collection of Real Estate Maps.
New Orleans Notarial Archives:
"One Lot of Ground in the Suburb Plaisance." Plan Book 75, fo. 28.
"Plan of a Lot in Suburb Plaisance." Plan Book 77, fo. 6.
"Plan of Forty Lots in Suburb Bouligny." Plan Book 20, fo. 23.
"Plan of 4 Lots with the Buildings." 1858. Plan Book 24, fo. 43.
"Plan of 99 lots in Town of Freeport." Plan Book 94, fo. 18.
"Plan of 165 Lots in Faubourg Avart." Plan Book 6, fo. 91.
"Plan of One Plot of Ground in Freeport." Plan Book 24, fo. 16.
"Plan of Property in City of Jefferson." Plan Book 77, fo. 20.
"Plan of 7 Lots in Jefferson City." 1854. Plan Book 83, fo. 20.
"Plan of the City of Jefferson." William H. Williams, 1860. Plan Book 64, fo. 41.
"Plan of 3 Lots of Land in Bouligny." 1856. Plan Book 25, fo. 38.
"Plan of 315 Lots in Faubourg Avart." Plan Book 6, fo. 7.
"Plan of Three Valuable Lots in Jefferson City." Plan Book 78, fo. 13.
"Plan of 2 Lots of Ground in Jefferson City." Plan Book 77, fo. 11.
"Plan of 2 Lots . . . with Right to Batture." 1865. Plan Book 77, fo. 24.
"Plan of Two Properties in Jefferson City." 1866. Plan Book 41, fo. 20.
"Plan of Valuable Property in Jefferson." 1853. Plan Book 73, fo. 7; Plan Book 77, fo. 23; Plan Book 78, fo. 7.
"Plan of Valuable Property, Sixth District." 1880. Plan Book 99, fo. 5.
"Survey of Division of Wiltz Property." July 8, 1811. Attached to Michel de Armas Acts 6/350.
"Survey of New Subdivision in East Bouligny." William H. Williams, 1881. Attached to E. Commagere Acts 9/90.
Samuel, J. Raymond Collection:
—"Map of New Orleans and Adjacent Towns." Charles Gardner, 1861.
—"Gardner's City Directory Map," 1867.
—"Topographical and Drainage Map of New Orleans prepared for
Joseph Jones by T.S. Hardee, Civil Engineer." 1880.
—"Map of the City of New Orleans prepared expressly for Jewell's *Crescent City Illustrated*," 1873.
—Zacharie, James S. *New Orleans Guide.* New Orleans: New Orleans News Co., 1885.
Security Homestead, Carrollton Office. "Map of the Sixth District and Carrollton." William H. Williams, 1871.
Tulane University, Howard-Tilton Memorial Library:
Rare Books and Manuscripts Section:
"Map of New Orleans and Carrollton." Springbelt & Pilie, 1839.

Southeastern Architectural Archive:
Insurance Maps of New Orleans, Louisiana. New York: Sanborn-Perris Map Co., 1887, 1893, 1896, 1909.
Walker & Avery, Inc. "Official Map of T12 & 13S, R11E, New Orleans & Carrollton." Valery Sulakowski, surveyor; George Grandjean, C.E. and U.S. Deputy Surveyor, 1873.

MANUSCRIPTS AND RECORDS

Acts, State of Louisiana:
No. 91, 1845; May 27, 1846; No. 93, 1850; March 4, 1852; April 29, 1853; March 18, 1856; March 15, 1859; Act 118, March 8, 1869; March 26, 1870.
Archdiocese of New Orleans, Archbishop Antoine Blanc Memorial. Correspondence Files.
Civil District Court Building:
—Jefferson Parish Conveyance Office Books.
—Orleans Parish Mortgage Office Records.
—New Orleans Conveyance Office Records.
—Notarial Archives: Orleans Parish Notarial Acts.
—Succession of P. Benjamin Buisson, No. 21816.
The Historic New Orleans Collection, Museum/Research Center. "Jefferson Parish Survey Book, Vol. 2."
Jefferson Parish Court House, Gretna, Louisiana:
—Jefferson Parish Mortgage Office Books.
—Jefferson Parish Notarial Records, Acts of François Enoul Dugué Livaudais.
New Orleans Public Library:
City Archives:
—"City Surveyor Records: Surveyor's Office, Permit Book Nov. 1883–Apr. 1887."
—"Surveyor's Office Specifications, February 10, 1869–April 3, 1873."
—Records of the City of Jefferson:
—"Names and addresses of business people in the City of Jefferson, November 25, 1869–January 1, 1870."
—"Minutes, Board of Aldermen, Vol. 1, September 1, 1857–May 20, 1861."
Fifth District Court Records.
Louisiana Division:
—"Jefferson City Surveyor's Office Correspondence Book, 1866–1870."
—"Jefferson City Surveyor's Office Plan Book, 1868–1869."
—Obituary Files.
National Archives, Washington, D.C. Records of Civil War Special Agencies: Index to Ledger of Property Seized in New Orleans and Ledger of Property Seized in New Orleans. Third Agency, Book 44: Record of Property (Real Estate and Personal) in New Orleans with Index.
New Orleans Certificates of Inspection. Nov. 25, 1879–Oct. 31, 1883.
New Orleans City Hall, Real Estate Office Records.
Tulane University, Howard-Tilton Memorial Library:
Louisiana Collection:
—Frank H. Boatner Photograph Collection.
—"Financial Condition of the City of Jefferson, August 1, 1869."
—Louisiana Landmarks Photograph Collection.
—Picture File.
—Scrapbooks (newspaper clippings).
—Vertical File.

Rare Books and Manuscripts Section:
  —"Charter of the New Orleans and Carrollton Rail Road Company, New Orleans, 1837."
  —"Field Survey Notebooks." William H. Williams and C. Milo Williams.
  —Municipal Papers, Box 17/Folder 30.
  —"Collection of Building Contracts and Excerpts, 1800–1900." Compiled by Samuel Wilson, Jr.
Southeastern Architectural Archive:
  —Seghers Collection.
  —Thomas Sully Records, Gift of Jeanne Sully West.

University of New Orleans, Earl K. Long Library. Supreme Court of Louisiana Archives Department.

ORLEANS PARISH, NOTARIAL ARCHIVES RECORDS

New Orleans Notarial Archives. Notaries studied—dates indicate their years as notaries:

Adolph, Fred. 1880–1922.
Alba, Louis R. 1910–1938.
Baldwin, Cuthbert. 1915–1969.
Barnett, Alphonse. 1847–1890.
Barnett, Edward. 1838–1872.
Barnett, John. 1872–1893.
Beard, Josph R. 1847–1850.
Beary, Allan R. 1906–1933.
Beck, A.S. 1870–1890.
Beer, Scott. 1905–1941.
Bendernagel, John. 1866–1891.
Benedict, Percy S. 1900–1944.
Bienvenu, Alexander E. 1846–1879.
Blache, Adolphe. 1868–1869.
Booth, Andrew B. Jr. 1918–1933.
Borgstere, J.R. 1850–1853.
Boswell, William. 1825–1838.
Boudousquie, Charles. 1837–1850.
Bouny, Eusebe. 1857–1896.
Brenan, Richard. 1852–1867.
Brewer, William F. 1888–1919.
Buchmann, Andrew. 1901–1929.
Cahill, A.J. 1896–1929.
Caire, Louis T. 1827–1850.
Casey, Joseph. 1918–1968.
Castell, William J. 1851–1885.
Cenas, Hilary Breton. 1834–1859.
Charbonnet, F.D. 1888–1935.
Chiapella, Achille. 1839–1857.
Christy, George W. 1865–1891.
Coffey, John French. 1852–1891.
Cohn, Joseph. 1854–1882.
Commagere, Ernest. 1856–1897.
Cuvillier, Joseph. 1830–1886.
Cuvellier, Pierre C. 1850–1874.
Davis, Pliny Earl. 1864–1867.
Danziger, Alfred D. 1908–1948.
Dart, Henry D. Jr. 1916–1942.
de Armas, Felix. 1823–39.
de Armas, Michel. 1808–1823.
de Armas, Octave. 1828–1889.
Deibel, Frederick. 1880–1937.
Dejan, Michel. 1875–1914.
Denechaud, Charles I. 1902–1949.
Denegre, W.D. 1889–1894.
Deutsch, Eberhard. 1926–1948.
Doriocourt, Andre D. 1843–1880.
Doriocourt, Antoine. 1847–1906.

Doyle, Frank T. 1921–1956.
Dresner, Jacob. 1914–1968.
Dresner, Meyer. 1928–1970.
Dreyfous, Abel. 1845–1892.
Dreyfous, Felix. 1881–1946.
Drouet, Onesiphore. 1844–1879.
Ducros, Marcel T. 1866–1896.
Duplantier, Guy. 1853–1887.
Emerson, Charles M. 1872–1881.
Eustis, John G. 1866–1911.
Fahey, James. 1869–1894.
Fernandez, Gabriel Jr. 1902–1936.
Flower, Samuel. 1880–1895.
Forcelle, Joseph H. Jr. 1905–1939.
Friedrichs, Carl C. 1903–1942.
Garland, Henry L. 1890–1899.
Gaudin, Felix W. 1921–1970.
Gautier, Sidney F. 1908–1945.
Gill, Charles G. 1898–1933.
Gottschalk, Edward G. 1853–1871.
Graham, James. 1850–1878.
Grima, Edgar. 1869–1930.
Grima, Felix. 1833–1885.
Grinage, James Boyd. 1903–1914.
Gurley, W. Morgan. 1892–1937.
Guyol, Theodore. 1845–1893.
Habans, Paul B. 1904–1907.
Hahn, Michael. 1862.
Hart, William O. 1880–1902.
Henriques, James C. 1896–1949.
Hermann, Lucien. 1839–1850.
Hero, Andrew Sr. 1863–1868.
Hero, Andrew Jr. 1865–1914.
Janin, Lawrence M. 1907–1929.
Kenny, Lawrence R. 1843–1852.
Ker, Robert J. 1850–1886.
Ker, William R. 1885–1922.
Kiam, Victor K. 1921–1932.
Kirschner, Ferdinand. 1885–1891.
Kleinpeter, William B. 1869–1878.
Kronenberger, George. 1897–1920.
Labatut, Henry P. 1895–1902.
Ladreyere, Cyprien C. 1849–1856.
Lafitte, Marc. 1810–1826.
Laresche, Paul E. 1845–1871.
Lautenschlaeger, Joseph. 1899–1946.
Leche, Richard W. 1925–1932.
LeGardeur, Gustave Jr. 1867–1909.
Legier, John. 1880–1906.
Leopold, Arthur B. 1897–1939.
Leverich, Watts K. 1914–1949.
Lewis, Edwin L. 1852–1857.
Lisbony, Joseph. 1848–1860.
Loomis, Harry L. Jr. 1893–1944.
Long, Oregon W. 1897–1910.
McCall, Henry. 1908–1946.
McGiehan, Theodore. 1920–1956.
Madden, Hugh. 1860–1866.
Magner, Selim. 1854–1870.
Maloney, Robert J. 1896–1908.
Manion, Martin H. 1897–1930.
Marx, Frederick C. 1899–1955.
Mazureau, Adolphe. 1829–1874.
Meunier, Jules F. 1876–1914.
Meunier, Roger. 1915–1941.
Michel, Herman. 1903–1918.

Michel, John T. 1862–1896.
Miller, W.V. 1917–1947.
Milling, Robert C. 1918–1919.
Milling, Wear F. 1916–1919.
Milner, Purnell. 1897–1926.
Morel, Octave. 1864–1894.
Murphy, Daniel J. 1902–1950.
O'Conner, Robert E. 1903–1943.
Olivier, Pierre. 1902–1950.
Ory, Benjamin J. 1877–1926.
Pascoe, William H. 1869–1910.
Pedesclaux, Pierre. 1788–1816.
Peters, Walter H. 1853–1867.
Peyroux, Edmund A. 1876–1889.
Philips, Alphonse Victor. 1884–1889.
Pitot, Armand Jr. 1867–1886.
Plough, Azzo Joseph. 1920–1969.
Pollock, Carlile. 1814–1845.
Pomes, Emile. 1896–1935.
Poole, William L. 1850–1881.
Preot, George C. 1881–1901.
Provosty, Michel. 1916–1958.
Puig, Felix J. 1894–1953.
Puneky, Cornelius W. 1920–1970.
Querens, Frederic C. 1915–1958.
Queyrouse, J. Maxime. 1897–1933.
Quintero, Lamar C. 1894–1918.
Racivitch, Herve. 1928–1970.
Ramos, Robert. 1920–1959.
Ray, Stanley. 1926–1936.
Rebentisch, Charles G. 1885–1919.
Renaudin, William. 1899–1914.
Rhodes, Henry I. 1884–1891.
Ricardo, Daniel I. 1844–1859.
Ricau, Gustave J. 1908–1941.
Rosser, James B. 1894–1931.
Rouen, Bussiere. 1883–1937.
Saal, Raymond. 1919–1943.
Sansum, Ernest L. 1897–1903.
Schneidau, Charles. 1900–1928.
Seghers, Theodore. 1828–1846.
Sessler, David. 1919–1937.
Seymour, William H. 1866–1913.

Shannon, William. 1850–1872.
Simeon, James. 1888–1915.
Simonds, Edward L. 1889–1905.
Simpson, Oramel H. 1909–1926.
Skinner, Edward K. 1888–1909.
Soniat, Charles T. 1872–1915.
Soniat, Meloncy C. 1885–1940.
Souchon, Harry. 1933–1970.
Spearing, James Z. 1885–1942.
Spitzfaden, Theodore. 1896–1909.
Stark, Theodore O. 1850–1871.
Stafford, Ethelred M. 1899–1932.
Stenzt, Valentine. 1902–1913.
Stifft, Peter. 1894–1948.
Talbot, William H. 1942–1969.
Taylor, Joseph Dewey. 1877–1907.
Theard, Charles J. 1882–1928.
Titche, Bernard. 1885–1934.
Toler, John L. 1927–1968.
Trist, Nicholas B. 1865–1904.
Untereiner, George Joseph. 1897–1931.
Upton, Charles B. 1888–1922.
Upton, John R. 1902–1936.
Upton, Robert P. 1884–1913.
Vidrine, Eraste. 1897–1945.
Von Behren, Wilhemina. 1924–1944.
Wagner, John. 1900–1949
Walshe, George C. 1894–1915.
Ward, John. 1890–1914.
Wegener, Edmund. 1914–1947.
Weil, Emanuel C. 1897–1942.
Weiss, Sol. 1912–1947.
Wells, Edmund G. 1858–1873.
Wenck, Jefferson C. 1889–1924.
West, William A. Jr. 1927–1970.
Wilson, Andrew H. 1885–1890.
Wolf, Benjamin. 1918–1957.
Woodville, John H. 1902–1940.
Woulfe, James J. 1885–1913.
Young, William W. Sr. 1910–1956.
Zengel, Frederick. 1880–1918.
Zengel, Frederick Jr. 1929–1939.

INVENTORY PHOTOGRAPH CREDITS

A.L. Schlesinger. Camp: 3427 (bottom right); Coliseum: 3704, 3715; Louisiana: 1216 (bottom center), 1224 (2).

Dr. Harold Wirth. Magazine: 3300 (2).

Sally K. Reeves. St. Charles: 4521 (Academy of the Sacred Heart, ca. 1890) (left center).

Robert J. Cangelosi, Jr. St. Charles: 4521 (Academy of the Sacred Heart; from *New Orleans, Louisiana, The Crescent City,* by George W. Engelhardt, ca. 1900) (bottom left).

Katherine McFetridge. Bordeaux: 1500 (bottom right); St. Charles: 4802 (now 1500 Bordeaux), 4812, 4814 (top right).

John Montgomery Family. Tchoupitoulas: 4109 (bottom center).

Koch and Wilson. St. Charles: 3513 (center).

Claire Creppel. St. Charles: 3811 (The Columns) (bottom left).

Samuel Wilson. St. Charles: 4010 (from *New Orleans, Illustrated in Photo Etching,* by James P. Craig, 1890) (top right).

Priscilla and Edgar Casey; photograph by Frank Masson. Louisiana: 1216 (top center).

Rare Books and Manuscripts Section, Howard-Tilton Memorial Library, Tulane University. Louisiana: 1030 (receipt).

Thomas Sully Office Records, Southeastern Architectural Archive, Howard-Tilton Memorial Library, Tulane University. Gift of Jeanne Sully West. Octavia: 1539–41 (center).

Southeastern Architectural Archive, Howard-Tilton Memorial Library, Tulane University. Gift of Samuel Wilson. St. Charles: 4026 (top center).

New Orleans Notarial Archives; photograph by Ben Myers. Bordeaux: 1500 (survey, 1887) (center).

Louisiana Collection, Howard-Tilton Memorial Library, Tulane University. Foucher: 830; Marengo: 526 (from *New Orleans, Louisiana, The Crescent City,* by George W. Engelhardt, 1903–04) (top right); Napoleon: 1204 (from *The City of New Orleans,* by George W. Engelhardt, 1894) (top left), 2037 (bottom right); Peniston: 1615 (top left); St. Charles: 3437–39 (from *The City of New Orleans,* by George W. Engelhardt, 1894) (bottom right), 3924 (bottom left), 4036 (ca. 1910) (top right), 4125 (ca. 1900) (bottom left), 4217 (ca. 1895) (bottom right), 4238 (center), 4417 (bottom right), 4433, 4534 (ca. 1908) (center), 4630 (ca. 1905), 4631 (ca. 1900) (bottom left), 4706 (ca. 1900) (center), 4900 (from *Architectural Art and Its Allies,* 1911), 4941 (ca. 1906) (top left).

Garrett G. Stearns. Delachaise: 1221 (2).

Warren G. Moses. Camp: 3435, 3602, 3622, 3937, 3945, 5300, 5301, 5349; Chestnut: 3939–41, 5357, 5432; Magazine: 5315–17, 5319–21, 5323–25.

C. Milo Williams Collection, Louisiana Division, New Orleans Public Library; photograph by Bert Myers. Jefferson: 1831 (Newman School, ca. 1904).

The Historic New Orleans Collection, Museum/Research Center (HNOC). Louisiana: 1312 (ca. 1905) (top left); Magazine: 5453 (Poydras Asylum, from *Crescent City Illustrated,* by Edwin L. Jewell, 1873) (center); Octavia: 1631 (New Orleans Conservatory of Music and School of Languages, 1895) (bottom right); St. Charles: 3924 (ca. 1893, from *Southern Garden,* 1895) (top left); Tchoupitoulas: 4608 (from *Crescent City Illustrated,* by Edwin L. Jewell, 1873) (bottom).

INDEX

PLAN
of the
CITY of JEFFERSON

1860.

Lithogr. by J. Manouvrier & Cº. 30 Camp Str. N.Orlº.

MISSISSIPPI

Wm. H. WILLIAMS, Surveyor & Civil Engineer